Visual Data Mining

Visual Data Mining

Techniques and Tools for Data Visualization and Mining

Tom Soukup
Ian Davidson

Wiley Publishing, Inc.

Publisher: Robert Ipsen
Executive Editor: Robert Elliott
Assistant Editor: Emilie Herman
Associate Managing Editor: John Atkins
New Media Editor: Brian Snapp
Text Design & Composition: John Wiley Production Services

Designations used by companies to distinguish their products are often claimed as trademarks. In all instances where John Wiley & Sons, Inc., is aware of a claim, the product names appear in initial capital or ALL CAPITAL LETTERS. Readers, however, should contact the appropriate companies for more complete information regarding trademarks and registration.

This book is printed on acid-free paper. ⊖

This publication is designed to provide accurate and authoritative information in regard to the subject matter covered. It is sold with the understanding that the publisher is not engaged in professional services. If professional advice or other expert assistance is required, the services of a competent professional person should be sought.

Library of Congress Cataloging-in-Publication Data:

Soukup, Tom, 1962-
  Visual data mining : techniques and tools for data visualization and
mining / Tom Soukup, Ian Davidson.
      p. cm.
"Wiley Computer Publishing."
Includes bibliographical references and index.
  ISBN 0-471-14999-3
 1. Data mining. 2. Database searching. I. Davidson, Ian, 1971- II.
Title.
  QA76.9.D343 S68 2002
  006.3—dc21   2002004004

Printed in the United States of America.

10 9 8 7 6 5 4 3 2 1

Advance Praise for *Visual Data Mining: Techniques and Tools for Data Visualization and Mining*

"This book is a wonderful contribution and important resource for anyone building visual data mining systems. It combines down-to-earth, practical advice with thoughtful examples."

Stephen G. Eick
Chief Technology Officer, Visual Insights

"Whenever I receive a new dataset, the first thing I do is to load it into my favorite data mining visualization tool to examine the distributions of all the variables. Because the mind processes visual information so quickly and instinctively, my eye is immediately drawn to the variables with suspicious outliers, the variables with only one value, the variables that are mostly null, the nominal variables that are being interpreted as continuous . . . And that is just the beginning! As this book shows, visualization plays an important role in every step of the data mining process. Soukup and Davidson take the reader through every detail of this process, providing sample SQL code for each practical example. In fact, much of their advice on project planning and data extract, transformation and cleaning is applicable to all data mining projects, visual or not."

Michael J. A. Berry
Founder, Data Miners, Inc.

"Data mining is a double-edged sword. Putting powerful tools that are visually driven into the hands of analysts can be encouragement to push beyond the boundaries of appropriate modeling. Soukup and Davidson's book provides not only excellent guidance about how to leverage, but not abuse, visualization's power. Their comprehensive view of the entire data mining process, from processing raw data to drawing final conclusions, is a model for all data miners to follow."

Thomas Warden
Assistant Vice President, Allstate Research and Planning Center

v

To Ed and my family for their encouragement.

—*TOM*

To my wife and parents for their support.

—*IAN*

CONTENTS

T his book would not have been possible without the generous help of many people.

We thank the reviewers for their timely critique of our work, and our editor, Emilie Herman, who skillfully guided us through the book-writing process.

We thank the Oracle Technology Network and SPSS Inc., for providing us evaluation copies of Oracle and Clementine, respectively. The use of these products helped us to demonstrate key concepts in the book.

Finally, we both learned a great deal from our involvement in Silicon Graphics' data mining projects. This, along with our other data mining project experience, was instrumental in formulating and trying the visual data mining method-ology we present in this book.

Tom Soukup and Ian Davidson

My sincere thanks to the people with whom I have worked on data mining projects. You have all demonstrated and taught me many aspects of working on successful data mining projects.

Ian Davidson

To all my data mining and business intelligence colleagues, I add my thanks. Your business acumen and insights have aided in the formulation of a suc-cessful visual data mining methodology.

Tom Soukup

Tom Soukup is a data mining and data warehousing specialist with more than 15 years experience in database management and analysis. He currently works for Konami Gaming Systems Division as Director of Business Intelligence and DBA.

Ian Davidson, Ph.D., has worked on a variety of commercial data-mining projects, such as cross sell, retention, automobile claim, and credit card fraud detection. He recently joined the State University of New York at Albany as an Assistant Professor of Computer Science.

Microsoft, Microsoft Excel, and PivotTable are either registered trademarks or trademarks of Microsoft Corporation in the United States and/or other countries.

Oracle is a registered trademark of Oracle Corporation.

SPSS is a registered trademark, and Clementine and Clementine Solution Publisher are either registered trademarks or trademarks of SPSS Inc.

MineSet is a registered trademark of Silicon Graphics, Inc.

Business intelligence solutions transform business data into conclusive, fact-based, and actionable information and enable businesses to spot customer trends, create customer loyalty, enhance supplier relationships, reduce financial risk, and uncover new sales opportunities. The goal of business intelligence is to make sense of change—to understand and even anticipate it. It furnishes you with access to current, reliable, and easily digestible information. It provides you the flexibility to look at and model that information from all sides, and in different dimensions. A business intelligence solution answers the question "What if . . . " instead of "What happened?" In short, a business intelligence solution is the path to gaining—and maintaining—your competitive advantage.

Data visualization and data mining are two techniques often used to create and deploy successful business intelligence solutions. By applying visualizations and data mining techniques, businesses can fully exploit business data to discover previously unknown trends, behaviors, and anomalies:

- *Data visualization tools and techniques* assist users in creating two- and three-dimensional pictures of business data sets that can be easily interpreted to gain knowledge and insights.

- *Visual data mining tools and techniques* assist users in creating visualizations of data mining models that detect patterns in business data sets that help with decision making and predicting new business opportunities.

In both cases, visualization is key in assisting business and data analysts to discover new patterns and trends from their business data sets. Visualization is a proven method for communicating these discoveries to the decision makers. The payoffs and return on investment (ROI) can be substantial for businesses that employ a combination of data visualizations and visual data mining effectively. For instance, businesses can gain a greater understanding of customer motivations to help reduce fraud, anticipate resource demand, increase acquisition, and curb customer turnover (attrition).

Overview of the Book and Technology

This book was written to assist you to first prepare and transform your raw data into business data sets, then to help you create and analyze the prepared business data set with data visualization and visual data mining tools and techniques. Compared with other business intelligence techniques and tools, we have found that visualizations help reduce your time-to-insight—the time it takes you to discover and understand previously unknown trends, behaviors, and anomalies and communicate those findings to decision makers. It is often said that a picture paints a thousand words. For instance, a few data visualizations can be used to quickly communicate the most important discoveries instead of sorting through hundreds of pages of a traditional on-line analytical processing (OLAP) report. Similarly, visual data mining tools and techniques enable you to visually inspect and interact with the classification, association, cluster, and other data mining models for better understanding and faster time-to-insight.

Throughout this book, we use the term visual data mining to indicate the use of visualization for inspecting, understanding, and interacting with data mining algorithms. Finding patterns in a data visualization with your eyes can also be considered visual data mining. In this case, the human mind acts as the pattern recognition data mining engine. Unfortunately, not all models produced by data mining algorithms can be visualized (or a visualization of them just wouldn't make sense). For instance, neural network models for classification, estimation, and clustering do not lend themselves to useful visualization.

The most sophisticated pattern recognition machine in the world is the human mind. Visualization and visual data mining tools and techniques aid in the process of pattern recognition by reducing large quantities of complicated patterns into two- and three-dimensional pictures of data sets and data mining models. Often, these visualizations lead to actionable business insights. Visualization helps business and data analysts to quickly and intuitively discover interesting patterns and effectively communicate these insights to other business and data analysts, as well as, decision makers.

IDC and The Data Warehousing Institute have sampled business intelligence solutions customers. They concluded the following:

1. Visualization is essential (Source: IDC).

   Eighty percent of business intelligence solution customers find visualization to be desirable.

2. Data mining algorithms are important to over 80 percent of data warehousing users (Source: The Data Warehousing Institute).

Visualization and data mining business intelligence solutions reach across industries and business functions. For example, telecommunications, stock exchanges, and credit card and insurance companies use visualization and data mining to detect fraudulent use of their services; the medical industry uses data mining to predict the effectiveness of surgical procedures, medical tests, medications, and fraud; and retailers use data mining to assess the effectiveness of coupons and promotional events. The Gartner Group analyst firm estimates that by 2010, the use of data mining in targeted marketing will increase from less than 5 percent to more than 80 percent (Source: Gartner).

In practice, visualization and data mining has been around for quite a while. However, the term data mining has only recently earned credibility within the business world for its abilities to control costs and contribute to revenue. You may have heard data mining referred to as knowledge discovery in databases (KDD). The formal definition of data mining, or KDD, is the extraction of interesting (non-trivial, implicit, previously unknown, and potentially useful) information or patterns in large database.

The overall goal of this book is to first introduce you to data visualization and visual data mining tools and techniques, demonstrate how to acquire and prepare your business data set, and provide you with a methodology for using visualization and visual data mining to solve your business questions.

How This Book Is Organized

Although there are many books on data visualization and data mining theory, few present a practical methodology for creating data visualizations and for performing visual data mining. Our book presents a proven eight-step data visualization and visual data mining (VDM) methodology, as outlined in Figure I.1. Throughout the book, we have stringently adhered to this eight-step VDM methodology. Each step of the methodology is explained with the help of practical examples and then applied to a real-world business problem using a real-world data set. The data set is available on the book's companion Web site. It is our hope that as you learn each methodology step, you will be able to apply the methodology to your real-world data sets and begin receiving the benefits of data visualization and visual data mining to solve your business issues.

Figure I.1 depicts the methodology as a sequential series of steps; however, the process of preparing the business data set and creating and analyzing the data visualizations and data mining models is an iterative process. Visualization and visual data mining steps are often repeated as the data and visualizations are refined and as you gain more understanding about the data set and the significance of one data fact (a column) to other data facts (other columns). It is rare that data or business analysts create a production-class data visualization or data mining model the first time through the data mining discovery process.

This book is organized into three main sections that correspond to the phases of a data visualization and visual data mining (VDM) project:

- Project planning
- Data preparation
- Data analysis

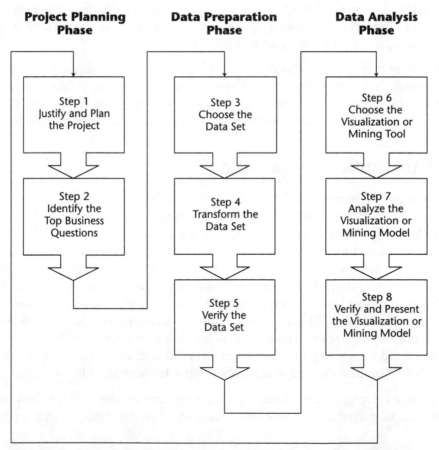

Figure I.1 Eight-step data visualization and visual data mining methodology.

Part 1: Introduction and Project Planning Phase

Chapter 1: "Introduction to Data Visualization and Visual Data Mining," introduces you to data visualization and visual data mining concepts used throughout the book. It illustrates how a few data visualizations can replace (or augment) hundreds of pages of traditional "green-bar" OLAP reports. Multidimensional, spatial (landscape), and hierarchical analysis data visualization tools and techniques are discussed through examples. Traditional statistical tools, such as basic statistics and histograms, are given a visual twist through statistic and histogram visualizations. Chapter 1 also introduces you to visual data mining concepts. This chapter describes how visualizations of data mining models assist the data and business analysts, domain experts and decision makers in understanding and visually interacting with data mining models such as decision trees. It also discusses using visualization tools to plot the effectiveness of data mining models, as well as to analyze the potential deployment of the models.

Chapter 2: "Step 1: Justifying and Planning the Data Visualization and Data Mining Project," introduces you to the first of the eight steps in the data visualization and visual data mining (VDM) methodology and discusses the business aspects of business intelligence solutions. In most cases, the project itself needs a business justification before you can begin (or get funding for the project). This chapter presents examples of how various businesses have justified (and benefited) from using data visualization and visual data mining tools and techniques. Chapter 2 also discusses planning a VDM project and provides guidance on estimating the project time and resource requirements. It helps you to define team roles and responsibilities for the project. The customer retention business VDM project case study is introduced, and then Step 1 is applied to the case study.

Chapter 3: "Step 2: Identifying the Top Business Questions," introduces you to the second step of the VDM methodology. This chapter discusses how to identify and refine business questions so that they can be investigated through data visualization and visual data mining. It also guides you through mapping the top business questions for your VDM project into data visualization and visual data mining problem definitions. Step 2 is then applied to the continuing customer retention VDM project case study.

Part 2: The Data Preparation Phase

Chapter 4: "Step 3: Choosing the Data," introduces you to the third step of the VDM methodology and discusses how to select the data relating to the data visualization and visual data mining questions identified in Chapter 3 from your operational data source. It introduces the concept of using an exploratory data mart as a repository for building and maintaining business data sets that address the business questions under investigation. The exploratory data mart is then used to extract, cleanse, transform, load (ECTL), and merge the raw operational data sources into one or more production business data sets. This chapter guides you through choosing the data set for your VDM project by presenting and discussing practical examples, and applying Step 3 to the customer retention VDM project case study.

Chapter 5: "Step 4: Transforming the Data Set," introduces you to the fourth step of the VDM methodology. Chapter 5 discusses how to perform logical transformations on the business data set stored in the exploratory data mart. These logical transformations often help in augmenting the business data set to enable you to gain more insight into the business problems under investigation. This chapter guides you through transforming the data set for your VDM project by presenting and discussing practical examples, and applying Step 4 to the customer retention VDM project case study.

Chapter 6: "Step 5: Verifying the Data Set," introduces you to the fifth step of the VDM methodology. Chapter 6 discusses how to verify that the production business data set contains the expected data and that all of the ECTL steps (from Chapter 4) and logical transformations (from Chapter 5) have been applied correctly, are error free, and did not introduce bias into your business data set. This chapter guides you through verifying the data set for your VDM project by presenting and discussing practical examples, and applying Step 5 to the customer retention VDM project case study.

Chapter 7: "Step 6: Choosing the Visualization or Data Mining Tool," introduces you to the sixth step of the VDM methodology. Chapter 7 discusses how to choose and fine-tune the data visualization or data mining model tool appropriate in investigating the business questions identified in Chapter 3. This chapter guides you through choosing the data visualization and data mining model tools by presenting and discussing practical examples, and applying Step 6 to the customer retention VDM project case study.

Part 3: The Data Analysis Phase

Chapter 8: "Step 7: Analyzing the Visualization or Data Mining Model," introduces you to the seventh step of the VDM methodology. Chapter 8 discusses how to use the data visualizations and data mining models to gain business insights in answering the business questions identified in Chapter 3. For data mining, the predictive strength of each model can be evaluated and compared to each other enabling you to decide on the best model that addresses your business questions. Moreover, each data visualization or data mining model can be visually investigated to discover patterns (business trends and anomalies). This chapter guides you through analyzing the visualizations or data mining models by presenting and discussing practical examples, and applying Step 7 to the continuing customer retention VDM project case study.

Chapter 9: "Step 8: Verifying and Presenting Analysis," introduces you to the final step of the VDM methodology. Chapter 9 discussed the three parts to this step: verifying that the visualizations and data mining model satisfies your business goals and objectives, presenting the visualization and data mining discoveries to the decision-makers, and if appropriate, deploying the visualizations and mining models in a production environment. Although this chapter discusses the implementation phase, a complete essay of this phase is outside the scope of this book. Step 8 is then applied to the continuing customer retention VDM project case study.

Chapter 10, "The Future of Visual Data Mining," serves as a summary of the previous chapters and discusses the future of data visualization and visual data mining.

The **Glossary** provides a quick reference to definitions of commonly used data visualizations and data mining terms and algorithms.

Who Should Read This Book

A successful business intelligence solution using data visualization or visual data mining requires the participation and cooperation from many parts of your business organization. Since this books endeavors to cover the VDM project from the justification and planning phase up to implementation phase, it has a wide and diverse audience. The following definitions identify categories and roles of people in a typical business organization and lists which chapters are most advantageous for them to read. Depending on your business organization, you may be responsible for one or more roles. (In a small organization, you may be responsible for all roles).

Data Analysts normally interact directly with the visualization and visual data mining software to create and evaluate the visualizations and data mining models. Data analysts collaborate with *business analysts* and *domain experts* to identify and define the business questions and get help in understanding and selecting columns from the raw data sources. We recommend data analysts focus on all chapters.

Business Analysts typically interact with previously created data visualizations and data mining models. Business analysts help define the business questions and communicate the data mining discoveries to other analysts — *domain experts* and *decision makers*. We recommend that business analysts focus on Chapters 1 through 4 and Chapters 8 and 9.

Domain Experts typically do not create data visualizations and data mining models, but rather, interact with the final visualizations and models. Domain experts know the business, as well as what data the business collects. *Data analysts* and *business analysts* draw on the domain expert to understand and select the right data from the raw operational data sources, as well as to clarify and verify their visualization and data mining discoveries. We recommend domain experts focus on Chapters 1 through 4 and Chapters 6 and 9.

Decision Makers typically have the power to act on the data visualization and data mining discoveries. The visualization and visual data mining discoveries are presented to decision makers to help them make decisions based on these discoveries. We recommend decision makers focus on Chapters 1, 2, and 9. Chapter 10 focuses on the near future of visualization in data mining. We recommend that all individuals read it.

Table I.1   How This Book Is Organized and Who Should Read It

CHAPTER	TOPIC AND VDM STEP DISCUSSES	DATA ANALYSTS	BUSINESS ANALYSTS	DOMAIN EXPERTS	DECISION MAKERS
1	Introduction to Data Visualization and Visual Data Mining	√	√	√	√
2	Step 1: Justifying and Planning the Data Visualization/ Data Mining Project	√	√	√	√
3	Step 2: Identifying the Top Business Questions	√	√	√	
4	Step 3: Choosing the Data Set	√	√	√	
5	Step 4: Transforming the Data Set	√			
6	Step 5: Verifying the Data Set	√		√	
7	Step 6: Choosing the Visualization or Data Mining Model	√			
8	Step 7: Analyzing the Visualization or Data Mining Model	√	√		

CHAPTER	TOPIC AND VDM STEP DISCUSSES	DATA ANALYSTS	BUSINESS ANALYSTS	DOMAIN EXPERTS	DECISION MAKERS
9	Step 8: Verifying and Presenting the Analysis	√	√	√	√
10	The Future of Visualization and Visual Data Mining	√	√	√	√

Software Tools Used

There are numerous visualization software tools, and more are being developed and enhanced each year that you can use for data preparation, data visualization, and data mining. The graphical and data mining analysis capabilities of software tools vary from package to package. We have decided to limit our selection to four core packages for illustrating the data preparation and data analysis phases: Oracle, Microsoft Excel, SGI MineSet, and SPSS Clementine. These software packages are not required for reading or understanding this book, as the data visualization and data mining techniques described in the book are similar to those available in the majority of data visualization and data mining software packages.

Oracle

The majority of query examples in the book are written using ANSI standard structured query language (SQL) syntax. For the data preparation extraction, cleanse, transform, and load (ECTL) tasks, we chose to use Oracle SQL*Loader syntax. For some of the logical transformation tasks, we chose to use Oracle procedural language SQL (PL/SQL). The majority of queries, ECTL, and logical transformation tasks can be accomplished using similar functions and tools in other popular RDBMS products, such as Microsoft SQL server, Sybase, Informix, DB2, and RedBrick.

Microsoft Excel

Excel is the most widely used spreadsheet and business graphics software tool. Excel provides comprehensive tools to help you create, analyze, and share spreadsheets containing graphs. We chose to use Excel to illustrate core data visualization types such as column, bar, pie, line, scatter, and radar graphs. These traditional graph types are common to most visualization tool suites.

SGI MineSet

Although no longer commercially available, we chose to use MineSet to illustrate advanced data visualization types, such as tree, statistics, and the 3D scatter graphs. These advanced graph types are common in most data mining software suites, such as ANGOSS Knowledge Studio, Oracle Darwin, IBM Intelligent Miner, and SAS Enterprise Miner.

SPSS Clementine

Clementine supports a variety of data mining techniques, such as prediction, classification, segmentation, and association detection. We chose to use Clementine to illustrate these core data mining techniques. These core data mining techniques are common in most of the data mining software suites previously listed.

What's on the Web Site

The companion Web site (www.wiley.com/compbooks/soukup) contains Web links to the data visualization and visual data mining software tools discussed throughout this book. It also contains Web links to the extraction, cleansing, transformation, and loading (ECTL) tools referenced in Chapter 4, as well as, other software tools discussed in other chapters.

To demonstrate the eight-step data visualization and visual data mining methodology, we used a variety of business data sets. One business data set we used frequently was from a home equity loan campaign. We have included the entire home equity loan campaign prepared business data set on the Web site. For ease of transport and download, we have saved it as an Excel spreadsheet containing 44,124 records and 20 columns.

At the end of Chapters 2 through 9, we applied each of the VDM steps to an ongoing customer retention case study. However, the size of the operations data sources, as well as the final two business data sets, is fairly large. For instance, the INVOICE.TXT file contains over 4.6 million rows. Therefore, we are providing the operational data sources and business data sets as an Access database file, casestudy.mdb, which is 180 MB. In addition, we are providing a 10 percent sample of each of the operational sources files, as well as the prepared business data sets as Excel spreadsheets, namely:

- 10 percent sample of the CUSTOMER.TXT, CONTRACT.TXT, INVOICE.TXT, and DEMOGRAPHIC.TXT operational source files

- 10 percent sample of the untransformed business data sets, *customer_join* and *customer_demographics*

- 10 percent sample of the prepared production business data sets, *customer_join* and *customer_demographics*

Beware, if you use the sample Code Figure SQL on the 10 percent sample files instead of the complete data set your results may not exactly match those demonstrated in the book. However, depending on the capacity of your computer system and what database you are using, the 10 percent sample files may be easier for you to work with than the complete files contained in the Access database file. The decision of which set of files to use is up to you; nevertheless, we encourage you to work though the methodology steps with the customer retention operational data source files and business data set files as you read the book.

Summary

The process of planning, preparing the business data set, and creating and analyzing data visualizations and data mining models, is an iterative process. Visualization and visual data mining steps as described in the visualization and visual data mining (VDM) methodology are frequently repeated. As you gain more understanding of the data set and the significance of one data fact (a column) to other data facts (other columns), the data and visualizations are refined. It is rare that data or business analysts create a production-class data visualization or data mining model the first time through the data mining discovery process. Often the data must be further transformed or more data is necessary to answer the business question. In some cases, discoveries about the data set lead to refining the original business questions. The power of visualization provides you the ability to quickly see and understand the data set and data mining model so you can improve your analysis interactively.

We hope that this book helps you develop production-class visualizations and data mining models that address your business questions. Furthermore, we hope that this book gives you the essential guidance to make your VDM project a success. The next chapter introduces you to data visualization and visual data mining concepts used throughout the book.

PART ONE

Introduction and Project Planning Phase

Introduction to Data Visualization and Visual Data Mining

When you read a newspaper or magazine, or watch a news or weather program on TV, you see numerous data visualizations. For example, bar and column graphs are often used to communicate categorical and demographic discoveries such as household or population survey results or trends, line graphs are used to communicate financial market time-based trends, and map graphs are used to communicate geographic weather patterns. Have you ever asked yourself why? Could it be that two- and three-dimensional data visualizations are the most effective way of communicating large quantities of complicated data? In this book, not only do we emphasize the benefits of data visualization to analyze business data sets and communicate your discoveries, but we also outline a proven data visualization and visual data mining methodology that explains how to conduct successful data mining projects within your organization.

Chapter 1 introduces you to a variety of data visualization tools and techniques that you can use to visualize business data sets and discover previously unknown trends, behavior, and anomalies. It also introduces you to a variety of data visualization tools and techniques for visualizing, analyzing, and evaluating popular data mining algorithms.

This book discusses two broad classes of visualizations—(1) data visualization techniques for visualizing business data sets and (2) visual data mining tools and techniques for visualizing and analyzing data mining algorithms and exploring the resultant data mining models. The distinction is as follows:

- *Data visualization tools and techniques* help you create two- and three-dimensional pictures of business data that can be easily interpreted to gain knowledge and insights into those data sets. With data visualization, you act as the data mining or pattern recognition engine. By visually inspecting and interacting with the two- or three-dimensional visualization, you can identify the interesting (nontrivial, implicit, perhaps previously unknown and potentially useful) information or patterns in the business data set.

- *Visual data mining tools and techniques* help you create visualizations of data mining models to gain knowledge and insight into the patterns discovered by the data mining algorithms that help with decision making and predicting new business opportunities. With visual data mining tools, you can inspect and interact with the two- or three-dimensional visualization of the predictive or descriptive data mining model to understand (and validate) the interesting information and patterns discovered by the data mining algorithm. In addition, data visualization tools and techniques are used to understand and evaluate the results of the data mining model. The output from a data mining tool is a *model* of some sort. You can think of a model as a collection of generalizations or patterns found in the business data set that is an abstraction of the task. Just as humans may use their previous experience to develop a strategy to handle, say, difficult people, the data mining tool develops a model to predict people who are likely to leave a service organization. Depending on the data mining tool, an explanation of why a decision was made is possible. Some data mining tools provide a clear set of reasons as to why a particular decision was made, while others are black boxes, making decisions but not telling you why.

In both cases, visualization is key in helping you discover new patterns and trends and to communicate these discoveries to the decision makers. The payoffs and ROI (return-on-investment) can be substantial for businesses that use a combination of data visualization and visual data mining effectively. A base knowledge of various types of data visualization and visual data mining tools is required before beginning the eight-step data visualization and data mining (VDM) methodology discussed in Chapters 2 through 9. A good working knowledge of the visualization types will aid you in the project planning, data preparation, and data analysis phases of your VDM project.

Visualization Data Sets

The majority of business data sets are stored as a single table of information composed of a finite number of columns and one or more rows of data. Chapter 4 discusses how to choose the data from your operational data warehouse or other business data sources. However, before we begin introducing you to the visualization tools and techniques, a brief explanation of the business data set is necessary. Table 1.1 shows an example of a simple business data set with information (data) about weather.

The information (data facts) about the *WEATHER* subject data set is interpreted as follows:

- WEATHER is the file, table, or data set name. A city's weather on a particular day is the subject under investigation.

- CITY, DATE, TEMPERATURE, HUMIDITY, and CONDITION are four *columns* of the data set. These columns describe the kind of information kept in the data set—that is, attributes about the weather for each city.

- ATHENS, 01-MAY-2001, 97.1, 89.2, SUNNY is a particular *record* or *row* in the data set. Each unique set of data (data fact) should have its own record (row). For this row, the data value "Athens" identifies the CITY, "01-MAY-2001" identifies the DATE the measurement was taken, "97.1" identifies TEMPERATURE in degrees Fahrenheit, "89.2" identifies the HUMIDITY in percent, and "Sunny" identifies the CONDITION.

- The level of detail or granularity of data facts (experimental unit) is at the city level.

Data visualization tools and techniques are used to graphically display the data facts as a 2-D or 3-D picture (representation) of the columns and rows contained in the business data sets.

Table 1.1 Business Data Set Weather

CITY	DATE	TEMPERATURE	HUMIDITY	CONDITION
Athens	01-MAY-2001	97.1	89.2	Sunny
Chicago	01-MAY-2001	66.5	100.0	Rainy
Paris	01-MAY-2001	71.3	62.3	Cloudy

Visualization Data Types

Columns in a business data set (table or file) contain either discrete or continuous data values. A *discrete column*, also known as a *categorical variable*, is defined as a column of the table whose corresponding data values (record or row values) have a finite number of distinct values. For instance, discrete data type columns are those that contain a character string, an integer, or a finite number of grouped ranges of continuous data values. The possible data values for a discrete column normally range from one to a few hundred unique values. If there is an inherent order to the discrete column, it is also referred to as an *ordinal variable*. For instance, a discrete column whose unique values are SMALL, MEDIUM, or LARGE is considered an ordinal variable.

A *continuous column*, also known as a numeric variable or date variable, is defined as a column of a table whose corresponding data values (record or row values) can take on a full range (potentially an infinite number) of numeric values. For instance, continuous data type columns are those that contain dates, double-precision numbers, or floating-point numbers. The possible unique data values for a continuous column normally range from a few thousand to an infinite number of unique values. Table 1.2 shows examples of the discrete and continuous columns.

Table 1.2 Discrete and Contin uous Column Examples

COLUMN DATA TYPE	COLUMN NAME	EXAMPLE ROW VALUES	DATA VALUE RANGE
Discrete	CITY	Athens, Chicago, Paris	Finite number of cities in the world
Discrete	CONDITION	Sunny, Rainy	Finite number of weather conditions, such as Sunny, Partly Cloudy, Cloudy, Rainy
Ordinal	EDUCATION	Unknown, High School	Finite number of educational degree categories, such as High School, Bachelor, Master, Doctorate
Discrete	GENDER	M, F, U	Finite number of values, such as M for male, F for female, U for unknown
Ordinal	AGE_GROUPS	0-21, 22-35	Finite number of age range groups
Discrete	PURCHASE_ MONTH	January, February	Finite number of months
Continuous	DATE	01-MAY-2001, 02-MAY-2001	All possible dates
Continuous	TEMPERATURE	97.1, 66.2, 71.3	All possible numeric temperatures in degrees Fahrenheit
Continuous	HUMIDITY	89.1, 100.0, 62.3	All numbers between 0 and100 percent
Continuous	TOTAL_SALES	1.00, $1,000,000.00	All possible total sales amounts

Visual versus Data Dimensions

Take care not to confuse the terms visual dimension and data dimension. *Visual dimension* relates to the spatial coordinate system. *Data dimension*, on the other hand, relates to the number of columns in a business data set. Visual dimensions are the graphical x-, y-, and z-axis of the spatial coordinate system or the color, opacity, height, or size of the graphical object. Data dimensions are the discrete or continuous columns or variables contained within the business data set.

If we use the business data set from Table 1.1, the data dimensions of the weather data set are the columns CITY, DATE, TEMPERATURE, HUMIDITY, and CONDITION. To create a two- or three-dimensional visualization of the weather data set, the columns under investigation are selected from the business data set to create a graphical data table. The graphical data table is used to map the column values of the business data set to corresponding data points in an x-, y-, or z-axis coordinate system.

Figure 1.1 illustrates a column graph visualization comparing the TEMPERATURE and HUMIDITY continuous data dimensions by the CITY discrete data dimension for the weather data set. The corresponding graphical data table values for the TEMPERATURE and HUMIDITY columns are represented by the height of the bars. A pair of bars is drawn for each corresponding CITY value. Normally, the graphical data table is not part of the visualization; however, in this example, the table is included to illustrate how the column graph was created.

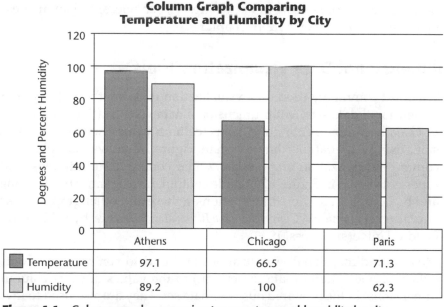

	Athens	Chicago	Paris
Temperature	97.1	66.5	71.3
Humidity	89.2	100	62.3

Figure 1.1   Column graph comparing temperature and humidity by city.

Since the WEATHER data set only contained summer temperatures ranging from 32 to 120 degrees Fahrenheit, the same y-axis scale can be used for both HUMIDITY and TEMPERATURE. For a data set with different HUMDITY and TEMPERATURE ranges, two y-axes would be required—one for the HUMIDITY scale (0 to 100 percent) and one for the TEMPERATURE scale (−65 to 150 degrees Fahrenheit).

Data Visualization Tools

Data visualization tools are used to create two- and three-dimensional pictures of business data sets. Some tools even allow you to animate the picture through one or more data dimensions. Simple visualization tools such as line, column, bar, and pie graphs have been used for centuries. However, most businesses still rely on the traditional "green-bar" tabular report for the bulk of the information and communication needs. Recently, with the advance of new visualization techniques, businesses are finding they can rapidly employ a few visualizations to replace hundreds of pages of tabular reports. Other businesses use these visualizations to augment and summarize their traditional reports. Using visualization tools and techniques can lead to quicker deployment, result in faster business insights, and enable you to easily communicate those insights to others.

The data visualization tool used depends on the nature of the business data set and its underlying structure. Data visualization tools can be classified into two main categories:

- Multidimensional visualizations
- Specialized hierarchical and landscape visualizations

Choosing which visualization technique or tool to use to address your business questions is discussed in Chapter 7. Using and analyzing the visualization to discover previously unknown trends, behaviors, and anomalies in your business data set is covered in Chapter 8.

Multidimensional Data Visualization Tools

The most commonly used data visualization tools are those that graph multidimensional data sets. Multidimensional data visualization tools enable users to visually compare data dimensions (column values) with other data dimensions using a spatial coordinate system. Figure 1.2 shows examples of the most common visualization graph types. Other common multidimensional graph types not shown in Figure 1.2 include contour, histogram, error, Westinghouse, and box graphs. For more information on these and other graph types refer to *Information Graphics: A Comprehensive Illustrated Reference,* by R. Harris (Oxford: Oxford University Press, 1999).

Most multidimensional visualizations are used to compare and contrast the values of one column (data dimension) to the values of other columns (data dimensions) in the prepared business data set. They are also used to investigate the relationships between two or more continuous or discrete columns in the business data set. Table 1.3 lists some common multidimensional graph types and the types of column values they can compare or the kinds of relationships they can investigate.

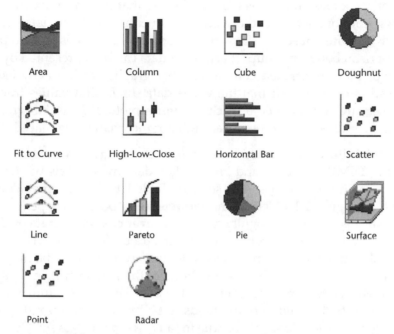

Area	Column	Cube	Doughnut
Fit to Curve	High-Low-Close	Horizontal Bar	Scatter
Line	Pareto	Pie	Surface
Point	Radar		

Figure 1.2   Multidimensional data visualization graph types.

Table 1.3   Graph Types and Column Types

GRAPH TYPE	TYPE OF COLUMN VALUES TO COMPARE
Column and bar	Used to compare discrete (categorical) column values to continuous column values
Area, stacked column or bar, line, high-low-close, and radar	Used to compare discrete (categorical) column values over a continuous column
Pie, doughnut, histogram, distribution, and box	Used to compare the distribution of distinct values for one or more discrete columns
Scatter	Used to investigate the relationship between two or more continuous columns

Column and Bar Graphs

Column and bar graphs, such as clustered column and clustered bar graphs, compare continuous data dimensions across discrete data dimensions in an x- and y-coordinate system. Column graphs plot data dimensions much like a line graph, except that a vertical column is drawn from the x-axis to the y-axis for the value of the data dimension. Bar graphs are identical to column graphs, except the x-axis and y-axis are switched so that the bar graphical entities are drawn horizontally instead of vertically. In either case, the data values associated with different sets of data are grouped by their x-axis label to permit easy comparison between groups. Each set of data can be represented by a different color or pattern. Stacked column and bar graphs work exactly like the non-stacked version, except that the y-axis data dimension values from previous data sets are accumulated as each column is plotted. Thus, bar graphical entities appear to be stacked upon each other rather than being placed side by side.

Figure 1.1 illustrates a multidimensional column graph visualization comparing the TEMPERATURE and HUMIDITY data dimensions by the CITY data dimension for the weather data set from Table 1.1. The interpretation of the bar graph in Figure 1.1 is left to the viewer—who posssesses perhaps the most sophisticated pattern recognition machine ever created. What conclusions can be discovered from the column graph illustrated in Figure 1.1? You may conclude the rule is that (in most cases) temperature tends to be higher than the humidity. However, in the case of Chicago, the rule is broken. Despite this, if you must also take into consideration the CONDITION column, you can refine the rule to be that temperature tends to be higher than humidity unless it is raining. Now the rule would be true for all rows in the data set. Obtaining more records for the data set and plotting them would help you visually test and refine your rule.

Distribution and Histogram Graphs

An extremely useful analytical technique is to use basic bar and column graphs to display the distribution of values for a data dimension (column). Distribution and histogram graphs display the proportion of the values for discrete (nonnumeric) and continuous (numeric) columns as specialized bar and column graphs. A *distribution graph* shows the occurrence of discrete, nonnumeric column values in a data set. A typical use of the distribution graph is to show imbalances in the data. A *histogram*, also referred to as a frequency graph, plots the number of occurrence of same or distinct values in the data set. They are also used to reveal imbalances in the data. Chapters 4, 5, and 6 use distribution and histogram graphs to initially explore the data set, detect imbalances, and verify the correction of these imbalances. Chapters 7 and 8 use distribution and histogram graphs to discover and evaluate key business indicators.

Figure 1.3 shows a distribution graph of the INVOICE DATE data dimension for 2,333 billing records for the first four months of 2000. From the distribution graph, you can visually see that the month of February 2000 had the most invoices. Since you can verify the number of records by month against the original operational data source, the distribution graph provides you a method for verifying whether there are missing records in your business data set.

Figure 1.4a shows a histogram graph of the number of invoices by REGION and Figure 1.4b shows a histogram graph of the number of invoices by BILLING RATE groupings for the first four months of 2000 from the same accounting business data set. In both of these graphs, you can visually see the *skewness* (lack of symmetry in a frequency distribution) in the column value distribution. For instance, the histogram graph of invoices by REGION (Figure 1.4a) is skewed toward the Eastern region while the histogram graph of invoice by BILLING RATE (Figure 1.4b) is skewed toward billing rates of $15.00 an hour or less.

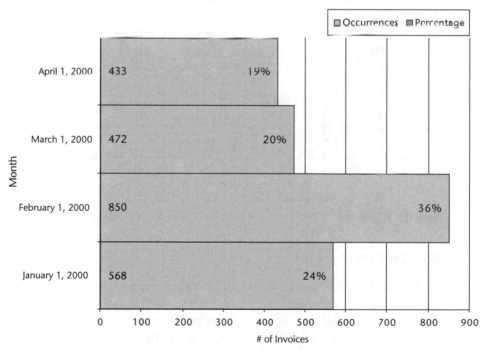

Figure 1.3   Distribution graph of invoices for the first four months of 2000.

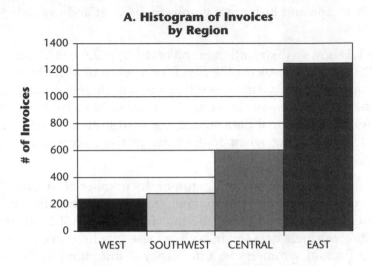

A. Histogram of Invoices by Region

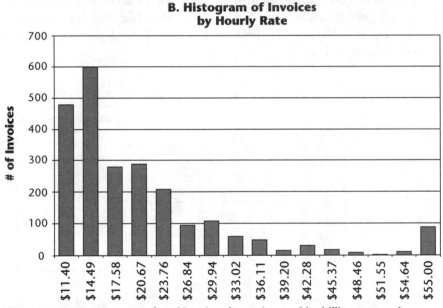

B. Histogram of Invoices by Hourly Rate

Figure 1.4 Histogram graphs of invoices by region and by billing rate regions.

Box Graphs

Understanding descriptive statistical information about the column's values has typically been accomplished by analyzing measurements of central tendency (such as mean, median, and mode), measurements of variability (such as standard deviation and variance), and measures of distribution (such as kurtosis and skewness). For more information about central tendency, variability, and distribution measurements, refer to *Statistics for the Utterly Confused* by L. Jaisingh (New York: McGraw-Hill, 2000). Table 1.4 shows some of the common descriptive statistics derived from the values of the continuous column BILLING RATE.

Table 1.4 Descriptive Statistics for BILLING RATE

BILLING_RATE	
Mean	19.59751
Standard error	0.271229
Median	15
Mode	12
Standard deviation	13.10066
Sample variance	171.6274
Kurtosis	16.48715
Skewness	3.196885
Range	159
Minimum	7
Maximum	166
Sum	45721
Count	2333
Confidence level (95.0%)	0.531874

A variation on the histogram graph is the *box plot graph*. It visually displays statistics about a continuous column (numeric and date data types). Figure 1.5 shows two box plots for the BILLING RATE and INVOICE DATE.

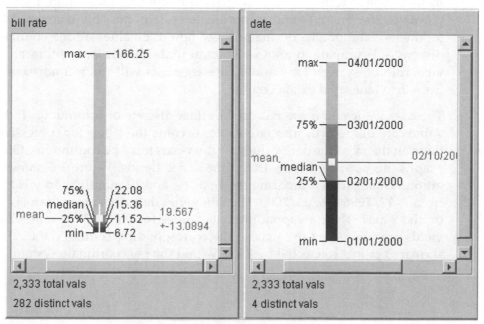

Figure 1.5 Box graph of BILLING RATE and INVOICE DATE.

The box graphs display the following for each continuous column in the data set:

- The two quartiles (25th and 75th percentiles) of the column's values. The quartiles are shown as lines across a vertical colored bar. The length of the bar represents the difference between the 25th and 75th percentiles. From the length of the bar you can determine the variability of the continuous column. The larger the bar, the greater the spread in the data.

- The minimum, maximum, median, and mean of the column's values. The horizontal line inside the bar represents the median. If the median is not in the center of the bar, the distribution is skewed.

- The standard deviation of the column's values. The standard deviation is shown + and – one standard deviation from the column's mean value.

The box plots visually reveal statistical information about the central tendency, variance, and distribution of the continuous column values in the data set. The statistics graphs in Figure 1.5 show the position of the descriptive statistics on a scale ranging from the minimum to the maximum value for numeric columns. They are often used to explore the data in preparation for transformations and model building. Similar to the distribution and histogram graph, statistics graphs are frequently used to reveal imbalances in the data. Chapters 4, 5, and 6 use statistics graphs to initially explore the data set, detect imbalances, and verify the correction of these imbalances.

Line Graphs

In its simplest form, a *line graph* (chart) is nothing more than a set of data points plotted in an x- and y-coordinate system, possibly connected by line segments. Line graphs normally show how the values of one column (data dimension) compare to another column (data dimension) within an x- and y-coordinate system. Line and spline segments will connect adjacent points from the values of the data column.

The data values for the x-axis can be either discrete or continuous. If the data values are discrete, the discrete values become the labels for successive locations on the axis. The data values for the y-axis must be continuous. Often line graphs are used to demonstrate time series trends. Figure 1.6 shows a line graph visualization comparing the 1-, 3-, 6-, and 12-month bond yield indices from 1/17/1996 to 6/23/2000. The time series data dimension (date) is plotted on the x-axis. The corresponding data values for the 1-, 3-, 6-, and 12-month yields are plotted on the y-axis. The corresponding column data values are shown as points connected by a line within the x-y coordinate system.

Figure 1.6 is the compilation of four individual line graphs. It allows you to quickly see how the yield indices compare to one another over the time dimension by the positions of the lines in the x- and y-coordinate system. In this single data visualization, over 4,500 pieces of information are communicated (1,136 individual daily readings of 4 values). Various trends may have been missed if you were only looking at column after column of numbers from a green-bar report.

A *high-low-close graph* is a variation on the line graph. Instead of a single x-y data point, the high, low, and close column values are displayed as hash markers on a floating column (the floating column being defined by the high and low values) within the x- and y- coordinate system. A typical use of high-low-close graphs is to show stock trends. Another variation on the line graph is the *radar graph*, which shows radars with markers at each data point in a 360-degree coordinate system instead of the traditional 90-degree x-y coordinate system. Figure 1.7 shows a radar graph of the bond yield indices comparing the 1- and 6-month bond yields. In Chapters 7 and 8, line and radar graphs are used to discover and analyze time-based trends.

Figure 1.6 Line graph of bond yield indices.

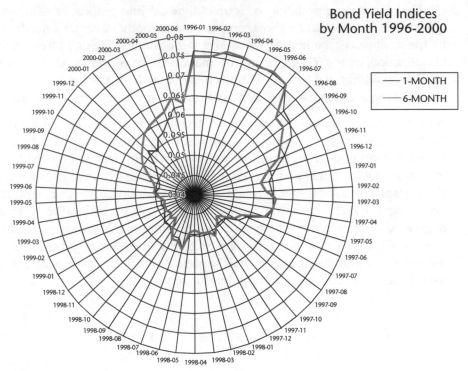

Figure 1.7 Radar graph of bond yield indices.

Scatter Graphs

Scatter graphs (sometimes referred to as scatter plots) are typically used to compare pairs of values. A scatter graph enables you to visualize the business data set by mapping each row or record in the data set to a graphical entity within a two- or three-dimensional graph. In contrast to the line graph, a scatter graphs displays unconnected points on an x-, y-, or z-coordinate system (3-D). In its simplest mode, data dimensions from the data set are mapped to the corresponding points in an x- and y-coordinate (2-D). The *bubble graph* is a variation of a simple scatter graph that allows you to display another data dimension of the data set as the size of the graphical entity, as well as its position within the x- and y-coordinate system. Figure 1.8 illustrates how you can use a scatter graph to investigate the relationship between the number of store promotions and the weekly profit. In Chapters 7 and 8, scatter graphs are used to discover and evaluate cause and effect relationships.

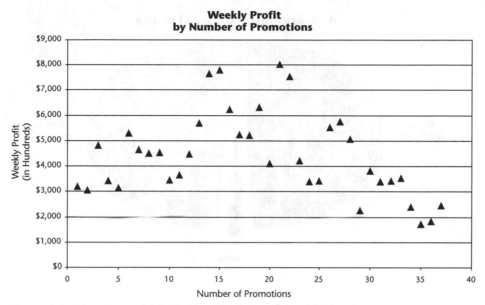

Figure 1.8 Scatter graph of weekly profit by number of promotions.

Pie Graphs

Pie graphs display the contribution of each value to the sum of the values for a particular column. Discrete column values become the labels for the slices of the pie, while the continuous column values are summarized into contribution per the discrete column value. Figure 1.9a shows a pie graph comparing the percent contribution of the total votes cast for each candidate in the state of Florida during the 2001 U.S. presidential race. Pie graphs are also very useful in showing column value distributions. In Chapters 4, 5, and 6, they are used to compare column value distributions before and after data preparation steps.

The doughnut graph is a variation on the pie graph. It can be used to compare and contrast multiple continuous columns at the same time. For instance, using a doughnut graph, you could show the voting percentages per U.S. presidential candidate in Florida, Wisconsin, and other states within the same visualization. This allows you to not only compare the vote percentages per candidate in Florida but also to compare those percentages against the other states that were visualized. Figure 1.9b shows a doughnut graph of the presidential vote in Florida.

A. Presidential Vote in Florida

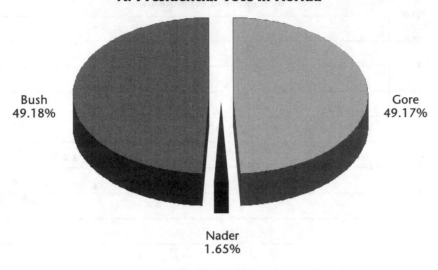

Bush
49.18%

Gore
49.17%

Nader
1.65%

B. Presidential Vote in Florida

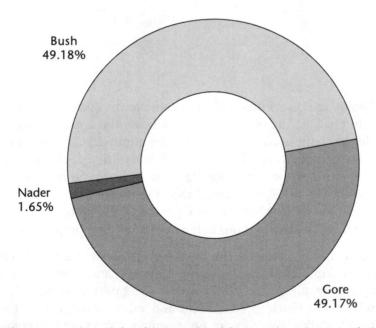

Bush
49.18%

Nader
1.65%

Gore
49.17%

Figure 1.9　Pie and doughnut graphs of the presidential vote in Florida.

Hierarchical and Landscape Data Visualization Tools

Hierarchical, landscape, and other specialized data visualization tools differ from normal multidimensional tools in that they exploit or enhance the underlining structure of the business data set itself. You are most likely familiar with an organizational chart or a family tree. Some business data sets possess an inherent hierarchical structure. Tree visualizations can be useful for exploring the relationships between the hierarchy levels. Other business data sets have an inherent geographical or spatial structure. For instance, data sets that contain addresses have a geographical structure component. Map visualization can be useful for exploring the geographical relationships in the data set. In other cases, the data set may have a spatial versus geographical structure component. For instance, a data set that contains car part failures inherently has spatial information about the location of the failure within the car. The failures can be "mapped" to a diagram of a car (a car landscape). Another data set may contain where in the factory the failing part was manufactured. The failure can be "mapped" to a diagram of the factory (a factory landscape) to explore whether the failed part has any significance to the location where it was manufactured.

Tree Visualizations

The *tree graph* presents a data set in the form of a tree. Each level of the tree branches (or splits) based upon the values of a different attribute (hierarchy in the data set). Each node in the tree shows a graph representing all the data in the sub-tree below it. The tree graph displays quantitative and relational characteristics of a data set by showing them as hierarchically connected nodes. Each node contains information usually in the form of bars or disks whose height and color correspond to aggregations of data values (usually sums, averages, or counts). The lines (called *edges*) connect the nodes together and show the relationship of one set of data to its subsets.

Figure 1.10 illustrates the number of families on Medicaid from a 1995 Census data set using a tree graph. The "root" node, or start of the tree, shows the total number of families on Medicaid (the small, darker colored column on the right) and not on Medicaid (the taller, lighter colored column on the left) that occur in the entire data set. You can see the number of families on Medicaid is very small, as the height of the lighter column is much greater than the darker column. The second level of the tree represents the number of families on

Medicaid by the various family types. By visualizing the data in this way, you may be able to find some combination attributes and values that are indicative of families having a higher than normal chance of being on Medicaid. As you can see from tree visualization, some types of families have a significantly higher chance of being on Medicaid than others (related subfamily and second individual family types versus non-family householders).

Map Visualizations

To explore business data sets for strong spatial (typically geographical) relationships, you can use a map visualization. The corresponding column values are displayed as graphical elements on a visual map based on a spatial key. Although the data set contains a geographic data dimension, what is not contained in the data set is the information that says there are 50 states in the United States, that California and New York are 3,000 miles apart, that California is south of Oregon, or what the latitude or longitude coordinates are for the states. For instance, you can plot your total sales by state, state and county, and zip code.

Figure 1.11 is a map visualization of a business data set that contains information about the number of new account registrations by state. Using a corresponding color key, the states are colored based on the number of registrations by state. You can quickly determine from the map which sales locations (states and regions) are signing up more new customers than others. You can also see the geographic significance of the best-producing state or regions compared with other states and regions.

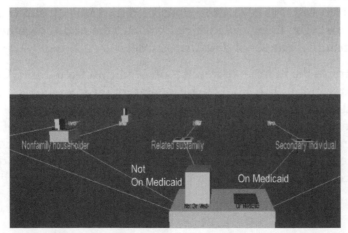

Figure 1.10   Tree visualization of proportion of families on Medicaid by family type and region.

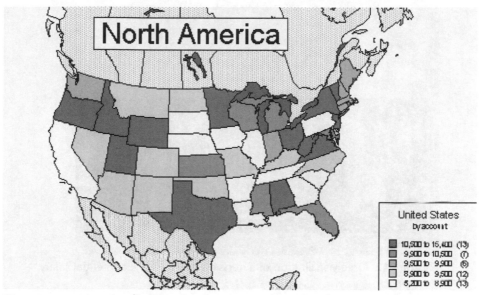

Figure 1.11   Map visualization of new account registrations by state.

Visual Data Mining Tools

Visual data mining tools can be used to create two- and three-dimensional pictures of the how the data mining model is making its decision. The visualization tool used depends on the nature of data set and the underlying structure of the resulting model. For example, in Figure 1.12 a decision tree model is visualized using a hierarchical tree graph. From this visualization you can more easily see the structure of the model.

Unfortunately, not all data mining algorithms can be readily visualized with commercially available software. For instance, neural network data mining models simulate a large number of interconnected simple processing units segmented into input, hidden, and output layers. Visualizing the entire network with its inputs, connections, weights, and outputs as a two- or three-dimensional picture is an active research question.

Visualization tools are also used to plot the effectiveness of the data mining model, as well as to analyze the potential deployment of the model. A *gains chart* is a line graph that directly compares a model's performance at predicting a target event in comparison to always guessing it occurs. The *cumulative gain* is the proportion of all the target events that occur up to a specific percentile. Figure 1.13 illustrates a cumulative gains chart. The population series refers to

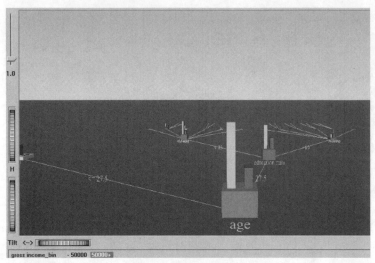

Figure 1.12 Tree visualization of a decision tree to predict potential salary.

our random-guess model. From this line graph, you can compare and contrast the performance of different data mining models. You can also use these visualizations to compare and contrast the performance of the models at the time they are built and once they are deployed. You can quickly visually inspect the performance of the model to see if it is performing as expected or becoming stale and out-of-date. Other multidimensional data visualization tools are useful in analyzing the data mining model results, as well as comparing and contrasting multiple data mining models.

The tree visualization in Figure 1.12 and the line visualization in Figure 1.13 are just two examples of how you can use data visualization to explore how data mining models make their decisions and evaluate multiple data mining models. Choosing which visual data mining tool to use to address your business questions is discussed in Chapter 7. Analyzing the visualization of the data mining model to discover previously unknown trends, behaviors, and anomalies in business data set is discussed in Chapter 8.

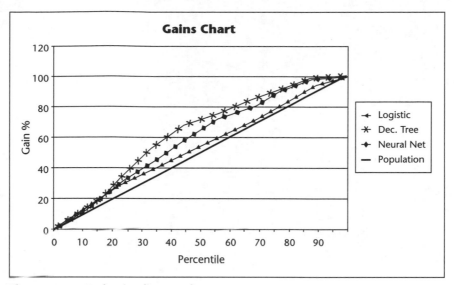

Figure 1.13 Evaluation line graph.

Summary

Chapter 1 summarized data visualization and visual data mining tools and techniques that can be used to discover previously unknown trends, behaviors, and anomalies in business data. In the next chapter, we help you justify and plan a data visualization and data mining project so you can begin to exploit your business data with data visualization and visual data mining to gain knowledge and insights into business data sets and communicate those discoveries to the decision makers. Chapters 2 through 9 present and teach you a proven eight-step VDM methodology that we have used to create successful business intelligence solutions with data visualization and visual data mining tools and techniques.

Step 1: Justifying and Planning the Data Visualization and Data Mining Project

S tep 1 of the eight-step data visualization and data mining (VDM) methodology is composed of both the project justification and the project plan. Chapter 1 provided you with an introduction to visualization and data mining tools and techniques. This chapter shows you how to justify and plan the VDM project. Before the first row of data is visualized or mined, a project justification and plan needs to be developed to ensure the success of the project. The purpose of the project justification is to identify quantitative project objectives and develop a sound business case for performing the project, and to gain executive support and funding from the decision makers for the project. The *project justification* defines the overall business stimulus, return-on-investment (ROI) targets, and visualization and data mining goals for the project. The purpose of a *project plan* is to define the scope, high-level tasks, roles, and responsibilities for the project. The project plan establishes a roadmap and project timeline. It defines the roles and responsibilities of all participants who will be involved in the project and serves as an "agreement" of individual responsibilities among the operations and data warehousing, the data and business analyst, the domain expert, and the decision maker teams.

A closed-loop business model is often helpful in modeling the business aspects of the project. The closed-loop model ensures the resulting visualizations or data mining models feed back into the initial data set sources. This feedback loop enables you to refine, improve, and correct your production visualizations or data mining models through time. Other feedback loops within the business model ensure your project stays focused, makes business sense, and remains within the scope of the project.

This chapter begins by discussing three types of projects:

- Proof-of-concept
- Pilot
- Production

We then introduce using a closed-loop business model, provide guidance to estimating the project timeline and resources, and define team roles and responsibilities for the project. At the end of this chapter, we introduce the case study of a customer retention business problem. We then apply the concepts discussed in this chapter to the case study to illustrate Step 1 of the VDM methodology.

Classes of Projects

The overall scope of your VDM project can be categorized into three classes of projects: proof-of-concept, pilot, or production. Often a successful proof-of-concept or pilot project later leads to a production project. Therefore, no matter which type of project is planned, it helps to keep the overall structure of the project justification and plan consistent. This enables you to quickly turn a proof-of-concept project justification and plan into a pilot or production project without starting over from scratch or wasting time and resources. Among other factors, the type of project will determine the following:

- The difficulty and number of the business questions investigated
- The complexity and amount of data analyzed
- The quality and completeness of the data
- The project costs (personnel, software, and hardware cost)
- The duration of the project
- The complexity and number of resultant visualizations and models created

A *proof-of-concept* VDM project has a limited scope. The overall scope of a proof-of-concept project is to determine whether visualization and data mining will be beneficial to your business, to prove to the decision makers the value of visualization and data mining, and to give your organization experience with visualization and data mining concepts. Typically, one or two relatively trivial business questions are investigated. The data set analyzed is limited to a small sample of existing data. The average duration of a proof-of-concept project normally is a few weeks.

A *pilot* VDM project also has a limited scope. The overall scope of the pilot project is to investigate, analyze, and answer one or more business questions to determine if the ROI of the discoveries warrants a production project. The data set analyzed is limited to representative samples from the real data sources. Often you will need to purchase limited copies of the visualization and data mining tools. However, since the pilot project may not be implemented, you may not have to purchase the production hardware or copies of the visualization and data mining tools for everyone. The average duration of a pilot project is normally a few months.

A *production* VDM project is similar to the pilot project in scope; however, the resulting visualizations and data mining models are implemented into a production environment. The overall scope of the production project is to fully investigate, analyze, and answer the business questions and then to implement an action plan and measure the results of the production visualizations and data mining models created. You will need to purchase licenses for the visualization and data mining tools for all production users and buy the production hardware. The average duration of a production project ranges from a few months to a year. The actual project deployment may last many years.

Depending on the visualization and data mining experience level of your staff, you may need to augment it. For production projects, you will need a dedicated and trained staff to maintain the production environment. Many times after you see the benefits and ROI from the project, you will want to use visualization and data mining to answer other business questions or use VDM in other departments in your organization.

Project Justifications

After you have decided which class of project to do, you next need to create a project justification. The *project justification* defines the overall business stimulus, ROI targets, and visualization and data mining goals for the project. Developing a project justification begins by identifying a high-level business issue your business needs to address. Table 2.1 lists a few of the business issues that can be addressed by VDM projects.

Attempt to state your overall project goal in a single statement, for instance, "To discover segments of ideal customers who share the same characteristics and who are the best candidates for our new cable modem service offering." You may need to interview various departments within your organization before deciding on your project goal. For proof-of-concept projects, keep the overall project goal simple. For pilot or production projects, the overall project goal may be more complex. Use the examples in Table 2.1 to establish your own project objective.

Table 2.1 Business Issues Addressed by Visualizations or Visual Data Mining Projects

BUSINESS ISSUE	VDM PROJECT OBJECTIVES
Target marketing	To discover segments of "ideal" customers who share the same characteristics, such as income level, and spending habits, with the best candidates for a specific product or service
Cross-marketing	To discover co-relations and associations between product sales and make predictions based on these associations to facilitate cross-marketing
Customer profiling	To create models to determine what types of customers buy which products
Identification of customer requirements	To discover the best product matches for different segments of customers and use predictions to find what factors will attract new customers
Financial planning and asset evaluation	To create descriptive or predictive models to aid in cash flow analysis and predictions, contingent claim analysis, and trend analysis to evaluate assets
Resource planning	To create descriptive or predictive models to aid in analyzing and comparing resources and spending
Competitive analysis	To segment customers into classes for class-based pricing structures and set pricing strategies for highly competitive markets
Fraud detection	To create descriptive or predictive models to aid in analyzing historical data to detect fraudulent behaviors in such industries as medical, retail, banking, credit card, telephone, and insurance
Attrition modeling and analysis	To create descriptive or predictive models to aid in the analysis of customer attrition
Chemical and pharmaceutical analysis	To create descriptive or predictive models to aid in molecular pattern modeling and analysis, as well as drug discovery and clinical trial modeling and analysis

Perhaps the most difficult part of the project's business justification is determining realistic ROI objects and expected outcomes. You will often need the assistance of the business analysts or line-of-business manager to help quantify the cost of continuing to do business "status quo." Your aim should be to create a document that contains the project ROI objectives; describes the content, form, access, and owners of the data sources; summarizes the previous research; explains the proposed methodology; and forecasts the anticipated outcome. When preparing the justification document, keep in mind the class of project you are planning, as well as your target audience—the decision makers and business experts.

As reference material for your business justification, include industry examples of visualization and data mining success stories. Choose those success stories that relate to the business issues you are trying to address. Our companion Web site (www.wiley.com/compbooks/soukup) has links to the majority of the commercially available data visualization and visual data mining software providers. For example, you can find the following success stories on the SPSS, SAS, and Oracle Web sites.

Dayton Hudson Corp. Success Story

Retail is a very competitive industry. The Dayton Hudson Corp. (DHC) success story highlights how they use data mining to grow their business and improve customer satisfaction.

For instance, the DHC research and planning department also uses data mining to help select new store sites. By analyzing trade and demographic data for 200 to 300 potential new sites with descriptive, correlation, and regression data mining models, the research group can quantitatively determine which sites have the best potential market success for each of its store lines: Target, Mervyn's, Dayton's, Hudson's, and Marshall Field's.

The DHC consumer research department also uses data mining to target customer satisfaction issues. Often respondent surveys include data files with several hundred thousand cases from DHC stores, as well as, competitive stores. These surveys are analyzed with data mining to gain knowledge about what is most important to customers and to identify those stores with customer satisfaction problems. The data mining results are used to help management better allocate store resources and technology, as well as improve training.

For more information on the DHC success story, refer to the SPSS Web site at www.spss.com/spssatwork/template_view.cfm?Story_ID=4 (SPSS, 2002).

Marketing Dynamics Success Story

Customer direct marketing is another industry that benefits from data visualization and data mining. The Marketing Dynamics success story highlights how they use visual data mining to develop more profitable direct marketing programs for their clients.

Marketing Dynamics has access to large amounts of customer marketing data; however, the trick is to turn that data into insights. Through the use of data mining analysis, Marketing Dynamics is able to develop more profitable target marking programs for their clients, such as Cartier, Benjamin Moore & Company, SmithKline Beecham, American Express Publishing, and several prominent catalog companies.

Marketing Dynamics uses analysis tools such as list analysis, data aggregation, cluster analysis, and other data mining techniques to deliver predictive models to their clients who then use these models to better understand their customers, discover new markets, and deploy successful direct marketing campaigns to reach those new markets.

For more information on the Marketing Dynamics success story, refer to the SPSS Web site at www.spss.com/spssatwork/template_view.cfm?Story_ID= 25 (SPSS, 2002).

Sprint Success Story

Telecommunications is yet another fiercely competitive industry that is benefiting from data visualization and data mining. The Sprint success story highlights how they use visual data mining for customer relationship management (CRM).

Within the sphere of CRM, Sprint not only uses data mining to improve customer satisfaction, but also uses data mining for cross-selling, customer retention, and new customer acquisition. Sprint uses SAS to provide their marketing departments with a central analytic repository. Internal sales and marketing groups access this repository to create better target marketing programs, improve customer relationships, and cross-sell to existing customers. The central repository enables them to integrate multiple legacy systems and incorporate feedback loops into their CRM system.

For more information on the Sprint success story, refer to the SAS Web site at www.sas.com/news/success/sprint.html (SAS, 2002).

Lowestfare.com Success Story

Similar to the traditional retail industry, the Internet online travel industry may be even more brutally competitive. The Lowestfare.com success story highlights how they used data mining to target those customers most likely to purchase over the Internet.

Lowestfare.com built a data warehouse with the most important facts about customers. By analyzing these data sets, they were able to better understand their customers in order to sell them the right products through the best channels, thus increasing customer loyalty. Developing successful target-marketing models helped Lowestfare.com increase profits for each ticket sold.

Lowestfare.com augmented their customer data warehouse with 650 pieces of demographic information purchased from Acxiom. This enabled them to not only better understand who their customers were, but it also helped them to build predictive cross-selling models. Through data mining, they were able to identify the top (87) pieces of demographic information that profiled their customers. Then they were able to build data mining C&RT models that produced customer profiles based on purchase behavior and deploy these models into their Internet site.

For more information on the Lowestfare.com success story, refer to the Oracle Web site at http://otn.oracle.com/products/datamining/pdf/lowestfare.pdf, "Lowestfare.com Targeting Likely Internet Purchasers."

Challenges to Visual Data Mining

Many challenges exist for justifying your VDM project. The various stakeholders in the organization may not understand data mining and what it can do. Following are some common objections to visual data mining approaches.

Data Visualization, Analysis, and Statistics are Meaningless

This objection is often due to a lack of familiarity with the process and benefits that visual data mining can provide. The objection can be overcome by explaining that data analysis is part of most decision-making processes. Whether consciously or subconsciously, individuals, teams, and organizations make decisions based on historical experience every day. Data mining can be easily compared to this decision-making process. For instance, if you view all your previous experiences as a large data set that can be investigated and analyzed, then the processes of drawing actionable conclusions from this data set can be likened to the task of data mining. A critical aspect of the VDM methodology is validation (discussed fully in Chapter 9). VDM tools and techniques only find the interesting patterns and insights. It is the various stakeholders, such as the decision makers and domain experts, that validate whether or not these discoveries are actionable, pragmatic, and worth implementing.

Why Are the Predictions Not 100 Percent Accurate?

One of the benefits of data mining is that it provides you with quantification of error. To some, the very fact that an insight or model has error at all is cause to discount the benefits of visual data mining. After all, shouldn't the model be 100 percent accurate before it is deployed? The accuracy of a model is only one measure that can be used to value its worth. The ability to easily explain the model to regulators and domain experts and the ease of implementation and maintenance are other important factors. Often, analyzing the errors or false prediction cases leads to greater insight into the business problem as a whole. Similarly, visually comparing the model with line graphs (discussed in Chapter 8) assists you in evaluating and selecting the "best" models based on your project objectives.

Our Data Can't Be Visualized or Mined

Data integrity is very important for building useful visualizations and data mining models. How does an organization determine that its data has the level of integrity needed to make a positive impact for the firm? At what point is the data good enough?

The issue of data integrity unfortunately prevents many companies who would benefit from data mining capabilities from getting started on building what is potentially a valuable future core competency. Very few organizations possess data that is immediately suitable for mining unless it was collected for that purpose. A key part of the VDM methodology is data preparation (fully discussed in Chapters 4, 5, and 6), which explicitly involves making the data good enough to work with. Furthermore, it is quite feasible to measure the potential financial success of a visual data mining project by working with historical data. Often the VDM data preparation steps can help your organization pinpoint integrity problems with your existing historical data, as well as implement new standards to ensure the integrity of new business data before and as it is gathered.

Closed-Loop Business Model

Whether you are planning a proof-of-concept, pilot, or production project, consider using a closed-loop business model. A business model is considered closed-loop when the output of the final stage feeds back into the initial step. The interactions among and between stages reveal the iterative nature of the business model.

Most VDM projects can be diagrammed as a closed-loop business model. Figure 2.1 shows the business stages and interactions of a closed-loop business model for a VDM project. This model may be applied to a multitude of visualization and data mining projects, such as projects that:

- Prevent customer attrition
- Cross-sell to existing customers
- Acquire new customers
- Detect fraud
- Identify most profitable customers
- Profile customers with greater accuracy

The business model can also be used for VDM projects that detect hidden patterns in scientific, government, manufacturing, medical, and other applications, such as:

- Predicting the quality of a manufactured part
- Finding associations between patients, drugs, and outcomes
- Identifying possible network intrusions

As illustrated in Figure 2.1, the closed-loop business model contains the data preparation and data analysis phases of the eight-step VDM methodology described throughout this book. However, the implementation phase is outside the book's scope. We have included the entire closed-loop business model to provide you with a business framework for justifying and planning your VDM project. Our companion Web site has links to the majority of the commercially available data visualization and "visual" data mining software providers where you can find information on the implementation phase of a VDM project.

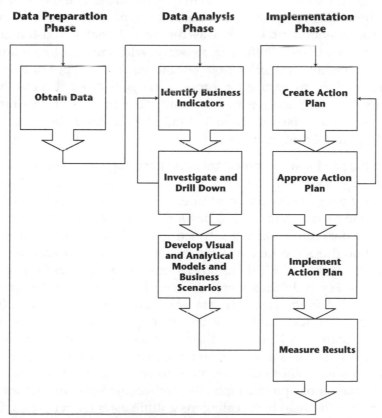

Figure 2.1 Closed-loop business model.

The following section discusses how to use the closed-loop business model for a customer attrition VDM project. The overall business goal of a customer attrition project was to reduce customer attrition from 30 percent to 25 percent. You may be saying to yourself that a 5 percent improvement doesn't seem to be a very valuable goal. However, in this particular case, 5 percent of approximately 4 million customers equates to 200,000 customers. Given the average customer represents $240.00 a year in sales, a 5 percent improvement equates to approximately $48 million in sales a year.

The overall business strategy of the customer attrition project was to create, analyze, and deploy visualization and data mining models to discover profiles of customers who switched services to a competitor, to understand why they switched services, and to find current customers who have similar profiles and then to take corrective action to keep them from switching to the competition. The process of developing the business strategy and identifying the business questions is the second step of the VDM methodology, which we discuss in Chapter 3.

Using the Closed-Loop Business Model

The first stage in the business model is to obtain and select the raw data from the data warehouse and business data repositories pertaining to customers. In the customer retention project, it was discovered that a "customer" was defined differently in the multiple databases. In addition, "customer attrition" was defined differently by different organizations. These types of data issues need to be resolved to ensure the proper data is selected. Unless they are resolved, the resulting analysis may be faulty. The process of obtaining and selecting the data are Steps 3, 4, and 5 of the VDM methodology and are discussed in Chapters 4 through 6.

Identifying the key business indicators is the next stage in the business model. Once all the project teams agreed on the business rules (definitions) of who constitutes a "customer," and what constitutes "customer attrition," visualization and data mining tools were used to begin the process of identifying the key business indicators for classifying satisfied versus lost customers. In the customer retention project, common indicators or profiles that define a satisfied customer as compared to a lost customer were discovered from the historical data. After the key indicators were discovered, the investigation and drill-down stage started. In this stage the data set is further investigated to gain business insights and understanding of behavior (patterns and trends) of lost customers. As shown in Figure 2.1, these business stages feed back into one another. If a key business indicator cannot be substantiated or doesn't make good business sense, other indicators need to be identified. Sometimes a key business indicator looks promising on the surface, but upon further investigation, it doesn't really help in revealing insightful customer behaviors. During the customer retention project, it was discovered that customers who had originally selected a particular service rate plan were extremely likely to begin shopping around for a better rate after about 9 months of service. In addition, after a year of service, customers wanted new equipment. The process of identifying and analyzing the key business indicators and drilling down into the data is Step 7 of the VDM methodology, which we discuss in Chapter 8.

The development of visual and analytical models for different business scenarios is the next stage. For instance, a model that identifies which customers are most likely to switch to the competition unless they are sent updated equipment may be too cost-prohibitive, whereas a model for changing a customer from one service plan to another may be more cost-effective. In this stage, the visualization and data mining models are used to help develop different business scenarios. The process of developing the visualizations and analytical models is also part of Step 7 of the VDM methodology, discussed in Chapter 8.

Creating an action plan and gaining approval for the "best" strategic use of the models, visualizations, and insights that produce the best ROI based on the business goals is the next stage in the business model. In this stage, the visualizations and data mining models are used to communicate the findings to the decision makers and other business analysts. These business stages feed back into one another, as shown in Figure 2.1. There may be high-level business reasons for choosing one scenario over another. For instance, during the presentation of the customer attrition project findings to the decision makers, the vice president of finance suggested that upgrading the customers to newer equipment would not be as cost-prohibitive as originally thought (or modeled). The VP of finance had just renegotiated a contract with the equipment manufacturer that greatly reduced the cost of the equipment. The process of evaluating the "best" models is discussed in Chapter 8. Creating a presentation of the analysis is Step 8 of the VDM methodology, which we discuss in Chapter 9.

Implementing the action plan once it has been approved is the next stage in the business model. In this stage, the visualizations or data mining model are prepared for production. For example, during the customer retention project, the rules from a data mining model were coded into the C language, and weekly batch procedures flagged customers who had a high probability of switching to the competition. The customer support center was given this list of customers at the beginning of each week. The customer support center then contacted each customer on the list throughout the week and either offered to upgrade them to newer equipment or to switch them to a different rate plan.

Measuring the results of the action plan against the model is the next stage in the business model. For example, during the customer retention project, those customers offered and upgraded to the newer equipment were monitored for a full year to determine the actual ROI of the project. The decision tree model had estimated that the "upgrade" campaign would reduce customer attrition by

2.5 percent—$24 million. However, after 6 months, the actual measured results were only around 2 percent—$20 million. The initial data set was augmented with the results, and more refined data mining models were developed and put into production that resulted in a 3 percent reduction in customer attrition—$29 million. In addition to the "upgrade" campaign, the customer attrition project implemented a different data mining model to identify customers who should be offered a different plan before they switched to a competitor that reduced customer attrition by another 2 percent.

Overall, the customer attrition project was deemed a success and added over $40 million to the bottom line. The customer retention project costs (personnel, software, and hardware) were approximately $800,000, resulting in a profit of $31 million for the first year. Using a closed-loop business model helped make the customer retention project a success. The feedback loops enabled the data and business analysts to focus and improve their data mining models to glean a higher rate of return.

Project Timeline

The project timeline will depend on the type of VDM project you are planning. Table 2.2 lists the average workdays per task for typical proof-of-concept, pilot, and production projects. We have compiled this list based on different real-world projects that we have completed. Of course, your "mileage" may vary depending on the business issues investigated, the complexity of the data, the skill level of your teams, and the complexity of the implementation, among other factors. Table 2.2 should give you a general guideline for estimating the project plan timeline for proof-of-concept, pilot, and production projects.

Project Resources and Roles

As illustrated in Table 2.2, schedule a few weeks if you are planning a proof-of-concept project, a month or more for a pilot project, and a few months to a year for a production project. When allocating your project resources, be sure to reach agreement with all teams. The project consists of multiple teams: operations and data warehousing, data and business analysts, domain experts, and decision makers. In the following sections, we will define each team and their responsibilities.

The time and resource demands for each team will depend on the type of VDM project you are planning. A successful business intelligence solution using data visualization or visual data mining requires the participation and cooperation from many parts of a business organization. Depending on the size of your business organization, you may be responsible for one or more roles. (In small organizations, you may be responsible for all roles.)

Table 2.2 Estimating the Project Duration

PROJECT PHASE	VDM METHODOLOGY STEP	TASK NAME	PROOF-OF-CONCEPT	PILOT	PRODUCTION
Planning					
	1	Justify and Plan Project	5	5	5
	2	Identify the Top Business Questions	3	5	10
		Estimated Project Planning Phase Days	8	10	15
Data Preparation					
	3	Choose the Data Set	1	2	5
	4	Transform the Data Set	3	10	15
	5	Verify the Data Set	1	2	5
		Estimated Data Preparation Phase Days	5	14	25
Data Analysis					
	6	Choose the Visualization or Mining Tools	3	10	15
	7	Analyze the Visualization or Mining Models	5	10	15
	8	Verify and Present the Visualization or Mining Models	2	10	15
		Estimated Data Analysis Phase Days	11	30	45
Implementation					
		Create Action Plan			10
		Approve Action Plan			5
		Implement Action Plan			20
		Measure Results			30
		Estimated Implementation Phase Days			65
		TOTAL PROJECT DURATION	24 days	54 days	150 days

Tables 2.3 through 2.6 list the average workdays per resource for typical proof-of-concept, pilot, and production projects. We have compiled this list based on different real-world projects that we have completed. As with the project timeline, your "mileage" may vary depending on the business issues investigated, the complexity of the data, the skill level of your teams, and the complexity of the implementation, among other factors.

Data and Business Analyst Team

The *data and business analyst team* is involved in all phases of the project; therefore, you can use Table 2.2 as a guideline for estimating the average workdays for typical proof-of-concept, pilot, and production projects.

For proof-of-concept, pilot, and production projects, the data and business analyst team is often responsible for the following:

- Justifying and planning the project to the decision makers and creating the project justification and planning document
- Identifying the top business questions to be investigated
- Mapping the top business questions into questions that can be investigated through visualization and data mining
- Creating extract procedures for historical and demographic data with the guidance of domain experts and data warehousing team
- Creating, analyzing, and evaluating the visualizations and data mining models with the guidance of domain experts
- Presenting the solution to the decision makers and assisting to create an action plan

During the implementation phase of a production project, the data and business analyst team is often responsible for the following:

- Implementing the solution's production environment and maintaining the solution's production environment until the operations team is trained
- Measuring the results of the solution and using the results to further refine, enhance, and correct the production visualizations and data mining models

Domain Expert Team

The role of the *domain expert team* is to act as consultants to the data and business analysts to ensure the correct data is obtained and valid business indicators are discovered. They also act as consultants to the decision maker team to ensure the solution makes sound business sense. Table 2.3 lists the average workdays for typical proof-of-concept, pilot, and production projects.

Table 2.3 Domain Expert Team Roles and Responsibilities

VDM METHODOLOGY STEP	TASKS	PROOF-OF-CONCEPT	PILOT	PRODUCTION
1	Justify and Plan Project	5	5	5
2	Identify the Top Business Questions	3	3	9
3	Choose the Data Set	1	2	5
4	Transform the Data Set	–	–	–
5	Verify the Data Set	1	2	5
6	Choose the Visualization or Mining Tools	–	–	–
7	Analyze the Visualization or Mining Models	1	2	4
8	Verify and Present the Visualization or Mining Models	1	2	4
	Create Action Plan			5
	Implement Action Plan			10
	Measure Results			15
	ESTIMATED DAYS	12 days	16 days	62 days

For proof-of-concept, pilot, and production projects, the domain expert team is often responsible for the following:

- Helping the data and business analysts justify and plan the project
- Helping the data and business analysts identify the top business questions to be investigated
- Validating the data obtained by operations and the data and business analysts
- Validating the key business indicators discovered by the data and business analysts

In addition, for the implementation phase of a production project, the domain expert team often has the following responsibilities:

- Helping the data and business analysts and decision makers to create a valid action plan
- Assisting in measuring the results of the project

Decision Maker Team

The role of the *decision maker team* is to evaluate the business scenarios and potentially approve the solution. Table 2.4 lists the average workdays for typical proof-of-concept, pilot, and production projects.

Table 2.4 Decision Maker Team Roles and Responsibilities

VDM METHODOLOGY STEP	TASKS	PROOF-OF-CONCEPT	PILOT	PRODUCTION
1	Justify and Plan Project	2	5	5
2	Identify the Top Business Questions	1	3	3
3	Choose the Data Set	–	–	–
4	Transform the Data Set	–	–	–
5	Verify the Data Set	–	–	–
6	Choose the Visualization or Mining Tools	–	–	–
7	Analyze the Visualization or Mining Models	–	–	–
8	Verify and Present the Visualization or Mining Models	3	3	3
	Create Action Plan			3
	Implement Action Plan			2
	Measure Results			3
	ESTIMATED DAYS	6 days	11 days	19 days

For proof-of-concept, pilot, and production projects, the decision maker team is often responsible for the following:

- Evaluating and approving the business justification and plan
- Championing the project to the rest of the organization at a high level
- Allocating the project funds

In addition, for the implementation phase of a production project, the decision maker team often has the following responsibilities:

- Providing feedback to the data and business analysts during the action plan creation
- Providing feedback to the measured results of the project

Operations Team

The role of the *operations team* is to provide network, database administration, and system administration assistance to the data and business analyst team. They help in obtaining the project data, implementing the production system, as well as measuring the results. Table 2.5 lists the average workdays for typical proof-of-concept, pilot, and production projects.

For proof-of-concept, pilot, and production project, the operations team is often responsible for the following:

- Identifying contact names for historical data, demographics data, network, and database administration services so the data and business analyst team can discuss questions and plan for obtaining the correct data
- Ensuring compatibility and integration of the visualization or data mining software and hardware with the existing network and production environment
- Creating any required databases required by the data and business analysts
- Providing system management of the environment during the proof-of-concept and pilot stages

In addition, for the implementation phase of a production project, the operations team is often responsible for the following:

- Helping to implement the production visualizations or data mining models
- Helping create procedures to measure the results

Table 2.5 Operations Team Roles and Responsibilities

VDM METHODOLOGY STEP	TASKS	PROOF-OF-CONCEPT	PILOT	PRODUCTION
1	Justify and Plan Project	2	3	3
2	Identify the Top Business Questions			
3	Choose the Data Set	1	2	5
4	Transform the Data Set			
5	Verify the Data Set			
6	Choose the Visualization or Mining Tools			
7	Analyze the Visualization or Mining Models			
8	Verify and Present the Visualization or Mining Models			
	Create Action Plan			5
	Implement Action Plan			20
	Measure Results			15
	ESTIMATED DAYS	3 days	5 days	48 days

Data Warehousing Team

Some large organizations have separated the operations and data warehousing teams. In other organizations, a data warehouse doesn't exist, so there isn't a data warehousing team. If your organization has a data warehouse, the role of the *data warehousing team* is to provide extract files from the data warehouse or other business sources to the data and business analyst team. They help in obtaining the project data. Table 2.6 lists the average workdays for typical proof-of-concept, pilot, and production projects. However, if your organization doesn't have a data warehouse, you will need to identify individuals from the operations team that can help you obtain the necessary data from the available business data sources. In this case, the same roles and responsibilities as listed in Table 2.6 will apply to obtaining the data from other business data sources.

Table 2.6 Data Warehousing Team Roles and Responsibilities

VDM METHODOLOGY STEP	TASKS	PROOF-OF-CONCEPT	PILOT	PRODUCTION
1	Justify and Plan Project	2	3	3
2	Identify the Top Business Questions			
3	Choose the Data Set	1	2	5
4	Transform the Data Set	3	10	15
5	Verify the Data Set	1	2	5
6	Choose the Visualization or Mining Tools			
7	Analyze the Visualization or Mining Models			
8	Verify and Present the Visualization or Mining Models			
	Create Action Plan			5
	Implement Action Plan			20
	Measure Results			15
	ESTIMATED DAYS	7 days	17 days	68 days

For proof-of-concept, pilot, and production projects, the data warehousing team is often responsible for the following:

- Setting up and maintaining the environment for extract files
- Creating the extract procedures from the data warehouse or other business sources

In addition, for the implementation phase of a production project, the data warehousing team is often responsible for the following:

- Initiating procedures to provide daily and weekly and monthly extract files for the data and business analyst team
- Helping create procedures to measure the results

Project Justification and Plan for the Case Study

The president of Big Cellular phone company wanted to find a new and cost-effective way of retaining customers. In the weekly status meeting, the VP asked the IT department head what could be done to reduce customer attrition. The IT department head agreed to investigate the problem and report in 2 weeks. Thus began the project justification and plan for the customer retention case study.

The project began by conducting interviews with the major stakeholders: the business analyst, domain expert, IT operations, and data warehousing staffs. We discovered from the customer service department that, according to its database, from 1996 through 1999, 182,319 contracts were canceled out of 501,424. On the surface, it would appear for this time period 36 percent of its customers dropped their service (churned). Reviewing the contract database, we learned that there were over 80 reasons given why customers canceled service. We discovered from the billing department, that over 58,000 contracts were terminated because the customer didn't pay his or her bills (or 32 percent of the assumed churners). We discovered from the data warehousing group that in the data warehouse, they had a wealth of information on every customer—over 300 pieces per customer. They also had an ongoing relationship with a demographics firm and had already augmented each customer in the warehouse with demographic data.

After the first round of interviews, we had a group meeting with the major stakeholders to discuss objects for a visualization and data mining (VDM) pilot project. We suggested that with the wealth of information that Big Cellular had on its customers, data mining was the appropriate tool for not only investigating why customers were canceling their service but for building proactive models to reduce customer attrition. Furthermore, we suggested using visual data mining to aid the data and business analysts in selecting the data to be used for data mining, as well as in understanding and interpreting the data mining models.

At the next meeting with the president of Big Cellular, the results of the interviews were presented. From the customer service department he was given a 4-year customer attrition rate of 36 percent; from the billing department, the 4-year rate was 24 percent; and from the data warehousing department, the 4-year rate was 18 percent. Big Cellular had just spent over $2 million over the past 2 years to build a data warehouse, so it was understandable that the president was not pleased to hear that no one knew for sure what the customer attrition rate was, nor did they know how to stop it.

As a result of the meeting, it was decided that a visual data mining pilot project would be funded to develop descriptive and predictive models that would identify which type of customers were churning and to see if anything could be done to reduce the customer attrition rate. We set our VDM project goal at reducing customer attrition by 15 percent or better. We explained that through visualization and data mining, we could help Big Cellular not only identify its actual churn rate and provide profiles of churn, but to develop models that would predict the likely churners and when they were most likely to churn and why. The president decided that if he was satisfied with the results of the pilot project, he would consider whether to implement a production project.

Table 2.7 shows the project plan for the customer retention VDM pilot project. The estimated project duration was 45 days. The estimated total resource time for the data and business analyst team was 45 days, for the domain expert team 20 days, for the operations team 6 days, and for the data warehousing team 18 days.

The data and business analyst team is involved in all phases of the customer retention VDM pilot project. In particular, this team is responsible for the following:

- Identifying the top business questions to be investigated with the guidance of the domain experts. This task is discussed in Chapter 3.

- Defining the extract procedures from the historical and demographic operational data sources with the guidance of the domain expert, operations, and data warehousing teams. These tasks are discussed in Chapter 4.

- Defining the logical transformations that need to be applied to the production business data set to enhance the information contained within the data set, to remove bias, and to facilitate visualizing and data mining of the business data set. These tasks are discussed in Chapter 5.

- Verifying that both the ECTL procedures, as well as the logical transformation operations, were applied correctly to the business data sets. These tasks are discussed in Chapter 6.

- Selecting which visualization techniques and visual data mining techniques are best suited for investigating the data visualization and visual data mining questions identified in Chapter 3. These tasks are discussed in Chapter 7.

- Creating, analyzing, and evaluating the visualizations and data mining models with the guidance of domain experts. These tasks are discussed in Chapters 7 and 8.

- Presenting the analysis to the decision makers. This task is discussed in Chapter 9.

Table 2.7 Project Plan for Case Study 1

PROJECT PHASE	VDM METHODOLOGY STEP	TASK NAME	DATA AND BUSINESS ANALYSTS	DOMAIN EXPERTS	OPERATIONS	DATA WAREHOUSING
Planning	1	Justify and Plan Project	3	3	1	1
	2	Identify the Top Business Questions	5	5		
Data Preparation	3	Obtain Data	10	3	3	10
	4	Transform the Data Set	5			5
	5	Verify the Data Set	2	2	2	2
Data Analysis	6	Choose the Visualization or Mining Tools	5			
	7	Analyze the Visualization or Mining Models	10	5		
	8	Verify and Present the Visualization or Mining Models	5	2		
Total Estimated Days			45	20	6	18

The domain expert team acts as consultants to the data and business analysts to ensure the correct data is obtained and valid business indicators and insights are discovered. In particular, this team is responsible for the following:

- Helping the data and business analysts identify the top business questions to be investigated. This task is discussed in Chapter 3.

- Determining the visualization and data mining analysis goals and success criteria. These tasks are discussed in Chapter 3.

- Verifying that both the ECTL procedures as well as the logical transformations operations were applied correctly to the business data sets. These tasks are discussed in Chapter 6.

- Providing business guidance to the business and data analysts in analyzing and evaluating the data visualizations and data mining models. These tasks are discussed in Chapter 8.

- Validating the key business insights discovered by the data and business analysts and evaluating potential deployment options. These tasks are discussed in Chapter 9.

The operations team provides network, database administration, and system administration assistance to the data and business analyst team. They help to obtain and validate the project data (both the historical and demographic data). In particular, this team is responsible for the following:

- Identifying the physical location of the historical data, demographics data, and other operational data required to create the business data sets. They are also responsible for any network or database administration required to facilitate the data and business analyst team in obtaining the correct data. These tasks are discussed in Chapter 4.

- Providing system management of the environment during the pilot stages.

The data warehousing team provides extract files from the data warehouse or other business sources and assists the data and business analyst team in creating business data sets. In particular, this team is responsible for the following:

- Setting up and maintaining the exploratory data mart environment for extract files. These tasks are discussed in Chapter 4.

- Creating any extract procedures from the data warehouse, as well as any demographic data extracts. These tasks are discussed in Chapter 4.

- Creating the logical transformations and applying them to the production business data set. These tasks are discussed in Chapter 5.

- Correcting any ECTL or logical transformation operations errors discovered while verifying the business data set. These tasks are discussed in Chapter 6.

The next step in the customer retention VDM pilot project is to identify the top business questions. The discussion of the customer retention project will continue at the end of the next chapter.

Summary

Chapter 2 described how to justify and plan the visualization and data mining project, which is Step 1 of the eight-step VDM methodology. The next step of the planning phase is to map the top business question into problem definitions that can be investigated with data visualization and data mining, which we will cover in Chapter 3.

Step 2: Identifying the Top Business Questions

S tep 2 of the VDM methodology is mapping the top business questions and project objectives into problem definitions and objectives that can be investigated through visualization and data mining techniques. In the previous chapter, we demonstrated how to justify and plan the VDM project. Chapter 3 focuses on how to rephrase your top business questions and project objectives. Throughout this chapter, we present industry examples that will help you rephrase your top VDM project business questions into visualization and data mining problem definitions. We will also present ROI and profit evaluation techniques that can assist you to map your VDM project ROI targets into achievable and measurable data mining goals. Finally, we apply Step 2 to the ongoing customer retention business case study.

Choosing the Top Business Questions

You must ascertain what business questions need to be investigated, as well as map those business questions to problem definitions that can be addressed by data visualizations and data mining models. Identifying the top business questions takes collaboration among the data and business analysts, domain experts, or line-of-business managers who understand the business. You must find out and clarify what exactly is expected as the output of the VDM project.

Is it a set of descriptive visualizations that provide insight into the business problem? Is it a deployable data mining model to predict potential prospects for a new product?

Identifying the business questions you plan to analyze and what the expected project output looks like helps you decide which visualization or data mining tools to use. For instance, even when data mining for new, descriptive patterns in the data, you need to start out with an idea of how many customer segments (clusters) or what degree of associations to search for. Chapter 7 is devoted to discussing which visualization or data mining tools to choose depending on the data and business questions. However, first the business questions need to be rephrased and mapped into data visualization or data mining problem definitions.

The domain experts and line-of-business manager typically have a list of business questions that they need addressed. However, they often don't know how to map those questions into data visualization or data mining problem definitions. This list of business questions may be limited by the individual's perception of what is technologically capable. The use of data mining may allow new types of questions to be addressed. Chapter 1 may help you explain the capabilities of data visualization and data mining to team members that aren't familiar with visual data mining.

As part of the VDM project plan, you may have gathered a list of potential business questions that you want to address through visualizations and data mining. The next step is to meet as a team (decision makers, domain experts, data and business analysts, and operations) and determine the importance of each potential business problem, estimate how difficult the visualization or data mining solution will be to discover, potentially deploy, and estimate the potential ROI and profit yields. The number and type of business questions identified and mapped into data visualization and data mining problem definitions depend on the type of VDM project you are planning, the resources assigned to the project, and the project timeframe.

Problems Data Mining Does Not Address

A common mistake that decision makers, business analysts, and domain experts make is to attempt to answer online analytical processing (OLAP) business questions with data visualization or data mining tools and techniques. An example of an OLAP business question is "Who are my top five resellers?" This type of business question is best addressed in an OLAP report. However, if the actual business problem is "What are the monthly trends of my top resellers and what are their profiles?", then this rephrased business question can be investigated with data visualization and data mining tools.

You may need to help the data analysts understand the difference between OLAP and visual data mining questions. For years, decision makers, business analysts, and domain experts have been relying on and have grown comfortable with traditional green-bar reports. Since visual data mining may be totally new to them, you may need to suggest potential business questions or help them translate a collection of OLAP questions into data visualization or visual data mining questions.

Data Visualization Problem Definitions

Rephrasing your top business questions into visual data mining questions depends on whether they are best investigated and analyzed by using data visualizations or by developing a data mining model to gain insight into the problem. In general, if you rephrase your business question into a multidimensional, comparative, geographic, or hierarchical question, it can be investigated, analyzed, and evaluated with data visualization tools and techniques. The following examples will help you determine what types of business questions you can answer through data visualization. In addition, you may be able to use these examples to help you rephrase your most important business questions into data visualization problem definitions. Chapter 7 will help you choose the best data visualization tools to address data visualization business questions, and Chapter 8 will help you analyze and evaluate the resulting visualizations. However, first you need to determine whether your business question is best addressed through data visualization or data mining.

Multidimensional or Comparative Visualization Problem Definitions

"What are the trends of my top suppliers by product categories?" is an example of a multidimensional or comparative data visualization question. These types of questions can be investigated and answered through the column, bar, or scatter visualization tools. You may need help from the business analysts or domain experts in defining what a "top supplier" means and how to rank them. If the data set also contains a time-based variable (date column), the real business question may actually be "What are the monthly trends of my top suppliers by product categories?" For time-based comparative questions, you may choose to use line, radar, or area visualization tools. If the product categories (or one of the dimensions) are hierarchical in nature, you may be able to use a tree or hierarchical visualization tool to investigate the top supplier relationships among the product category hierarchy.

For different businesses or subject areas, multidimensional or comparative visualization problem definitions may be defined as follows:

- What are the trends for my top-producing oil wells by energy types over the past five years?
- What are the trends in attribute types by the most active genes?
- Is there a correlation between airplane manufacturers and type of failure?
- Is there a correlation between insurance claims and automobile model?

Geographic or Spatial Data Visualization Problem Definitions

"Where are my most loyal customers located?" is an example of a geographic or spatial data visualization question. The question can be investigated and answered through map visualization tools. You may need the help of the business analysts or domain experts in defining what a "loyal customer" means and how to rank them. Some map visualization tools can also investigate subject areas other than geographic maps, such as a chromosome map, an airport map, or an automobile assembly map.

For different businesses or subject areas, geographic or spatial data technical problem definitions may be defined as follows:

- Is there a geographical trend based upon the location of my best-producing oil wells?
- Where are the most active gene sequences located on the chromosomes?
- Is there a spatial relationship between flight delays, and where the airline is located in the airport?
- Is there a correlation between failed automobile parts and where it was produced in the assembly plant?

Visual Data Mining Problem Definitions

Analytic data mining tools can address complex business questions that at their core consist of a specific task that humans often inherently perform. To use data mining techniques, you must map the business questions to one or more of these tasks. The output from a data mining tool is a *model* of some sort. You can think of a model as a collection of generalizations or patterns found in the business data set that is an abstraction of the task. Just as humans may use their previous experience to develop a strategy to handle, say, difficult people, the data mining tool develops a model to predict behaviors and trends, such as which customers are likely to leave a service organization. Data mining tools tend to address one specific decision, problem, or task at a time, such as classification, estimation, association groupings, clustering and segmentation, or prediction. Depending on the data mining tool, an explanation of why a decision was made is possible. Some data mining tools provide a clear set of reasons why a particular decision was made, while others are black boxes, making decisions but not telling you why.

Often you will need to use multiple data mining tools to fully address your business questions. The following descriptions of data mining tasks and examples will help you determine what types of business questions are best addressed through data mining tools. In addition, you may be able to use these examples to help you map your business questions into data mining questions. Chapter 7 helps you choose the best data mining tools for these problems, and Chapter 8 helps you analyze and evaluate the resulting data mining models.

Classification Data Mining Problem Definitions

Classification is the process of putting an object into a predetermined distinct category. Every day banks must categorize loan applications as acceptable or not acceptable, insurance companies must decide whether to investigate a suspicious claim or let it proceed, and e-businesses must determine what type of advertisement a particular type of customer is likely to respond to. "Which of my customers are switching to the competition and why?" is a popular example of a classification data mining question. You can investigate and answer these types of question through classification data mining tools. You may need help from the business analysts or domain experts in selecting the relevant data about each existing customer. Often, visualizing the discoveries from the data mining models helps you understand the profile of a customer who switched to the competition or who didn't. The more pertinent information available, the more precise and useful the answers to the questions will be. If the competitor the customer chose is available, you can discover the profile of the customers who went to each competitor. Otherwise, you can only discover a generalized profile of customers that left your business for a competitor. Similarly, if the reason the customer left the organization is available, you can investigate what reasons drove particular types of customers to leave the organization.

You can use data mining insights and predictions to enhance business applications such as customer relationship management (CRM), enterprise resource planning (ERP), Web portals, and wireless applications. For different businesses or subject areas, predictive classification questions may be as follows:

- Why are my oil wells not producing as well as last year?
- Which gene sequences cause which types of disease?
- Which airplane models are most likely to cause delays?
- Which failed automobile parts are related to the same subsystem failure?

Estimation Data Mining Problem Definitions

Estimation is very similar to classification, except that each object is associated with a continuous value. For example, a telecommunications company may assign a customer a lifetime value in terms of dollars, a credit card company may estimate the dollars an individual will spend in a year, and a warranty provider may estimate the number of claims a particular product is likely to generate. You can view estimation as classification, but with many ordered categories. Because humans often prefer to deal with categories, you may convert the estimation into categories based on intervals of the estimated value. Often you will map a customer's lifetime value into categories such as low, medium, and high.

Association Grouping Data Mining Problem Definitions

Association grouping consists of identifying which entities or items are likely to coexist in some situation. The quintessential example is market basket analysis. Each time a person goes shopping, if the store has the right equipment, it can determine what items the customer has bought (coexist) in his or her visit (situation). If the store were to look at all customers' buying transactions, it could determine if there are any pairs (or groups) of items that customers tend to buy at once. This information can be used for promotions, product placement, or pricing strategies. Association grouping has many other useful purposes. For example, a mobile provider of parts and services may determine what parts are most used in combination to determine how to better stock or restock their vans. Typically scatter graphs are used to investigate and analyze the results of an association grouping model. For different businesses or subject areas, descriptive association data mining problems definitions may be defined as follows:

- What energy types are produced together?
- What are the correlations between patients, drugs, and outcomes?
- What gene sequences occur together?
- What airplane models were delayed together?
- What automobile parts failed together?

Clustering and Segmentation Data Mining Problem Definitions

Clustering and segmentation is the process of dividing a population of objects into subgroups of similar items. You can view clustering as implicitly forming categories. For example, a retailer may segment its customers based on demographics and spending habits and then label each group based on the cluster description. Clustering is referred to as descriptive or exploratory data mining, as it provides insights into a data set that are often useful for other data mining tasks. For example, the retailer who segments his customers based on their demographic and spending habits may then initially send out product promotions that appeal to their different tastes. From the feedback from that campaign, he may then build models for each cluster that predicts which particular customers will respond to future campaigns.

For different businesses or subject areas, descriptive segmentation data mining problems definitions may be defined as follows:

- If I cluster by producing oil wells into three segments, what are their profiles?

- What are the top 10 groups of gene sequences, and how does each group differ from one another?

- What are the top three segments of failed automotive parts, and are there differences or similarities by car model?

A specialized task often associated with clustering is *outlier detection*. The clusters represent groups of similar records. However, there may be objects or rows that do not belong strongly to any one cluster. These are examples of outliers, anomalies, and misfits. Depending on the business data set, these outliers may, for example, represent fraudulent transactions or unusual customer behaviors or trends. Bar, column, histogram, distribution, and statistics graphs are often used to investigate and analyze the results of a cluster model.

Prediction Data Mining Problem Definitions

Many data mining models can be used for *prediction* if they are used to forecast some value for a case. The difference between using a model for classification and for prediction is quite subtle. You can use a classification tool to build a model to classify existing loan applications for explaining what characteristics are associated with loans that default. If you then use that same model to determine whether to give a loan to a new customer, then you are using the model for predictive purposes.

Which Data Mining Techniques Can Address a Business Issue?

Table 3.1 shows a typical mapping between data mining techniques and the typical business questions listed in Table 2.1 in Chapter 2. Often more than one data mining techniques is needed to better address a particular business problem. Table 3.1 shows which business questions the various data mining tasks can address. For more information on these and other visual data mining techniques refer to *Visual Clues*, by P. Keller and M. Keller (Los Alamitos: IEEE Computer Society Press, 1993), and *Data Mining Techniques: For Marketing, Sales, and Customer Support* by M. Berry and G. Linoff (New York: John Wiley and Sons, 1997).

Table 3.1   Which Visual Data Mining Techniques Can Address a Business Issue?

BUSINESS ISSUE	CLASSIFICATION	ESTIMATION	CLUSTERING	ASSOCIATIONS
Target marketing	√		√	
Cross-marketing	√			√
Customer profiling	√		√	
Identify customer requirements			√	
Financial planning and asset evaluation	√	√		
Resource planning		√		√
Competitive analysis			√	
Fraud detection	√		√	
Attrition modeling and analysis	√		√	
Chemical and pharmaceutical analysis	√		√	

For instance, retailers and database marketers can use predictive data mining to build marketing campaign applications that target those prospects that are most likely to respond to offers. The results can be integrated into production applications. Examples include predicting a customer's likelihood to churn, respond to a special offer, be a profitable customer, file a claim, or spend large amounts of money. Ebusinesses and Web sites can enhance Web searches using data mining to present other documents or items that are related or "associated" in use or content.

Once the data has been mined and the predictive models built, you can apply the models to "score" other data to make predictions. Scoring of data occurs in the database, and scores are then available for use by other applications. Data mining models stored in the database can provide insights and predictions on demand to interactive applications, such as call centers, that suggest "recommendations." For example, a call center application could use a customer's historical data together with responses from a call in progress to rate the customer's preferences and make personalized cross-sell recommendations.

Mapping the ROI Targets

For problems that involve using data mining tools for prediction, you can directly measure the success of the project in financial terms. Most visualization and data mining tools enable you to associate a confidence or degree of belief with a prediction. For example, a model may predict that with a 75 percent chance a particular customer will defect. By ordering the model's predictions in terms of their confidence, we can chart the performance of the model in a number of ways described in Chapter 8. By determining the revenue and cost associated with each prediction, you can convert the model's performance into financial terms.

Rather than referring to the top n predictions, the predictions can be divided into contiguous intervals of a fixed number of examples. Common intervals are quartiles (intervals of 25 percent of all examples), deciles (intervals of 10 percent of all examples) and percentiles (intervals of 1 percent of all examples). For instance, the 50th percentile means those observations that are in the 50th interval if the sorted examples are divided into intervals of width equal to 1 percent of all examples. Often the term *cumulative* is used when referring to charts based on percentiles, deciles, or quartiles. In this situation, the chart will show the model's performance up to and including the percentile, decile, or quartile referred to.

"At what point is the model's performance too poor to continue using?" is a valid question to ask. The pragmatic answer is when it is no longer profitable.

This cutoff point can be determined by using ROI charts and profit charts. The ROI chart shows the profit as a ratio of the cost multiplied by 100. You can turn the question around and ask, "Given a target ROI, what should the model's performance be?" This helps make the question of insight finding closed. It provides a goal that can be used to determine the success of the model-building process.

To calculate the ROI, you need to address all costs associated with using the model. These include one-time set up costs such as:

- Data collection and transformation
- Model building
- Model deployment into the information system infrastructure (if needed)
- Logistical changes to business processes to make use of the model

The use of visual data mining methods for prediction involves trying to correctly predict some important event. Not only do you need to predict the event, but you also need to associate a cost and revenue with each prediction. The simplest method of calculating ROI is to have a fixed cost and revenue for each prediction. For example, the data collected from a home equity loan campaign where customers were indiscriminately targeted could be used to build a model to identify individuals most likely to respond to future campaigns. Suppose every offer you send out costs $250 to create, mail, and follow up in person. The revenue you obtain due to a positive response is $500. Therefore, for every $250 you invest, you can get $500 in return if you pick a customer who responds to your offer. For every two guesses, if you guess right once, you will break even; if you do better, you will make a profit. The cost is the monies spent in reaction to the prediction, whereas the revenue is the monies gained if the prediction of the important event is correct. Figure 3.1 shows for this situation, the cumulative ROI chart for a model with the target ROI of 1.5, which represents a 50 percent return on every dollar spent.

The ROI for this project may seem spectacular, but remember, the setup costs haven't been factored in. More than likely, the costs associated with making and following up on a prediction are fixed, but the revenue may be variable depending on the customer. It is even possible that both the cost and revenue associated with each prediction is variable. Consider a retention campaign where the organization has assigned lifetime values to the customers. From the lifetime value, you can derive a potential revenue if you successfully retain a customer who was to defect. How much effort you spend to keep the customer (for example, the size of the discount) may be a proportion of his or her lifetime value. Most data mining tools facilitate automatically producing a ROI with varying costs and revenues if they are provided as additional columns in the data set (these columns are usually not used for model-building purposes).

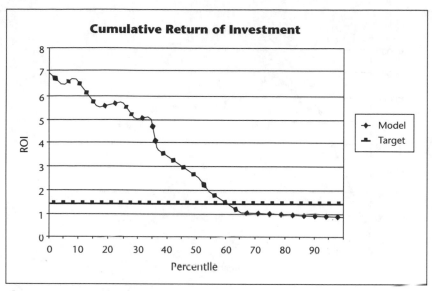

Figure 3.1 Cumulative ROI chart.

In the examples just discussed, the revenue of an incorrect prediction was assumed to be $0. However, in some situations such as insurance fraud, there is a negative cost associated with making an incorrect prediction of the target event occurring. This negative revenue may be associated with bad customer relations. For example, in the insurance fraud example, we could assume a customer wrongly accused of committing fraud will leave the organization; hence, the negative revenue is their lifetime value.

Another way to show the financial performance of the model is to consider a profit chart that is the sum of revenue less the expense. Figure 3.2 shows the profit chart for the model. You can see from this chart that the most money you could potentially make from this situation using this model is nearly $35,000.

From the cumulative ROI and profit charts, as expected, the ROI and profits progressively get smaller as the models' ability to correctly predict the target event diminishes.

Determining the Visualization and Data Mining Analysis Goals and Success Criteria

It is important to keep each business question "closed" by agreeing upon the number of production visualizations and data mining models to build. This helps to focus the project and stops the project from going off on perhaps important but tangential questions that were not agreed upon in the project scope.

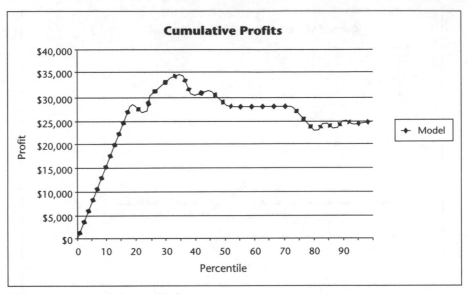

Figure 3.2 Cumulative profit chart.

Once the pertinent questions have been gathered, it is important to understand and agree upon how to measure the success of the project. The measures used and the definition of success will vary depending on if it is a proof-of-concept, pilot, or production project. It is easier to specify the criteria for success of the project using the current measures the organization uses. This can be achieved using the following steps:

1. Gather the reports that an organization creates to track key strategic areas.

2. Identify the measures that quantify the information that the organization tracks.

3. Decode the measures.

4. Identify those measures that quantify the business questions the VDM project addresses.

5. Establish a baseline of how well (quantitatively) the business is currently doing in respect to the business question to be invested in the VDM project. When the project is completed, the baseline can be used to compare and measure the results of the project.

If the criteria of the success of the project is in financial terms such as ROI and profit, then these need to be mapped onto the measures the organization tracks. After gathering the management reports, the VDM team needs to identify the measures that quantify the information that an organization tracks. Example business measures include:

- Percentage of households that purchased the product
- Number of responders to a marketing campaign
- Average sale price
- Average number of units purchased
- Average pound volume
- Total units purchased or amount financed

Once the measures are identified, it is important to validate the understanding of what the measures actually record. Analysts and information technologists often refer to these definitions as *business meta data*. You can think of business meta data as explanatory descriptions of business terms. For example, the meta data that describes profit may be simply "sales price of the item minus all costs to manufacture and sell the item." It is very important to have a fundamental understanding of the business meta data. Most meta data contains descriptions that require additional explanation, so it is important not to accept at face value meta data information. For instance in the previous example, you may need to research what "all costs to manufacture and sell the item" really represents. After the measures are identified, validated, and understood, the VDM team is prepared to understand the key performance indicators that measure the business questions to be addressed in the VDM project.

Before the project is implemented (in the case of a production VDM project), the current baseline values for the measures to be used should be collected for comparison. Deploying a data mining project requires affecting the business process that you are trying to improve. Your measures should consider all impacts of the project, not just the direct and obvious measures. For example, if you were to deploy a credit card fraud detection project, an obvious measure would be the percentage accuracy of the model's predictions. However, auxiliary measures should include all other potential impacts on the business processes, such as the time spent investigating each case and the dollar amount of the fraudulent transaction. A model that is very accurate may not be as desirable if the dollar amount of the transactions caught are small and took more time than normal to investigate.

Problem and Objective Definitions for the Case Study

Step 2 of the VDM methodology maps out or rephrases the top business questions and project objectives into problem definitions and objectives that can be investigated through visualization and data mining techniques. According to the VDM project plan outlined in Chapter 2, this step is estimated to take approximately 5 working days to complete. The tasks for Step 2 are assigned to the following teams:

- The data and business analyst team is responsible for identify and ranking the top business questions to be investigated with the guidance of the domain experts. They also map the top business questions into visualization and visual data mining problem definitions.

- The domain expert team is responsible for assisting the data and business analyst teams in identifying the top business questions. They also determine the visualization and data mining analysis goals and success criteria.

The overall goal of the customer retention project was to find a new and cost-effective way of retaining customers. However, from the discussion of the case study in Chapter 2, no one could determine exactly how big the customer attrition problem was or how much it was costing Big Cellular. The Big Cellular customer retention problem and estimating its cost can first be investigated and analyzed with data visualization tools and techniques. For instance, the attrition rate and cost questions can be mapped into the following data visualization questions:

- What are the monthly and yearly customer attrition trends for the past 3 years?

- What is the average monthly and yearly cost to Big Cellular from customer attrition for the past 3 years?

The answers to these business questions will enable Big Cellular to quantify the customer retention problem in terms of the number of lost customers, as well as the loss of monthly and yearly revenue caused by losing these customers. Future new marketing campaigns and visual data mining models can use these measurements to gauge the success or failure of the campaign or model.

In the case study section of Chapter 2, the visual data mining goals were to develop descriptive and predictive models that would identify which type of customers were churning and see if anything could be done to reduce the customer attrition rate. Another visual data mining goal was to help Big Cellular not only identify their actual churn rate and provide profiles of churners, but to develop models that would predict the likely churners and when they were most likely to churn and why. The overall VDM project goal was to reduce customer attrition by 15 percent or better.

These high-level visual data mining goals can be mapped into the following four key data mining business questions:

Question 1: What are the profiles of the individuals who are leaving Big Cellular?

Question 2: Can a data mining model be developed to predict *if* an individual is going to churn?

Question 3: Can a data mining model be developed to predict *when* an individual is going to churn?

Question 4: Can the data mining models explain *why* an individual will churn?

The data mining solution for question 1 involves profiling the lost customers. The solution can be achieved by clustering the lost customers into similar groups and then profiling each group. The data mining solution for question 2 involves developing a model to classify each record in the business data set into either a "churn" or "not churn" category. The data mining solution to question 4 requires explaining why the churn decision was made. The model generated to answer question 2 can be used for this purpose.

The data mining solution for question 3 is a difficult problem given the requirement to predict if a customer will leave and when. Since the approved project is a VDM pilot project, the solution will be to rephrase the question into a simpler data mining question. Question 3 will be rephrased as "Can a data mining model be developed to predict recent, midterm, or long-term defection chances?"

Summary

Chapter 3 described how to map your most important business questions and project objectives into problem definitions and objectives that can be investigated through visualization and data mining techniques. Step 2 also helped you determine and quantify your visualization and data mining analysis goals and success criteria. This step completes the planning phase of your VDM project. In the next chapter, we begin the first step of the data preparation phase. Step 3 selects and transforms operational data into business data sets that can be used to investigate the visualization and visual data mining business questions and objectives just identified.

PART TWO

Data Preparation Phase

CHAPTER 4

Step 3: Choosing the Business Data Set

M ost businesses collect an enormous amount of transactional and historical data. It is common for an Online Transaction Processing (OLTP) system to contain hundreds of relational database management system (RDBMS) tables. Some businesses have also implemented data warehouses, data marts, and other operational data stores to support decision-making information about their businesses. These warehouses, marts, and stores may also contain hundreds of RDBMS tables. So how do you select a business data set that contains the data facts (columns) you need to address your business questions from all these operational data sources?

Step 3 of the VDM methodology is choosing business data sets based on the technical definitions identified in the previous chapter. In this chapter, the focus is on creating an exploratory data mart to serve as the repository for one or more production business data sets. The exploratory data mart will contain one or more tables extracted, cleansed, transformed, and loaded from your operational data sources. To investigate different facets of the business questions, business data subsets can then be selected from the exploratory data mart repository. These business subsets may be used to create multiple data visualizations. Supersets such as the entire table or a combination of tables from the exploratory data mart may also be analyzed through data mining algorithms to create predictive and descriptive data mining models. Once the exploratory data mart containing the foundation tables is extracted, cleansed, transformed, and loaded from the operational data sources, you may need to logically transform and fine-tune them before creating meaningful data visualizations or data mining models. Logical transformations typically accomplished inside the data visualization or visual data mining tool is discussed in the next chapter. In this chapter, we address the issue of where to get the data, what type of data to select, and how much. We also address how to handle the extract, cleanse, transform, and load (ECTL) processes. We conclude by applying Step 3 to the ongoing business case study.

The class of VDM project you are planning (proof-of-concept, pilot, or production) dictates the complexity and amount of information required to address your business questions. In the project plan, you defined the scope of the project and identified the VDM team roles and responsibilities for choosing the business data set. With the assistance of the operations and data warehousing team, you can begin to identify the business data sources and develop ECTL procedures for populating your exploratory data mart. The domain expert team functions as consultants through the selection process to validate the completeness and correctness of extracted data.

Identifying the Operational Data

In Chapter 3, you identified the top business questions and mapped them into technical definitions. From this step, you may have already discussed possible operational data sources with the data and business analyst, domain expert, operations, and data warehousing teams. If your company has already created, populated, and deployed a data warehouse, a tremendous amount of work has already been done for you.

The exploratory data mart is designed to store information that answers the business questions under investigation. The class of VDM project you are planning and the complexity and number of raw business data sources (operational data sources) will define the scope of the exploratory data mart. In a sense, the exploratory data mart is a denormalized subset of the operational data typically contained in star schemas in a data warehouse; similarly, it can be a subject-oriented extract from OLTP systems. Because the exploratory data mart is organized to support a single business function, users will find it easy to traverse the data and create data visualizations and perform visual data mining.

When designing the exploratory data mart, keep in mind that it is designed primarily to support executives, senior managers, and business analysts in making complex business decisions. The primary objective of the exploratory data mart is to bring together information from disparate sources and put it into a format that is conducive to making business decisions. It is up to you, the data and business analyst, domain expert, IT operations, and data warehousing teams to define what data will populate your exploratory data mart.

In many cases, you must cleanse and translate the operational data before including it.

The term *operational data* is most often used to refer to data that is generated by your OLTP system. However, for an exploratory data mart, we have expanded the definition to include any data source that is used to maintain the day-to-day operations of your business as long as that data contains information pertaining to the business questions under investigation.

For example, operational data sources can include data from one or more of the following sources:

- Legacy data that has been collected and stored in relational or non-relational databases.
- Data collected and managed by customer service's database systems. These database systems are often used to manage and leverage relationships with your customers.
- Purchased external data from demographic information providers, such as Axiom, R.L. Polk, and others.
- Data collected and managed by Enterprise Resource Planning (ERP) systems.
- Other operational data exports or flat files.

Figure 4.1 diagrams the overall flow of data from the operational data sources to the exploratory data mart. The data selection operation is represented as a reduction arrow, since it denotes that you only need to select a subset of the data from the operational data sources. The ECTL process is illustrated as four separate tasks; however, using commercially available tools such as Microsoft's Data Transformation Service tool, you can accomplish all four tasks in one step.

Exploratory Data Mart

In its simplest form, the exploratory data mart can contain a single table, such as that shown in Table 4.1. For proof-of-concept and pilot VDM projects, you may only need a few tables in the exploratory data mart. For example, if your business question dealt with customer and product revenues, you would implement an exploratory data mart that contains one or more tables with information about the performance metrics of customers and product revenues. You would need to identify the operational source systems that contain raw revenue data, as well as determine the business rules that will help maintain those business data sets.

We strongly recommend that you store those tables in a relational database management system (RDBMS). Oracle Server, Microsoft SQL Server, and IBM DB2 are all examples of RDBMSs. The RDBMS provides management of computer resources, shared access, security, programming interfaces, and many

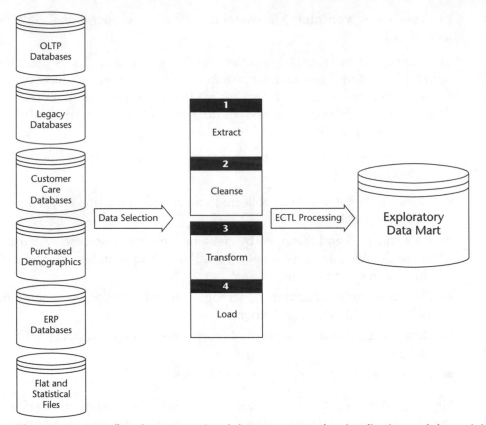

Figure 4.1 Data flow from operational data sources to the visualization and data mining tools.

other data manipulation and transformation functions that may be required for maintaining the business data sets for your VDM project. Another reason to store your data in an exploratory data mart is to keep the information consistent and maintain version control throughout your project. Later in this chapter we discuss creating and documenting the ECTL procedures.

For proof-of-concept and pilot VDM projects, you may want to have the operations team create a separate database instance to serve as your exploratory data mart. Optionally, you can simply have the team set up an RDBMS user and store the business data sets as independent tables within an existing database. For larger pilot and production VDM projects, you may need to have your own RDBMS installed on the machine you are using as the data visualization and data mining server.

Many VDM projects fail when an exploratory data mart isn't used. Performing numerous transformations against the operational data source and then against the business data set is prone to introduce errors into the data visualizations or data mining models. For instance, one large car manufacturer had completed a data mining and statistical analysis to determine whom to market their new car models to. Unfortunately, the business data set had gone through so many changes that logical and data consistency errors were introduced. It wasn't until one of the data analysts started to use visual data mining that the errors were uncovered. Weeks of hard work had to be abandoned, and the business data set had to be re-created almost from scratch.

Business Data Sets

The first task in choosing the business data set is to identify the data dimensions (columns) from the operational data sources. The process of identifying the business data sources begins by mapping the business questions identified by VDM Step 2 to raw tables and columns from your operational data sources. It is rare that you will create a definitive business data set the first time through the process. In addition, when visualizing or data mining the business data set, you may find that you have to refine your data selection to include more data facts or different data facts. For this reason, it is very important that you develop and document the extract procedures and use an exploratory data mart approach to storing and maintaining your business data sets.

The business data set concept was first introduced in Chapter 1 in the context of data visualization and visual data mining tools. In RDBMS terms, you can think of the business data set as the result of an SQL query that may join many tables together from multiple data operational sources into a single table or view in the exploratory data mart. The business data set can also be thought of as a report table that contains all the information necessary to answer the business question under investigation. For a particular visualization you may only use two or more columns selected from the exploratory data mart table. For a particular data mining algorithm you may select multiple columns from one or more tables in the exploratory data mart.

Table 4.1 is an example of a simple table with information (columns and rows) about a chain of department stores used to answer business questions about sales by store type for 1999. It is the result table created from the SQL query shown in Code Figure 4.1.

The SQL query in Code Figure 4.1 inserts one record for each store with the sum of all sales for that store for 1999 into the exploratory data mart table Tot_Store_Sales_99. In this case, we are using a database link indicated by SOURCE_TABLE_NAME@DBLINK to demonstrate that the operational data sources are from other database. In Code Figure 4.1, the operational data sources are the store and transaction RDBMS tables from the online transaction processing system database, *oltp_database*. Later in this chapter, we address how to select and convert raw data flat files into the exploratory data mart.

```
CREATE OR REPLACE TABLE Tot_Store_Sales_99 AS
SELECT
decode (store.regionid,
1, 'East',
2, 'Central',
3, 'West') REGION,
store.store_name STORE,
store.city LOCATION,
decode (store.planid,
1, 'Original',
2, 'Compact',
3, 'Modern') FLOOR_PLAN,
store.location_size SQ_FEET,
avg(transaction.year) S_YEAR,
sum(transaction.sales) SALES
FROM transaction@oltp_database,
store@oltp_database
WHERE
transaction.store_key = store.store_key and
transcation.year = 1999
GROUP BY
store.regionid,
store.store_name,
store.city,
store.planid,
store.location_size
ORDER BY
store.store_name
```

Code Figure 4.1   SQL query to build the total store sales table for 1999.

NOTE

In this book, we use standard SQL query statements for readability and to demonstrate how to select the business data set from the raw data sources into tables in the exploratory data mart. The exact SQL syntax varies from one RDBMS to another. For instance, you use the decode function shown in Code Figure 4.1 with Oracle SQL, but with other databases such as Microsoft SQL, you use the case function. A multitude of standard SQL query tools are available that enable you to create the SQL query through point-and-click graphical user interfaces (GUIs). For more detailed information on SQL and to determine if a point-and-click GUI is available, refer to the SQL reference manual of the RDBMS you are using.

The information (data facts) about the *store* subject data set is interpreted as follows:

- STORE is the file, table, or data set name. The subject under investigation is the total sales by store for 1999.

Table 4.1   Tot_Store_Sales_99

STORE	REGION	LOCATION	FLOOR_PLAN	SQ_FEET	S_YEAR	TOTAL_SALES
Store No. 1	East	New York	Modern	4000	1999	5,343.30
Store No. 3	East	Atlanta	Compact	2000	1999	2,312.72
Store No. 4	West	Los Angeles	Original	6000	1999	6,681.67
Store No. 5	West	San Francisco	Original	5000	1999	5,945.20
Store No. 7	East	Pittsburgh	Compact	3000	1999	3,945.25
Store No. 8	East	New Orleans	Original	8000	1999	4,846.10
Store No. 9	West	Seattle	Compact	1500	1999	3,861.45
Store No. 10	Central	Dallas	Original	3000	1999	4,453.50
Store No. 11	Central	Cincinnati	Original	5000	1999	6,987.12
Store No. 12	Central	Minneapolis	Compact	3000	1999	2,978.39
Store No. 13	Central	Louisville	Compact	2000	1999	2,134.00
Store No. 14	West	Phoenix	Original	5000	1999	3,487.94
Store No. 15	West	Denver	Compact	1500	1999	2,134.65
Store No. 16	Central	St. Louis	Original	5000	1999	3,134.03
Store No. 17	East	Washington	Original	4000	1999	3,314.99
Store No. 18	East	Miami	Compact	3000	1999	2,523.34
Store No. 19	East	Boston	Compact	5000	1999	3,003.75
Store No. 20	Central	Nashville	Original	7000	1999	5,341.34
Store No. 2	Central	Chicago	Original	5000	1999	5,532.33
Store No. 6	East	Philadelphia	Compact	1500	1999	3,343.00

■ STORE, REGION, LOCATION, FLOOR PLAN, SQ_FEET, S_YEAR, and TOTAL_SALES are seven *columns* or data dimensions of the data set. These columns describe the kind of information stored in the data set—that is, attributes or data dimensions about the store.

Data Types

Columns in an exploratory data mart table contain either discrete or continuous data values. A *discrete column*, also known as a categorical attribute, is defined as a column of the table whose corresponding data values (record or row values) have a finite number of distinct values. For instance, discrete data type columns are those that contain character string, integer, or a finite number of grouped ranges of continuous data values. The possible data values for a discrete column normally range from one to a few hundred unique values. The discrete columns from Table 4.1 are STORE, REGION, STORE, LOCATION, and FLOOR PLAN. Though column S_YEAR contains numeric data, it can be considered discrete because its values are limited to a finite number of values.

A *continuous column*, also known as a numeric attribute, is defined as a column of a table whose corresponding data values (record or row values) can take on a full range (potentially an infinite number) of continuous values. For instance, continuous data type columns are those that are double-precision or floating-point numbers. The possible unique data values for a continuous column normally range from a few thousand to an infinite number of unique values. Dates can be represented as continuous columns in some tools. Table 4.1 contains two continuous columns, SQ_FEET and TOTAL_SALES.

Experimental Unit

An important property of the exploratory data mart table (business data set) is that its rows or records all agree on the same *experimental unit*. In data mining terminology, an experimental unit is defined as the level, degree, or granularity of facts about the subject. For many data visualization tools, the rows in the business data set do not necessarily need to exist at the same experimental unit. However, if you plan to use the business data set for data mining, all the records in the data set *must agree* on the same experimental unit. That is, the data facts contained in a row must agree on the level or degree of information about the subject. Identifying the experimental unit for your business data set will guide you in choosing the columns from the raw business data sources.

For Table 4.1 the experimental unit is the individual store. Each row of data has information about a particular store at the store level. The experimental unit rule ensures that when you aggregate the data facts to a higher level, the information does not become skewed or meaningless. Adding the continuous column, state population, to each row would break the experimental unit rule for the store business data set. For instance, if you aggregate the table to the region level, the column values for state population would be skewed, since there are multiple cities in each state. The region column doesn't break the rule, since it is a discrete descriptive column. Mixing different levels of data (facts) in a single business data set often causes the data mining analysis to be invalid, as the patterns discovered are not useful or accurate.

Another example that illustrates the issue with the experimental unit can be found with most OLTP databases used for customer accounting. For instance, there are multiple levels of information that a business keeps about its customers and their accounts. The marketing and customer service databases may keep information at the customer level such as customer name, address, marital status, and other demographic information. However, the OLTP database may bill customers at the contract level, such as contract ID, balance, payments, and monthly charges. If you need to build a business data set that uses information from all three databases, you need to first define the experimental unit or the level of information required to answer the business question. Do you need information at the customer level or the contract level? To further exacerbate the problem, a "customer" in one database may not mean the same as a "customer" in the other database.

Often in the operational data sources, there can be one-to-many or many-to-many relationships for the entity under investigation. During the selection process, the entity record (all columns for a particular experimental unit) must agree on the level of information concerning that entity. For instance, in the customer accounting OLTP database, information may be recorded at the contract level. In the marketing and customer service databases the information may be recorded at the customer level. If customer demographic information from the marketing and customer services databases is included when contracts are analyzed, invalid predictive and descriptive patterns will be found. If you need to include demographic data, you must aggregate the contract information to the experimental unit of a customer. You could "distribute" the continuous column values over the experimental unit. Statistical normalization and other techniques for addressing these issues are discussed in Chapter 5.

Surveying Discrete and Continuous Columns with Visualizations

Data visualization tools such as histogram, distribution, and statistics graphs can help you survey and analyze discrete and continuous columns from the operational data sources. Inspecting the column values helps you decide if the operational data contains information you need to answer business questions. For instance, Figure 4.2 shows a distribution graph of the data from Table 4.1.

The distribution graph in Figure 4.2 shows the possible values for each discrete column grouped by distinct values. For the continuous columns,

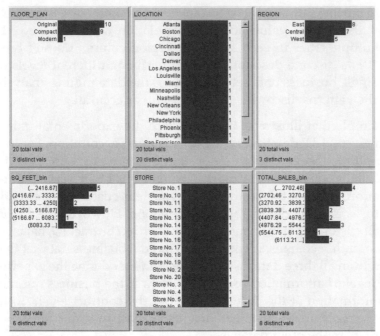

Figure 4.2 Distribution graph of total store sales table for 1999.

SQ_FEET and TOTAL_SALES, you can use a distribution graph after you have grouped the continuous column into value range groups. Inspecting these groups enables you to visually see the distribution of the values over the entire data set. For instance, a state column would have 50 distinct bars that display the count of records in the data set that correspond to each state. By using these graphs, you can visually see the *skewness,* or the lack of symmetry, in a frequency distribution of the column values. For continuous columns (numeric and date data types), the range of the column values is divided into subranges called *bins.* The count of the number of records within each bin is displayed next to the bin range. The number of bins is typically calculated using one of the following techniques:

Entropy. This technique chooses the value range group so that each group (bin) is similar, thus minimizing entropy or disorder among range groups. Entropy is a measure from information theory that refers to the degree of disorder of data. The higher the entropy of a data set, the more diverse and mixed its values.

Uniform range. This technique divides the data set into bins evenly distributed across the range of values for the column.

Uniform weight. This technique divides the data set into bins each with the same weight (or number of rows or records) of column values per bin group.

User-defined ranges. This user-defined technique is used when you want to see the distribution of records in specific range group. For instance, target marketers may want to know the distribution of ages in the groups 1 to 21, 22 to 30, 31 to 40, 41 to 50, and so on.

For more information on binning techniques, refer to *Data Preparation for Data Mining* by Dorian Pyle (San Diego: Academic Press, 1999).

Histogram graphs frequently reveal imbalances in the operational data. You can use histogram graphs to explore the operational data to help you decide whether the operational data contains the information required to answer your business questions and whether to include those columns in your exploratory data mart. Histogram graphs can also help you evaluate what further processing is required to prepare the column before continuing the visualization or data mining process. Often, discrete columns contain too many distinct values (over 25) that slow down data mining tools and make visually discovering significant patterns difficult. For example, you may discover that it is necessary to group distinct values into larger category groupings (supercategories). Chapter 5 discusses how to transform these types of columns into larger category groupings.

The *statistics graph*, also referred to as a box plot, in Figure 4.3 provides you even more information about the continuous columns, SQ_FEET and TOTAL_SALES. For each continuous column, the box plots display:

- The two quartiles (25th and 75th percentiles) of the column's values. The quartiles are shown as lines across a vertical colored bar. The length of the bar represents the difference between the 25th and 75th percentiles. From the length of the bar you can determine the variability of the continuous column. The larger the bar, the greater the spread in the data.

- The minimum, maximum, median, and mean of the column's values. The horizontal line inside the bar represents the median. If the median is not in the center of the bar, the distribution is skewed.

- The standard deviation of the column's values. The standard deviation is shown + and – one standard deviation from the column's mean value.

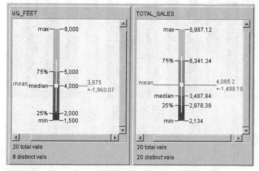

Figure 4.3   Statistics graph of total store sales table for 1999.

The box plots visually reveal statistical information about the central tendency, variance, and distribution of the continuous column values in the source operational data, showing the position of the descriptive statistics on a scale ranging from the minimum to the maximum value for numeric columns. These graphs are frequently used to reveal imbalances in the operational data. Some versions of statistics (box) graphs include whiskers. These are lines drawn from the boundaries of the 25th and 75th percentiles bar to the largest and smallest values that are not outliers. Outliers are values that are more than 1.5 bar lengths from the 25th or 75th percentile. Outliers are normally caused by recording errors, caused when the sample is from a skewed population distribution, when it is not from the same population, or simply due to a small sample size. For more information on outlier detection, refer to *Robust Regression and Outlier Detection* by P. Rousseeuw and A. Leroy (New York: John Wiley & Sons, 1987). Use statistics graphs to help decide whether the operational data contains the information required to answer your business questions and whether to include the source operational data column in your exploratory data mart.

Figure 4.4 is a histogram graph showing the interaction between the LOCATION discrete column and TOTAL_SALES continuous columns. You can use this type of histogram to determine the interaction of discrete and continuous columns in the operational data sources. Use these graphs to help decide whether the operational data contains the information required to answer

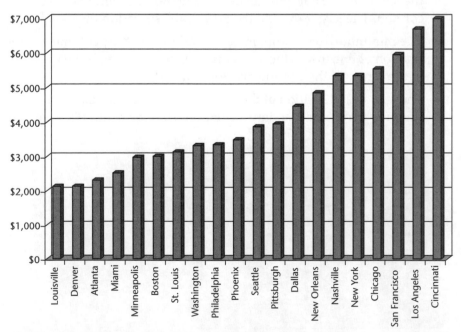

Total Store Sales 1999

Figure 4.4 Histogram graph of total store sales table for 1999.

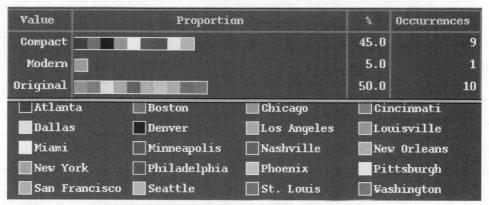

Value	Proportion	%	Occurrences
Compact		45.0	9
Modern		5.0	1
Original		50.0	10

☐ Atlanta ☐ Boston ☐ Chicago ☐ Cincinnati
☐ Dallas ☐ Denver ☐ Los Angeles ☐ Louisville
☐ Miami ☐ Minneapolis ☐ Nashville ☐ New Orleans
☐ New York ☐ Philadelphia ☐ Phoenix ☐ Pittsburgh
☐ San Francisco ☐ Seattle ☐ St. Louis ☐ Washington

Figure 4.5 Distribution graph of total store sales table for 1999.

your business questions and whether to include the source operational data columns in your exploratory data mart.

Figure 4.5 is a distribution graph showing the interaction between the FLOOR_PLAN and the LOCATION discrete columns. You can use the distribution graph to determine the interaction between columns in the operational data sources. Use distribution graphs to help decide whether the operational data contains the information required to answer your business questions and whether to include the source operational data columns in your exploratory data mart.

Selecting Columns from the Operational Data Sources

Data does not equal information. All the data, as it exists in your operational systems, may not be very useful in your exploratory data mart and thus not useful for creating data visualizations or visual data mining models to answer your business questions. The purpose of the exploratory data mart is to use a subset of the available data to provide information that you can use to answer your business questions. The information (columns from operational data sources) should be those columns that have been corrected, organized, and improved to make it more meaningful, accurate, and easy to use. Here are some common examples of problems with the data from operational data sources:

- The data from the operational data sources often contains codes that are unfriendly. For the sake of efficient data entry, operational systems extensively use codes that serve as shorthand for longer names. When a sales order is being processed, the order entry person may enter a code like "P1" to indicate that the order was placed by phone, as opposed to email, the Web, regular mail, or any of the other available means. Data entry personnel often memorize these codes and become quite comfortable using them. Others in the company will have no idea what order code P1 means. Transforming the order code column values with their expanded meaning adds value and understanding (information) to your business data set.

- The data from the operational data sources does not incorporate business rules, or the business rules are not consistent. Operational systems are not concerned with much of the information that you need for data visualization or data mining. For instance, the order entry person doesn't track profit, only unit quantity and price. On the other hand, the CEO, sales manager, and finance manager are very concerned about profit. Calculations necessary to determine profit are often performed separately by several people spread throughout various departments, each using a unique formula. Understanding what business rules are embedded within the operational data sources will help you correctly and consistently transfer this information into your exploratory data mart.

- The data from the operational data sources is "dirty." In other words, the data in its current form is not accurate and would therefore prove unreliable. If you include dirty data in your exploratory data mart, your resultant visualizations and data mining models may be inaccurate and lead to erroneous conclusions. Sometimes there are limits to how clean you can make the data, which forces you to determine a lesser, but acceptable, level of cleanliness that will still support your business objectives. Handling dirty data by ignoring it is not acceptable. Another point to keep in mind is that cleaning the data may benefit your operational systems, not just your exploratory data mart. When cleaning data, your aim should be to improve its quality, consistency, and usefulness. For example, if a particular column is known to be incorrectly populated, it is best to remove it even though it may potentially be very useful. Making sure that the columns that are visualized or mined are reliable will save you considerable rework.

Encoded Data Dimensions

A common mistake made while choosing the data for the exploratory data mart is to select *coded data dimensions* (columns). For example, if you are building a business data set to answer questions about hospital patient histories, you may want to include the type of procedure the patient underwent. However, the OLTP billing database for a particular patient may have code 890 for the type of procedure. In most cases, the end users of the visualization or data mining model aren't going to know what procedure code 890 means. During the selection process, you should decode the coded data dimensions into their full meanings. That is, the value of 890 should be replaced with the string "Basic Physical" from a lookup table in the database.

Many OLTP tables have been normalized to the third or higher normal forms. This technique has been historically used to keep the transaction and transaction detail tables as small as possible, to speed up the processing of the transactions, and to maintain referential integrity. However, it makes our job more difficult, since we in fact need to denormalize the data set. Often, multiple table joins are required to decode all "coded columns." Code Figure 4.1 shows the use of the SQL *decode* operator to decode the REGIONID and PLANID columns into their full meanings. Code Figure 4.2 demonstrates how to replace the *decode* operator with SQL table joins, since it may not be an SQL operator your database supports. Furthermore, if you have to decode more than just a few values, the SQL decode syntax can become extremely lengthy. In addition, if the operational data changes their coding scheme, you would need to modify your original SQL statement.

The (+) syntax on the *region* and *floorplan* table joins indicates to perform an outer join. The outer join ensures that in case there isn't a corresponding refer-ence in the *region* or *floorplan* tables, a row is still returned with a blank for the *region* or *floorplan* table lookup. To maintain the integrity of exploratory data mart tables, you should use outer joins. For complex business data sets, the number of joins grows dramatically. The operations and data warehousing teams can assist in the creation (and optimizing) of the SQL query statements.

```
CREATE OR REPLACE TABLE tot_store_sales_99 AS
SELECT
region.region_name REGION,
store.store_name STORE,
store.city LOCATION,
floorplan.floor_plan_name FLOOR_PLAN
store.location_size SQ_FEET,
avg(transaction.year) S_YEAR,
sum(transaction.sales) SALES
FROM transaction@oltp_database,
store@oltp_database,
region@oltp_database,
floorplan@oltp_database
WHERE
transaction.store_key = store.store_key and
transaction.year = 1999 and
store.regionid = region.regionid (+) and
store.planid = floorplan.planid (+)
GROUP BY
store.regionid,
store.store_name,
store.city,
store.planid,
store.location_size
ORDER BY
store.store_name
```

Code Figure 4.2 SQL query using joins to select the total store sales for 1999.

Data Dimension Consistency

Another problem you may face is *data dimension consistency*, an issue all data warehouse, data mart, and operational data store builders must deal with regularly. The classic example is the column GENDER. In the OLTP database, the GENDER column could be coded as a numeric 0, 1, and 2, where 0=Unknown, 1=Male, and 2=Female. In the purchased demographics data set, the same GENDER column may be coded as a text string whose values are either Unknown, Male, Female, or NULL (empty). In the customer support database, GENDER may be coded as a single character column whose values are U, M, F, or NULL.

The data warehouse, data mart, or operational data store builder must first decide on a consistent format for GENDER, then create procedures that convert the other formats before inserting or updating the records about the customer into the database. For more information on this and other issues involved in building a data warehouse, refer to *The Data Warehouse Toolkit* by Ralph Kimball (John Wiley & Sons, Inc.).

Business Rule Consistency

Business rule consistency is similar to data dimensional consistency in that the various operational data sources may use different rules to calculate a metric. For instance, the business rule to calculate profit may be different in the OLTP database than in the customer care database. Within the exploratory data mart, the domain experts and the data and business analysts need to determine the right formula as it pertains to the business question under investigation. The formula can then be documented in the ECTL procedures so that it's done once, automatically, and is then readily available to users of the exploratory data mart. Calculations, such as the one performed to determine profit, are the logical and mathematical translation of business rules. A number of business rules can be incorporated into the exploratory data mart in this manner, thus enforcing them with ease.

Unique Columns

Unique columns such as primary and foreign key are typically not very useful for data visualizations or data mining. Normally, you do not want to extract unique key columns from the operational data sources into your exploratory data mart, since they are not useful in discovering patterns in data visualizations or data mining. However, there are exceptions to this rule. You may need to keep one or more primary keys in the exploratory data mart tables. Although they may not be used for data visualization or data mining, you need to join your results back to the original records for the operations data sources. So if a target marketing data mining model was created, the primary key must join back to the name and address table to generate the targeted mailing list.

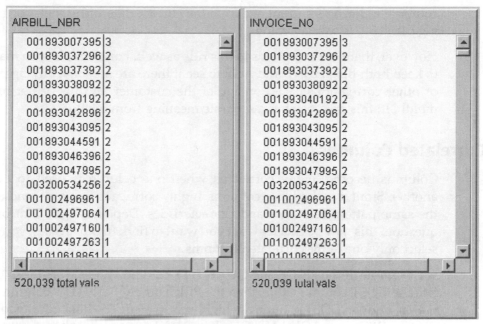

Figure 4.6 Unique columns displayed in a distribution graph.

Figure 4.6 illustrates unique or nearly unique columns from an OLTP ship-ment-tracking system. The columns AIRBILL_NBR and INVOICE_NO contain different values for almost every row in the operational data source. These types of columns do not lend themselves to meaningful data visualization, nor do they convey any useful information to data mining algorithms that are searching for patterns. Therefore, unless you need to use a unique column as a key for joining back to the original data set, there is no need to select these columns into your exploratory data mart.

Duplicate Columns

Duplicate columns are another type of column that you may not want to select from the operational data sources. Examples of duplicate columns are birthday and age that both indicate the age of the customer. Normally, you really only need to extract one of the columns. Since age can be determined by birthday, and only the age of the person in the data set is important to answering your business question, you only want to select either the BIRTHDAY or AGE column but not both. To help decide which column to select, compare a histogram of both BIRTHDAY and AGE. As a general rule of thumb, keep the column that has the fewest NULL values, which indicates that it has fewer unknown or empty values or contains the most up-to-date information. For instance, the AGE column values may not have been updated or maintained, but you can compute a person's current age from the current date using their corresponding BIRTHDAY column value.

However, there are exceptions to this rule as well. For example, you may want to keep both BIRTHDAY and AGE to see if there are seasonal buying patterns or other correlations based on age of the customer and his or her birthday month. In this case, age has a separate meaning from birthday.

Correlated Columns

Columns become highly correlated when one column is used to calculate another. Similar to duplicate columns, highly correlated columns tend to show the same pattern relevance and characteristics. Depending on your business question, this may be exactly what you want to find. In other cases, you should select only one of the correlated columns.

For example, if the PRICE and QUANTITY column values were used to calculate the COST column value, then the PRICE and QUANTITY column combination, and the COST column are highly correlated. The data mining tools will discover PRICE and QUANTITY column combination and COST column have nearly equivalent characteristics. However, we already know this, since the fields are highly correlated. To avoid finding known patterns, keep only one of the highly correlated columns or column combinations in exploratory data mart.

Not surprisingly, there are exceptions to this rule as well. For example, you may want to keep all three columns if you logically transform them into different category groupings or you are looking for association rules. For instance, if the column PRICE was binned into Low, Medium, and High groups, then both the COST and PRICE_BIN columns (but not the original PRICE column) could be used with most predictive and descriptive data mining algorithms.

Insignificant Columns

Insignificant columns are those columns that contain values for less than 2 percent of the source records (population of potential records). Often with purchased demographics, there are numerous columns that don't contain values other than NULL. As a rule of thumb, don't include insignificant columns in your exploratory data mart. In general, data visualizations or data mining will not find any significant patterns based on insignificant columns.

Figure 4.7 shows a distribution graph of column REGION_CODE. NULLs or unknown data values account for 99.29 percent of the values for REGION_CODE. Use distribution graphs and histograms to reveal insignificant columns in the data sources.

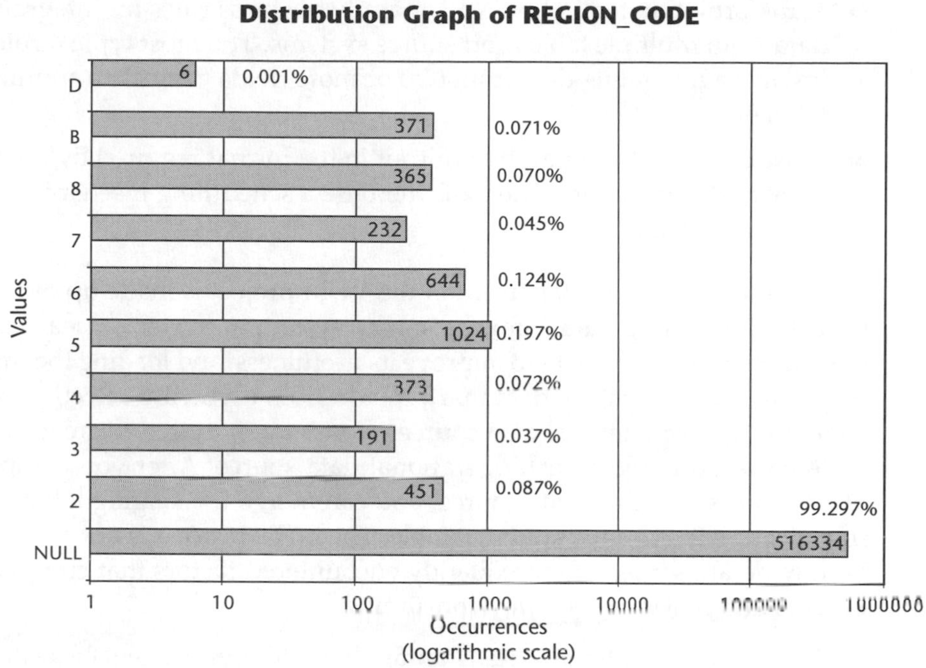

Distribution Graph of REGION_CODE

Figure 4.7   Distribution graph of REGION_CODE.

Developing and Documenting the ECTL Procedures

The ECTL process consists of all of the steps necessary to extract data from its current location, cleanse and transform the data from operational data sources to business data using your business rules, and load that data into your exploratory data mart. This four-step process is often carried out by a single toolset or a combination of toolsets and internal processes. Following are a few facts about ECTL tools:

- Extraction refers to the process of identifying and retrieving a set of data from an operational system. Many companies already have systems in place to extract flat files from their operational systems. But there are tools that enable administrators to execute more granular extractions where they only retrieve the files needed to load the exploratory data mart.

- Cleansing tools allow you to modify the source operational data before adding it to the exploratory data mart. The amount of cleansing depends on how dirty the source data is. If the source data is coming directly from a data warehouse, it may have already been cleaned.

- Transformation tools allow you to apply business rules for integrating data from multiple tables and source systems. The most typical rules involve aggregating data from two or more fields to create a summary table or total.

- Most ECTL tools format their output in the format required by the target database's load utility. The tools then use a scheduling mechanism to trigger the load.

Commonly, from 60 to 80 percent of the VDM project is made up of the ETCL process—extracting data from the source system or systems, cleansing dirty data, transforming the data to improve its usefulness, and loading the improved data into the exploratory data mart. In addition, if you are selecting columns from multiple operational data sources, you may first need to create a staging table corresponding to each operational data source. After you complete the ECTL process for each data source, you can merge the staging tables into the final production business data set table. The ECTL process is not a simple task. Following are some of the frequently encountered factors that complicate the process and make it more time-consuming:

- The source operational data is unfamiliar and cryptic. Legacy systems and even the more modern ERP systems have databases that are huge and cryptic. To ensure the success of your exploratory data mart, make sure you enlist the assistance of IT or operations, who know these databases (not just the structure, but what the data means). When this knowledge isn't readily available, you end up doing a great deal of work to acquire the database familiarity that you need.

- Operational source system databases are generally very complex. They're designed for transaction performance, not for friendly navigation. Data models can literally cover an entire wall of the DBA's office. The programming required to pull data together from a myriad of tables using complex join logic is very time-consuming.

- Sometimes the data that you need to answer your business questions simply does not exist in any form that you can access. This means that you need to figure out some way of getting that data into electronic form so that it can be included in the exploratory data mart. This can require an enormous amount of work.

- You need to determine how clean the data needs to be for the purposes of answering your business questions, then develop or acquire a means to cleanse the operational data before inserting it into the exploratory data mart. The most common example of dirty data is found in customer data. Names and addresses, in particular, are notorious for being entered into operational systems in inconsistent ways and with inconsistent spellings.

- It is inevitable that once you start looking closely at your source data and trying to extract it, you will discover problems that you didn't anticipate.

You need to spend up-front time exploring actual source data and experimenting with it to uncover these surprises as early as possible. This exploration and the resolution of the problems that are uncovered will increase the efficiency and effectiveness of your exploratory data mart for your VDM project.

- When you're dealing with multiple-source systems, the time consumption due to each of the preceding points is multiplied. You also face the challenge of trying to build a means to handle as much of the ECTL process as possible through a central mechanism that interacts with all of your source systems.

- Even though the tools that are specifically designed to handle ECTL tasks have now become viable, some source systems are so proprietary that ECTL tools cannot interact with them effectively. Your only choice in such a case is to use a tool or programming language that is specific to your proprietary source system. These tools are often primitive and thus difficult and inefficient to use. Even if you purchase one of the good ECTL tools, you will need to invest a fair amount of up-front time learning how to use it.

- You may need to include data sets stored in other formats or stored as flat files in your exploratory data mart. Not only do you need to transfer the data, but you also need to transform the data types. Unfortunately, not all data types are stored in a consistent format. Continuous-column data types like numbers with decimal points and dates are normally the most difficult to transfer between statistical packages or from flat files. This process is not only time-consuming, but it is also error-prone. For those data sets with many columns (hundreds) or a variety of data types such as decimal numbers and dates, converting the data set from one software package to another becomes a serious impediment.

Data Cleaning

As part of the ECTL procedure you must address the quality of the data from the operational data sources before including it in your exploratory data mart. Data in the real world tends to be incomplete and inconsistent, with a lot of noise. For example, in theory, discrete columns such as GENDER from a customer database should only contain M and F for male and female. However, often they contain other values or no value at all. Another example of noise is in discrete columns such as USA_STATE that contained more than 50 distinct values (51 if you include District of Columbia). Likewise, the continuous column AGE from a customer operational data source may contain negative age values or age values over 120. During the ECTL procedure you need to develop methods for handling these data quality issues.

There are various techniques for handing these data quality anomalies. The following three are the most widely used:

Ignore the operational data source column or record while loading it into the exploratory data mart. This method is the fastest way to fix the data quality anomalies. However, it is also the most dangerous. This technique may bias your production business data set and lead to less accurate data mining models and data visualizations, since you are ignoring potentially useful information. Before using this method, decide whether the column should be ignored or whether to ignore the entire record. In some cases, you may determine that the column is insignificant to answering your business question and can be safely ignored.

Use a global constant to fill in the missing or fix the inconsistent value for discrete columns. Though very time-consuming, this method tends to produce more accurate data mining models and data visualizations. Depending on the ECTL tool you are using, you can programmatically "fix" the missing or inconsistent value. Using the GENDER example, you could replace all values that are not M or F with U to indicate unknown. Using the USA_STATE example, you could replace invalid state codes with NA to indicate the state value is not available.

Use a calculated value to fill in the missing or fix the inconsistent value for continuous columns. This method is also extremely time-consuming, but it tends to produce more accurate data mining models and data visualizations. Using the AGE example, you could replace all values that were outside the range of ages 0 to 120 with the calculated mean, mode, or median value of the entire data set or a random sample of the data set. Another method is to replace the inconsistent or incomplete values with the most probable value by calculating the value using a data mining model. For example, you could use regression (curve fitting) or inference tools. Likewise, you could use other methods such as nearest neighbor (estimates values by setting them to the value of the nearest known data point, with respect to the distance metric), linear interpolation (interpolated from closest values in same row or column or both), or based on statistical variance.

The problem with all these methods is that they may unfairly bias your production data set. A column or record is biased if, in the long run, it consistently over- or underestimates the value and adversely skews the entire column. For instance, if you used the third method to calculate the AGE value by using the mean of the other AGE values, you may be introducing bias. If only younger female customers supplied their ages while older female customers didn't, using the mean age would underestimate the older female ages. Likewise, if historically, customer ages in the operational data source weren't updated or maintained frequently in the operational data source, the mean age would reflect a younger population than in reality.

For detailed information on handling data noise, NULLs, and techniques and tools for replacing missing and empty value, refer to *Data Preparation for Data Mining* by D. Pyle (San Diego: Academic Press, 1999). The ECTL tool you use to populate your exploratory data mart typically contains some basic data cleansing or data scrubbing tools and functions. In addition, numerous commercial software packages are available to assist in cleansing the data, such as Firstlogic's i.d. Centric, Qualitative Marketing Solutions, Group 1 Software, The Trillium Software System, Innovative Solutions, MatchWare, DataFlux Data Quality Workbench, Electronic Digital Documents' DataCleanser, People-Smith, and Intelligent Search Technology's NameSearch, among others. Refer to our companion Web site (www.wiley.com/compbooks/soukup) for more information on these and other ECTL tools.

Techniques for Handling Data Noise, NULLs, and Missing Values

You can determine the best technique by assessing the operational data sources using histogram, distribution, and statistics graphs to detect data quality problems. The domain expert and the data and business analyst teams need to discuss what technique to use to correct the data quality problems on a case-by-case basis. Once you've discussed each column, you can choose to handle the data noise, NULLs, and missing values by:

- Not including the column in your exploratory data mart
- Not including the records that contain the data noise, NULLs, or missing values in your exploratory data mart
- Replacing the data noise, NULL, or missing value with a default value that defines the value as unknown
- Replacing the data noise, NULL, or missing value with a derived value
- Keeping the column or record and addressing the problem inside the data visualization or data mining tool

There are a few simple and practical techniques for handling data noise in the operational data source. These include converting all characters to upper- or lowercase and range-checking continuous and discrete columns during the selection of the columns from the operational data sources. Code Figure 4.3 implements some simple and practical techniques for reducing data noise, NULLs, and missing data in your exploratory data mart.

```
CREATE OR REPLACE TABLE tot_store_sales_99 AS
SELECT
UPPER (region.region_name) REGION,
UPPER (store.store_name) STORE,
UPPER (store.city) LOCATION,
UPPER (floorplan.floor_plan_name) FLOOR_PLAN
store.location_size SQ_FEET,
avg(transaction.year) S_YEAR,
sum(transaction.sales) SALES
FROM transaction@oltp_database,
store@oltp_database,
region@oltp_database,
floorplan@oltp_database
WHERE
transaction.store_key = store.store_key and
transaction.year = 1999 and
store.regionid = region.regionid (+) and
store.planid = floorplan.planid (+) and
store.location_size between 0 and 10000 and
transaction.sales between 0 and 1000000
GROUP BY
store.regionid,
store.store_name,
store.city,
store.planid,
store.location_size
ORDER BY
store.store_name
```

Code Figure 4.3 SQL query using selection constraints to minimize data anomalies.

In Code Figure 4.3, the selection constraints and string functions are shown in bold print. For instance, the UPPER function automatically corrects regions names like East, east, EasT that exist in the *region* and *floorplan* tables by translating them all to EAST. The range checks on the continuous column values store.location_size, transaction.sales excludes all records that didn't satisfy those ranges, including NULL values. The domain experts and the data and business analysts will need to decide on the appropriate ranges for continuous variable. By excluding records, the sum of transaction.sales column will be numerically inaccurate. But including extreme values (outliers) causes inaccuracy in the data set as a whole. Many data visualization and data mining algorithms rely on the minimum, maximum, and mean values to decide on the scale of an axis or how to segment the column. Removing the outliers aids these tools in finding better and more accurate patterns on the entire data set.

You could also remove the (+) outer join from the *region* and *floorplan* table joins to ensure there are no blank regions or floorplans. However, if there isn't a corresponding reference in the *region* or *floorplan* tables, the transaction.sales column will again be numerically inaccurate. In this case, you do not want to exclude the record (unless it fails the range check). To handle potential blank or NULL *region* or *floorplan* values, you can issue an SQL update statement to globally replace all blank or NULL *region* or *floorplan* values with a string constant such as NA or UNKNOWN.

Handling NULLs

Some data mining algorithms handle NULLs and blanks better than others. For example, association rule generators and decision trees can typically deal with NULLs better than other algorithms. Other data mining algorithms have trouble dealing with blanks and NULLs, and they experience longer training times and produce less accurate models. While you can associate different semantics with NULLs, usually NULLs represent missing or unknown values. The difference is that a missing value for a column is one that has not been entered or captured in the operational data. An empty value for a column is one that has no real-world value. For example, if an operational data record contained the following columns: FIRSTNAME, MIDDLENAME, LASTNAME, and if a person's MIDDLENAME was not given at the time the customer was entered into the customer database, it is usually represented by the NULL or blank value in the database. This type of NULL indicates that the value is missing. On the other hand, if there are no flights between Las Vegas and Dallas, a query such as "find the average flight time from Las Vegas to Dallas" yields a NULL value. This time, the NULL indicates the value is unknown.

Some databases, such as Oracle RDBMS, do not distinguish between NULL and empty strings. In such a case, it is not possible to differentiate between an unknown middle name and a person who does not have a middle name. On the other hand, Sybase RDBMS distinguishes between NULL and empty strings. To complicate the issue, not all data visualization and data mining tools can handle NULLs. Therefore, you need to develop a strategy for consistently handling NULLs when selecting columns from the operational data sources. You also need to know how NULLs are treated by the data visualization and data mining software. In some cases, the visualization or data mining tool will give you the option of excluding the NULLs.

For instance, Microsoft Excel treats discrete column NULLs as empty cells. There are three ways that Excel can plot an empty cell in the data range: don't plot the data point, interpolate the data point, or plot it as a zero value. Normally, Excel does not plot a point for that cell. For example, where there is no value for a time-series column, there will be a break in the line graph. The solution is to have Excel interpolate the data point. In this case, Excel averages the data from the surrounding values to estimate the missing data. If the empty cell actually reflects a zero value, your chart can also reflect a zero value.

Table 4.2 Six Transactions Records for Customer 1000.

RECORD	TOTAL_SALES
1	3000
2	2000
3	NULL
4	4000
5	1000
6	0

In most relational database systems, a column value can be tested using the IS NULL condition operator to indicate that it contains no data (not even zero) and IS NOT NULL to indicate that it contains some data (even zero).

Table 4.2 contains NULLs for continuous columns to illustrate why you need to either replace the NULLs or remove the records. Many times you will aggregate the operational data sources to the experimental unit of the business question under investigation. If your experimental unit is at the customer level, you will aggregate all the detail sales transactions about each customer to the individual customer level. However, NULL values are ignored when the SUM, AVG, MIN, MAX, and COUNT aggregation operations are computed.

The aggregation operator sum(TOTAL_SALES) would produce $10,000 for customer 1000. In some tools, the aggregation operator count(TOTAL_SALES) would produce 5, even though there are 6 transaction records in the data set. The aggregation operator avg(TOTAL_SALES) would produce $2,000. In this case, the NULL is ignored but the 0 isn't. However, if you calculated the customer's average with the expression sum(TOTAL_SALES) / count(CUSTOMER_NUMER), you would get $1,666.67. As you can see, the accuracy of your aggregation is dependent on how NULLs are being processed. A rule of thumb to avoid biasing your production business data set is to not allow NULLs in any continuous columns you are selecting for your exploratory data mart.

Sampling the Operational Data Sources

Depending on the business question and what types of visualizations and data mining you will perform, you may be able to reduce the size of the tables contained in the exploratory data mart by sampling the data from the operational data source. A query that joins multiple million-row tables can take hours or days to complete. What happens when you discover in a later VDM step that you really needed to select a different column or perform a different join? One technique to reduce the time to create data sets, models, and visualizations is *random sampling*.

Often the number of rows in the tables from the raw data sources is in the millions. In some case you can use random sampling to reduce the number of records selected for your business data set. For a proof-of-concept or pilot project, you may be able to use random sampling if your source data sets are large (over 50,000 rows) to speed up your visualization and analysis efforts. There are a variety of reasons to sample the original data, including:

- Increasing the performance of the data visualization or data mining tool.

- Paring down a large data set, such as one with millions of records. Using random sampling, you can pass a random sample to generate a model that is usually as accurate as one derived from the full data set.

- Training a neural network or other classification algorithms. You should reserve a sample for training and a sample for testing.

However, you should use sampling with caution if the target event of interest is rare. For example, if your aim is to predict insurance claim fraud, even though you may have millions of records, only a small proportion of these are examples of the event of interest.

Depending on the business question and type of VDM project you are planning, sampling can cut hours or days out of the visualization and visual data mining process. Not only can you create your initial business data set faster, but also the data visualization tools and visual data mining tools complete faster when working on a smaller data set. We often use random sampling to test the business data set to ensure we have chosen the correct columns from the raw data sources and to build some initial data visualizations and data mining models.

Most data mining software packages support a transformation operation that allows you to create a random sample of a preexisting business data set. However, if you need to sample the raw data source table to create a new business data set, you could use SQL (in most versions) to perform the random sampling. For instance, the Oracle SQL select statement supports sampling syntax called the *sample_clause*. This clause enables you to select a random sample of rows from the table, rather than from the entire table. However, you can only use the sample clause in a query that selects from a single table. Joins are not supported.

The disadvantage with the SQL sample syntax is that it doesn't work on table joins. However, you can achieve the same results by using a CREATE TABLE ... AS SELECT query to materialize a sample of an underlying table and then rewrite the original query to refer to the newly created table sample. If you wish, you can write additional queries to materialize samples for other tables. Code Figure 4.4 demonstrates using the Oracle SQL select sample syntax to select a random sample from multiple raw data source tables.

```
CREATE OR REPLACE TABLE temp_transactions_sample AS
SELECT
     transaction.year, transaction sales
FROM transaction
WHERE transaction.year = 1999 sample (10);
CREATE OR REPLACE TABLE tot_store_sales_99_sample AS
SELECT
region.region_name REGION,
store.store_name STORE,
store.city LOCATION,
floorplan.floor_plan_name FLOOR_PLAN
store.location_size SQ_FEET,
avg(sample_transaction.year) S_YEAR,
sum(sample_transaction.sales) SALES
FROM sample_transaction, store, region, floorplan
WHERE
transaction.store_key = store.store_key and
transaction.year = 1999 and
store.regionid = region.regionid and
store.planid = floorplan.planid and
GROUP BY
store.regionid,
store.store_name,
store.city,
store.planid,
store.location_size
ORDER BY
store.store_name
```

Code Figure 4.4 Creating a 10 percent random sample of total store sales for 1999.

First, you must identify the largest table that you need to sample to reduce the size of the resulting business data set. In Code Figure 4.4 the *transaction* table was chosen. Compared to the *store*, *region*, and *floorplan* tables, it was by far the largest. Next, you create a sample of that table with only the column required for the business data set. In this case, it was *transaction.year* and *transaction.sales*. Finally, you perform the table joins using and referring to the newly created sample table instead of the original table. This technique circumvents the restriction that you cannot specify the sample syntax in join queries. You can use this technique for most data visualization and data mining software if you are using ODBC connections for the raw data source tables and the RDBMS supports random sampling SQL select statement syntax.

Avoiding Biased Sampling

We have described the benefits of sampling, but there are also drawbacks. If you don't use random sampling to select the truly random subset from all the potential rows, you could be introducing bias into your business data set. For example, if you selected the first 50,000 rows from a million-row table, your business data set could be biased. Are the first 50,000 rows really representative of the information contained within the entire table? Perhaps the first 50,000 rows correspond to your earliest customers.

Figure 4.8 shows a map visualization of the first 50,000 rows of a 5-million-row OLTP transaction table. In the map visualization, you see that the majority of the monthly profit by state ranges between $15,900 and $24,600. There are 45 states that fall into this range. The most profitable states are represented by the darkest shade. There are 12 states whose monthly store profits range between $21,700 and $30,400. However, are the first 50,000 rows truly representative of the entire 5-million-row data set?

Insert Figure 1 shows a map visualization of the average store profit by month using random sampling to select 50,000 rows. The first thing you notice is the profit per month has increased. There was a product increase during the third and fourth quarter that only affected transactions later in the year. If you selected only the first 50,000 rows, your business data set would be missing transactions that show the effects on profit by the product increase. In Insert Figure 1, you can also see that stores in some states are very profitable or not very profitable. There are 22 states whose store profits range from $28,400 to $50,600 per month. Conversely, store profits in 22 other states range between $16,800 and $19,900. If you were using store profitability to decide which stores to close, the sampling bias illustrated in Figure 4.8 would lead you to choose the wrong stores to close.

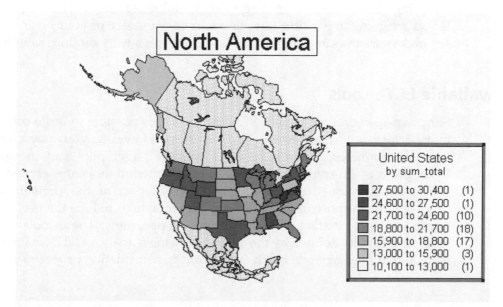

Figure 4.8   Map visualization of the first 50,000 rows of average store profit by month.

Perhaps the following true story will help further demonstrate the effect that biased sampling can have on your results. In 1936, the Democratic candidate for U.S. president was Franklin Delano Roosevelt, just finishing his first term as president. The Republican candidate was Alfred M. Landon, governor of Kansas. The editors of a well-known magazine, *The Literary Digest*, decided to conduct a poll to predict the winner in the election. The problem facing the editors was how to obtain a random list of names of those to be queried. The editors hired pollsters who compiled their target list of people to contact from telephone books and lists of registered car owners from all over the United States. They concluded from the survey that Mr. Landon would win the election. However, Roosevelt overwhelmingly won in all states except Maine and Vermont, the biggest electoral-college victory in U.S. history. What went wrong with *The Literary Digest* polling?

During the Great Depression, more Republicans owned telephones and cars than did Democrats. So the random sample was biased toward Republicans and not a true random sample of the population of eligible U.S. voters. The pollsters thought they were asking the question, "Who are most American citizens going to vote for president?" However, because of the bias, they were asking, "Who are most Republicans going to vote for president?" And the election's answer was the same as the poll's answer. Most Republicans *did* vote for Landon. However, during the depression there were many more Democratic voters than Republican voters.

This example, as well as more detailed information about sampling bias, can be found in *Statistics*, 3d ed., by D. Freedman, R. Pisani, and R. Purves (New York: W. W. Norton & Company, 1998). The election-poll sampling story shows how sampling bias can result in incorrect data visualizations or data mining models. If you are going to perform sampling to reduce the size of your business data set, make sure the sampling mechanism gives you a truly random sample.

Available ECTL Tools

For proof-of-concept and pilot VDM projects, it is possible to write programs that perform and manage the ECTL process. However, you may consider using a commercially available ECTL tool for larger pilot and production VDM projects. (In some cases, these vendor software tools are referred to as ETL tools, because they consider cleansing a part of the transformation process.) The purpose of ECTL tools is to eliminate or reduce the need for in-house coding of extract and transformation programs. These tools operate according to rules defined by the data and business analyst and domain expert team. Often they generate batch extract and transformation programs (in C or

COBOL, for example) based on those rules, or they interpret the rules at run time while extracting source data into the exploratory data mart.

The main benefit of ECTL tools that generate code is that they usually support more complex data transformations than interpretive ECTL products and are therefore particularly well suited to VDM production projects involving large amounts of legacy data. If necessary, you can customize the generated code or enhance it using in-house coded exit routines. One problem with code-generation tools, however, is that they often create large numbers of batch programs that are difficult to manage, especially if you need to update the extract and transformation rules frequently and regenerate the program code. Examples of ECTL tool code generators include Informix/Ardent's Warehouse Executive, Evolutionary Technologies International's ETI-Extract tool suite, and Microsoft's Data Transformation Service.

The current direction of ECTL vendors is to offer an alternative to the code generation approach by supplying products that incorporate their own language for defining ECTL tasks. Instead of generating code, these tools interpret the definitions during ECTL routines. Many also supply customizable templates for extracting data from transaction processing packages such as ERP systems. The key benefit of these tools is that they are faster, cheaper, and easier to install and use than code generation products. Consequently, they are ideal for proof-of-concept and pilot projects that require rapid development times. Examples of interpretive ECTL tools include Informix/Ardent DataStage, IBM Visual Warehouse (now called DB2 Warehouse Manager), Informatica Corp.'s PowerCenter, and Oracle's Data Mart Suites.

Documenting the ECTL Procedures

Documenting the ECTL procedures, although a tedious process, enables you to ensure the integrity and accuracy of data, as well as maintain the production business data sets in the exploratory data mart. In Chapter 6, we discuss verifying the business data set. These documents will prove invaluable for accomplishing this VDM step.

Some ECTL tools include a meta data repository tool that helps document the location of the data source, the transformation applied, and the data target in the exploratory data mart. If your ECTL tool doesn't have a meta data repository tool, you can keep the meta data in an Excel workbook. At a minimum, you need to document the meta data concerning each column in the production business data set that is shown in Table 4.3. This table illustrates the type of documentation you need to maintain for each production business data set table in the exploratory data mart. The table shows the descriptive data for Table 4.1.

Table 4.3 ECTL Table-Level Documentation

META DATA ELEMENT	META DATA (DESCRIPTION)
Table name	Tot_Store_Sales_99
Description	Total store sales for 1999
Experimental unit	Data is aggregated at the individual store level
Update frequency	One time
Table data sources	OLTP database tables transactions, store, region, and floorplan

Table 4.4 illustrates the type of documentation you need to maintain for each column in a particular production business data set. This table shows the descriptive meta data using the ECTL procedure from Code Figure 4.3. The exploratory data mart column value ranges show the descriptive meta data from the histogram graph in Figure 4.2 and the statistics graph in Figure 4.3.

Choosing the Business Data Set for the Case Study

Step 3 of the VDM methodology is choosing business data sets based on the technical definitions identified in Chapter 3. In this step, the selected columns from operational data are extracted, cleansed, transformed, and loaded into an exploratory data mart. According to the VDM project plan outlined in Chapter 2, this step is estimated to take 10 working days to complete. The tasks for Step 3 are assigned to the following teams:

- The data and business analyst team is responsible for defining the extract procedures from the historical and demographic operational data sources with the guidance of domain expert, operations, and data warehousing teams.

- The operations team is responsible for identifying the physical location of the historical data, demographics data, and other operational data required to create the business data sets. They are also responsible for any network or database administration required to facilitate the data and business analyst teams in obtaining the correct data.

- The data warehousing team is responsible for setting up and maintaining the environment for extract files. They are also responsible for creating any extract procedures from the data warehouse, as well as any demographic data extracts.

Table 4.4   ECTL Column-Level Documentation for Table Tot_Store_Sales_99

| | SOURCE | | | EXPLORATORY DATA MART | | |
ECTL STEP	TABLE NAME	COLUMN NAME	COLUMN NAME	COLUMN DATA TYPE	COLUMN VALUE RANGE	ECTL TRANSFORMATIONS
1	OLTP region	regionid and region_name	REGION	Discrete	East, Central, West	Decode of regionid to region_name and TO_UPPER
2	OLTP store	store_name	STORE	Discrete	Stores 1-20	TO_UPPER
3	OLTP store	City	LOCATION	Discrete	Cities in the USA	TO_UPPER
4	OLTP floorplan	planid and floor	FLOOR_PLAN	Discrete	Original Compact Modern	Decode of plan id to floor and TO_UPPER
5	OLTP store	location_size	SQ_FEET	Continuous	1500 - 8000	Range Check 0-10000
6	OLTP transaction	Year	S_YEAR	Discrete	1999	Range Check 1999
7	OLTP transaction	Sales	TOTAL_SALES	Continuous	2,134.00 - $6,987.12	Range Check 0-1000000

The overall objective of Step 3 for the customer retention VDM pilot project is to create and document an ECTL process that creates an accurate, complete, and useful picture of each Big Cellular customer. Since this project is a pilot project, we need to categorically document the process so that it can be replicated if the pilot project gains management approval to be deployed into production.

Identifying the Operational Data Sources

For the customer retention project, the project team (after hours of meetings) identified three in-house operational data sources and one purchased demographic source that contained information to address the business questions identified in Chapter 3.

The operational data sources tables were as follows:

- CUSTOMER.TXT contained 641,369 historical records about current and past customers. Nine columns from the customer service database were selected: CUSTOMERID, CITY, STATE, ZIP, ACTIVATEDDATE, PGR-CODE, CURRENTBALANCE, BIRTHDATE, and CREDIT_SCORE. This file was extracted from the customer service database.

- CONTRACT.TXT contained 641,369 historical records about contracts held by customers. Seven columns from the customer billing database were selected: CUSTOMERID, CONTRACTID, TM_CODE, DESCRIPTION_TM_CODE, ENT_DATE, REASON_DESCRIPTION, and ACCESS_FEE. This file was extracted from the customer billing database.

- INVOICE.TXT contained 4,596,319 historical records about invoices sent to the customers. Five columns from the OTLP database were selected: CUSTOMERID, INVOICE_DATE, OPEN_AMOUNT, INVOICE_AMOUNT, and TOTAL_PAID. This file was extracted from the customer billing database.

For another marketing project, the company had purchased demographic information on 100,000 of their customers. The domain experts and the data and business analysts decided that since the demographic data was less than 6 months old, it might prove useful in answering the business question of why customers were leaving. However, it was also decided that two production business data sets would be created. The first business data set would only contain the results of merging the customer, contract, and invoice operations data sets. The second business data set would be a subset of the first business data set, with only those customers who had matching records in the demographic data set.

The demographic source table contained the following information:

- DEMOGRAPHIC.TXT contained 100,000 records purchased from a demographic information provider. The purchased demographic data set contained the following 16 columns: CUSTOMERID, AGE, OCCUPATION_1ST, OCCUPATION_2ND, HOME_OWNER, LENGTH_RESIDENCE, MARTIAL_STATUS, SECOND_GENDER, WORKING_WOMAN, BANK_CARD, GAS_DEPT_RETAIL_CARD, T_E_CARD, CREDIT_CARD_BUYER, PREMIUM, UPSCALE, AGE_2ND, and ESTIMATED_INCOME.

To keep pilot project costs down, it was decided to not purchase a formal ECTL tool but rather to use the tools, utilities, and functions within the RDBMS to extract, cleanse, transform, and load the exploratory data mart. The CUSTOMER, CONTRACT, and INVOICE files were extracted from the legacy mainframe as ASCII comma-delimited flat files. All strings where enclosed in double quotes, numbers contained decimal places, and dates were in MM/DD/YYYY format.

Because a formal ECTL tool would not be used, the Oracle's sqlload utility was used to perform the majority of the ECTL functions. However, first each file was loaded independently into the exploratory data mart. After they were loaded and partially cleaned, they were joined to create the production business data sets. Since all the tables contained the same primary key, the join operation was relatively simple. In many cases, to prevent loading missing and dirty data, the table creation scripts enforced many NOT NULL table constraints.

Figure 4.9 diagrams the ECTL process that will be applied to the CUSTOMER, CONTRACT, INVOICE, and DEMOGRAPHIC operational data sources to the exploratory data mart business data sets. For each operational data source, we will demonstrate the following steps:

- How to evaluate the operational data source using histograms and statistics graphs. In this step, the entire operational data source file is loaded into the exploratory data mart (as is). We use visualizations to evaluate the columns and their value ranges to determine what ECTL processing is necessary.

- How to create the interim exploratory data mart table and the ECTL processing script to populate the table.

- How to evaluate and document the ECTL process.

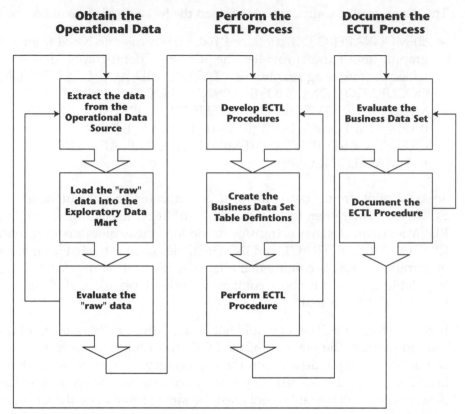

Obtain the Operational Data   **Perform the ECTL Process**   **Document the ECTL Process**

Figure 4.9 Overview of the ECTL process.

ECTL Processing of the Customer File

After the "raw" customer file is loaded into the exploratory data mart, histogram, distribution, and statistics graphs can be used to evaluate the columns and contents of the CUSTOMER.TXT data file. Since the operations team extracted from the mainframe system, there may be some conversion issues. The visualizations also help pinpoint data quality issues.

Figure 4.10 highlights some of the problems discovered with the "raw" CUSTOMER.TXT data file.

The problems and their solutions are discussed in the next few paragraphs.

The range of the column ACTIVATEDDATE is from 09/23/1996 through 08/12/1999. The distribution looks normal—that is, the mean is fairly close to the middle of the range of values and most of the observations are close to the mean. From the 25 percent and 75 percent quartiles, we can see that most customers were activated in 1998 and 1999. However, the raw data file is missing

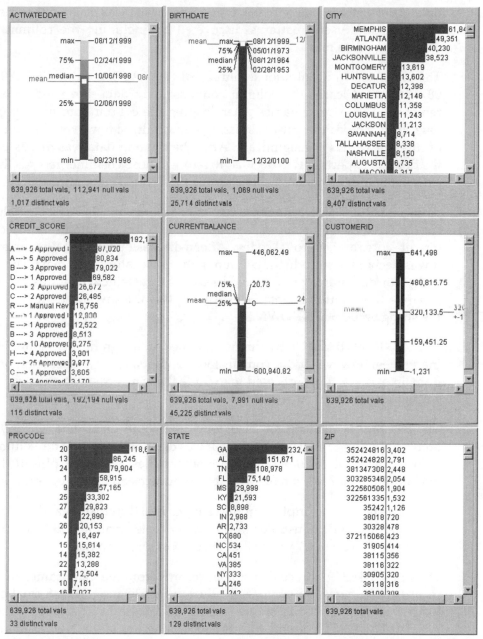

Figure 4.10   Distribution and statistics graphs of the raw customer table.

112,941 values, or approximately 18 percent of the total population. After a discussion about the missing data with the operations team, it was discovered that there had been a few historical software bugs where the ACTIVATEDDATE values were not captured. Basically, there was no way to recapture this missing data. After a discussion with the domain experts, it was decided that there still may be some useful patterns discovered by including the column in the exploratory data mart.

The range of the continuous column BIRTHDATE is from 12/32/0100 to 08/12/1999. Clearly, the column contains dirty data. We need to address removing the extreme values when loading the column into the exploratory data mart. The column also is missing a few values; however, the percentage of missing values is insignificant. After the missing data was discussed with the domain experts, it was decided to remove those customer records that had extreme values or missing values for the BIRTHDATE column.

Approximately 30 percent of the customer records are also missing values for the CREDIT_SCORE column. In addition, the column contains multiple codes (credit scores and approval codes). After a discussion with the domain experts, it was decided to include the column in the exploratory data mart. The visualization or data mining tool would be used to create new columns that would separate these multiple data facts. All empty values would be replaced with the string value of UNKOWN.

The CURRENTBALANCE column contained an insignificant amount of missing values; however, it did contain some outliers. After a discussion with the domain experts, it was decided to exclude those records with extreme values, since the majority of customers had a current balance around $20.00.

The STATE discrete column also contained some dirty data. Clearly, there aren't 129 states in the United States. It was decided to include the column, and before joining the customer table with other tables, a 50-state (plus the District of Columbia) validation table would be used to clean up the incorrect states.

The next step was to implement the changes into the creation and load scripts. Code Figure 4.5 demonstrates the customer table creation and load scripts to load the CUSTOMER.TXT file into the exploratory data mart.

Out of the 641,369 extracted customer records from the mainframe, only 2,517 records (0.39 percent) were rejected during the cleaning, transformation, and load process. Figure 4.11 shows the results of the ECTL process. Only the ACTIVATEDDATE column was not constrained to allow NULLs or missing values. The NULLs or missing data for column CURRENTBALANCE were set to 0, and the NULLs or missing values from CREDIT_SCORE were set to UNKNOWN. A unique constraint was placed on the CUSTOMERID to ensure no duplicate records were loaded.

```
—First Create the RDBMS table
CREATE TABLE customer (
customerid NUMBER(10)    CONSTRAINT nn_customer_customerid NOT NULL,
city       VARCHAR(50)   CONSTRAINT nn_customer_city NOT NULL,
State      VARCHAR(2)    CONSTRAINT nn_customer_state NOT NULL,
zip        VARCHAR(10)   CONSTRAINT nn_customer_zip NOT NULL,
activateddate DATE,
prgcode    VARCHAR(2)    CONSTRAINT nn_customer_prgcode NOT NULL,
currentbalance NUMBER(10,2)
                         CONSTRAINT nn_customer_currentbalance NOT NULL,
Birthdate  DATE          CONSTRAINT nn_customer_birthdate NOT NULL,
Credit_Score VARCHAR(50),
                         CONSTRAINT pk_customer_customerid PRIMARY KEY
                         (customerid))

—customer.ctl Oracle SQLLDR control file
LOAD data
INFILE 'customer.txt'
INSERT
INTO TABLE customer
FIELDS TERMINATED BY   ,
TRAILING NULLCOLS
(
customerid,
    city enclosed by '"'        "UPPER(:city)",
    state enclosed by '"'       "SUBSTR(UPPER(:state),1,2)",
    zip enclosed by '"'         "SUBSTR(:zip,1,5)",
    activateddate               DATE "MM/DD/YYYY",
    prgcode enclosed by '"',
    currentbalance              "NVL(:currentbalance, 0)",
    birthdate                   DATE "MM/DD/YYYY",
    credit_score enclosed by '"' "NVL(:credit_score, 'UNKNOWN')"
```

Code Figure 4.5 Customer table creation script and load scripts.

There are still data quality problems with the transformed table; however, many of them will be addressed by constraining which records are used during joins to the other tables to create the final production business data set. Table 4.5 shows a useful state validation table that has been loaded into the exploratory data mart. Not only will it validate the STATE column in the customer table, but also it can be used to augment the state information. For instance, when we join the tables together, we can also include the region information. Adding the region information may help in finding regional trends if no state trends are discovered.

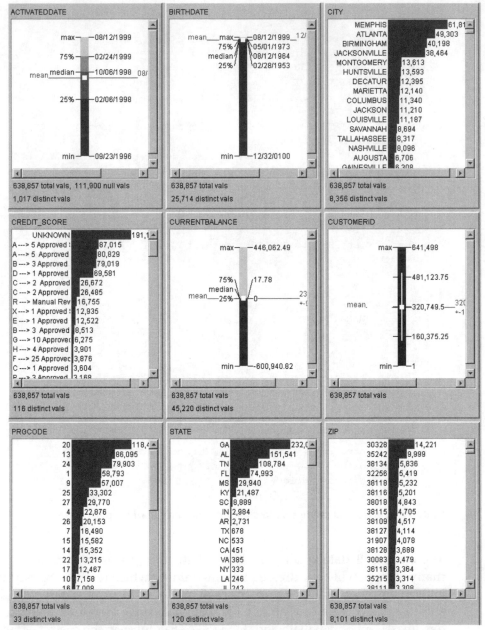

Figure 4.11 Distribution and statistics graphs of the transformed customer table.

Table 4.5   State Validation Table

RECORD	FIPS STATE NUMERIC CODE	FIPS STATE ALPHA CODE	REGION	EAST OR WEST
1	01	AL	E_S_CENTRAL	USA_E
2	02	AK	AK	USA_W
3	04	AZ	MOUNTAIN	USA_W
4	05	AR	W_S_CENTRAL	USA_W
5	06	CA	PACIFIC	USA_W
6	08	CO	MOUNTAIN	USA_W
7	09	CT	NEW_ENGLAND	USA_E
8	10	DE	MID_ATLANTIC	USA_E
9	11	DC	S_ATLANTIC	USA_E
10	12	FL	S_ATLANTIC	USA_E
11	13	GA	S_ATLANTIC	USA_E
12	15	HI	HI	USA_W
13	16	ID	MOUNTAIN	USA_W
14	17	IL	E_N_CENTRAL	USA_E
15	18	IN	E_N_CENTRAL	USA_E
16	19	IA	W_N_CENTRAL	USA_W
17	20	KS	W_N_CENTRAL	USA_W
18	21	KY	E_S_CENTRAL	USA_E
19	22	LA	W_S_CENTRAL	USA_W
20	23	ME	NEW_ENGLAND	USA_E
21	24	MD	S_ATLANTIC	USA_E
22	25	MA	NEW_ENGLAND	USA_E
23	26	MI	E_N_CENTRAL	USA_E
24	27	MN	W_N_CENTRAL	USA_W
25	28	MS	E_S_CENTRAL	USA_E
26	29	MO	W_N_CENTRAL	USA_W
27	30	MT	MOUNTAIN	USA_W
28	31	NE	W_N_CENTRAL	USA_W

(continues)

Table 4.5 State Validation Table *(Continued)*

RECORD	FIPS STATE NUMERIC CODE	FIPS STATE ALPHA CODE	REGION	EAST OR WEST
29	32	NV	MOUNTAIN	USA_W
30	33	NH	NEW_ENGLAND	USA_E
31	34	NJ	MID_ATLANTIC	USA_E
32	35	NM	MOUNTAIN	USA_W
33	36	NY	MID_ATLANTIC	USA_E
34	37	NC	S_ATLANTIC	USA_E
35	38	ND	W_N_CENTRAL	USA_W
36	39	OH	E_N_CENTRAL	USA_E
37	40	OK	W_S_CENTRAL	USA_W
38	41	OR	PACIFIC	USA_W
39	42	PA	MID_ATLANTIC	USA_E
40	44	RI	NEW_ENGLAND	USA_E
41	45	SC	S_ATLANTIC	USA_E
42	46	SD	W_N_CENTRAL	USA_W
43	47	TN	E_S_CENTRAL	USA_E
44	48	TX	W_S_CENTRAL	USA_W
45	49	UT	MOUNTAIN	USA_W
46	50	VT	NEW_ENGLAND	USA_E
47	51	VA	S_ATLANTIC	USA_E
48	53	WA	PACIFIC	USA_W
49	54	WV	S_ATLANTIC	USA_E
50	55	WI	E_N_CENTRAL	USA_E
51	56	WY	MOUNTAIN	USA_W

Documenting ECTL Procedure for the Customer File

Table 4.6 shows the table-level documentation for the customer table. Table 4.7 shows the column-level documentation. The values in the column named *column value range* will be used to constrain the selection of the customer table to remove outliers while it is being joined to the other tables. For instance, the BIRTHDATE column will be constrained to include only cellular customers that are from 10 years old to 100 years old.

Table 4.6 ECTL Table-Level Documentation for the Customer Table

META DATA ELEMENT	META DATA (DESCRIPTION)
Table name	Customer
Description	Details about individual cellular phone customers, such as where they live and their financial credit score
Experimental unit	Unique customerid
Update frequency	One time
Table data sources	Extract file from the mainframe customer billing system

ECTL Processing of the Contract File

After the "raw" contract file is loaded into the exploratory data mart, histogram, distribution, and statistics graphs can be used to evaluate the columns and contents of the CONTRACT.TXT data file. Since the operations team extracted from the mainframe system, there may be some conversion issues. The visualizations also help pinpoint data quality issues.

Figure 4.12 highlights some of the problems discovered with the "raw" CONTRACT.TXT data file. These problems, along with their solutions, are as follows:

- The CUSTOMER_ID column from the contract file closely resembles the CUSTOMERID column from the customer file. The column CONTRACT_ID can be removed, since we only need the CUSTOMERID column to join the tables.

- The ACCESS_FEE column seems to contain valid data. No additional cleaning or transformations are necessary. It was decided to rename this column CONTRACT_FEE to provide a more descriptive name.

- The DESCRIPTION_TM_CODE and TM_CODE columns are duplicate columns. Since the DESCRIPTION_TM_CODE column is the decode meaning of the TM_CODE column, the duplicate column TM_CODE column will be removed.

- The ENT_DATE column seems to contain only one year's worth of data. After a discussion with the operations and domain expert teams, it was discovered that the ENT_DATE represents when customers renew their contract. Since the majority of contracts are renewed yearly, the data seems relatively clean. There are a few outliers that will be removed during the table joins. It was decided to rename the column RENEWAL_DATE.

Table 4.7 ECTL Column-Level Documentation for the Customer Table

	SOURCE		EXPLORATORY DATA MART		
TABLE NAME	COLUMN NAME	COLUMN NAME	COLUMN DATA TYPE	COLUMN VALUE RANGE	ECTL TRANSFORMATIONS
Mainframe customer table	CUSTOMERID	CUSTOMERID	Continuous	1 to 641,498	Unique Constraint
Mainframe customer table	ACTIVATEDDATE	ACTIVATEDDATE	Continuous (DATE)	09/23/1996 to 08/12/1999	VALID DATE
Mainframe customer table	BIRTHDATE	BIRTHDATE	Continuous (DATE)	01/01/1900 to 01/01/1990	VALID DATE
Mainframe customer table	CITY	CITY	Discrete	Valid Cities	TO_UPPER
Mainframe customer table	CREDIT and SCORE	CREDIT_SCORE	Discrete	A–Z	NULLs transformed to UNKNOWN
Mainframe customer table	CURRENTBALANCE	CURRENTBALANCE	Continuous	-$1,000 to $1,000	NULLs transformed to $0.00
Mainframe customer table	PRGCODE	PRGCODE	Discrete	1 to 33	None
Mainframe customer table	STATE	STATE	Discrete	50 USA States Plus District of Columbia	TO_UPPER
Mainframe customer table	ZIPCODE	ZIP	Discrete	Valid Zip Codes	Sub-string 5 characters

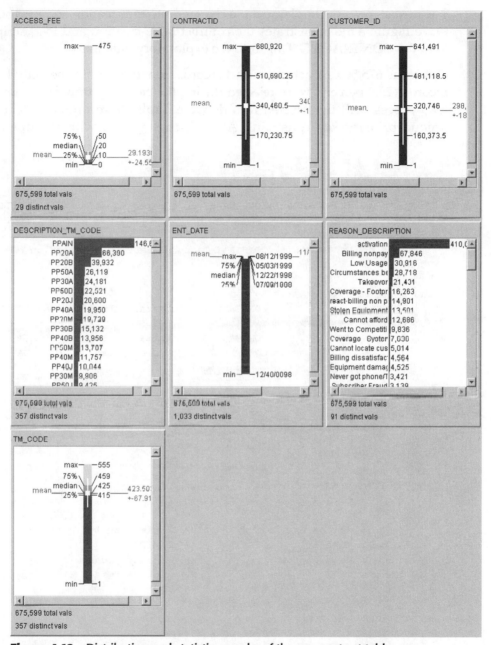

Figure 4.12 Distribution and statistics graphs of the raw contract table.

- The REASON_DESCRIPTION column shows reasons the customers gave for not renewing or for dropping their cellular service. However, if the reason description is "ACTIVATION", it indicates the customer hasn't churned. Therefore, the REASON_DESCRIPTION column values can be used to segment the records into those churners and non-churners, depending on whether the REASON_DESCRIPTION = "ACTIVATION".

The next step was to implement the changes into the creation and load scripts. Code Figure 4.6 demonstrates the contract table creation and load scripts to load the CONTRACT.TXT file into the exploratory data mart.

Out of the 675,599 extracted contract records from the mainframe, only 174,175 records (25.9 percent) were rejected during the cleaning, transformation, and load process. All the rejected records were duplicate records and failed the unique primary key constraint. After discussing this with the operations

```
—First Create the RDBMS table
CREATE TABLE contract (
customerid       NUMBER(10) CONSTRAINT nn_contract_customerid NOT NULL,
filler1          NUMBER,
filler2          NUMBER,
tm_description VARCHAR(6) CONSTRAINT nn_contract_tm_description NOT
NULL,
renewal_date     DATE,
churn_reason     VARCHAR(40)
                          CONSTRAINT nn_contract_churn_reason NOT NULL,
contract_fee     NUMBER (10,2)
                          CONSTRAINT nn_contract_contract_fee NOT NULL,
                          CONSTRAINT pk_contract_customerid PRIMARY KEY
                             (customerid))

—contract.ctl Oracle SQLLDR control file
LOAD data
INFILE 'contract.txt'
INSERT
INTO TABLE contract
FIELDS TERMINATED BY  ','
TRAILING NULLCOLS
(
customerid,
    tm_description enclosed by '"'  "UPPER(:tm_description)",
    renewal_date                    DATE "MM/DD/YYYY",
    churn_reason enclosed by '"'    "UPPER(:churn_reason)",
    contract_fee                    "NVL(:contract_fee, 0)"
)
—drop the columns filler1 and filler2
ALTER TABLE CONTRACT
DROP ("FILLER1", "FILLER2") CASCADE CONSTRAINTS
```

Code Figure 4.6 Contract table creation script and load scripts.

teams, they discovered that their extract procedure from the mainframe selected all active and renewed customer contracts. Therefore, to use only the most current contracts, the CONTRACT.TXT file was sorted by CONTRACTID, then CUSTOMERID before it was loaded into the exploratory data mart. This enabled us to only insert the most current customer contracts. Insert Figure 2 shows the results of the ECTL process.

Documenting ECTL Procedure for the Contact File

Table 4.8 shows the table-level ECTL documentation, and Table 4.9 shows the column-level ECTL documentation for the contract table. The column value range values will be used to constrain the selection of the customer table to remove outliers while it is being joined to the other tables. For instance, the RENEWAL_DATE column will be constrained to only include cellular contracts within the potential range of dates while customer activated the cellular plans.

ECTL Processing of the Invoice File

After the "raw" invoice file is loaded into the exploratory data mart, histogram, distribution, and statistics graphs can be used to evaluate the columns and contents of the INVOICE.TXT data file. Since the operations team extracted from the mainframe system, there may be some conversion issues. The visualizations also help pinpoint data quality issues.

Table 4.8   ECTL Table-Level Documentation for the Contract Table

META DATA ELEMENT	META DATA (DESCRIPTION)
Table name	Contract
Description	Details about the contract held by individual cellular phone customers, such as renewal date. Sorted by CONTRACTID, CUSTOMERID in descending order to ensure only the most recent contracts are loaded.
Experimental unit	Unique customerid
Update frequency	One time
Table data sources	Extract file from the mainframe contract system

Table 4.9 ECTL Column-Level Documentation for the Contract Table

TABLE NAME	SOURCE COLUMN NAME	COLUMN NAME	COLUMN DATA TYPE	EXPLORATORY DATA MART COLUMN VALUE RANGE	ECTL TRANSFORMATIONS
Mainframe contract table	CUSTOMERID	CUSTOMERID	Continuous	1 to 641,498	Unique Constraint
Mainframe contract table	ACCESS_FEE	CONTRACT_FEE	Continuous	$0.00 to $500.00	None
Mainframe contract table	TM_CODE_ DESCRIPTION	TM_DESCRIPTION	Discrete	Valid terms (rate plans)	TO_UPPER
Mainframe contract table	ENT_DATE	RENEWAL_DATE	Continuous (DATE)	09/23/1996 to 08/12/1999	Valid Date
Mainframe contract table	REASON_ DESCRIPTION	CHURN_REASON	Discrete	Free-flow textual description	TO_UPPER

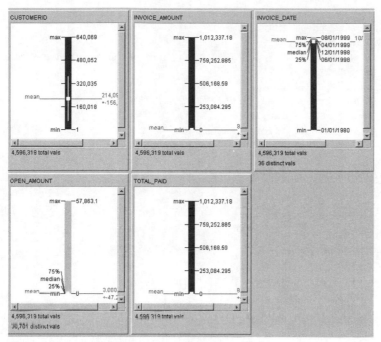

Figure 4.13   Distribution and statistics graphs of the raw invoice file.

Figure 4.13 highlights some of the problems discovered with the "raw" INVOICE.TXT data file. These are as follows:

- The CUSTOMER_ID column is within the same range as the customer file. Notice that it is skewed toward earlier (numerically smaller) customer numbers. This is expected since these customers have received more invoices over the date range.

- The columns INVOICE_AMOUNT, OPEN_AMOUNT, and TOTAL_PAID clearly contain some dirty data. However, the columns' means are within reason. After a discussion with the domain expert team, it was decided to remove any records whose amounts were over $1,000.00.

- The INVOICE_DATE column shows that there are also some extreme dates (outliers). After a discussion with the domain expert team, it was decided to remove any records whose INVOICE_DATE did not fall between 09/23/1996 and 08/12/1999 to be consistent with the customer table.

The next step was to implement the changes into the creation and load scripts. Code Figure 4.7 demonstrates the invoice table creation and load scripts to load the INVOICE.TXT file into the exploratory data mart.

```
-- First Create the RDBMS table
CREATE TABLE Invoice (
customerid NUMBER(10)      CONSTRAINT nn_Invoice_customerid NOT NULL,
Invoice_Date DATE,
Open_Amount NUMBER (10,2)
CONSTRAINT nn_Invoice_open_amount NOT NULL,
Invoice_Amount NUMBER (10,2)
CONSTRAINT nn_Invoice_Invoice_amount NOT NULL,
Total_Paid NUMBER (10,2) CONSTRAINT nn_Invoice_total_paid NOT NULL
)
-- Invoice.ctl Oracle SQLLDR control file
load data
infile 'invoice.txt'
insert
into table invoice
fields terminated by ','
trailing nullcols
(
CustomerID,
Invoice_Date enclosed by '"' "TO_DATE(:invoice_date,'YYYY/MM')",
Open_Amount,
Invoice_Amount,
      Total_Paid
)
```

Code Figure 4.7 Invoice table creation script and load scripts.

Since the invoice table is not the same experimental unit as the customer and contract table, it needs to be aggregated to the customer level; that is, it must be aggregated by CUSTOMERID so that there is only one record per customer. The SQL statement WHERE-*conditions* will remove all records that have suspect amounts from the aggregation, as shown in Code Figure 4.8.

The aggregation transformation is typically considered a logical transformation. Aggregations and other logical transformations are covered in detail in Chapter 5. However, we have included the aggregation of the invoice table

```
CREATE TABLE invoice_aggregate AS
SELECT      customerid,
        SUM(open_amount) TOT_OPEN_AMT,
        SUM(invoice_amount) TOT_INVOICE_AMT,
        SUM(total_paid) TOT_PAID_AMT,
        COUNT(invoice_date) NUM_INVOICES
```

Code Figure 4.8 Aggregating the invoice table.

```
FROM invoice
WHERE       open_amount < 1000 and
            invoice_amount < 1000 and
            total_paid < 1000 and
            invoice_date between
TO_DATE('09/23/1996','MM/DD/YYYY') and
TO_DATE('08/12/1999','MM/DD/YYYY')
GROUP BY CUSTOMERID
```

Code Figure 4.8 Aggregating the invoice table. *(continued)*

here, since later in this section we will join the aggregated invoice table to the customer and contract table to create the *customer_join* business data set.

Figure 4.14 shows the results of the aggregation. After seeing the resulting statistics graphs, the domain experts pointed out that the aggregated invoice data is now very clean. The SQL WHERE condition cleaned up the outliers. You will notice that the mean TOT_INVOICE_AMT of $728 is approximately equal to the sum of the means of TOT_PAID_AMT and TOTAL_OPEN_AMT. More on techniques for verifying the production business data set is covered in Chapter 6.

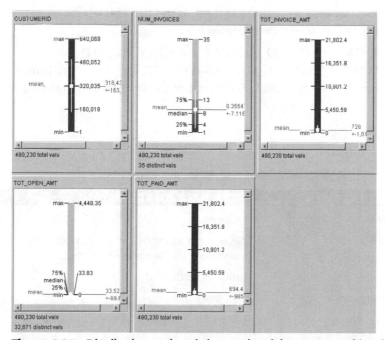

Figure 4.14 Distribution and statistics graphs of the aggregated invoice table.

Documenting ECTL Procedure for the Invoice File

Table 4.10 shows the table-level ECTL documentation, and Table 4.11 shows the column-level ECTL documentation for the invoice table. The column value range values will be used to constrain the selection of the customer table to remove outliers while it is being joined to the other tables. For instance, the RENEWAL_DATE column will be constrained to only include cellular contracts within the potential range of dates while customer activated the cellular plans.

ECTL Processing of the Demographic File

After the "raw" demographic file is loaded into the exploratory data mart, histograms, distribution, and statistics graphs can be used to evaluate the columns and contents of the DEMOGRAPHIC.TXT data file. We need to evaluate whether the demographic file will be useful in our VDM pilot project. The visualizations also help pinpoint data quality issues.

Figure 4.15 highlights some of the problems and observations discovered with the "raw" DEMOGRAPHIC.TXT data file. Following are notes about the columns:

- The CUSTOMERID column shows a balanced distribution of customers. Therefore, it doesn't appear to be a biased sample of the customer base.

- The AGE column is a duplicated field of the BIRTHDATE column from the customer file, so it can be removed.

- The AGE_2ND, SECOND_GENDER, OCCUPATION_1ST, OCCUPATION_2ND, T_E_CARD, WORKING_WOMAN columns are missing between 50 and 90 percent of the population and will not be used.

Table 4.10 ECTL Table-Level Documentation for the Invoice Table

META DATA ELEMENT	META DATA (DESCRIPTION)
Table name	Invoice
Description	Aggregated monthly invoices amounts by individual cellular phone customers
Experimental unit	Unique customerid
Update frequency	One time
Table data sources	Extract file from the mainframe customer billing system

Table 4.11 ECTL Column-Level Documentation for the Invoice Table

	SOURCE		EXPLORATORY DATA MART		
TABLE NAME	COLUMN NAME	COLUMN NAME	COLUMN DATA TYPE	COLUMN VALUE RANGE	ECTL TRANSFORMATIONS
Mainframe invoice table	CUSTOMERID	CUSTOMERID	Continuous	1 to 641,498	Unique Constraint
Mainframe invoice table	OPEN_AMOUNT	TOT_OPEN_AMT	Continuous	Aggregated total of amount < $1000	None
Mainframe invoice table	INVOICE_AMOUNT	TOT_INVOICE_AMT	Continuous	Aggregated total of amount < $1000	None
Mainframe invoice table	TOTAL_PAID	TOT_PAID_AMT	Continuous	Aggregated total of amount < $1000	None
Mainframe invoice table	INVOICE_DATE	NUM_INVOICES	Continuous	Count of invoices between 09/23/1996 and 08/12/1999	TO_DATE

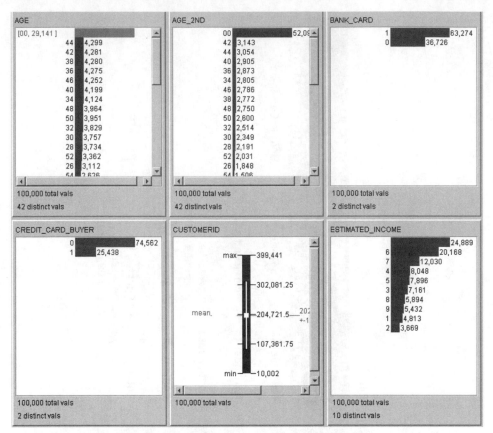

Figure 4.15 Partial distribution and statistics graphs of the raw demographic file.

- The BANK_CARD, ESTIMATED_INCOME, CREDIT_CARD_BUYER, GAS_DEPT_RETAIL, HOME_OWNER, LENGTH_RESIDENCE, and MARITAL_STATUS columns appear to have valid data and will be loaded. Empty and blank records will be converted to "E" to represent that the value was empty. In some cases, a "U" was already recorded to indicate unknown.

- The PREMIUM and UPSCALE columns also appear to have valid data and will be loaded.

The next step was to implement the changes into the creation and load scripts. Code Figure 4.9 demonstrates the demographic table creation and load scripts to load the DEMOGRAPHIC.TXT file into the exploratory data mart. The insignificant or duplicate columns will be removed from the table before it is joined to the other tables. Only the columns that we keep will be constrained to not accept NULLs.

```
--First Create the RDBMS table
CREATE TABLE demographic (
filler1 VARCHAR(5),
filler2 VARCHAR(2),
filler3 VARCHAR(2),
home_owner VARCHAR(1)
CONSTRAINT nn_demographic_home_owner NOT NULL,
yrs_residence VARCHAR(2)
CONSTRAINT nn_demographic_yrs_residence NOT NULL,
marital_status VARCHAR(1)
CONSTRAINT nn_demographic_martial_status NOT NULL,
gender VARCHAR(1)
CONSTRAINT nn_demographic_gender NOT NULL,
filler4 VARCHAR(5),
filler5 VARCHAR(5),
bank_card VARCHAR(1)
CONSTRAINT nn_demographic_bank_card NOT NULL,
consumer_card VARCHAR(1)
CONSTRAINT nn_demographic_consumer_card NOT NULL,
filler6 VARCHAR(5),
credit_buyer VARCHAR(1)
CONSTRAINT nn_demographic_credit_buyer NOT NULL,
premium VARCHAR(1)
CONSTRAINT nn_demographic_premium NOT NULL,
upscale VARCHAR(1)
CONSTRAINT nn_demographic_upscale NOT NULL,
filler7 VARCHAR(5),
estimated_Income VARCHAR(1)
CONSTRAINT nn_demographic_estimated_Income NOT NULL,
customerid NUMBER(10)
CONSTRAINT nn_demographic_customerid NOT NULL,
CONSTRAINT pk_demographic_customerid PRIMARY KEY (customerid))
--demographic.ctl Oracle SQLLDR control file
load data
infile 'demographic.txt'
insert
into table demographic

fields terminated by ','

trailing nullcols
(
filler1 enclosed by '"',
filler2 enclosed by '"',
filler3 enclosed by '"',
home_owner enclosed by '"'
"decode(:home_owner,' ','E',:home_owner)",
yrs_residence enclosed by '"'
```

Code Figure 4.9 Demographic table creation script and load scripts. *(continues)*

```
"decode(:yrs_residence,' ','E',:yrs_residence",
marital_status enclosed by '"',
gender enclosed by '"'
    "decode(:gender,' ','E',:gender)",
filler4 enclosed by '"',
filler5 enclosed by '"',
bank_card enclosed by '"',
consumer_card enclosed by '"',
filler6 enclosed by '"',
credit_card_buyer enclosed by '"',
premium enclosed by '"',
upscale enclosed by '"',
filler7 enclosed by '"',
estimated_Income enclosed by '"'
"decode(:estimated_Income,' ','E',:estimated_Income)",
customerid enclosed by '"'
)
-- SQL to DROP Insignficant and duplication columns
ALTER TABLE DEMOGRAPHIC
DROP ("FILLER1", "FILLER2", "FILLER3", "FILLER4",
"FILLER5", "FILLER6", "FILLER7")
```

Code Figure 4.9 Demographic table creation script and load scripts. *(continued)*

All of the 100,000 raw demographic records were loaded successfully into the exploratory data mart. The ECTL process replaced the missing or blank values with an "E". Figure 4.16 shows the result of the ECTL procedure.

Documenting ECTL Procedure for the Demographic File

Table 4.12 shows the table-level ECTL documentation, and Table 4.13 shows the column-level ECTL documentation for the demographic table. The column value range values were used to fill in blank and missing values during the ECTL procedure.

Table 4.12 ECTL Table-Level Documentation for the Demographic Table

META DATA ELEMENT	META DATA (DESCRIPTION)
Table name	Demographic
Description	Purchased demographic information on 100,000 customers
Experimental unit	Unique customerid
Update frequency	One time
Table data sources	Originally used for another marketing program less than 6 months ago

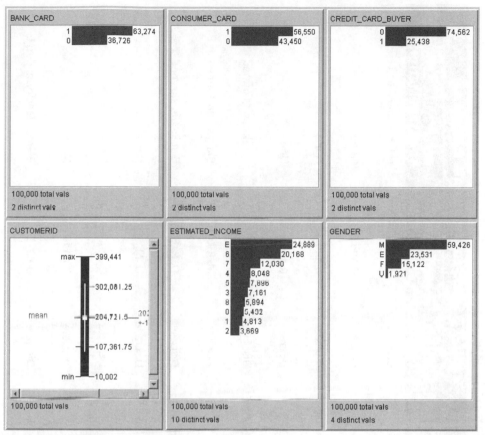

Figure 4.16 Partial distribution and statistics graphs of the transformed demographic table.

Creating the Production Business Data Set

Finally, we are able to combine the customer, contract, and aggregated invoice tables into our first production business data set. Code Figure 4.10 shows how the three tables are joined together to produce the first production business data set. Code Figure 4.11 shows how the demographic information from the demographics table was added to the *customer_join* table to create the second production business data set.

All of the validation and range checking is performed in the SQL WHERE condition. The customer table validation and range-checking rules are documented in Table 4.7, and the contract table validation and range-checking rules are documented in Table 4.9. The invoice table validation and range checking were already completed during the aggregation process.

Table 4.13 ECTL Column-Level Documentation for the Demographic Table

	SOURCE		EXPLORATORY DATA MART		
TABLE NAME	COLUMN NAME	COLUMN NAME	COLUMN DATA TYPE	COLUMN VALUE RANGE	ECTL TRANSFORMATIONS
Purchased Demographics	CUSTOMERID	CUSTOMERID	Continuous	1 to 641,498	Unique Constraint
Purchased Demographics	BANK_CARD	BANK_CARD	Discrete	0 and 1	None
Purchased Demographics	GAS_DEPT_RETAIL_CARD	CONSUMER_CARD	Discrete	0 and 1	None
Purchased Demographics	CREDIT_CARD_BUYER	CREDIT_CARD_BUYER	Discrete	0 and 1	None
Purchased Demographics	ESTIMATED_INCOME	ESTIMATED_INCOME	Discrete	1-9, E	Blanks transformed to E
Purchased Demographics	GENDER	GENDER	Discrete	M, F, U, E	Blanks transformed to E
Purchased Demographics	HOME_OWNER	HOME_OWNER	Discrete	O, R, E	Blanks transformed to E
Purchased Demographics	MARITAL_STATUS	MARITAL_STATUS	Discrete	U, M, S, A, B	None
Purchased Demographics	PREMIUM	PREMIUM	Discrete	0 and 1	None
Purchased Demographics	UPSCALE	UPSCALE	Discrete	0 and 1	None
Purchased Demographics	LENGTH_RESIDENCE	YRS_RESIDENCE	Discrete	0-99, E	Blanks transformed to E

```
CREATE TABLE customer_join AS
SELECT        cust.customerid,
              cust.activateddate,
              cust.birthdate,
              cust.city,
              cust.state,
              cust.zip,
              state.st_region region,
              cust.credit_score,
              cust.currentbalance,
              cust.prgcode,
              cont.contract_fee,
              cont.renewal_date,
              cont.churn_reason,
              inv.tot_open_amt,
              inv.tot_invoice_amt,
              inv.tot_paid_amt,
              inv.num_invoices
FROM customer cust, contract cont, invoice_aggregate inv, state
WHERE         cust.customerid = inv.customerid AND
              cust.customerid = cont.customerid AND
              cust.state = state.st_st AND
              cust.activateddate between
              TO_DATE('09/23/1996','MM/DD/YYYY') and
TO_DATE('08/12/1999','MM/DD/YYYY')AND
              cust.birthdate between
TO_DATE('01/01/1900','MM/DD/YYYY') and
TO_DATE('01/01/1990','MM/DD/YYYY') AND
              cust.currentbalance between -1000 and 1000 AND
              cont.contract_fee < 500 AND
              cont.renewal_date between
TO_DATE('09/23/1996','MM/DD/YYYY') and
TO_DATE('08/12/1999','MM/DD/YYYY')
```

Code Figure 4.10   Joining the customer, contract, and invoice tables.

```
CREATE TABLE customer_demographic AS
SELECT        cust.customerid,
              cust.activateddate,
              cust.birthdate,
              cust.city,
              cust.state,
              cust.zip,
              cust.region,
```

Code Figure 4.11   Adding the demographic table to the *customer_join* table. *(continues)*

```
cust.credit_score,
cust.currentbalance,
cust.prgcode,
cust.contract_fee,
cust.renewal_date,
cust.churn_reason,
cust.tot_open_amt,
cust.tot_invoice_amt,
cust.tot_paid_amt,
cust.num_invoices,
demographic.home_owner,
demographic.yrs_residence,
demographic.marital_status,
demographic.gender,
demographic.bank_card,
demographic.consumer_card,
demographic.credit_card_buyer,
demographic.premium,
demographic.upscale,
demographic.estimated_Income
FROM customer_join cust, demographic
WHERE
     cust.customerid=demographic.customerid
```

Code Figure 4.11 Adding the demographic table to the *customer_join* table. *(continued)*

Review of the ECTL Procedures for the Case Study

The selection and ECTL process has been completed. For each of the operational data sources, we have demonstrated the following ECTL processing steps:

- Evaluating the operational data source using histograms and statistics graphs. In this step, the entire operational data source file was loaded into the exploratory data mart (as is). We used visualizations to evaluate the columns and their value ranges to determine what ECTL processing was necessary.

- Creating the interim exploratory data mart tables and the ECTL processing script to populate the table.

  - Code Figure 4.5 demonstrated how to create and perform the ECTL processing for the customer table.

  - Code Figure 4.6 was used to create and perform the ECTL processing for the contract table.

- Code Figure 4.7 was used to create and perform the ECTL processing for the invoice table. Code Figure 4.8 was used to perform the logical transformation of the invoice table.

- Code Figure 4.9 was used to create and perform the ECTL processing for the demographic table.

■ Evaluating and documenting the ECTL process.

Our exploratory data mart now contains two business data sets: *customer_join* and *customer_demographic*, as demonstrated in Code Figures 4.10 and 4.11. Our next step is to logically transform these business data sets into formats that can be used by the data visualization and visual data mining tools. We will perform these steps at the end of the next chapter.

Summary

Choosing the business data set includes creating an exploratory data mart to store the production business data sets and using ECTL tools to populate the exploratory data mart. The business case study in this chapter illustrated the many data quality issues faced in the ECTL process and demonstrated techniques for resolving these issues. In the next chapter, we help you logically transform the business data set into a format that can be used by data visualization and visual data mining tools. By doing so, you can begin to exploit your business data sets with data visualization and visual data mining to gain knowledge and insights into business data sets and communicate those discoveries to the decision makers.

CHAPTER 5

Step 4: Transforming the Business Data Set

O ften the data facts contained in the business data set need to be transformed into information. You may need to transform the format of the data set itself to make it easier to visualize, mine, or investigate different facets of the business question. Moreover, you may need to use logical transformations to remove embedded bias to create more accurate data mining models.

Step 4 of the VDM methodology is logical transformations to enhance the information contained within the data set, to remove bias, and to facilitate visualizing and data mining of the business data set. In this chapter the focus is on how to perform useful and often necessary operations on the production business data sets created in VDM Step 3. In most cases, the logical transformation operators are included as part of the RDBMS or embedded within the data visualization or visual data mining tool. If the transformation will be used globally—that is, it is required for every visualization or data mining model—you perform the transformation operation as part of the ECTL procedures and documentation discussed in Chapter 4. In this chapter, we address the table-level logical transformations, such as removing weighted records bias and data set aggregations, and column-level logical transformations, such as column value grouping (binning) and creating new columns or removing existing columns. Furthermore, we apply Step 4 to the ongoing business case study to illustrate implementing this step in your own VDM project.

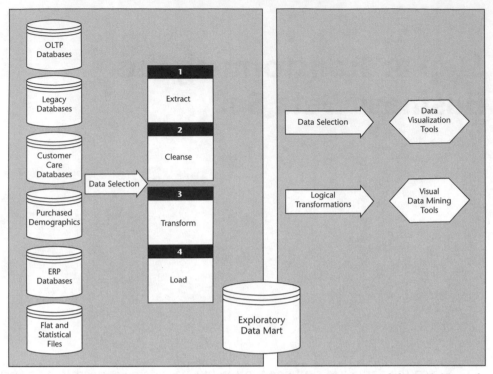

Figure 5.1 Data flow from exploratory data mart to the visualization and data mining tools.

Figure 5.1 diagrams the overall flow of data from the operational data sources to the exploratory data mart (VDM Step 3), as well as the flow from the exploratory data mart to the data visualization and data mining tools (VDM Step 4). In Step 4, the data selection operation is represented as a reduction arrow, since it denotes that often you will only select a subset of business data sets or aggregate the business data set before you visualize or mine it. The logical transformation arrow is also represented as a reduction arrow, since it denotes that you frequently will reduce the value range of columns using a column grouping or other column-level transformations.

Types of Logical Transformations

As mentioned in Chapter 4, the class of VDM project you are planning (proof-of-concept, pilot, or production) determines the complexity and amount of data in your business data set. The class of VDM project also dictates how you will implement the logical transformations. There are basically two levels of logical transformations that you may need to consider before you visualize or perform data mining of the business data set: table-level and column-level logical transformations. Many of the logical transformations depend on the type data visualization or visual data mining tool you are using and the facet of the business question you are investigating.

The number and type of logical transformations you need to apply depends on the quality of data in the production business data set. It also depends on the type of data visualization or data mining model you are using to investigate the business question. Performing the logical transformation using the data visualization or data mining transformation tool runs relatively quickly. However, for larger data sets and those used in production VDM project, you may need to perform the logical transformation while selecting the production business data set and make these logical transformations part of the ECTL procedures, as discussed in Chapter 4.

Table-Level Logical Transformations

Table-level logical transformations affect the structure and number of rows within the entire production business data set. Logical transformations, such as transforming weighted and time series data sets, increase the number of records in the data set and often reduce the number of columns. Other logical transformations, such as aggregating and filtering the data set, decrease the number of records in the data set but usually keep the same number of columns. Some of the common table-level logical transformations are as follows:

Transforming weighted data sets.   These are logical transformations that replace column and record weights from the data set with additional rows that mimic the original weighting. Not all data visualization and visual data mining software packages can deal with one or more weights. This table-level logical transformation creates a new data set by adding new rows based on the column or record weights.

Transforming time series data sets.   These are logical transformations that restructure time series data sets. Many data visualization tools required time series data sets in this format: object of interest followed by numerous observations of the object at time 1 through to n. However, some data mining algorithms may require that you restructure the time series data set into this format: object of interest, time dimension. This table-level logical transformation creates a new data set by adding new rows based on the number of time series. Alternatively, a time series data set can be transformed into records of length m, where m represents the maximum number of time series events that can occur. The table-level logical transformation creates a new data set where each column represents a particular time dimension.

Aggregating data sets. Depending on the data visualization, you may need to aggregate the data set to a higher experimental unit. For instance, map visualizations require the data set to be aggregated to the map unit level. If the map unit level is at the state level, the data set needs to be aggregated to the state level. For data mining, the data set should be aggregated at the experimental unit defined by the business question.

Filtering data sets. You may want to use a filter to refine your selection of records from the data set to investigate different aspects of the business question. This table-level transformation enables you to create subsets of the data set based on your filtering condition.

Transforming Weighted Data Sets

Sometimes the original business data set contains one or more *weighted* columns, especially if you included files from statistical software packages in your exploratory data mart. You can think of a weighted column as table short-hand. The column weight indicates how much influence the record or column within the record has when compared to other records. Not all data mining algorithms or data visualization software packages can decipher weighted columns or records. Therefore, to avoid introducing bias into your analysis, you may need to remove the column or record weights.

For instance, most data mining tools assume that all records have equal importance in the data set. If one record weight is 5 and another record weight is 1, most data mining algorithms won't give the first record five times more consideration than the second record. Bias in this sense is different from the notion of a biased sample explained in Chapter 4. A column or record weight is positively biased if it tends to overestimate the experimental unit and a column or record weight is negatively biased if it tends to underestimate the experimental unit.

Table 5.1 shows a fictitious gene data set that contains two column weights per row of data. The HAIR_WEIGHT column weight applies to hair color, and the EYE_WEIGHT column weight applies to eye color. The embedded information contained within the column weights for the gene data set is that the gene X causes 3 out of 5 people to have brown hair and 4 out of 5 people to have blue eyes and gene Y causes 2 out of 5 people to have black hair and 1 out of 5 people to have green eyes.

Table 5.1 GENE table with Multiple Column Weights per Record

GENE_NAME	HAIR_COLOR	HAIR_WEIGHT	EYE_COLOR	EYE_WEIGHT
X	Brown	3	Blue	4
Y	Black	2	Green	1

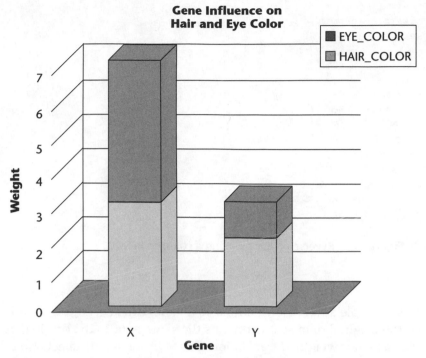

Figure 5.2 Column graph of gene showing the influence of column weights.

Not all visualization tools require that you remove the column and record weights. For example, Figure 5.2 illustrates a column graph of the gene table showing the influence of column weights. The column graph can be used to visually show that gene X has more influence on the population then gene Y. Also, you can visually compare the influence each gene has on each physical trait. In this case, the column weight is considered a data fact or dimension about the gene data set. However, we cannot explicitly tell the visualization or visual data mining tool that the Hair Weight column weights the Hair Color column.

Transforming Column Weights

For the many data visualization and data mining tools, you must remove the column and record weight to satisfy the requirement that all rows in the data set be unbiased. The first step is to make sure that each record has only one weight. For example, Table 5.1 is the result of a pivot operation (aggregation grouped by HAIR_COLOR and EYE_COLOR). To remove these aggregations, you can use a reverse pivot operation to achieve this. Code Figure 5.1 demonstrates how to perform a reverse pivot operation in standard SQL with the UNION operator.

```
CREATE or REPLACE VIEW view gene_rev_pivot AS
SELECT
gene.gene_name,
'Hair' ATTRIBUTE,
gene.hair_color COLOR,
gene.hair_weight WEIGHT
     FROM gene
UNION
SELECT
gene.gene_name,
'Eyes' ATTRIBUTE,
gene.eye_color COLOR,
gene.eye_weight WEIGHT
     FROM gene
```

Code Figure 5.1 Reverse pivoting weighted columns in SQL.

In this example a new view (similar to a table) called *gene_rev_pivot* is created from the original data set. It contains the same data as the original gene data set but as a nonweighted translation. The SQL statement selects first the gene and its influence on the hair trait. The output of this selection is joined with the selection of the gene and its influence on the eye color trait using the SQL UNION operator. Table 5.2 shows the results of the reverse pivot operation. From the table, you will notice that the gene and the gene column observations all have the same influence and the data set is no longer biased by column weights. However, each record still carries a record weighted.

Insert Figure 3 illustrates a scatter graph of the record weighted data set. In this visualization, the record weight is actually considered a data fact about the data set. As shown in Insert 3, the record weight is indicated by the size of the graphical entity. The location of the graphical entity is determined by the other column dimensions: GENE_NAME, ATTRIBUTE, and COLOR. The 3-D scatter graph enables you to compare all four data dimensions of the data set at the same time within the same visualization.

Table 5.2 GENE Table with Only a Record Weight

GENE_NAME	ATTRIBUTE	COLOR	WEIGHT
X	Hair	Brown	3
Y	Hair	Black	2
X	Eyes	Blue	4
Y	Eyes	Green	1

Transforming Record Weights

If your data visualization or visual data mining tools do not support row or record weights, you must transform the data set into new rows based on record weights. The record weight column indicates how many rows to create. For instance, the first row of Table 5.2 has a record weight of 3. To transform the record, you need to translate the first row into three new rows containing GENE_NAME=X, ATTRIBUTE=Hair, COLOR=Brown. For the second row with a record weight of 2, you would need to translate the row into two new rows, and so on.

Code Figure 5.2 demonstrates how to transform the record weights into new rows based on the value of the record weight. It is written in PL/SQL and implements a PL/SQL cursor to step through the weighted data set one row at a time. For each row, it adds new rows into the *gene_table_flattened* table based on the value of the record weight. This technique is often referred to as "flattening" a weighted data set.

The PL in PL/SQL stands for *procedural language*. This coding language extends the limited functionality of SQL by providing numerous third- and fourth-generation language constructs, such as the ability to conditionally change an SQL statement and loop through records one at a time (cursors) and the ability to apply conditional logic (if-then-else), among others.

```
DECLARE
v_gene_name      gene.gene_name%TYPE;
v_attribute      gene.attribute%TYPE;
v_color          gene.color%TYPE;
v_weight           gene.weight%TYPE;
-- define the PL/SQL cursor to step through the table
-- a record at a time
CURSOR cursor_weight (
p_gene_name gene.gene_name%TYPE,
p_attribute gene.attribute%TYPE,
p_color gene.color%TYPE,
p_weight gene.weight%TYPE)
IS
SELECT
gene_name,
attribute,
color,
weight
FROM gene;
-- Open the PL/SQL cursor and loop through the records
BEGIN
OPEN cursor_weight(v_gene_name, v_attribute,v_color,v_weight);
```

Code Figure 5.2   Flattening a weighted table using PL/SQL. *(continues)*

```
LOOP -- fetch rows outer loop
FETCH cursor_weight into
v_gene_name, v_attribute, v_color, v_weight;
EXIT WHEN cursor_weight%NOTFOUND;
-- Inner loop to insert new rows based on the value of
-- of the original record weight
WHILE v_weight > 0
LOOP
INSERT into gene_table_flattened
(gene_name, attribute, color)
VALUES
(v_gene_name, v_attribute, v_color);
v_weight := v_weight -1;
END LOOP; -- inner loop
END LOOP; -- outer loop to fetch rows
close cursor_weight;
END;
```

Code Figure 5.2 Flattening a weighted table using PL/SQL. *(continued)*

The process begins by defining a PL/SQL cursor to hold the original data set. Then for each row in the data set, rows are inserted into the new table called *gene_table_flattened* for the count of the record weight. The new table *gene_table_flattened* contains one row per the number of record weights from the original table. Table 5.3 shows the results of the flattening technique.

Table 5.3 Unbiased GENE Table with the Record Weight Removed

GENE_NAME	ATTRIBUTE	COLOR
X	Hair	Brown
X	Hair	Brown
X	Hair	Brown
Y	Hair	Black
Y	Hair	Black
X	Eyes	Blue
X	Eyes	Blue
X	Eyes	Blue
X	Eyes	Blue
Y	Eyes	Green

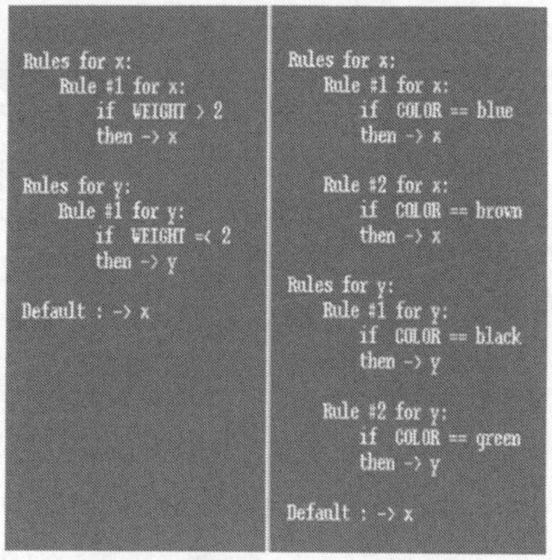

```
Rules for x:              Rules for x:
    Rule #1 for x:            Rule #1 for x:
        if  WEIGHT > 2           if  COLOR == blue
        then -> x                then -> x

Rules for y:                  Rule #2 for x:
    Rule #1 for y:               if  COLOR == brown
        if  WEIGHT =< 2          then -> x
        then -> y
                          Rules for y:
Default : -> x                Rule #1 for y:
                                 if  COLOR == black
                                 then -> y

                              Rule #2 for y:
                                 if  COLOR == green
                                 then -> y

                          Default : -> x
```

Figure 5.3 Data mining rules.

Why is transforming column and record weight necessary? Depending on the data visualization and what you are showing, it may not be. However, it is normally required to achieve more accurate data mining models. Figure 5.3 illustrates two rule sets for predicting the gene label The left-hand decision tree rule set was built using the GENE table with a record weight (Table 5.2). The rules clearly show that only the weighted column is taken into consideration and not the physical traits at all. Keeping the record weight as a data fact caused the creation of an erroneous data mining model. The right-hand decision tree rule set was built using the unbiased GENE table with the record weight removed (Table 5.3). Not only does this model take into consideration the physical traits, but it predicts the correct gene 100 percent of the time based on the physical traits rather than the record weight. Therefore, if you plan to use data mining with the business data set, you may need to perform multiple weighted column and record transformations before using the business data set. Chapters 6 and 7 discuss creating and analyzing data mining model in more detail.

Transforming Time Series Data Sets

For creating data visualizations, a data set formatted as a time series table is very useful. For instance, Chapter 1 contained examples of how a time series table can be used to create insightful line and area graphs. However, many data mining tools require you to reverse pivot the time series data set. Similar to record weights, the algorithms assume each column in the data set to be independent of all the other columns. Table 5.4 lists the first few records from a data set containing yield index information. The format of the data set illustrates the most common format for time series data sets. That is, the first column is the

Table 5.4 Yield Index Data Set

IDX_DATE	IDX_10D	IDX_1M	IDX_3M	IDX_6M	IDX_12M
1/17/1996	0.0759	0.076	0.0752	0.0747	0.0739
1/18/1996	0.0759	0.0765	0.0758	0.0753	0.0747
1/19/1996	0.0759	0.076	0.0755	0.0749	0.0743
1/22/1996	0.0759	0.076	0.0753	0.0748	0.0742
1/23/1996	0.0759	0.0761	0.0756	0.0749	0.0744
1/24/1996	0.0759	0.076	0.0755	0.0748	0.0741
1/25/1996	0.0759	0.076	0.0753	0.0746	0.0738
1/26/1996	0.0759	0.076	0.0753	0.0746	0.0738
1/29/1996	0.0759	0.0761	0.0756	0.0748	0.0741
1/30/1996	0.0759	0.076	0.0755	0.0748	0.074
1/31/1996	0.0759	0.0761	0.0756	0.0741	0.0729
2/1/1996	0.0759	0.076	0.0753	0.074	0.0728

object of interest and the subsequent columns are observations of that object at different time intervals. In the case of Table 5.4, the first column is the date of the bond index, the second and subsequent columns are the bond index yield rate for 10 days, 1 month, 3 months, 6 months, and so on.

Code Figure 5.3 demonstrates how to reverse pivot the time series data set from Table 5.5 into independent columns and records. The SQL UNION operator is used to create a view of the yield data set in the format of date of the index (object of interest), day range (observation time), and index value (observation). In the transformed format, the view *yield_rev_pivot* satisfies the data mining requirement that the columns in the business data set are independent of one another.

```
CREATE or REPLACE VIEW yield_rev_pivot AS
-- Transform the series Into the new format
SELECT
yield.idx_date IDX_DATE,
'10' DAYS,
yield.idx_10d IDX
```

Code Figure 5.3 Reverse pivoting a time series data set.

```
     FROM yield
-- Use the UNION operator to combine the previous series with
-- the next transformation
UNION
SELECT
yield.idx_date IDX_DATE,
'30' DAYS,
yield.idx_1m IDX
FROM yield
-- Use the UNION operator to combine the previous series with
-- the next transformation
UNION
SELECT
yield.idx_date IDX_DATE,
'91' DAYS,
yield.idx_6m IDX
FROM yield
-- Use the UNION operator to combine the previous series with
-- the next transformation
UNION
SELECT
yield.idx_date IDX_DATE,
'183' DAYS,
yield.idx_6m IDX
FROM yield
-- Use the UNION operator to combine the previous series with
-- the next transformation
UNION
SELECT
yield.idx_date IDX_DATE,
'365' DAYS,
yield.idx_12m IDX
FROM yield
```

Code Figure 5.3   Reverse pivoting a time series data set. *(continued)*

Table 5.5 illustrates the results of the reverse pivot SQL query for the first two records from the original yield index data set. You can use similar procedures to reverse pivot with one or more time series columns. The data mining algorithms can now detect patterns based on the observation object, the observation time dimension, and the observed value.

Table 5.5 Yield_Rev_Pivot Index Data Set

IDX_DATE	DAYS	IDX
1/17/1996	10	0.0759
1/17/1996	30	0.076
1/17/1996	91	0.0752
1/17/1996	183	0.0747
1/17/1996	365	0.0739
1/18/1996	10	0.0759
1/18/1996	30	0.0765
1/18/1996	91	0.0758
1/18/1996	183	0.0753
1/18/1996	365	0.0747

Aggregating the Data Sets

Many of the data visualization and visual data mining tools include aggregation functions. An aggregation transformation provides a way to group information according to your business question and to generate statistics about that information. The aggregation function normally provides the following functions that you can apply to continuous input columns: COUNT, COUNT DISTINCT, SUM, AVG, MAX, MIN, STDDEV, and VARIANCE. You typically aggregate by one or more discrete or continuous columns in the data set. The aggregation transformation is often used to create summary data sets from hierarchical, spatial, and geographic data sets.

The business question helps you determine the level of aggregation required for the visualization or the level to use for the data mining algorithm. For instance, if your business question is "What is the average price of cars purchased by year by state?" and your experimental unit level of your production business data set is at the individual car purchase level, you would need to aggregate to the state and year level. Table 5.6 illustrates the first 10 rows from the car sales data set as it may exist in the exploratory data mart to answer this question.

Table 5.6 Car Sales Business Data Set

STATE	P_YEAR	P_PRICE
GA	1995	43,132
GA	1996	37,324
GA	1996	20,090
TX	1995	20,300
TX	1996	53,900
TX	1996	60,000
GA	1995	29,800
TX	1999	30,480
TX	1998	45,000
GA	1999	60,000

You could accomplish the required aggregation in a variety of ways. Code Figure 5.4 demonstrates how to use a standard SQL statement to create a new data set or view *car_sales_year_state* that aggregates the data set by the discrete columns STATE and P_YEAR.

Table 5.7 illustrates the results of the aggregation. From the view, you would be able to visualize a map of the United States, showing the number of cars purchased by year, as well as the average sales price by state.

```
CREATE OR REPLACE VIEW car_sales_year_state AS
SELECT
p_year,
state,
count(p_price)P_COUNT,
avg(p_price) AVG_PRICE
FROM car purchases
GROUP BY state, p_year
```

Code Figure 5.4 Aggregating using standard SQL.

Table 5.7 Aggregation View of the Car Sales Business Data Set

P_YEAR	STATE	P_COUNT	AVG_PRICE
1995	GA	2	36466
1996	GA	2	28707
1999	GA	1	60000
1995	TX	1	20300
1996	TX	2	56950
1998	TX	1	45000
1999	TX	1	30480

Figure 5.4 shows two map visualizations of the aggregation view of the car sales business set. The map in Figure 5.4a shows the data set for 1996 when the average sales price per car in Texas was $56,950, compared to $28,707 in Georgia. The map in Figure 5.4b shows the data set for 1999 when the average sales price per car in Texas was $30,480, compared to $60,000 in Georgia.

Filtering Data Sets

You may want to use a filter to refine your selection of records from the data set to investigate different aspects of the business question. This table-level transformation enables you to create subsets of the data set based upon your filtering condition or a boolean expression. Only records for which the condition or expression evaluates to TRUE are kept. During the selection of the business data set for the case study in Chapter 4, many filtering operations were performed on the operational data set to remove extreme values (outliers) before loading the data into the exploratory data mart. Logical filtering of the production business data set uses filtering to change the focus of the data set.

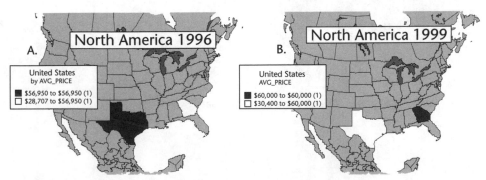

Figure 5.4 Map visualizations of the aggregated car sales data set.

```
SELECT       YIELD_REV_PIVOT.IDX_DATE,
YIELD_REV_PIVOT.DAYS,
YIELD_REV_PIVOT.IDX
FROM YIELD_REV_PIVOT YIELD_REV_PIVOT
WHERE
YIELD_REV_PIVOT.IDX_DATE BETWEEN '01-JAN-1998' AND '31-DEC-1998'
AND YIELD_REV_PIVOT.DAYS = '10'
```

Code Figure 5.5   SQL query to filter only 10-day yield indices for 1998.

Using the data set generated from Code Figure 5.5, you could use filtering to focus your attention on a specific year or yield maturity day index. To accomplish the filtering, you can use either standard SQL or the embedded filtering tools within the data visualization and data mining tools. If your production business data set is large, you may want to perform the filtering as an ODBC query. Code Figure 5.5 shows an SQL query generated by filtering only 10-day indexes and selecting data for only 1998.

In addition, most data visualization and data mining tools also support sampling of the data set to create a subset of the production business data set. However, to avoid sampling bias, make sure the tool is creating a *random* sample and not just selecting the first X number of rows. Refer to the discussion on avoiding sampling bias in Chapter 4.

Column-Level Logical Transformations

Column-level logical transformations affect the structure of the columns within the entire production business data set. Simple column transformations such as adding or removing a column and changing the number and type of columns of the data set typically do not change the number of records in the data set. Other logical transformations such as column value grouping and transforming NULL values change the column values but do not change the number of columns in the data set. Some of the common column-level logical transformations are as follows:

Simple column transformations.   These are logical column transformations such as remove column, change column data type, or create new column based on an expression. These column-level transformations enable you to manipulate the data set. Often, you can combine multiple columns (data facts) into a single column that aids you in visualizing or enhancing the accuracy of the data mining model.

Column value grouping transformations. These are logical transformations to group ranges of continuous and discrete values into larger groupings. These column-level transformations enable you to improve the understandability of your visualizations and boost the probability of discovering patterns of the data mining algorithms.

Simple Column Transformations

Simple column transformations include removing, adding, and changing the column's data type. Depending on whether you want to globally alter the business data set, you can perform many of the simple column transformations within the data visualization or data mining tool. In other cases, if you want the column changes to affect all visualizations and data mining, you should update your ECTL procedures to not select the column or add or change the column from the operational data source before loading the data into the exploratory data mart. Other times, you may want to remove, add, or change the column temporarily to see what effect it has on the data mining algorithm. For instance, if you are using association rules, you may want to keep correlated columns (that's what you're looking for). However, for predictive data mining algorithms, you should remove all but one of the correlated columns.

Each data visualization and data mining tool has its own unique column transformation language. For continuous (numeric) columns, most tools have simple math functions like add, multiply, and divide. For discrete (string) columns, most tools have simple string functions like substring() and isnull(). In addition, most tools allow for "if-then-else" and other higher-level conditional functions, as well as comparison operators.

Remove Column Transformation

Perhaps the simplest column transformation is the remove column transformation. This transformation removes the column from the production business data set. Normally, you use this transformation when you want to remove unique, duplicate, or highly correlated columns from the data set.

Add Column Transformation

Another simple column transformation is the add column transformation. This transformation adds a column to your production business data set based on a mathematical expression. You generally use this transformation to create a new column based on other columns within the data set, usually to combine other columns or to create new data facts. For example, if the production business data set contains the columns QUANTITY and PRICE, but the sales price is needed to answer the business question, you could create a new column SALES_PRICE as defined as QUANTITY times PRICE. In most cases, you would then remove the QUANTITY and PRICE columns from the data set, since they will be highly correlated to the newly created SALES_PRICE column.

Often you can use the add column transformation to decipher a column's meaning or to use a column as more than one data fact. For instance, suppose you have the column SALES_DATE in the format DD-MON-YYYY and you are looking for seasonal (time series) trends. You may want to use the add column transformation to convert the SALES_DATE into one or more of the following time series data facts: SALES_YEAR, SALES_QUARTER, SALES_MONTH, SALES_WEEK, and SALES_WEEKDAY. Code Figure 5.6 demonstrates how you could create the new column within SQL. For more date format conversions, refer to your RDBMS SQL manuals.

Change Column Data Type Transformation

The change column data type transformation is another simple column transformation. This transformation changes a column's data type when possible. For instance, a continuous column containing numbers that represent four-digit years can easily be converted to a four-character discrete column. Another example of a change type column transformation is a three-character string that contains the quantity of a product sold. You could easily convert it into a continuous (numeric) column. Often you will find that the operational data sources use a data type that isn't appropriate for your data visualization or data mining efforts. For instance, the column PART_NUMBER is most likely stored as a continuous (numeric) column in the operational data source; however, its true meaning is a discrete, categorical column. For instance, it is insignificant to know the numeric sum of all PART_NUMBER parts. However, it may be significant to know how many PART_NUMBER=0123456789 parts failed. The visualization and data mining tools do make a distinction between continuous and discrete columns, so you can use the change column data type transformation to convert the columns into their logical meanings.

```
SELECT
--- To transform the sales_date Into a calendar Year
    TO_CHAR(sales_date,'YYYY') SALES_YEAR,
--- To transform the sales_date Into a calendar Quarter
    TO_CHAR(sales_date,'Q') SALES_QUARTER,
--- To transform the sales_date Into a calendar Month
    TO_CHAR(sales_date,'MON') SALES_MONTH,
--- To transform the sales_date Into the calendar Week
    TO_CHAR(sales_date,'WW') SALES_WEEK,
--- To transform the sales_date Into day of the week
    TO_CHAR(sales_date,'DAY') SALES_DAY
FROM source_table
```

Code Figure 5.6 Add column date transformations.

Sometimes the original data source column used a numeric data type instead of a character data type column definition to save disk space. For example, the column GENDER may contain the numeric whose values are either 0 or 1. However, the logical meaning of the value 0 is Male and the logical meaning of the value 1 is Female for the GENDER column. If you don't change the column type, a rule induction algorithm may find a rule that contains the expression "GENDER value of 0.3". But the value 0.3 (though numerically closer to female than male) doesn't help define a business rule. In most cases, you want to know whether to market to male or female customers, not to 0.3 type customers. Therefore, you need to use the change type transformation to change the GENDER column from continuous to discrete.

In addition, for readability of the visualization or data mining model, you may want to decode the GENDER column. For instance, you can add a column called GENDER_FULL that is defined by the following expression:

```
if ('GENDER' = 0) then ("Male") else ("Female")
```

Note that if the values for the column can contain the values 0, 1, or NULL (?), all three possible cases may need to be considered depending on the original column's values:

```
if ('GENDER'= 0) then ("Male")
else (if ('GENDER' = 1) then ("Female")
else ("Unknown"))
```

Column Grouping Transformations

One of the most useful logical column transformations is a column grouping transformation. This transformation creates a new column based on a range selection criteria imposed on the original column. It can be applied to both discrete and continuous columns. Following are the methods for each:

- For discrete columns, the new group column value is a superset of individual values. For instance, if your business question dealt with searching for pattern for drug interactions, you may find that transforming the SPECIFIC_DRUG column into a DRUG_CLASS may assist in visualizing and data mining the data set. Most data visualization and data mining tools perform poorly (don't find predictive or descriptive patterns) when the number of distinct column values is over 30. Developing techniques to reduce the number of distinct values to 30 or less can be very useful.

- For continuous columns, the new group column value is also a superset of individual column values. This process is often referred to as *binning* continuous columns. Once the continuous column values are binned into the range group, the new column can be considered a discrete column. For instance, the U.S. census uses predefined income range groups. If your data set contained a customer's individual income, you may consider binning the INCOME column into range groups. Most data visualization and data mining tools can benefit from binning to discover predictive or descriptive patterns.

The domain expert and the data and business analyst teams will need to decide the degree of grouping to apply to discrete and continuous column within the production business data set. In addition, you must decide whether to perform these column grouping transformations within the data visualization and data mining tools or as part of your ECTL procedures. A rule of thumb is if you end up repeating the same column groupings for every production visualization or data mining model, you want to perform the column grouping as part of the ECTL procedures. However, if you perform different column grouping transformations to investigate different aspects of the business data set, you would not want to be locked into a predefined column grouping transformation accomplished as part of the ECTL procedure. On the other hand, most data visualization and data mining tools are not as efficient at performing transformations as an ECTL tool is. Especially for iterative data mining processes, you may want to let the ECTL tool perform the transformation for overall efficiency and performance.

Grouping Transformation on Discrete Columns

In general, for data visualization and data mining, discrete columns that take on more than 30 values are not very useful for showing trends or discovering patterns. For instance, one Internet service provider's RATE_PLAN column contained 194 distinct rate plans for its 75,860 customers, as illustrated by the middle histogram, Rate Plan Original, in Figure 5.5.

After a talk with the domain experts, it was discovered that actually only the first two digits of the RATE_PLAN column signified the rate plan. The third digit was used to indicate the billing cycle. Therefore, a column grouping transformation needs to be applied to the RATE_PLAN column to remove the billing cycle information. In Figure 5.5, the right-hand histogram graph, Rate Plan Substring, demonstrates the effects of using a substring column transformation on the original RATE_PLAN column to create the Rate Plan Substring column. As you can see from Figure 5.5, there are really only 60 rate plans available. However, 60 distinct values may still be too many to be useful, especially for data visualizations. If you look at the Rate Plan Substring histogram graph, the first few rate plans really contain the majority of customers (the majority of the rate plan variance among customers).

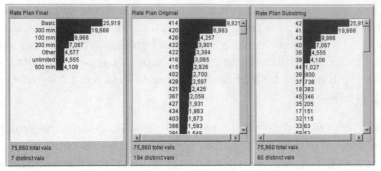

Figure 5.5   Distribution graph of rate plan transformations.

One common technique to further reduce the number of distinct values for a column is to combine insignificant column values into an "Other" catchall group. Normally, you can group those distinct values that account for less than 2 percent of the total records into the "Other" group. At this point, you may also want to decode the RATE_PLAN into a user-friendly format. For instance, you could decode rate plan value 42 into its business meaning "Basic," and so on from the rate plan description lookup table. The resulting column grouping transformations (and one decode transformation) are shown in the left-hand histogram graph, Rate Plan Final.

Code Figure 5.7 illustrates a sample grouping transformation procedure written in Oracle PL/SQL. The sample procedure is passed two parameters. The first parameter is the threshold percentage of the distinct values groupings to keep. The second is the replacement string to use for those groups that fall below the threshold. For example, you could call the procedure from SQL with the following syntax: execute group_column (2,'Other'). The procedure uses a PL/SQL cursor to create a list of distinct values for the column and a frequency count for each distinct value. Then the procedure counts all the records in the data set to be able to calculate the percentage distribution of distinct column values to the whole. Finally, the parameter string 'Other' is used to replace those values whose distinct count percentages fall below the threshold parameter.

You could modify this or develop similar procedures to perform column grouping transformations on discrete columns within your business data set. If the column grouping will be global in all your visualizations and data mining efforts, make the procedure part of the ECTL process when initially creating the business data set in the exploratory data mart. Otherwise, you may first want to make a copy of the business data set before applying the procedure, since it updates the column values in the given data set.

```
CREATE OR REPLACE PROCEDURE group_column
(p_percent_input        NUMBER,
p_fill_value            VARCHAR)
IS
-- Variables used by the procedure
v_percent_input              NUMBER;
v_fill_value                 VARCHAR2(255);
v_rec_total              NUMBER;
v_column_value               VARCHAR2(255);
v_column_value_count         NUMBER;
v_percent_calc               NUMBER;
-- PL/SQL cursor to hold the distinct values and their count
CURSOR c_column IS
SELECT rate_plan,
count(rate_plan)
FROM copy_of_business_data_set
GROUP BY rate_plan
ORDER BY count(rate_plan) asc;
BEGIN
-- Load the passed parameters
v_percent_input          := p_percent_input;
v_fill_value          := p_fill_value;
-- Get the total record count In the data set
SELECT count(rate_plan) INTO v_rec_total
FROM copy_of_business_data_set;
-- Open and Loop through the PL/SQL cursor
OPEN c_column;
LOOP
FETCH c_column INTO v_column_value,v_column_value_count;
EXIT WHEN c_column%NOTFOUND;
-- Calculate the percentage of the record count for a
-- the current distinct value
v_percent_calc := v_column_value_count/v_rec_total*100;

-- Check If the calculate percentage Is less than the
-- percentage passed to the procedures
IF v_percent_calc <= v_percent_input
THEN
UPDATE copy_business_data_set
SET rate_plan = v_fill_value
WHERE rate_plann      = v_column_value;
END IF;
END LOOP;
CLOSE c_column;
END;
```

Code Figure 5.7 PL/SQL procedure to perform the grouping transformation.

Grouping Transformation on Continuous Columns

For data visualization and data mining of continuous columns, you may want to consider grouping continuous values into range groups before you visualize or mine the business data set. For instance, many target marketers want to know which age ranges of customers to market to, rather than specific ages. Date range grouping is another common continuous column grouping transformation you may need to apply. In both of these instances, you know what predefined groups you want to specify.

Many data visualization and data mining tools include a binning transformation option that enables you to specify custom bin groups as a transformation to the opened data set. In addition, these binning transformations may also let you automatically bin continuous column values into range groups using mathematical formulas when you don't have predefined groupings. Many visualization and data mining tools use a trimming fraction of 0.05. This excludes the 5 percent of the records with the most extreme values (2.5 percent with the lowest values in the range and 2.5 percent with the highest values). Trimming tends to reduce the influence of outliers on the generation of thresholds.

Figure 5.6 shows a histogram of the AGE continuous column. From the histogram, you can see that the majority of ages range from 20 to 55. However, it is very unlikely that there are as many 100-year-olds as 55-year-olds.

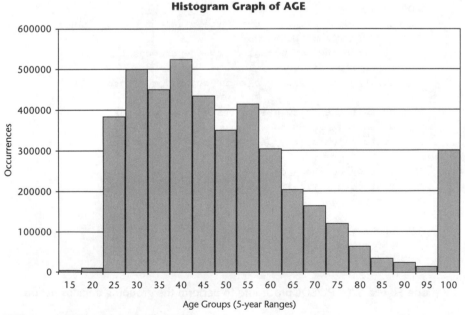

Figure 5.6 Histogram graph of AGE.

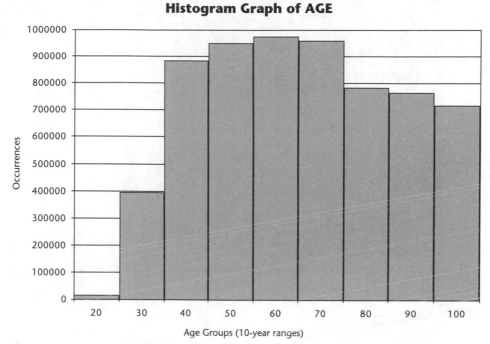

Figure 5.7 Histogram graph of AGE using a 10-year grouping transformation.

Often with columns like age, your company will have predetermined age groupings that you want to investigate. For instance, a common range grouping for ages is 1 to 20, 21 to 30, 41 to 50, 51 to 60, and so on. Your data visualization or data mining tool may allow you to specify range groups; otherwise, you can code the age range groupings in your SQL query. Figure 5.7 shows the histogram of ages using a 10-year range grouping. It also removes the outliers to provide a clearer indication of the AGE column's population. From the histogram graph, you can create a filter that automatically creates 10-year range age groupings.

Documenting the Logical Transformations

Documenting the logical transformations, although tedious, helps you ensure the integrity and accuracy of data, as well as maintain the production business data sets in the exploratory data mart. In Chapter 6, we discuss verifying the business data set. These documents will prove invaluable for accomplishing this VDM step.

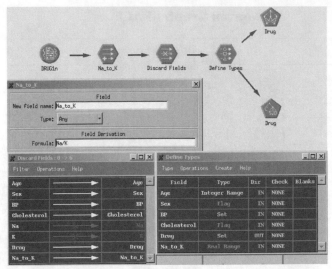

Figure 5.8 History of logical transformations in SPSS's Clementine.

Some data visualization and data mining tools include a history of applied transformations that helps document all the logical transformations applied by the tool. For instance, most tools allow you to edit the history of, delete, change, or add new transformation steps to the logical transformation stream in the form of a data flow interface. Figure 5.8 shows the history of logical transformations applied to a drug business data set in SPSS. IBM's Intelligent Miner and SAS's Enterprise Miner have similar interfaces that allow the user to visually review and edit a complete history of all transformations applied to the data set.

As illustrated in Figure 5.8, three logical transformations were applied to the drug business data set. The Na_to_K transformation (derive node in SPSS terminology) creates a new column based on a mathematical calculation performed on two original columns. The Discard Fields transformation (filter node in SPSS terminology) removes the two original columns, since they were used to create the new column Na_to_K and are highly correlated. The Define Types transformation (type node in SPSS terminology) defines and constrains the range of values to be used for the data mining algorithms—in this case, a neural network and C5.0 rule induction algorithm. Figure 5.9 shows the type of constraints used in the define types transformation.

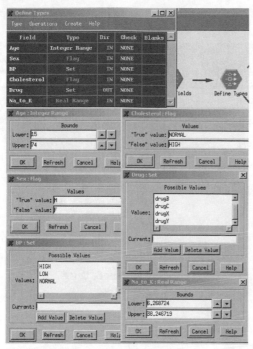

Figure 5.9   Define type of logical transformation in SPSS's Clementine.

You can set the type for a field to any of the following:

- For integer ranges, you can define the lower and upper bounds, such as 0 to 100.

- For real ranges, you can define the lower and upper bounds, such as 0.50 to 1.25.

- For set types, you can define the multiple symbolic (discrete column values), such as Small, Medium, or Large.

- For flag types, you can define two symbolic (discrete column values), such as Yes or No.

- For typeless, no information is gathered about the business data set column.

As part of the ECTL column-level documentation discussed in Chapter 4, the column value ranges have already been defined and documented. For the logical transformations documentation, you need to document any table-level or column-level logical transformation you performed on the production business data set. For example, Table 5.8 documents the logical transformations applied to the Drug1n business data set.

Table 5.8 Logical Transformations Column-Level Documentation for Business Data Set Drug1n

BUSINESS DATA SET COLUMN NAME	LOGICAL TRANSFORMATION	COLUMN VALUE RANGE	NEW COLUMN NAME
Na and K	Na/K		Na_to_K
Na and K	Delete Columns		
Na_to_K	Range Check	6.268724 – 38.246719	
Age	Range Check	15 – 74	
Sex	Column Decode	M set to True and F set to False	
BP	Column Decode	Normal set to True and High set to False	
Drug	Range Check	DrugA, DrugB, DrugC, DrugX, DrugZ	

Logically Transforming the Business Data Set for the Customer Retention VDM Case Study

Step 4 of the VDM methodology is applying logical transformations to the production business data set to enhance the information contained within the data set, to remove bias, and to facilitate visualizing and data mining of the business data set. According to the VDM project plan outlined in Chapter 2, this step is estimated to take approximately 5 working days to complete. The tasks for Step 4 are assigned to the following teams:

- The data and business analyst team is responsible for defining logical transforms that must be applied to the production business data set to enhance the information contained within the data set, to remove bias, and to facilitate visualizing and data mining of the business data set.

- The data warehousing team is responsible for creating and applying those logical transformations to the production business data set.

In Chapter 4, the operational data sources were extracted, cleansed, and transformed, and loaded into the exploratory data mart. The selection criterion for the business data sets was based on the business question of which customers were leaving and why. Before creating data visualizations or performing data mining to address these business questions, logical transformations need to be applied to the business data sets. During data visualization and data mining, you may also discover you need other logical transformations. However, many of the logical transformations can be accomplished before visualization and data mining by surveying the columns and their value ranges in the production business data sets and applying those logical transformations that make good business sense. The domain experts and data and business analysts need to review the production business data set and the ECTL documentation and define and document all logical transformations that need to be applied to the production business data set.

For the customer retention visual data mining pilot project, two production business data sets were extracted, cleansed, transformed, and loaded from the operational data sources into the exploratory data mart:

- The *customer_join* business data set joined selected data facts from the customer, contract, and invoice operational data sources. After the ECTL and join operations, the resulting data set contained 464,916 records.

- The *customer_demographic* business data set joined the information from the *customer_join* data set with selected data facts from the purchased demographics file. After the ECTL and join operations, the resulting business data set contained 96,258 records.

During VDM Step 5, Verifying the Business Data Set, covered in Chapter 6, the VDM project team will verify that all ECTL and logical transformation operations were applied correctly and didn't introduce any errors or bias into the business data set. Therefore, it is necessary to make a backup copy of the *customer_join* and *customer_demographic* tables, applying any logical transformations. This can be accomplished in SQL by creating new tables, such as *customer_join_audit* and *customer_demographic_audit*. Code Figure 5.8 demonstrates the standard SQL statements to use.

If you use standard SQL to implement the logical transformations, it is common to make mistakes. The audit backup copies serve as baseline tables, so you can undo and redo logical transformation steps by starting over with the baseline. During the visualization and data mining process, you may discover that some of the column grouping percentages need to be lower or you need to define different continuous column grouping ranges.

```
-- Create the audit copy of customer_join
CREATE TABLE customer_join_audit AS
SELECT *
FROM customer_join
-- Create the audit copy of customer_demographic
CREATE TABLE customer_demographic_audit AS
SELECT *
FROM customer_demographic
```

Code Figure 5.8 Creating audit backup copies for the business data sets.

Logically Transforming the *customer_join* Business Data Set

During the ECTL procedures, all table-level logical transformations were applied to the *customer_join* data set. Each record in the resulting business data set represents information about a unique customer and agrees with the experimental unit of individual customer. However, there are many column-level transformations that need to be applied.

The domain expert and the data and business analyst teams meet and decide to apply the following logical transformations to the *customer_join* business data set.

- The ACTIVATEDDATE column is currently a continuous date column containing values from 09/23/1996 to 08/12/1999. It will be logically transformed into the new columns ACTIVATED_YEAR and ACTIVATED_MONTH, and then removed from the *customer_join* table. This column grouping and remove column transformation enables the data visualizations and data mining tools to discover historical trends by customer activation year and month rather than a specific day in the 1,053-day range.

- The BIRTHDATE column is currently a continuous data column containing values from 01/01/1900 to 01/01/1990. It will be logically transformed into the new column AGE and then removed from the *customer_join* table. This add column and remove column transformation enables the data visualization and data mining tools to discover historical trends by customer AGE rather than specific birthday. The new age column AGE will then be grouped into uniform 10-year ranges, since we are interested in customer age groups and not their specific ages. The new column AGE_RANGE will contain values such as 20s, 30s, 40s, 50s, 60s, 70s, 80s, and 90s. The AGE column will then be removed.

- The CREDIT_SCORE column is currently a discrete column. It will be logically transformed into the new column CREDIT_APPROVAL and then removed from the *customer_join* table. A substring filtering transformation will convert values such as "A—> 5 Approved" to "5 Approved". The lower 0.5 percent of the CREDIT_APPROVAL will be grouped into an OTHERS category using the column grouping procedure demonstrated in Code Figure 5.12. Many data visualization and data mining tools do not perform well when the number of distinct values is over 30. Grouping the distinct values also removes the outliers. Column grouping and filtering the column will enhance the readability and understandability of data visualization and resulting data mining models.

- The PRGCODE column is currently a discrete column and contains 33 distinct values. The lower 5 percent of distinct values will be grouped into an OTHERS category using the column grouping procedure demonstrated in Code Figure 5.12. The remaining distinct values will be decoded into logical meanings to create a new column called CONTACT_METHOD. For instance, the value 20 means that the customer initially purchased the cellular service at a retail store. The operations team will provide all the decode values. Decoding the column will enhance the readability and understandability of data visualization and resulting data mining models.

- The CHURN_REASON column currently has 81 distinct values. The lower 0.5 percent of the CHURN_REASONS will be grouped into an OTHERS category using the column grouping procedure demonstrated in Code Figure 5.12. Many data visualization and data mining tools do not perform well when the number of distinct values is over 30. Grouping the distinct values also removes the outliers. Performing a column grouping transformation will enhance the readability and understandability of data visualization and resulting data mining models.

- The TM_DESCRIPTION column currently has 350 distinct values. The lower 5 percent of the distinct values will be grouped into an OTHERS category using the column grouping procedure demonstrated in Code Figure 5.12. The TM_DESCRIPTION column will also be logically transformed into the new column RATE_PLAN and then removed from the *customer_join* table. The new RATE_PLAN column will contain the logical meanings of the rate plans. The operations team will provide all the decode values. Decoding the column will enhance the readability and understandability of data visualization and resulting data mining models.

- The RENEWAL_DATE column is currently a continuous date column containing values from 09/23/1996 to 08/12/1999. It will be logically transformed into the new columns RENEWAL_YEAR and RENEWAL_MONTH and then removed from the *customer_join* table. This column grouping and remove column transformation enables the data visualizations and data mining tools to discover historical trends by customer renewal year and month rather than a specific day in the 1,053-day range.

Code Figures 5.9 to 5.15 demonstrate how to accomplish these logical transformations in standard SQL and PL/SQL procedures. You may want to use histogram, distribution, and statistics graphs to visually inspect the columns before and after the transformations to verify the accuracy of the transformations.

Code Figure 5.9 demonstrates how to transform the ACTIVATEDDATE into columns ACTIVATED_YEAR and ACTIVATED_MONTH.

```
-- First add the new columns to the table
    ALTER TABLE customer_join
ADD     ("ACTIVATED_YEAR" VARCHAR2(4),
"ACTIVATED_MONTH" VARCHAR2(3))
-- Next calculate the values for the new ACTIVATED_YEAR and
-- ACTIVATED_MONTH columns
    UPDATE customer_join
SET activated_year = TO_CHAR(activateddate,'YYYY')
UPDATE customer_join
SET activated_month = TO_CHAR(activateddate,'MON')
-- Remove the ACTIVATEDDATE column
    ALTER TABLE customer_join
DROP ("ACTIVATEDDATE") CASCADE CONSTRAINTS
```

Code Figure 5.9   Logically transforming the ACTIVATEDDATE column.

Code Figure 5.10 demonstrates how to transform the BIRTHDATE columns into AGE and AGE_RANGE.

```
-- First add the new columns to the table
    ALTER TABLE customer_join
ADD     ("AGE" NUMBER(3),
"AGE_RANGE" VARCHAR(4))
-- Next calculate the values for the new AGE column
    UPDATE customer_join
SET age = ROUND(TO_NUMBER(sysdate - birthdate)/365)
-- Next change AGE_RANGE to UNK for any outliers
UPDATE customer_join
    SET age_range = 'UNK'
        WHERE age < 12 or age > 100
-- Next calculate the values for the new AGE_RANGE column
UPDATE customer_join
    SET age_range = 'TEEN'
        WHERE age < 20
    UPDATE customer_join
    SET age_range = '20S'
        WHERE age between 20 and 29
UPDATE customer_join
    SET age_range = '30S'
        WHERE age between 30 and 39
UPDATE customer_join
    SET age_range = '40S'
        WHERE age between 40 and 49
UPDATE customer_join
```

Code Figure 5.10   Logically transforming the BIRTHDATE column.

```
        SET age_range = '50S'
            WHERE age between 50 and 59
UPDATE customer_join
    SET age_range = '60S'
            WHERE age between 60 and 69
UPDATE customer_join
    SET age_range = '70S'
            WHERE age between 70 and 79
UPDATE customer_join
    SET age_range = '80S'
            WHERE age between 80 and 89
UPDATE customer_join
    SET age_range = '90S'
            WHERE age between 90 and 99
-- Remove the AGE and BIRTHDATE columns
    ALTER TABLE customer_join
DROP ("AGE", "BIRTHDATE") CASCADE CONSTRAINTS
```

Code Figure 5.10   Logically transforming the BIRTHDATE column. *(continued)*

Code Figure 5.11 demonstrates how to filter the CREDIT_SCORE column into the CREDIT_APPROVAL column. Then a grouping transformation is applied to the CREDIT_APPROVAL column, grouping all column values that account for less than 0.05 percent of the population into the OTHERS category.

Code Figure 5.12 demonstrates an example of the column grouping transformation for the PGRCODE column. The procedure is used to group insignificant columns and outliers into an OTHERS category. As shown, the procedure group_column_pgrcode is specific to the PRGCODE column; however, by replacing "pgrcode" with "credit_approval", "tm_description", or "churn_reason", the procedure will work for all four columns.

```
-- First add the new columns to the table
ALTER TABLE customer_join
ADD("CREDIT_APPROVAL" VARCHAR2(20))
UPDATE customer_join
    SET credit_approval = substr(credit_score,7,20)
-- Column grouping procedure to remove outliers
    exec group_column_credit_approval(0.5,'OTHER');
-- Remove the CREDIT_SCORE column
    ALTER TABLE customer_join
DROP ("CREDIT_SCORE") CASCADE CONSTRAINTS
```

Code Figure 5.11   Logically transforming the CREDIT_SCORE column.

```
CREATE OR REPLACE PROCEDURE group_column_pgrcode
(p_percent_input        NUMBER,
p_fill_value            VARCHAR)
IS
-- Variables used by the procedure
v_percent_input              NUMBER;
v_fill_value            VARCHAR2(255);
v_rec_total             NUMBER;
v_column_value               VARCHAR2(255);
v_column_value_count         NUMBER;
v_percent_calc               NUMBER;
-- PL/SQL cursor to hold the distinct values and their count
CURSOR c_column IS
SELECT prgcode,
count(prgcode)
FROM customer_join
GROUP BY prgcode
ORDER BY count(prgcode) asc;
BEGIN
-- Load the passed parameters
v_percent_input              := p_percent_input;
v_fill_value            := p_fill_value;
-- Get the total record count In the data set
SELECT count(prgcode) INTO v_rec_total
FROM customer_join;
-- Open and Loop through the PL/SQL cursor
OPEN c_column;
LOOP
FETCH c_column INTO v_column_value,v_column_value_count;
EXIT WHEN c_column%NOTFOUND;
-- Calculate the percentage of the record count for a
-- the current distinct value
v_percent_calc := v_column_value_count/v_rec_total*100;

-- Check If the calculate percentage Is less than the
-- percentage passed to the procedures
IF v_percent_calc <= v_percent_input
THEN
UPDATE customer_join
SET prgcode = v_fill_value
WHERE prgcode      = v_column_value;
END IF;
END LOOP;
CLOSE c_column;
END;
```

Code Figure 5.12   Column-grouping PL/SQL procedure.

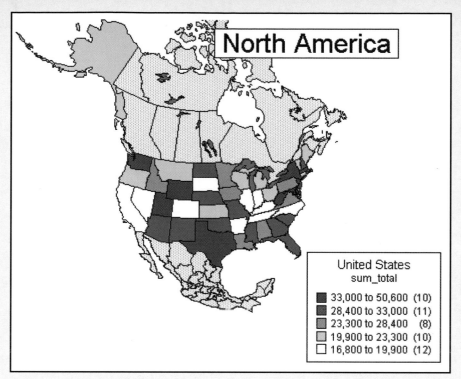

Insert 1: Map visualization of a random sample of 50,000 rows of Average Store profit by month.

United States
sum_total

■ 33,000 to 50,600 (10)
■ 28,400 to 33,000 (11)
■ 23,300 to 28,400 (8)
□ 19,900 to 23,300 (10)
□ 16,800 to 19,900 (12)

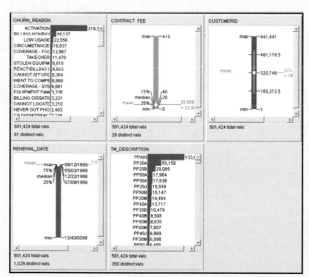

Insert 2: Distribution and statistic graphs of the transformed contract table.

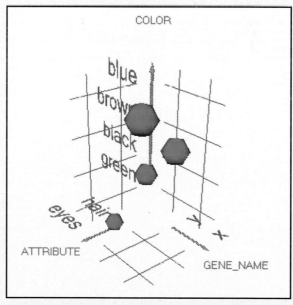

Insert 3: Scatter graph of the gene data set using the record weight as the entity size.

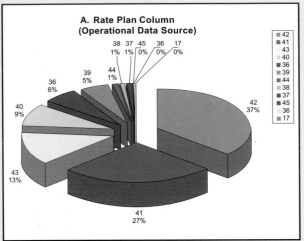
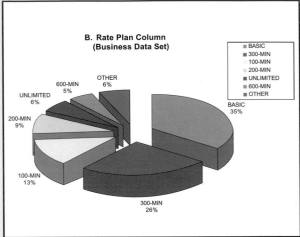

Insert 4: Using distribution pie graphs to verify logical column grouping operations.

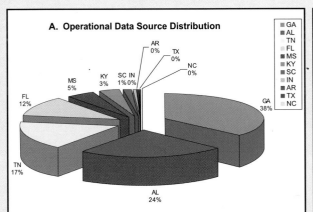
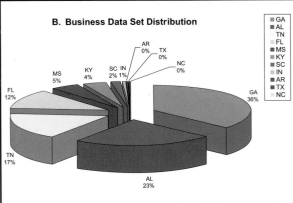

Insert 5: Using distribution pie graphs to verify the ECTL operations on the State column.

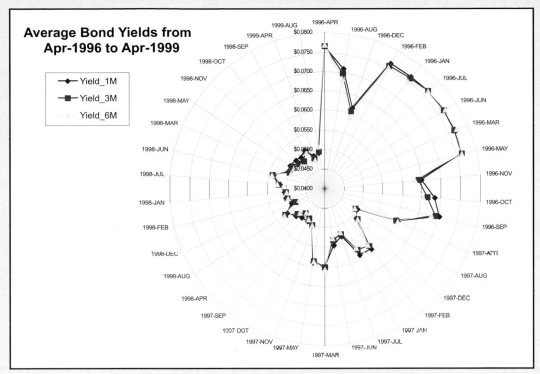

Insert 6: Radar graph of average bond yields.

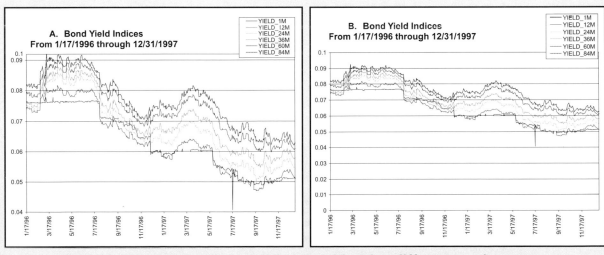

Insert 7: Line graphs of average bond yields using different y-axis ranges.

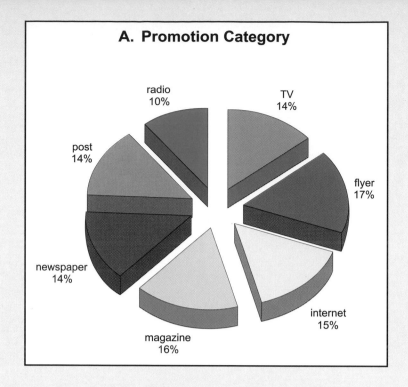

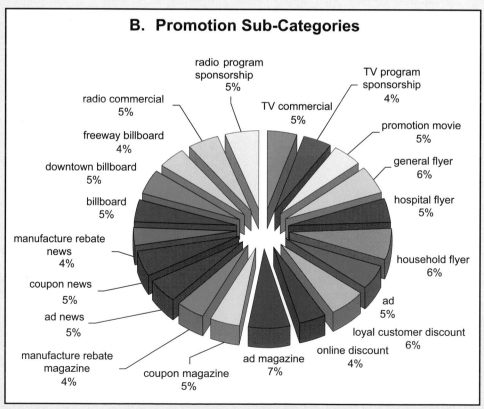

Insert 8: Distribution pie graphs of average cost by promotion and sub-promotion categories.

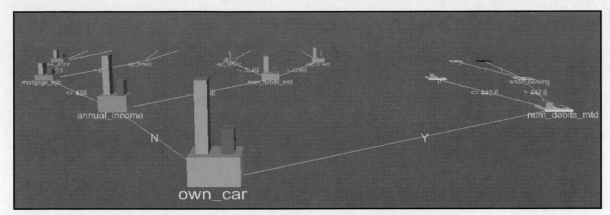

Insert 9: Tree graph of a decision tree model.

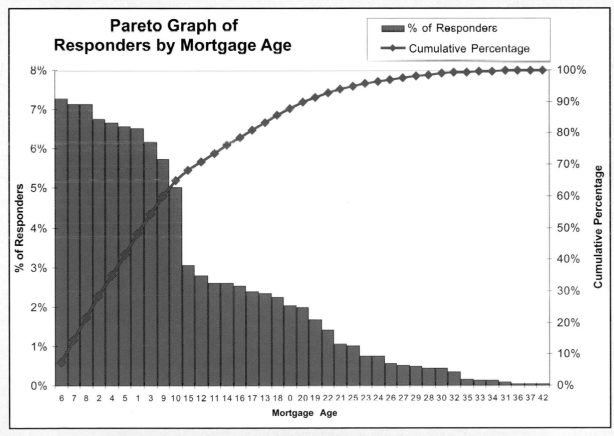

Insert 10: Pareto graph of responders by their mortgage age.

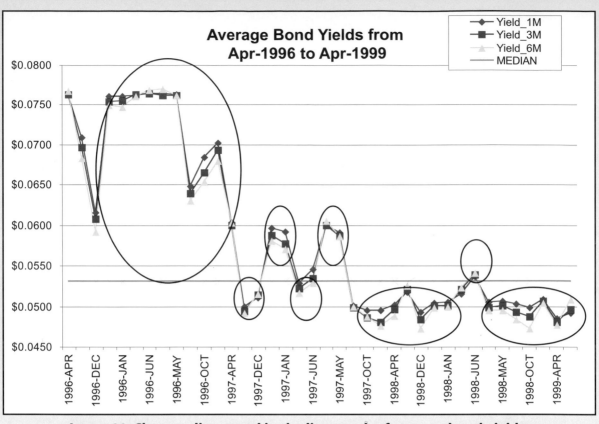

Insert 11: Clusters discovered in the line graph of average bond yields.

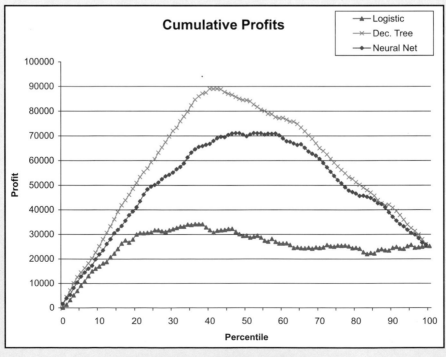

Insert 12: Cumulative profit chart.

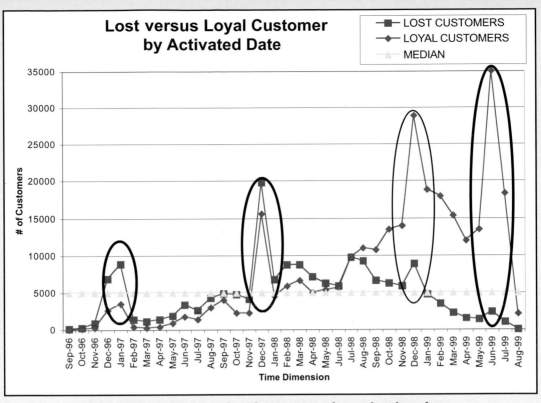

Insert 13: Lost versus loyal customers by activation date.

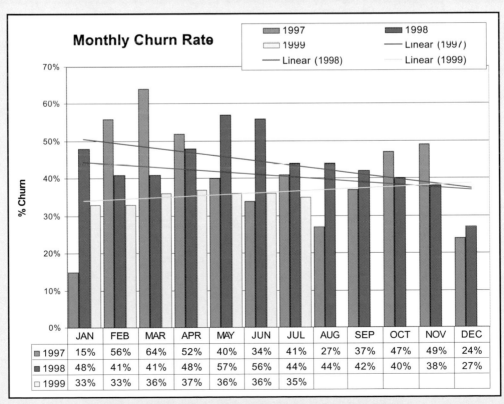

	JAN	FEB	MAR	APR	MAY	JUN	JUL	AUG	SEP	OCT	NOV	DEC
1997	15%	56%	64%	52%	40%	34%	41%	27%	37%	47%	49%	24%
1998	48%	41%	41%	48%	57%	56%	44%	44%	42%	40%	38%	27%
1999	33%	33%	36%	37%	36%	36%	35%					

Insert 14: Monthly churn rate trends comparison.

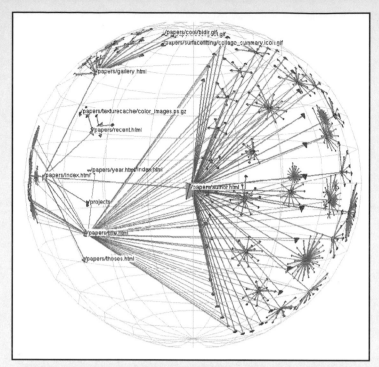

Insert 15: Three-dimensional hyperbolic tree visualizations of the structure of a Web site. (Used with permission from T. Munzer.)

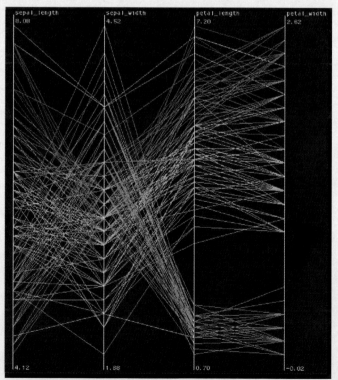

Insert 16: A parallel coordinate visualization. (Used with permission from Matthew O. Ward.)

```
-- First add the new column to the table
    ALTER TABLE customer_join
ADD     ("CONTACT_METHOD" VARCHAR2(15))
-- Next decode the column values
    UPDATE customer_join
SET CONTACT_METHOD = 'RETAIL SALE' WHERE PRGCODE='20'
UPDATE customer_join
SET CONTACT_METHOD = 'INTERNET SALE' WHERE PRGCODE='9'
UPDATE customer_join
SET CONTACT_METHOD = 'PHONE SALE' WHERE PRGCODE='24'
UPDATE customer_join
SET CONTACT_METHOD = 'FAMILY SALE' WHERE PRGCODE='1'
UPDATE customer_join
SET CONTACT_METHOD = 'MALL SALE' WHERE PRGCODE='13'
UPDATE customer_join
SET CONTACT_METHOD = 'OTHER' WHERE PRGCODE='OT'
-- Remove the PRGCODE column
    ALTER TABLE customer_join
DROP ("PRGCODE") CASCADE CONSTRAINTS
```

Code Figure 5.13 Logically transforming the PRGCODE column.

Code Figure 5.13 demonstrates filtering the PRGCODE column by decoding it into its logical meaning. For instance, after the column grouping performed in Code Figure 5.12, only five PRGCODE values remain to be decoded.

The operations group determined that only the first three characters of the TM_DESCRIPTION column were used for determining the RATE_PLAN. So first a temporary column is created to hold the first three characters of the TM_DESCRIPTION column, as shown in Code Figure 5.14. Next, the column grouping function is applied to group the lower 5 percent of the distinct values into an OTHERS category. Then the filtering transformation is applied to decode TM_DESCRIPTION into its logical meaning. After the column grouping, only 5 TM_DESCRIPTION values remain to be decoded.

```
-- First add the temporary and new column to the table
    ATLER TABLE customer_join
    add ("TM_SHORT" VARCHAR(3),
    "RATE_PLAN" VARCHAR(15))
-- Update the temporary column TM_SHORT with the
```

Code Figure 5.14 Logically transforming the TM_DESCRIPTION column. *(continues)*

```
-- first three characters of TM_DESCRIPTION
UPDATE customer_join
SET tm_short = substr(tm_description,1,3)
-- Perform the column grouping procedure, grouping the
-- lower 5% of distinct values Into the OTHERS category
    EXEC group_column_tm_short(5,'OTH')
-- Decode the TM_SHORT Into Its logical meaning
    UPDATE customer_join
SET RATE_PLAN = '200 MINUTE' WHERE TM_SHORT='PP2'
UPDATE customer_join
SET RATE_PLAN = '300 MINUTE' WHERE TM_SHORT='PP3'
UPDATE customer_join
SET RATE_PLAN = '100 MINUTE' WHERE TM_SHORT='PP4'
UPDATE customer_join
SET RATE_PLAN = 'UNLIMITED' WHERE TM_SHORT='PP5'
UPDATE customer_join
SET RATE_PLAN = 'BASIC' WHERE TM_SHORT='PPA'
UPDATE customer_join
SET RATE_PLAN = 'OTHER' WEHRE TM_SHORT='OTH'
-- Remove the PRGCODE column
    ALTER TABLE customer_join
DROP ("TM_DESCRIPTION", "TM_SHORT") CASCADE CONSTRAINTS
```

Code Figure 5.14   Logically transforming the TM_DESCRIPTION column. *(continued)*

Code Figure 5.15 demonstrates how to transform the RENEWAL_DATE into the columns RENEWAL_YEAR and RENEWAL_MONTH.

```
-- First add the new columns to the table
    ALTER TABLE customer_join
ADD    ("RENEWAL_YEAR" VARCHAR2(4),
"RENEWAL_MONTH" VARCHAR2(3))
-- Next calculate the values for the new RENEWAL_YEAR and
-- RENEWAL_MONTH columns
    UPDATE customer_join
SET renewal_year = TO_CHAR(renewal_date,'YYYY')
UPDATE customer_join
SET renewal_month = TO_CHAR(renewal_date,'MON')
-- Remove the RENEWAL_DDATE column
    ALTER TABLE customer_join
DROP ("RENEWALDATE") CASCADE CONSTRAINTS
```

Code Figure 5.15   Logically transforming the RENEWAL_DATE column.

Documenting the Logical Transformations for the Business Data Set *customer_join*

As part of the ECTL column-level documentation discussed in the business case study section of Chapter 4, the *customer_join* column value ranges have already been defined and documented. For the logical transformations documentation, you need to document any table-level or column-level logical transformation you performed on the production business data set. For example, Table 5.9 documents the logical transformations applied to the *customer_join* business data set.

Table 5.9 Logical Transformations Column-Level Documentation for Business Data Set *customer_join*

BUSINESS DATA SET COLUMN NAME	LOGICAL TRANSFORMATION	COLUMN VALUE RANGE	NEW COLUMN NAME
ACTIVATEDDATE	TO_CHAR (activateddate,'YYYY')	1996-1999	ACTIVATED_YEAR
ACTIVATEDDATE	TO_CHAR (activateddate,'MON')	Jan-Dec	ACTIVATED_ MONTH
ACTIVATEDDATE	Remove Column		
BIRTHDATE	ROUND (TO_NUMBER (sysdate - birthdate)/ 365)	0 – 100	AGE
New column AGE	Column Grouping	UNK, TEEN, 20S, 30S, 40S, 50S, 60S, 70S, 80S, 90S	AGE_RANGE
CREDIT_SCORE	Column Filter	Normal set to True and High set to False	CREDIT_ APPROVAL
CREDIT_APPROVAL	Grouping Transformation	Lower 0.5% of the distinct values converted to the OTHERS category	CREDIT_ APPROVAL
PRGCODE	Grouping Transformation	Lower 5% of the distinct values converted to the OTHERS category	
PRGCODE	Decode Column Filter	FAMILY SALE, INTERNET SALE, MALL SALE, PHONE SALE, RETAIL SALE, OTHER	CONTACT_ METHOD

(continues)

Table 5.9 Logical Transformations Column-Level Documentation for Business Data Set *customer_join* (Continued)

BUSINESS DATA SET COLUMN NAME	LOGICAL TRANSFORMATION	COLUMN VALUE RANGE	NEW COLUMN NAME
PRGCODE	Remove Column		
TM_DESCRIPTION	SUBSTR (TM_DESCRIPTION, 1,3)	First 3 characters of TM_DESCRIPTION	TM_SHORT (temporary staging column)
TM_SHORT (temporary staging column)	Grouping Transformation	Lower 5% of distinct values converted to OTHERS category	
TM_SHORT	Grouping Transformation	Lower 2% of the distinct values converted to the OTHERS category	
TM_SHORT	Decode Column Filter	100 MINUTE, 200 MINUTE, 300 MINUTE, BASIC, OTHER, UNLIMITED	RATE_PLAN
TM_SHORT, TM_DESCRIPTION	Remove Column		
CHURN_REASON	Grouping Transformation	Lower 0.5% of the distinct values converted to the OTHERS category	
RENEWAL_DATE	TO_CHAR (activateddate,'YYYY')	1996-1999	RENEWAL_YEAR
RENEWAL_DATE	TO_CHAR (activateddate,'MON')	Jan-Dec	RENEWAL_MONTH
RENEWAL_DATE	Remove Column		

Logically Transforming the *customer_demographic* Business Data Set

During the ECTL procedures, all table-level logical transformations were applied to the *customer_demographic* data set. Each record in the resulting business data set represents information about a unique customer and agrees with the experimental unit of individual customer. However, there are many column-level transformations that need to be applied. Since the *customer_demographic* data set is a superset of the *customer_join* data set and demographic data set and the *customer_join* data set has already been logically transformed, only column-level transformations need to be applied to the columns added from the demographic data set.

The domain expert and the data and business analyst teams meet and decide to apply the following logical transformations to the *customer_join* business data set:

- The majority of the columns are a single character string containing either a 0 or a 1. To enhance readability, the 0 will be converted to "NO" and the 1 will be converted to "YES" for the columns BANK_CARD, CONSUMER_CARD, CREDIT_BUYER, PREMIUM, and UPSCALE.

- The column ESTIMATED_INCOME will be decoded into its logical meaning. The new column INCOME will contain the decoded meaning.

- The columns GENDER, HOME_OWNER, MARITAL_STATUS, and GENDER will be expanded and decoded. For instance, the GENDER column value M will be decoded to MALE, F will be decoded to FEMALE, E will be decoded to NULL, and U will be decoded to UNKNOWN.

Code Figures 5.16 through 5.18 show how to accomplish these logical transformations in standard SQL. You may also want to use histogram, distribution, and statistics graphs to visually inspect the columns before and after the transformations to verify the accuracy of the transformation.

Code Figure 5.16 demonstrates how to re-create the *customer_demographic* table by adding the demographic columns to the logically transformed *customer_join* table.

```
CREATE TABLE customer_demographic as
SELECT cust.*,
demographic.home_owner,
demographic.yrs_residence,
demographic.marital_status,
demographic.gender,
demographic.bank_card,
demographic.consumer_card,
demographic.credit_card_buyer,
demographic.premium,
demographic.upscale,
demographic.estimated_Income
FROM customer_join cust, demographic
WHERE
cust.customerid=demographic.customerid
-- Create the audit copy of customer_demographic
CREATE TABLE customer_demographic_audit AS
SELECT *
FROM customer_demographic
```

Code Figure 5.16 Creating the CUSTOMER_DEMOGRAPHIC table.

```
ALTER TABLE customer_demographic
MODIFY(""BANK_CARD" VARCHAR2(3),
"CONSUMER_CARD" VARCHAR2(3),
"CREDIT_CARD_BUYER" VARCHAR2(3),
"PREMIUM" VARCHAR2(3),
"UPSCALE" VARCHAR2(3))
-- Decode the columns
UPDATE customer_demographic
SET bank_card='YES' where bank_card='1'
UPDATE customer_demographic
SET bank_card='NO' where bank_card='0'
UPDATE customer_demographic
SET consumer_card='YES' where consumer_card='1'
UPDATE customer_demographic
SET consumer_card='NO' where consumer_card='0'
UPDATE customer_demographic
SET credit_card_buyer='YES' where credit_card_buyer='1'
UPDATE customer_demographic
SET credit_card_buyer='NO' where credit_card_buyer='0'
UPDATE customer_demographic
SET premium='YES' where premium='1'
UPDATE customer_demographic
SET premium='NO' where premium='0'
UPDATE customer_demographic
SET upscale='YES' where upscale='1'
UPDATE customer_demographic
SET upscale='NO' where upscale='0'
```

Code Figure 5.17   Replacing 0 and 1 with YES and NO values.

Code Figure 5.17 demonstrates how to transform the BANK_CARD, CONSUMER_CARD, CREDIT_BUYER, PREMIUM, and UPSCALE columns' values 0 and 1 by replacing 1 with "YES" and 0 with "NO".

Code Figure 5.18 demonstrates how to transform the HOME_OWNER, GENDER, MARITAL_STATUS, and INCOME columns into their logical meanings.

```
ALTER TABLE customer_demographic
MODIFY("HOME_OWNER" VARCHAR2(4),
"MARITAL_STATUS" VARCHAR2(15),
"GENDER" VARCHAR2(10),
"ESTIMATED_INCOME" VARCHAR2(4))
-- Update HOME_OWNER
```

Code Figure 5.18   Logically transforming the HOME_OWNER, GENDER, MARITAL_STATUS, and INCOME columns.

```
UPDATE customer_demographic
SET home_owner='OWN' where home_owner='O'
UPDATE customer_demographic
SET home_owner='RENT' where home_owner='R'
UPDATE customer_demographic
SET home_owner='NULL' where home_owner='E'
-- Update GENDER
UPDATE customer_demographic
SET gender='MALE' where gender='M'
UPDATE customer_demographic
SET gender='FEMALE' where gender='F'
UPDATE customer_demographic
SET gender='UNKNOWN' where gender='U'
UPDATE customer_demographic
SET gender='NULL' where gender='E'
-- Update MARITAL_STATUS
UPDATE customer_demographic
SET marital_status='MARRIED' where marital_status='M'
UPDATE customer_demographic
SET marital_status='SINGLE' where marital_status='S'
UPDATE customer_demographic
SET marital_status='UNKNOWN' where marital_status='U'
UPDATE customer_demographic
SET marital_status='DVRD MALE' where marital_status='A'
UPDATE customer_demographic
SET marital_status='DVRD FEMALE'
where marital_status='B'
-- Update INCOME
UPDATE customer_demographic
SET estimated_Income='30-' where estimated_Income='3'
UPDATE customer_demographic
SET estimated_Income='40' where estimated_Income='4'
UPDATE customer_demographic
SET estimated_Income='50' where estimated_Income='5'
UPDATE customer_demographic
SET estimated_Income='60' where estimated_Income='6'
UPDATE customer_demographic
SET estimated_Income='70' where estimated_Income='7'
UPDATE customer_demographic
SET estimated_Income='80' where estimated_Income='8'
UPDATE customer_demographic
SET estimated_Income='100' where estimated_Income='9'
UPDATE customer_demographic
SET estimated_Income='150' where estimated_Income='1'
UPDATE customer_demographic
SET estimated_Income='150+' where estimated_Income='2'
UPDATE customer_demographic
SET estimated_Income='NULL' where estimated_Income='E'
```

Code Figure 5.18 Logically transforming the HOME_OWNER, GENDER, MARITAL_STATUS, and INCOME columns. *(continued)*

Documenting the Logical Transformations for the Business Data Set *customer_demographic*

As part of the ECTL column-level documentation discussed in the business case study section of Chapter 4, the *customer_demographic* column value ranges have already been defined and documented. For the logical transformations documentation, you need to document any table-level or column-level logical transformation you performed on the production business data set. For example, Table 5.10 documents the logical transformations applied to the *customer_demographic* business data set.

Review of the Logical Transformation Procedures for the Case Study

The logical transformation process has been completed for both the *customer_join* and *customer_demographic* business data sets, as demonstrated in Code Figures 5.9 through 5.18. Recall that in the previous chapter, we also performed a table-level aggregation transformation on the invoice table before joining it with the customer and contract tables.

Table 5.10 Logical Transformations Column-Level Documentation for Business Data Set *customer_demographic*

BUSINESS DATA SET COLUMN NAME	LOGICAL TRANSFORMATION	COLUMN VALUE RANGE
BANK_CARD	Column filtering	YES, NO
CONSUMER_CARD	Column filtering	YES, NO
CREDIT_CARD_BUYER	Column filtering	YES, NO
PREMIUM	Column filtering	YES, NO
UPSCALE	Column filtering	YES, NO
HOME_OWNER	Column filtering	OWN, RENT, NULL
GENDER	Column filtering	MALE, FEMALE, UNKNOWN, NULL
MARITAL STATUS	Column filtering	MARRIED, SINGLE, UNKNOWN, DVRD MALE, DVRD FEMALE
ESTIMATED_INCOME	Column filtering	30, 40, 50, 60, 70, 100, 125, 150, 150+, NULL

In this chapter, we have demonstrated multiple column-level transformation processing steps on both the *customer_join* and *customer_demographic* business data sets. The data sets are almost ready for us to begin visualizing and data mining. The last task in the data preparation phase is to verify that the ECTL procedures (Chapter 3) and logical transformations (this chapter) did not introduce errors or bias into the data sets. We will perform these steps at the end of the next chapter.

Summary

Chapter 5 described a variety of table and column-level logical transformations that may be necessary to apply to the production business data set in preparation for data visualization or visual data mining. The business case study illustrated numerous column-level logical transformations that will enhance the readability and understandability of data visualization and resulting data mining models. In the next chapter, we will help you begin to exploit your transformed production business data sets with data visualization and visual data mining to gain knowledge and insights into business data sets and communicate those discoveries to the decision makers.

CHAPTER 6

Step 5: Verify the Business Data Set

I n Chapter 4, we described how the operational data sources were identified and how columns were selected. We also demonstrated how the source data was extracted, cleansed, transformed, and loaded (the ECTL process) into the exploratory data mart to become the foundation of the business data set. In Chapter 5, we described how to logically transform this foundation data set into a business data set so that it can be used to create data visualizations and be mined to discover historical patterns and trends with data mining tools. In this chapter, we discuss how to verify that the resulting business data set is accurate and that the previous data preparation steps did not introduce errors or bias into the business data set. This is the last step in the data preparation phase of the VDM project.

In this chapter, we focus our attention on verifying that the business data set is a true, error-free, bias-free representation of the information extracted from operational data set. The first step is to verify the integrity and accuracy of the data preparations ECTL operations. This step includes techniques to verify ECTL operations performed on both discrete and continuous columns. The next step is to verify the integrity and accuracy of the logical transformation operations. This step includes techniques to verify the logical table-level and column-level operations. We will then apply Step 5 to the ongoing business case study.

It is not uncommon to have performed 10, 20, or even hundreds of ECTL and logical transformation actions on the operational data source data sets before arriving at a business data set that you can use for data visualization or data mining. No matter how careful you have been and how well you documented the ECTL procedures and logical transformations, they often contain errors that result in inaccurate data visualizations and data mining models. For instance, a large automotive company had to postpone the launch of a new car model because they discovered that the business data set used for target marketing analysis was flawed. Had this company taken the time to verify its business data set, it could have saved millions of dollars caused by the delay. Verifying the business data sets can save you a considerable amount of rework.

Another consideration when verifying the business data set is that you may need to perform this step more than once. Remember that data visualization and data mining is an iterative process. It is not uncommon that during the visualization and data mining steps you discover you need more data or need the data in a different format to address the business questions. Many errors have been introduced into the production business data set because new columns were selected or new logical transformations were applied but the entire business data set wasn't reverified. Therefore, to minimize the chances of introducing errors and bias into your production business data set, you need to create a verification procedure that is easy to reexecute.

Verification Process

In most VDM projects, the operations, data warehousing, or data and business analyst teams performed the data preparation operations and documentation. The domain experts may have also helped define the value ranges for the selected column, as well as helped decipher the business logic embedded in the operational data sources. The verification process is a VDM project team effort. The operations, data warehousing, or data and business analyst teams need to develop and document a verification procedure to confirm the production business data set is a true, error-free, and unbiased representation of the operational data source information. If integrity, accuracy, or logic errors are discovered, they need to be corrected and the ECTL and logical transformation documentation updated. Through the verification process, the domain experts act as advisors to make sure that the business rules are respected and the production business data set answers the business question under investigation.

Often you can use standard SQL and various visualization and data mining techniques to help you ensure the accuracy of the business data set, detect ECTL and logical transformation errors, and detect bias, such as sampling bias. Verifying the business data set can be broken down into two parts:

- The first part is to verify the integrity and accuracy of the data preparation operations. For each ECTL and logical column or table transformation, you need to verify that the data preparation operations were applied correctly and are error-free. For example, if you used a column decode operation as part of your ECTL procedure, you need to verify that a column decode ECTL operation was applied correctly.

- The second part is to verify the logic of the data preparation operations. For each ECTL transformation and logical column or table transformation, you need to verify that the logic of the transformation didn't distort or bias the data. For example, if you applied a sampling operation as part of your ECTL procedure, you need to verify that the sampling didn't bias the business data set. In this case, you need to ensure that the sampling was random and didn't introduce bias into the business data set.

Perhaps the easiest way to devise a verification process is to start with the ECTL and logical transformation documentation. You will want to add the columns Integrity Verified and Logic Verified to each ECTL and logical transformation operation.

In the following sections, we look more closely at the two parts of verifying the business data set.

Verifying the Integrity of the Data Preparation Operations

Since many of the ECTL and logical transformation operations eliminated outliers (extreme values) from the business data set, the descriptive statistics, such as mean, standard deviation, and others, for the business data set may not exactly match those of the operational data sources. For instance, you may have applied a filtering logical transformation to remove the extreme values from an AGE column because they were negative or over 100. If you compare an SQL SUM of the AGE column in the data source with an SQL SUM on the transformed AGE column in your business data set, the two sums will be different. However, if you compare an SQL AVG (average) between the business data set and operational data source, the averages should be relatively close. Likewise, if you compare the record count on the operational data source and your business data source, the record counts will be different. These differences don't mean that the integrity and accuracy of the business data set has been compromised. Especially for data mining, you are looking for general trends and patterns; so as long as the averages between the operational data sources and the business data sets are within reason to one another, you can be confident that your business data set is an accurate and reasonable representation of the operational data.

If the average (or mean) of continuous column values or the distribution percentage of distinct values of discrete column values varies more than 2 to 5 percent between the operational data sources and the business data set, the ECTL or logical transformations operations may have introduced bias into the data set. You need to re-verify the correctness and accuracy of the ECTL and logical transformation operations for each column that varies more than 2 to 5 percent. Of course, there are exceptions to this rule. For example, if the operational data set contained extremely dirty data (extreme value outliers) or numerous empty (NULL) values, the average between the operational data source and the business data set would be much higher than 2 percent. Likewise, there may be numerous records that couldn't be joined when creating a business data set from multiple operational data sources. These and all other exceptions should be part of the verification process documentation. Dorian Pyle devotes entire chapters on techniques for verifying that the business data set contains an accurate, non-biased representation of the operational data sources. For more information on these issues, refer to *Data Preparation for Data Mining* by Dorian Pyle (San Diego: Academic Press, 1999).

Table 6.1 is a copy of the ECTL procedure documentation from the example data set of total store sales for 1999 first introduced in Chapter 4 as Table 4.4. If you recall for this business data set, the experimental unit (level of the information) was aggregated to the individual store level. The operational data sources for the business data set were the OLTP data base transactions, store, region, and floorplan tables.

Discrete Column Verification Techniques

In Table 6.1, ECTL Steps 1 through 4 and 6 are data preparation operations on discrete columns. To verify the integrity of these data preparation operations on discrete columns, we will use a discrete column verification technique. This technique uses SQL queries to compare the distinct values, their associated record counts, and distribution percentages between the operational data source column and the business data set column. This technique is shown in Code Figure 6.1 for the discrete column REGION. Following are some notes regarding the figure:

- The first query in Code Figure 6.1 queries the operational data source table. The query retrieves the distinct column values, their corresponding record counts, and the distribution percentage of the distinct column from the operational data source table. The distribution percentage is calculated as the record count for the distinct value divided by the record count for the entire table multiplied by 100.

- The second query in Code Figure 6.1 queries the business data set table. This query retrieves the distinct column values, their corresponding record counts, and the distribution percentage of the distinct column from the business data set table in the exploratory data mart.

Table 6.1   ECTL Column-Level Documentation for Table Tot_Store_Sales_99

	SOURCE		EXPLORATORY DATA MART			
ECTL STEP	TABLE NAME	COLUMN NAME	COLUMN NAME	COLUMN DATA TYPE	COLUMN VALUE RANGE	ECTL TRANSFORMATIONS
1	OLTP region	regionid and region_name	REGION	Discrete	East, Central, West	Decode of regionid to region and TO_UPPER
2	OLTP store	store_name	STORE	Discrete	Stores 1-20	TO_UPPER
3	OLTP store	city	LOCATION	Discrete	Cities in the USA	TO_UPPER
4	OLTP floorplan	planid and floor	FLOOR_PLAN	Discrete	Original, Compact, Modern	Decode of planid to floor and TO_UPPER
5	OLTP store	location_size	SQ_FEET	Continuous	1500 – 8000	Range Check 0-10000
6	OLTP transaction	year	S_YEAR	Discrete	1999	Range Check 1999
7	OLTP transaction	sales	TOTAL_SALES	Continuous	$2,134.00 - $6,987.12	Range Check 0-1000000

```
-- Retrieve the distinct value, the record count and the
-- distribution percentage for each distinct value for the
-- column from the operational source table
SELECT      store.regionid,
            count(store.regionid),
            count(store.regionid)/(SELECT count(store.regionid)
FROM transaction@oltp_database,
     store@oltp_database
WHERE transaction.store_key = store.store_key and
     transaction.year = 1999) * 100 distribution
FROM transaction@oltp_database,
store@oltp_database
WHERE
transaction.store_key = store.store_key and
transaction.year = 1999
GROUP BY
store.regionid
ORDER BY store.regionid;
-- Retrieve the distinct value, the record count and the
-- distribution percentage for each distinct value for the
-- column from the business data set table
SELECT      store.store_name,
            count(store.store_name),
            count(store.store_name)/(SELECT count(store.store_name)
FROM tot_store_sales_99) * 100 distribution
FROM tot_store_sales_99
GROUP BY
store.regionid
ORDER BY store.store_name;
```

Code Figure 6.1 SQL queries to perform discrete column verification.

This technique enables you to compare the column before and after the ECTL operation to verify the correctness of the operation. It also allows you to determine if the ECTL operation introduced any bias. If there is a large difference in the distribution of the distinct values from the two SQL queries, the operation may have introduced bias into your business data set. You will need to investigate the operation if the difference between the distributions is greater than 2 to 5 percent.

Table 6.2 shows the results of the discrete column verification technique for the REGION column. The operational source data distribution for the column values is exactly the same as the business data set (target) distribution. Therefore, you can conclude that the ECTL operation is error-free.

You can use also use data visualizations to help you verify the ECTL operations. Figure 6.1 illustrates how to use a pie graph to compare an operational data source column before the ECTL operation (Figure 6.1a) with its corresponding business data set column after the ECTL operation (Figure 6.1b). For discrete columns that contain numerous distinct values, the number and size of the pie slices in the distribution pie graph may become too small and difficult to compare. In these cases, you can use a histogram or distribution graph to compare the distribution of distinct column values between the operational source and the business data set.

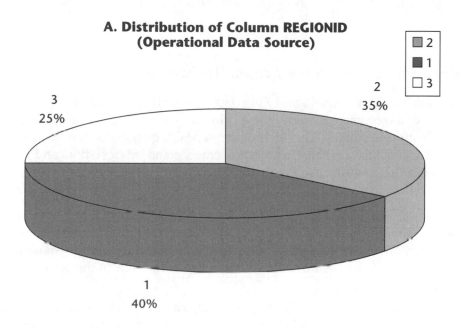

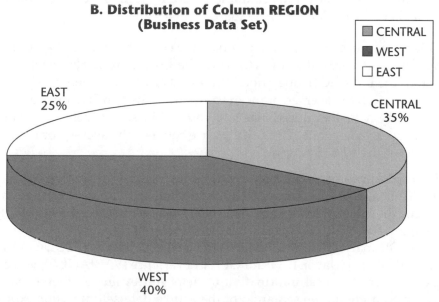

Figure 6.1 Using distribution pie graphs to perform discrete column verification.

Table 6.2   Results of the SQL Queries to Perform Discrete Column Verification

SOURCE REGIONID	COUNT OF REGIONID	SOURCE DISTRIBUTION	TARGET REGION	COUNT OF REGION	TARGET DISTRIBUTION
2	7	35	CENTRAL	7	35
1	8	40	WEST	8	40
3	5	25	EAST	5	25

Continuous Column Verification Techniques

In Table 6.1, ECTL Steps 5 and 7 are data preparation operations performed on continuous columns. To verify these columns, we will use a continuous column verification technique. This technique uses SQL queries to compare the minimum and maximum value, numeric average, standard deviation, and variance between the operational data source column and the business data set column. This technique is shown in Code Figure 6.2 for the continuous column TOTAL_SALES. Following are some notes regarding the figure:

- The first query in Code Figure 6.2 queries the operational data source table. The query retrieves the minimum, maximum, average, standard deviation, and variance of the continuous column from the operational data source table.

- The second query in Code Figure 6.2 queries the business data set table. This query retrieves the minimum, maximum, average, standard deviation, and variance of the continuous column from the business data set table in the exploratory data mart.

This technique enables you to compare the column before and after the ECTL operation to verify the correctness of the operation. It also enables you to determine if the ECTL operation introduced any bias. If there is a large difference between the average or mean values from the two SQL queries, the operation may have introduced bias into your business data set. You will need to investigate the operation if the difference between the average or mean values is greater than 2 to 5 percent.

Table 6.3 shows the results of the continuous column verification technique for the TOTAL_SALES column. The operational data source average value is exactly the same as the average value of business data set for the TOTAL_SALES column. Therefore, you can conclude that the ECTL operation is error-free. With SQL analytical functions such as standard deviation (STDDEV), variance (VAR POP), correlation (CORR POP), and variance (VARIANCE), you can also glean other statistical information to help you evaluate whether you have extracted a good representation of the source data set into your exploratory data mart.

```
-- Retrieve the miniumum and maximum values
-- compute the average, standard deviation and variance for the
-- column from the operational source table
SELECT      MIN(sales) MIN_SALES,
            MAX(sales) MAX_SALES,
            AVG(sales) AVG_SALES,
            STDDEV(sales) STDDEV_SALES,
            VARIANCE (sales) VARIANCE_SALES
FROM transaction@oltp_database,
store@oltp_database
WHERE
transaction.store_key = store.store_key and
transcation.year = 1999
-- Retrieve the miniumum and maximum values
-- compute the average, standard deviation and variance for the
-- column from the business data set table
SELECT      MIN(total_sales) MIN_TOTAL_SALES,
MAX(total_sales) MAX_TOTAL_SALES,
AVG(total_sales) AVG_TOTAL_SALES,
STDDEV(total_sales) STDDEV_TOTAL_SALES,
VARIANCE (total_sales) VARIANCE_TOTAL_SALES
FROM tot_store_sales_99
```

Code Figure 6.2 SQL queries to perform continuous column verification.

You can also use data visualizations to help you verify the ECTL operations. Figure 6.2 illustrates how to use a box plot to compare an operational data source column before the ECTL operation with its corresponding business data set column after the ECTL operation. The first box plot graphs the minimum value, the "-STD DEV", the mean, the "+STD DEV", and the maximum value for the continuous column from the operational data source. You can compare this to the second box plot that graphs the exact same statistics for the continuous column from the business data set. This visualization allows you to quickly evaluate whether the minimum, maximum, mean, and negative and positive standard deviation values are dramatically different before and after the ECTL operation. In most cases, the black bars (+/- standard deviation) should be within reason of one another. If you also cleaned up outliers

Table 6.3 Results of the SQL Queries to Perform Continuous Column Verification

SOURCE SALES	SOURCE STATISTIC VALUE	TARGET TOTAL_SALES	TARGET STATISTIC
MIN_SALES	2134	MIN_TOTAL_SALES	2134
MAX_SALES	6987	MAX_TOTAL_SALES	6987
AVG_SALES	4065	AVG_TOTAL_SALES	4065
STDDEV_SALES	1498	STDDEV_TOTAL_SALES	1498
VARIANCE_SALES	2244555	VARIANCE_TOTAL_SALES	2244555

as part of the ECTL operation, the minimum and maximum values for the target column may be dramatically different. In Figure 6.2, the negative standard deviation value (-STD DEV) is shown as the start of the black bar and is calculated by subtracting the standard deviation from the column average value. The positive standard deviation value (+STD DEV) is shown as the end of the black bar and is calculated by adding the standard deviation to the column average value.

Verifying Common ECTL Data Preparation Operations

You can also use the discrete and continuous column verification techniques for verifying the accuracy of data dimensional consistency and the removal of unique, correlated, and insignificant column ECTL data preparation operations.

Normally, data dimensional consistency ECTL operations are accomplished in the same manner as encoded data dimensions. For instance, as long as you standardized on a decode method for a column such as GENDER by decoding the values as MALE, FEMALE, UNKNOWN, you can use SQL distinct and count functions to verify the source and target column values no matter if they were represented in multiple different formats in the operational data sources. Likewise, if you decoded empty and NULL values in the operational data sources as UNKNOWN or EMPTY in the business data set, you can still use the distinct and count functions to verify the column that had values. You can then use an SQL condition, such as where *total_sales* is NULL, to count the number of NULLs or EMPTY values and compare that with the count of the UNKNOWN label in the business data set.

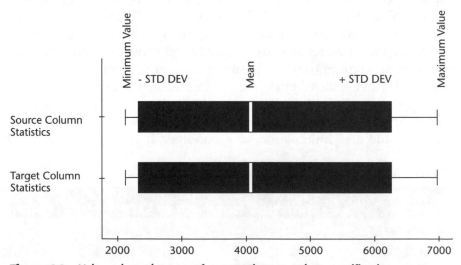

Figure 6.2 Using a box plot to perform continuous column verification.

In Chapter 4, we discussed why you remove unique, duplicate, insignificant, and correlated columns from the business data set. The only time you have to revisit these decisions is if your original column selection criterion has changed. If you modify which columns you are selecting from the operational data sources or change the entire data source, you may want to review whether a column that was marked as unique, duplicated, insignificant, or correlated is still valid for the new business data set.

In Chapter 4, we also discussed reasons why you may want to sample the operational data sources or even create a sample from the business data set. If you use SQL queries and visualizations to verify the source and target columns, you quickly realize that the counts don't correspond to one another. For example, if you had taken a 20 percent sample from the operational data source, you would need to multiply your discrete column counts by a 1.8 to verify that the counts match; however, the distribution percentages should match or be within 2 to 5 percent of one another. For continuous columns, the average or mean should be similar (or be within 2 to 5 percent of one another). You may also want to compare the variance between the operational data source and the business data set to ensure that you have captured a representative sample.

Verifying the Logic of the Data Preparation Operations

Verifying the logic of the data preparation operations is necessary to ensure that complex ECTL or logical transformation operations didn't introduce bias into the business data sets. For instance, if you use sampling, you need to ensure that you are capturing as much of the column value variance that exists in the operational data set as possible. You can use both the discrete and continuous column verification techniques to verify the majority of the logical transformation. In addition, you can use histogram, distribution, pie, and line graphs to visually verify the data before and after the logical transformation operation to compare the column value variance.

Verifying Common Logical Transformation Operations

In Chapter 5, we discussed both table-level and column-level logical transformation operations. Transforming weighted and time series data set table-level logical transformations are reverse pivot operations. For instance, a table in the form of object of interest, observation 1 and observation 2 through observation N may need to be reverse pivoted into the object of interest, observation weight or time name (1, 2, ... n), observation value. An example of a reverse pivot operation is when you transform each single row of a table with multiple time observations, such as,

```
row 1: object_name, time-1 value, time-2 value, time-3 value
```

into a new table containing multiple rows corresponding to the original table row, such as,

```
row 1: object_name, 1, value
row 2: object_name, 2, value
row 3: object_name, 3, value.
```

You can use the discrete and continuous column verification techniques already discussed to verify that the logical transformation was error-free. For example, if you list the distinct values of the object of interest, it should be the same between the operational data source and the business data set. However, the count of the distinct value records will be quite different. To resolve this difference, you must divide the count of the business data set by the number of pivots (or UNION operators). Then distinct value record counts between the operational data source and business data set will match. The average of the observation value in the business data set should be equivalent to the average of the averages of each individual observation 1, 2, through N. Unlike the ECTL operations, you aren't modifying the data values in a reverse pivot operation. You are simply reformatting the table structure.

Unfortunately, there is no bona fide method to verify that a table-level aggregation or filtering logical transformation operation is accurate, error-free, and unbiased. However, you can use before-and-after SQL queries and data visualization to help you manually check these types of logical transformations. You can also use SQL queries and data visualizations to verify column-level logical transformations similar to those discrete and continuous column verification techniques used to verify ECTL data preparation operations. Figure 6.3 shows a distribution graph of a discrete column whose column type was logically changed from continuous to discrete. In the operational data source, the continuous column values were numeric 0 and 1. After the change column type logical transformation operations, the column values were transformed to "NO" and "YES".

Change Column Type Verfication

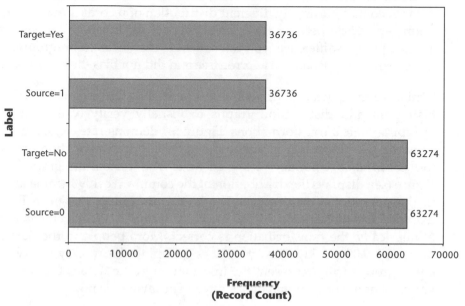

Figure 6.3   Distribution graph used to verify the change column type operation.

Insert Figure 4 shows how distribution pie graphs can be used to verify a column-grouping logical transformation operation. This technique is basically the same as the discrete column verification technique already discussed; however, the technique is slightly modified. The pie graph in Insert 4a shows the distribution of the RATE_PLAN column as it existed in the operational source data. The pie graph in Insert 4b shows the distribution after the column-grouping operation. You will also notice that the column values have been decoded into their descriptive meanings—that is, 42 has been decoded into BASIC, 41 has been decoded into 300 MIN, and so on. The column-grouping transformation grouped all column values with less than a 1 percent record count into the OTHER category. So, operational rate plans 44, 38, 37, 18, 45, 35, and 17 were grouped into the OTHER category in the business data set.

You will notice some differences in the distribution percentages. Since outliers (extreme values) were removed from the operational data source, the business data set contains a slightly different distribution of records. Because the distribution percentages between the operational data and business data set are within a 2 to 5 percent difference, you can conclude that the column-grouping logical transformation operation was error-free and did not bias the business data set.

Similar to the logical change column type verification technique, you can use histogram and distribution graphs to visually verify continuous column-grouping logical transformations. Figure 6.4 demonstrates a histogram graph showing the before and after column-grouping transformation operation on the continuous column Weekly Income. The histogram graph shown in Figure 6.4a displays the distribution of the column Weekly Income as it existed in the operational data source. The histogram graph shown in Figure 6.4b displays the distribution of the logically grouped Weekly Income column. Numerically, the transformation is correct. More people in the data set earn under $500.00 weekly. However, does grouping the weekly salary into four equal groups truly represent the information in the data set and capture the variance of the operational data source? The answer is no.

Figure 6.5 demonstrates distribution graphs showing more accurate grouping of the Weekly Income continuous column. The histogram graph shown in Figure 6.5a captures the distribution of the column Weekly Income as it existed in the operational data source. The histogram graph shown in Figure 6.5b demonstrates more clearly that the variance of the Weekly Income operational data source column has been captured in the business data set.

You can use distribution pie graphs and other data visualization to help you verify the logic of transformation operations applied to the business data set. For instance, you can use this visual technique, as well as the distribution pie graph technique, to verify the business data set before and after a sampling operation to ensure that the sampling operation did not introduce any bias. Since the distribution and pie graphs show the distribution rather than the records count, a graph of the sampled data set that is equivalent to the sample can help you verify the logic of the sampling operation.

Figure 6.6 shows before and after histogram graphs of a TEASER_RATE column. In this case, the histogram graph for the population shown in Figure 6.6a looks identical to the histogram graph shown in Figure 6.6b. The only difference is that the Figure 6.6a graph summarizes 80,000 records, while the Figure 6.6b graph only summarizes a 20 percent random sample of the population (16,000 records). From these graphs, you can conclude that the 20 percent random sample was successful and did not bias your data set.

**A. Before Grouping
Distribution Graph of Weekly Income**

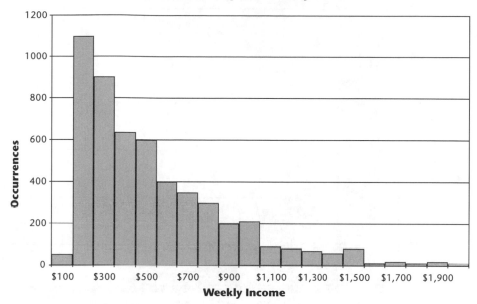

**B. After Grouping
Distribution of Weekly Income**

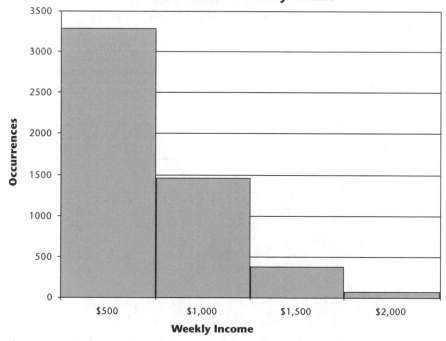

Figure 6.4   Before and after histogram graphs of grouping weekly income into four groups.

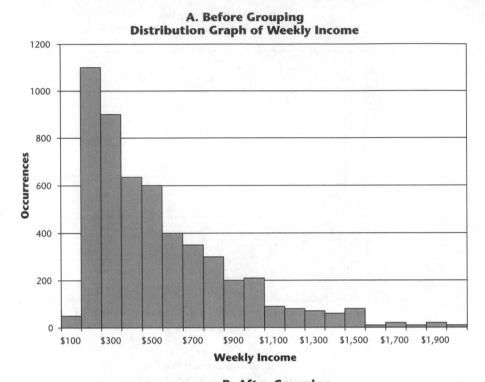

A. Before Grouping
Distribution Graph of Weekly Income

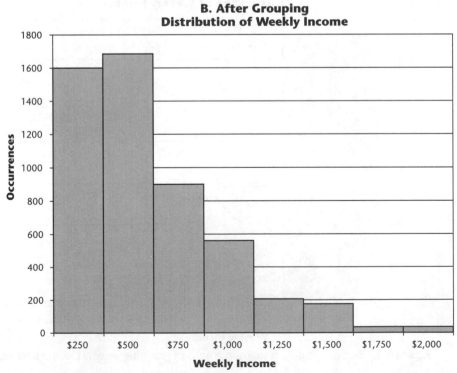

B. After Grouping
Distribution of Weekly Income

Figure 6.5 Before and after histogram graphs of grouping weekly income into eight groups.

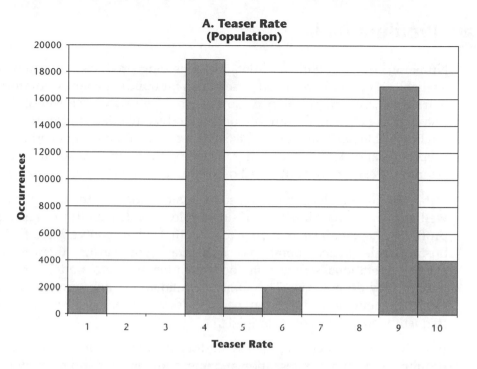

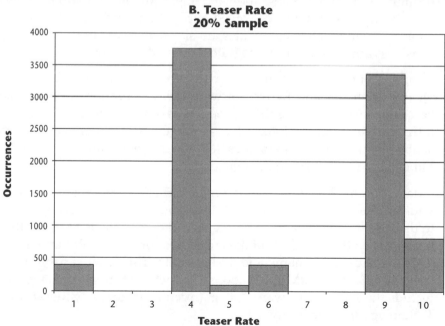

Figure 6.6 Before and after histogram graphs of grouping TEASER_RATE.

Data Profiling Tools

Numerous data profiling and data reengineering products are commercially available. You may have already used them for building your exploratory data mart. If not, you may be able to use these tools to verify the business data set. These tools help you thoroughly understand source data and check for data quality problems. If problems do exist, you can use data reengineering tools to preprocess and clean the data prior to loading the operational data source data set into the exploratory data mart or to clean an existing business data set.

Data profiling involves analyzing source data to identify the data element, as well as to apply data integrity business rules. A side benefit from using data profiling and data reengineering tools is that when you've identified these business rules in the operational source data, you can use them to update existing operational source data documentation and data models, or to create them if they do not exist. The ability to validate existing operational source data documentation is important because documentation for legacy systems is frequently out-of-date or incomplete.

In addition to maintaining the exploratory data mart, you can also use data profiling tools in data integration and migration projects and for moving data from legacy systems into packaged applications such as ERP and CRM systems. Some innovative companies are also using data profiling to implement ebusiness applications and integrate them with back-office systems.

Examples of products that focus on data profiling include the Informix/Ardent Quality Manager and Evoke Software Inc.'s Migration Architect. Although you could classify both of these products as data profiling tools, they are quite different. Migration Architect places stronger emphasis on data discovery and analysis to uncover business rules in the operational source data, while Quality Manager focuses more on data validation.

If data profiling identifies quality problems in the operational source data or in your production business data set, then you can use data reengineering tools to thoroughly investigate the problems and correct them. Many of these products focus on the extraction of data from free-form text fields and the cleansing and consolidation of name and address data. This latter capability is particularly important for CRM applications. Products that support data reengineering include the Trillium Software System (recently acquired by Merant) and Vality Technology Inc.'s Integrity.

Depending on the type of VDM project you are planning, the complexity of the operational data source and production business data sets, as well as the complexity of the business questions, you may choose to use one or more data profiling and data reengineering tools; however, in this chapter standard SQL and data visualization tools to create a verification procedure were used.

Whether or not you use data profiling and data reengineering tools, the verification concepts discussed will help you verify your production business data set.

Verifying the Data Set for the Case Study

In Chapter 4, the operational data sources were extracted, cleansed, transformed, and loaded into the exploratory data mart. The selection criterion for the business data sets was based on the business question of which customers were leaving and why. In Chapter 5, logical operations were applied to the business data set to make it easier to visualize and mine. Verifying the business data set is Step 5 of the VDM methodology, and it is the last step in the data preparation phase of the VDM project. A verification procedure and documentation will be created for the customer retention case study that verifies both the ECTL procedure and the logical transformation operations that were applied to the business data sets.

According to the VDM project plan outlined in Chapter 2, this step is estimated to take approximately 2 working days. The tasks for Step 5 are assigned to the following teams:

- The data and business analyst team works with the domain experts to verify that both the ECTL procedure and the logical transformation operations were applied correctly to the business data sets.

- The data warehousing team is responsible for correcting any ECTL or logical transformation operations errors discovered while verifying the business data set.

For the customer retention VDM pilot project, two production business data sets were extracted, cleansed, transformed, and loaded from the operational data sources into the exploratory data mart. They were then logically transformed based on the recommendation from the domain expert and the data and business analyst teams. The two data sets are as follows:

- The *customer_join* business data set joined selected data facts from the customer, contract, and invoice operational data sources. After the ECTL and join operations from Chapter 4, the resulting data set contained 464,916 records. The logical transformation operations from Chapter 5 only transformed column values but did not alter the record count.

- The *customer_demographic* business data set joined the information from the *customer_join* data set with selected data facts from the purchased demographics file. After the ECTL and join operations from Chapter 4, the resulting business data set contained 96,258 records. The logical transformation operations from Chapter 5 only transformed column values but did not alter the record count.

Table 6.4 ECTL Column-Level Documentation for the Customer Table

	SOURCE		EXPLORATORY DATA MART			
ECTL STEP	**TABLE NAME**	**COLUMN NAME**	**COLUMN NAME**	**COLUMN DATA TYPE**	**COLUMN VALUE RANGE**	**ECTL TRANSFORMATIONS**
1	Mainframe customer table	CUSTOMERID	CUSTOMERID	Continuous	1 to 641,498	Unique Constraint
2	Mainframe customer table	ACTIVATEDDATE	ACTIVATEDDATE	Continuous (DATE)	09/23/1996 to 08/12/1999	VALID DATE
3	Mainframe customer table	BIRTHDATE	BIRTHDATE	Continuous (DATE)	01/01/1900 to 01/01/1990	VALID DATE
4	Mainframe customer table	CITY	CITY	Discrete	Valid cities	TO_UPPER
5	Mainframe customer table	CREDIT and SCORE	CREDIT_SCORE	Discrete	A-Z	NULLs transformed to UNKNOWN
6	Mainframe customer table	CURRENTBALANCE	CURRENTBALANCE	Continuous	-$1,000 to $1,000	NULLs transformed to $0.00
7	Mainframe customer table	PRGCODE	PRGCODE	Discrete	1 to 33	None
8	Mainframe customer table	STATE	STATE	Discrete	50 U.S. states	TO_UPPER
9	Mainframe customer table	ZIPCODE	ZIP	Discrete	Valid zip codes	Substring 5 characters

Verifying the ECTL Procedures

Before any logical transformations were applied, a backup copy of the *customer_join* and *customer_demographic* tables was created to make the verification process easier. These tables were called *customer_join_audit* and *customer_demographic_audit*, respectively. They will be used as a baseline to verify the logical transformation operations. However, first we must verify that the ECTL procedure steps are accurate and error-free and that they did not introduce any bias into the business data set. Many of the ECTL procedures performed the same type of data preparation operations. In most cases, we can use the discrete and continuous column verification techniques to verify each ECTL step. To verify many of the ECTL operations performed on the customer, contract, invoice, and demographic files, you can use the before and after distribution and statistics graphs from the case study section from Chapter 4.

Verifying the ECTL Data Preparation Step for the Customer Table

Table 6.4 shows the ECTL column-level documentation for the customer table. Only those columns that underwent an ECTL operation need to be verified. You will notice the ECTL Steps 2 and 3 are basically the same, as are Steps 4, 8, and 9.

Since many of the same types of ECTL data preparation operations are applied to different columns in the operational data sources, we will only illustrate one of each type of ECTL step. For the customer table, the operational data source table, *customer_raw*, contains 639,926 customer records. It will be verified against the business data set audit table, *customer_join_audit*, that contains 464,916 joined customer records. Recall that the customer table was joined to the contract and invoice table to create the *customer_join* business data set.

Code Figure 6.3 demonstrates how to use the continuous column verification technique to verify the continuous column CUSTOMERID. The two queries compute the average, minimum, maximum, standard deviation, and variance for the columns. The first query calculates the statistics for the operational data set; the second query calculates the statistics for the business data set. To verify CURRENTBALANCE, you would replace all instances of CUSTOMERID with CURRENTBALANCE.

```
-- Retrieve the distinct value, the record count and the
-- distribution percentage for each distinct value for the
-- column from the operational source table
SELECT      MIN(customerid) MIN_CUSTOMERID,
            MAX(customerid) MAX_CUSTOMERID,
```

Code Figure 6.3 Discrete column verification technique to perform an integrity check on the CUSTOMERID column. *(continues)*

```
              AVG(customerid) AVG_CUSTOMERID,
              STDDEV(customerid) STDDEV_CUSTOMERID,
              VARIANCE (customerid) VARIANCE_CUSTOMERID
FROM customer_raw;
-- Retrieve the distinct value, the record count and the
-- distribution percentage for each distinct value for the
-- column from the business data set table
SELECT      MIN(customerid) MIN_CUSTOMERID,
MAX(customerid) MAX_CUSTOMERID,
AVG(customerid) AVG_CUSTOMERID,
STDDEV(customerid) STDDEV_CUSTOMERID,
VARIANCE (customerid) VARIANCE_CUSTOMERID
FROM customer_join_audit;
```

Code Figure 6.3 Discrete column verification technique to perform an integrity check on the CUSTOMERID column. *(continued)*

Table 6.5 lists the statistics returned by the queries for the CUSTOMERID column from the operational data (SOURCE) and the CUSTOMERID column from the business data set (TARGET). The CUSTOMERID ECTL transformation and join to the other operational sources can be considered error-free since the average value is within 1.9 percent.

Table 6.6 lists the statistics for CURRENTBALANCE column from the operational data (SOURCE) and the CURRENTBALANCE column from the business data set (TARGET). If you review the statistics graphs from Figures 4.10 and 4.11 from Chapter 4 for the CURRENTBALANCE column, you see that the average value before the ECTL step was $24 and after was $23 (4.2% difference). However, after the filtering logical transformation and joining the customer table to the contract and invoice tables, the average value increased to $29 (20% difference) for the business data set. The first step to investigating this large difference is to re-verify that the ECTL and logical transformation operations didn't contain errors by the operations and data warehousing teams. They discovered that the join operation to the invoice file caused the large difference. The join operations were discussed with the domain experts, and it was discovered that the cause of the large difference was due to intermixing corporate and personal accounts. The customer and contract files contained both corporate accounts and personal accounts, whereas the invoice file

Table 6.5 Verification Statistics for the CUSTOMERID Column

	AVG	MIN	MAX	STDDEV	VARIANCE
SOURCE	320,219	1,231	641,498	185,250	3.4318E+10
TARGET	314,208	27	640,069	182,660	3.365E+10

Table 6.6 Verification Statistics for the CURRENTBALANCE Column

	AVG	MIN	MAX	STDDEV	VARIANCE
SOURCE	24	-600,940	446,062	967	935,739
TARGET	29	-996	998	83	6,950

only contained personal accounts. It was decided not to change the join operation, as the focus of the analysis was at the personal customer level, not the corporate and personal level.

Code Figure 6.4 demonstrates how to use a slightly modified version of the continuous column verification technique to verify ECTL Step 2 for the continuous column ACTIVATEDDATE from the customer table. You will notice that the date is converted into an eight-digit number so we can compute the average, minimum, maximum, standard deviation, and variance for the data continuous columns. The first query calculates the statistics for the operational

```
-- Retrieve the miniumum and maximum values
-- compute the average, standard deviation and variance for the
-- column from the operational source table
SELECT      AVG(TO_NUMBER(TO_CHAR(activateddate,'DDDDDDDDD'))) AVG_acti-
vateddate,
MIN(TO_NUMBER(TO_CHAR(activateddate,'DDDDDDDDD'))) MIN_activateddate,
MAX(TO_NUMBER(TO_CHAR(activateddate,'DDDDDDDDD'))) MAX_activateddate,
STDDEV(TO_NUMBER(TO_CHAR(activateddate,'DDDDDDDD'))) STDDEV_activated-
date,
VARIANCE (TO_NUMBER(TO_CHAR(activateddate,'DDDDDDDD'))) VARIANCE_acti-
vateddate
FROM customer_raw
-- Retrieve the miniumum and maximum values
-- compute the average, standard deviation and variance for the
-- column from the business data set table
SELECT      AVG(TO_NUMBER(TO_CHAR(activateddate,'DDDDDD')))
            AVG_activateddate,
            MIN(TO_NUMBER(TO_CHAR(activateddate,'DDDDDD')))
            MIN_activateddate,
            MAX(TO_NUMBER(TO_CHAR(activateddate,'DDDDDDD')))
            MAX_activateddate,
            STDDEV(TO_NUMBER(TO_CHAR(activateddate,'DDDDDDDD')))
            STDDEV_activateddate,
            VARIANCE (TO_NUMBER(TO_CHAR(activateddate,'DDDDDDDD')))
            VARIANCE_activateddate
FROM customer_join_audit
```

Code Figure 6.4 Continuous column verification technique to perform an integrity check on the ACTIVATEDDATE column.

data set; the second query calculates the statistics for the business data set. To verify BIRTHDATE, you would replace all instances of ACTIVATEDDATE with BIRTHDATE. You will also notice that the dates were converted into numbers to allow for the statistical calculations.

Table 6.7 lists the statistics returned by the queries for the ACTIVATEDDATE column from the operational data (SOURCE) and the ACTIVATEDDATE column from the business data set (TARGET). The ACTIVATEDDATE ECTL transformation and join to the other operational sources can be considered error-free since the average value is within 0.16 percent. The BIRTHDATE column can be verified using this same technique.

Code Figure 6.5 demonstrates how to use the discrete column verification technique to verify ECTL Step 4 for the CITY discrete column from the customer table. The two queries display the distinct column value and the number of records that correspond to that distinct column value. The first query displays this information for the operational data set; the second query displays this information for the business data set. To verify CITY and ZIP, you would replace all instances of STATE with CITY or ZIP. To verify the ZIP column, you would need to use the substring operations on the operational data source as well.

Table 6.8 lists the record counts returned by the queries for the STATE column from the operational data (SOURCE) and the STATE column from the business data set (TARGET). This table shows that the order of the states that contain the most customers remains constant and their record counts are within reason. However, a more exact technique would be preferable. Insert Figures 5a and 5b illustrate how distribution pie charts can help give a better measurement as to the accuracy of the ECTL transformation. Insert 5a shows a distribution pie chart of the STATE distribution of the operational data source. It can easily be compared to Insert Figure 5b, which shows the STATE distribution of the business data set after the transformation.

Table 6.7 Verification Statistics for the ACTIVATEDDATE Column

	AVG	MIN	MAX	STDDEV	VARIANCE
SOURCE	191,043	1,001	36,636,631	11,388,268	1.2969E14
TARGET	190,724	1,001	36,636,631	11,453,207	1.3118E14

```
-- Retrieve the distinct value, the record count and the
-- distribution percentage for each distinct value for the
-- column from the operational source table
SELECT      state,
            count (state),
            count (state) / (SELECT count(state)
FROM customer_raw) * 100 distribution
FROM customer_raw
GROUP BY state
ORDER BY count (state) desc
-- Retrieve the distinct value, the record count and the
-- distribution percentage for each distinct value for the
-- column from the business data set table
SELECT      state,
count (state),
count (state) / (SELECT count(state)
    FROM customer_join_audit) * 100 distribution
    FROM customer_join_audit
    GROUP BY state
    ORDER BY count (state) desc
```

Code Figure 6.5 Discrete verification technique to perform an integrity check on the STATE column.

Table 6.8 Verification for the STATE Column

SOURCE TARGET STATE	COUNT	DISTRIBUTION	BUSINESS DATA SET STATE	COUNT	DISTRIBUTION
GA	232,408	36.31	GA	169,477	36.45
AL	151,671	23.70	AL	106,382	22.88
TN	108,978	17.03	TN	78,148	16.81
FL	75,140	1.74	FL	55,575	11.95
MS	29,999	4.69	MS	21,853	4.7
KY	21,593	3.37	KY	17,692	3.81
SC	8,898	1.39	SC	7,190	1.55
IN	2,988	0.47	IN	2,522	0.54
AR	2,733	0.43	AR	1,884	0.41
TX	680	0.11	TX	557	0.12
NC	534	0.08	NC	438	0.09

Table 6.9 ECTL Column-Level Documentation for the Contract Table

	SOURCE		EXPLORATORY DATA MART			
ECTL STEP	TABLE NAME	COLUMN NAME	COLUMN NAME	COLUMN DATA TYPE	COLUMN VALUE RANGE	ECTL TRANSFORMATIONS
1	Mainframe contract table	CUSTOMERID	CUSTOMERID	Continuous	1 to 641,498	Unique Constraint
2	Mainframe contract table	ACCESS_FEE	CONTRACT_FEE	Continuous	$0.00 to $500.00	None
3	Mainframe contract table	TM_CODE_DESCRIPTION	TM_DESCRIPTION	Discrete	Valid terms (rate plans)	TO_UPPER
4	Mainframe contract table	ENT_DATE	RENEWAL_DATE	Continuous (DATE)	09/23/1996 to 08/12/1999	Valid Date
5	Mainframe contract table	REASON_DESCRIPTION	CHURN_REASON	Discrete	Free-flow textual description	TO_UPPER

You can use distribution pie charts similar to Inserts 5a and 5b to help verify discrete columns like CITY, ZIP, and other discrete columns. The distribution pie charts enable you to visually compare the column distribution before and after the transformation operation. Recall that the operational data source contains 175,010 more records than the business data set. Therefore, the 1 or 2 percent difference that you see on some states, such as GA and AL, is within reason, and you can conclude that the ECTL transform and join operations were error-free and didn't introduce bias into the business data set.

Verifying the ECTL Data Preparation Step for the Contract Table

Table 6.9 shows the ECTL column-level documentation for the contract table. The techniques already discussed can be used to verify each step. You can use these techniques to verify the correctness of the ECTL operation and the integrity of the business data set.

- For ECTL Steps 1 (CUSTOMERID) and 2 (ACCESS_FEE) in Table 6.9, you can use the continuous column verification technique to verify the ECTL operations. Since both CUSTOMERIID and ACCESS_FEE are continuous columns, you can compare the average, minimum, maximum, standard deviation, and variance of the operational data source column to the exploratory data mart table column.

- For ECTL Step 4 (RENEWAL_DATE) in Table 6.9, you can use the modified continuous data column verification technique described in Code Figure 6.4 to verify the ECTL operation. Since RENEWAL_DATE is a continuous date column, you can convert the date into an eight-digit number and then compare the average, minimum, maximum, standard deviation, and variance of the operational data source column to the exploratory data mart table column.

- For ECTL Steps 3 (TM_CODE_DESCRIPTION) and 5 (REASON_ DESCRIPTION) in Table 6.9, you can use the discrete column verification technique to verify the ECTL operations. Since both TM_CODE_ DESCRIPTION and REASON_DESCRIPTION are discrete columns, you can compare the record counts of the distinct column values of the operational data source column to the exploratory data mart table column or use distribution graphs.

Verifying the ECTL Data Preparation Step for the Invoice Table

Table 4.11 from Chapter 4 lists the column-level ECTL documentation for the invoice table. The ECTL operations performed on the invoice operational source table are different from the data preparation performed on the customer and contract table. The operational data source invoice table contains historical detail transaction records that were aggregated to the experimental unit of the business data set (customer level). Only continuous column data can be aggregated. To verify the ECTL aggregation, we can use some simple SQL statements to compare the sum of the continuous column in the operational data source with the sum of the continuous column in the business data source. For instance, Code Figure 6.6 shows how to perform this verification for the TOT_INVOICE_AMT column.

Table 6.10 shows the results of the verification queries. When the aggregated invoice table was joined to the customer and contract table to create the *customer_join* business data set, approximately 5.2 percent of the customer records were removed because they contained dirty data. However, the average total invoice amount between the operational data set and the business data set is within 2.2 percent. Therefore, we can conclude that the aggregation was successful and that we didn't bias the business data set. This same aggregation verification technique can be used for the other ECTL transformation steps on the invoice table, such as TOT_OPEN_AMT and TOT_PAID_AMT.

```
-- Retrieve the sum, number of customers and average amount
-- per customer of the invoice_amount column from
-- the operational source table
SELECT    sum(invoice_amount) GRAND_TOTAL,
          count(distinct(customerid)) CUST_TOTAL,
          sum(invoice_amount)/count(distinct(customerid))
CUST_AVERAGE
FROM invoice
WHERE
open_amount < 1000 and
invoice_amount < 1000 and
total_paid < 1000 and
invoice_date between
TO_DATE('09/23/1996','MM/DD/YYYY') and
TO_DATE('08/12/1999','MM/DD/YYYY')
-- Retrieve the sum, number of customers and average amount
-- per customer of the TOT_INVOICE_AMT column from
-- the operational source table
SELECT    sum (tot_invoice_amt) GRAND_TOTAL,
          count(distinct(customerid)) CUST_TOTAL,
          sum(tot_invoice_amt)/count(distinct(customerid))
               CUST_AVERAGE
     FROM customer_join
```

Code Figure 6.6 Continuous aggregation verification technique.

Table 6.10 Results of the Aggregation Verification Technique

	GRAND TOTAL	NUMBER OF CUSTOMERS	AVERAGE PER CUSTOMER
Operational Data Source	356,750,498	490,230	727.720657
Business Data Set	330,735,742	464,916	711.388169
Difference	7.3%	5.2%	2.2%

Verifying the ECTL Data Preparation Step for the Demographic Table

Table 4.13 from Chapter 4 lists the column-level ECTL documentation for the demographic table. For the demographics table, only four ECTL operations were applied to the operational data source table. In all four cases, the blank column values were decoded as an "E" to represent empty. You can use the discrete column verification technique to verify each transformation.

Verifying the Logical Transformations

As described in Chapter 5, to make the verification process easier, a backup copy of the *customer_join* and *customer_demographic* tables is created before applying any logical transformations. These tables were called *customer_join_audit* and *customer_demographic_audit*, respectively. They will be used as a baseline to verify the logical transformation operations. In most cases, we can use the discrete or continuous column verification technique to verify the integrity of the transformations that were applied to the *customer_join* business data set.

For instance, the logical transformation applied to the ACTIVATEDDATE column to create the ACTIVATED_YEAR column can be verified by slightly modifying the discrete verification technique. You can compare the distinct column value counts and their distribution percentages to verify the logical transformation operations, as demonstrated in Code Figure 6.7.

The logical transformation steps applied to the BIRTHDATE column to create the AGE_RANGE column can be verified by using a histogram and distribution graph. Figure 6.7 illustrates this technique. The histogram graph shown in Figure 6.7a displays the record distribution of the years in which the customers were born. As you can see, the majority of the customers were born after 1960, so they are 40 years old or younger. You can compare these age groups to

A. Histogram Graph of Customer Age

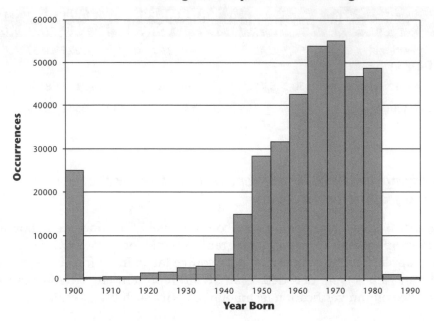

B. Distribution Graph of Customer Age Groups

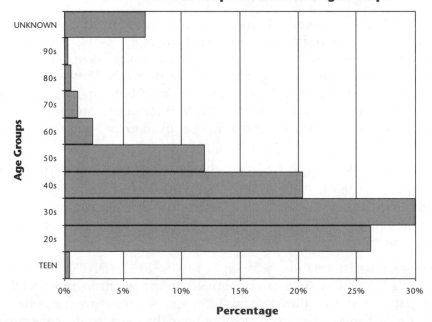

Figure 6.7   Histogram and distribution graph of customer age.

```
-- Retrieve the distinct column value, count of the distinct value
-- and distribution percentage from the before logical
-- transformation audit table
SELECT    to_char(activateddate,'YYYY'),
          count(activateddate),
          count(activateddate)/(SELECT count(activateddate)
          FROM customer_join_audit) * 100 distribution
FROM      customer_join_audit
GROUP BY to_char(activateddate,'YYYY')
-- Retrieve the distinct column value, count of the distinct value
-- and distribution percentage from the
-- production business data set
SELECT     activated_year,
count(activated_year),
count(activated_year)/(SELECT count(activated_year)
FROM customer_join) * 100 distribution
FROM customer_join
GROUP BY activated_year
```

Code Figure 6.7   Discrete column verification technique for logical transformations.

the distribution graph shown in Figure 6.7b. As you can see, most customers fall into the 30s and 20s age groups. You could also use standard SQL statements to verify the counts of the specific age ranges before and after the logical transformation.

The remainder of the logical transformation applied to the *customer_join* business data set can be verified with one of these or the discrete and continuous column verification techniques. Likewise, you can use these techniques to verify the logical transformations applied to the *customer_demographic* business data set.

Summary

There are numerous verification techniques and ways to use data visualizations to help you verify that ECTL and logical transformation data preparation operations are accurate, error-free, and do not introduce bias into your production data set. The verification step is the last step in the data preparation phase of a VDM project. In the next chapter, we start the data analysis phase of a VDM project. We will help you begin to exploit your prepared and verified production business data sets by selecting the appropriate data visualization and visual data mining tools.

PART THREE

Data Analysis Phase and Beyond

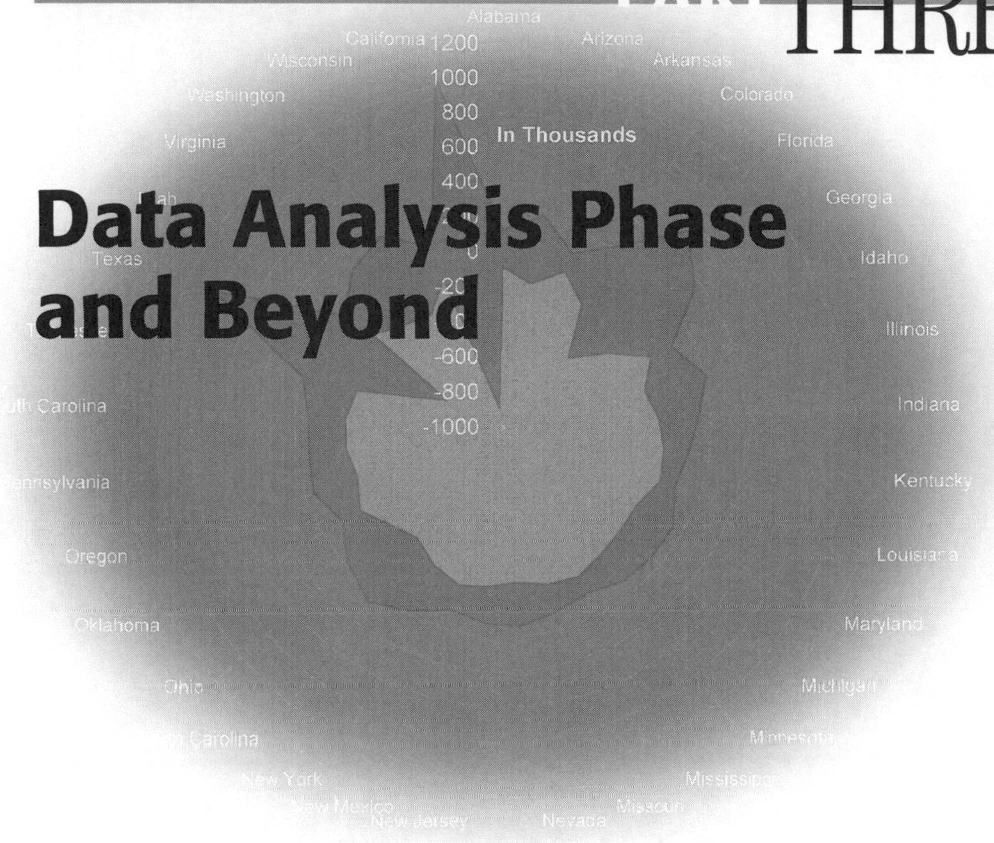

CHAPTER 7

Step 6: Choosing the Visualization or Data Mining Tool

The first step of the data analysis phase is choosing the appropriate data visualization or data mining tool to help you investigate your business data set and answer your business questions. Step 6 of the VDM methodology is selecting which visualization techniques are best suited for investigating data visualization questions such as how are my shipping costs distributed over my sales regions or what are my sales trends year-to-date. Step 6 also focuses on selecting which data mining techniques are suitable to address data mining questions such as why are my customers leaving, which customer segment is most likely to buy my new product, or which customers are most likely to upgrade their service.

Data visualizations send a very powerful message to people. The use of images makes a much more vivid impact than a traditional green-bar report or a set of numbers or rules from an amorphous data mining algorithm. Data visualizations also have the capability to strengthen implications about the business data set based on graph type used, the color used in the graph, and the graphical entities used. Therefore, care must be taken to choose the right data visualization tool that effectively communicates accurate and significant information and data mining discoveries to other business analysts and the decision makers.

In this chapter, we discuss which multi-dimensional graph types are appropriate for investigating comparative business questions identified in Chapter 3. For example, column and bar visualizations are better suited for investigating yearly sales over categorical values like regions or product class than are scatter graphs. Next we discuss which specialized landscape and hierarchical visualizations, such as map and tree graphs, are best suited for investigation hierarchical or geographical business questions. In the second part of Chapter 6, we first discuss which data mining tools are appropriate for investigating your data mining business questions and then discuss how to evaluate which tools are best, based upon your specific situation. Finally, we apply Step 6 to the ongoing customer retention business case study.

Choosing the Right Data Visualization Tool

The goals of data visualization tools and techniques are to assist you in creating two- and three-dimensional pictures of your prepared business data set that can be easily interpreted to gain knowledge and insights and to use the resulting data visualization, such as column, bar, and pie graphs, to share your insights with other data and business analysts and decision makers. The human mind is a very sophisticated pattern-recognition-processing engine. With data visualization, you act as the data mining tool. By visually inspecting and interacting with the two- or three-dimensional visualization, you can identify the interesting (nontrivial, implicit, perhaps previously unknown and potentially useful) information or patterns from the prepared business data set.

Choosing the right data visualization tool or technique depends on the nature of the business data set and its underlying structure. Data visualization tools can be classified into two main categories:

- Multidimensional visualization tools, such as scatter, line, column, bar, and pie graphs
- Specialized landscape and hierarchical visualization tools, such as map and tree graphs

Keep in mind that most graph types focus on a small facet of the business data set at a time. Often, your business data set will contain 20 or more columns. However, most graph types only allow you to analyze two columns at once. In most cases, the prepared business data set must be aggregated to the experimental unit being illustrated in the graph. For instance, if you want to create a graph of sales by region, your business data set needs to be aggregated to the region level. If you want to create a graph to investigate sales by floor plan, you need to aggregate at the floor plan level. The lowest level that you can investigate is the experimental unit of the prepared business data set. If you adhered to the data preparation steps in the previous chapters, you will be able to aggregate to higher levels without introducing errors or bias into your business data set.

Code Figure 7.1 demonstrates how you can use a standard SQL query to aggregate the business data set TOT_STORE_SALES_99 to the FLOOR_PLAN level. In this example, the resulting data table will contain TOTAL_SALES by FLOOR_PLAN. Refer to Chapter 4, Table 4.1 for more details about this business data set. For instance, if you are using Microsoft Excel as your data visualization tool, you can use an ODBC connection to the exploratory data mart to automatically return the results of the query to your worksheet. In this book, we refer to the columns and rows returned from the query as the graphical *data table*. This data table is the information (in row and column format) that is used to create the data visualization. It is a subset of the business data set that has been aggregated to the level of information you are investigating in the data visualization.

In most cases, you want to create the data table in either ascending or descending order. The most common is ascending order. Creating a data table in ascending order is often used to show an upward trend when graphed, whereas creating a data table in descending order is normally used to show a downward trend. However, if you are aggregating by a time-based column, such as year or quarter, you want to ORDER BY year or quarter in ascending order to conform to the standard calendar.

```
SELECT       floor_plan,
SUM(total_sales)
FROM tot_store_sales_99
GROUP BY     floor_plan
ORDER BY     SUM(total_sales) asc
```

Code Figure 7.1 SQL query to create a data table for the graph from the total store sales business data set.

Multidimensional Visualizations

Most multidimensional visualizations are used to compare and contrast the values of one column (data dimension) to the values of other columns (data dimensions) in the prepared business data set. They are also used to investigate the relationships between two or more continuous or discrete columns in the business data set. Table 7.1 lists some common multidimensional graph types, the column types under investigation, as well as usage suggestions.

Column and Bar Graphs

Like most data visualization types, column and bar graphs can be used to graphically display summarized data from your prepared business data set. The most common use for these graphs is to investigate trends or to compare discrete (categorical) column values. The categorical column can be either a discrete column with a finite number of distinct values or a continuous column that has been grouped into a finite number of distinct values, such as a continuous date column grouped into year, quarter, or month categories. To display the prepared business data set, you must first create a graphical data table or subset of the business data set that is aggregated by the category column you want to use. For instance, if you want to visually investigate shipping costs by state, you need to aggregate the shipping costs by each state to create a graphical data table. Depending on what facet of the business data set you are investigating, you can choose to use either the average or summation operator. However, take care when aggregating the business data set that you don't introduce errors or bias. Following is a discussion of these graph types.

Table 7.1 Graph Type, Column Type under Investigation, and When to Choose

GRAPH TYPE	COLUMN TYPE	WHEN TO CHOOSE
Column and Bar[1]	Discrete	Use column graphs to investigate trends among distinct values for one or more discrete columns. Use bar graphs to compare and contrast distinct values for one or more discrete columns.
Area, line, high-low-close, and radar	Continuous	Use line, high-low-close, and radar to investigate trends among the values for one or more continuous columns.

Table 7.1   *(Continued)*

GRAPH TYPE	COLUMN TYPE	WHEN TO CHOOSE
Histogram, distribution, pie, and doughnut[2]	Discrete	Use histogram, distribution, and pie graphs to compare the frequency of distinct values for a discrete column. Use doughnut graphs to compare the frequency of distinct values for multiple discrete columns.
Box	Continuous	Use box plots to investigate the frequency of values for a continuous column.
Scatter	Continuous	Use scatter graphs to investigate the relationships between two or more continuous columns.

[1]The stacked version of the column graph can be used to investigate trends or compare and contrast distinct values for multiple discrete columns. The stacked column graph displays the values for two or more discrete columns using a single column for each interval. The multiple discrete values are "stacked" vertically on top of one another.

[2]The stacked version of the bar graph can be used to compare and contrast distinct values for multiple discrete columns. The stacked bar graph displays the values for two or more discrete columns using a single bar for each interval. The values are "stacked" horizontally next to one another.

Column Graphs

These graphs compare distinct items or show single items at distinct time intervals. With column graphs, the discrete column categories are arranged along the horizontal axis and the continuous summarized values along the vertical axis. Column graphical entities are drawn vertically on the graph. A very common use for column graphs is to investigate how continuous column values change over discrete units of time, for instance, yearly sales or profit changes by month or year.

Bar Graphs

Bar graphs are like column graphs because they also compare distinct items or show single items at distinct intervals. Normally, a bar graph is laid out with discrete column categories (distinct values) along the vertical axis and aggregated continuous column values along the horizontal axis. In other words, the bar graphical entities are horizontally placed on the graph. Bar graphs are useful for comparing discrete column categories that are in competition, so it makes sense to place the longest bar on top and the others in descending order beneath it. With bar graphs, you should avoid using a time-based scale as the discrete category. Studies have shown that this use is generally confusing for people. Instead, use a column graph when working with times or date type columns.

Figures 7.1 and 7.2 illustrate an appropriate use for a bar graph to compare the store's floor plan to the total sales for 1999. The graphical data table was created by the query shown in Code Figure 7.1.

When you visually compare the column and bar charts from Figures 7.1 and 7.2, you can see the impact of sorting the graphical data table. In the column and bar graphs from Figure 7.1, it is more difficult to see the business trend between COMPACT, MODERN, and ORIGINAL floor plans, whereas in Figure 7.2, the trend is displayed more clearly. Since the discrete column, FLOOR_PLAN, isn't a date or time-based column, choosing whether to use a column or bar graph is your preference. Both the column and bar graphs can be used to illustrate the same trend information. In Chapter 8, we discuss analyzing and deriving conclusions from the graphs in more detail.

Code Figure 7.2 demonstrates how you can use an SQL query to aggregate the bond yield business data set by the month and year. In this example, the resulting graphical data table will contain the average 1-, 3-, and 6-month bond yields by month and year. Refer to Chapter 5, Tables 5.4 and 5.5 for more details about the bond yield business data set. In Code Figure 7.2, the AVG (average) SQL operator is used instead of the SUM (summation) operator, since our investigation focus is looking for general bond yield trends.

Figure 7.3 shows a bar and column graph using a continuous date column as the categorical column. In this example, the continuous date column is actually converted into a discrete column formatted as YYYY-MON: four-digit year followed by the three-character month. As you can see from Figure 7.3, the column graph (Figure 7.3a) is much easier to understand than the bar graph (Figure 7.3b). In this example, the graphs are used to compare three data dimensions (YIELD_1M, YIELD_3M, and YIELD_6M) over a time series dimension (YIELD_DATE) from the yield business data set.

```
SELECT     TO_CHAR(yield_date,'YYYY-MON') yield_date,
           AVG(yield_1m) yield_1m,
           AVG(yield_3m) yield_3m,
           AVG(yield_6m) yield_6m
FROM yield
GROUP BY   TO_CHAR(yield_date,'YYYY-MON')
```

Code Figure 7.2 SQL query to create a data table for the graph from the bond yield business data set.

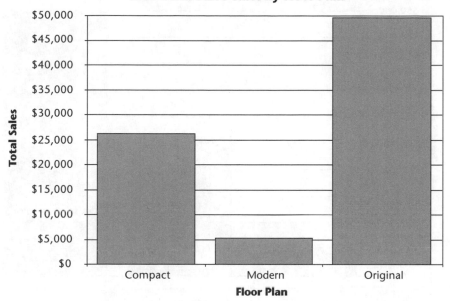

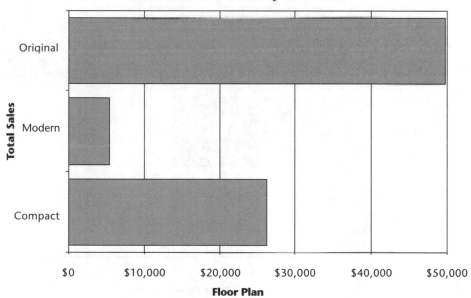

Figure 7.1   Column and bar graphs of total store sales by floor plan (data table not sorted).

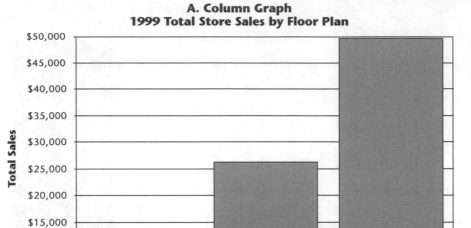

A. Column Graph
1999 Total Store Sales by Floor Plan

B. Bar Graph
1999 Total Store Sales by Floor Plan

Figure 7.2 Column and bar graphs of total store sales by floor plan (data table sorted in ascending order).

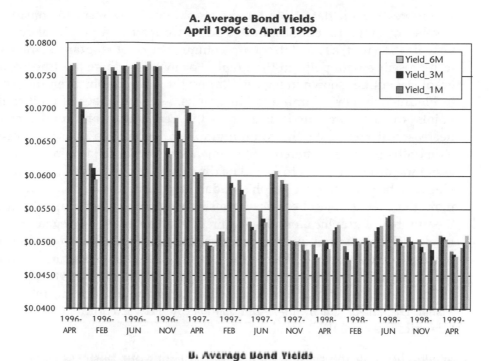

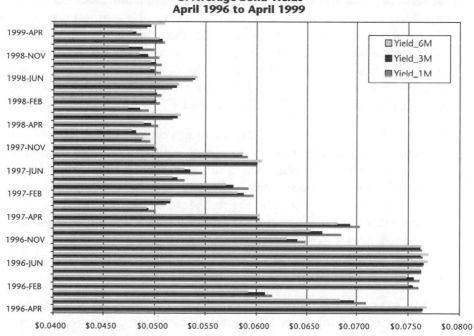

Figure 7.3 Column and bar graphs of average monthly bond yields from April 1996 to April 1999.

When creating the data table for the graph, you may want to consider the number of graphical entities. In this book, we refer to a graphical entity (or visualization unit) as the dot, square, column, bar, or other graph symbol used to represent a data point in the graph. For instance, there are three column graphical entities shown in Figure 7.2a and three bar graphical entities shown in Figure 7.2b. For column and bar graphs, as the number of entities (data points to be represented) increases, the readability and understanding decreases. For instance, the column graph in Figure 7.3a is used to display 38 months for three different data dimension, or 114 data points. Although assigning different colors to each data dimension series, as well as using a 3-D view, can help increase the graph's readability, normally you don't want to use more than 100 graphical entities for a single column or bar graph. To reduce the number of graphical entities required, you can either aggregate to a high level, such as year and quarter, or reduce the time series length to only select one or two years instead of three full years' worth of data. For more information on selecting the number of data points and data dimensions to use, as well as the principles of graphical excellence, integrity and design, refer to *The Visual Display of Quantitative Information* by Edward Tufte (Cheshire, CT: Graphics Press, 2001).

When choosing the right visualization tool for your business data set, you need to take into consideration the readability of the graph type you choose. As demonstrated in Figure 7.3a and 7.3b, the number of graphical entities can affect readability and understandability. You also need to consider your target audience. For instance, are they other data and business analysts or are they decision makers? Keep in mind that the goal of using data visualization is to be able to communicate your findings easily.

Figure 7.4 shows a column and a bar graph of the average cost of promotion categories for a large computer company. Both graphs were created using the same aggregated graphical data table. However, the bar graph (Figure 7.4b) tends to be easier to read and interpret as compared to the column graph (Figure 7.4a). The column graph (Figure 7.4a) can be used to show an upward trend by category, whereas the bar graph (Figure 7.4b) can be used to compare and contrast the discrete promotion categories. In this case, the business question was simply comparative, so the bar graph is more appropriate to answer the business question.

In this example, the prepared data set had contained over 50,000 records that were aggregated into only 20 promotion categories. However, since the category description (distinct discrete column values) is up to 27 characters in length, the column graph becomes difficult to read. On the other hand, in the bar graph, you can easily associate the category description to the graphical entity (bar). Another option is to use the column graph and place the labels on a 45-degree angle. Depending on the label length, the label uniformity (approximately the same number of characters per label), and total number of labels, using this technique can also greatly improve readability of the column graph.

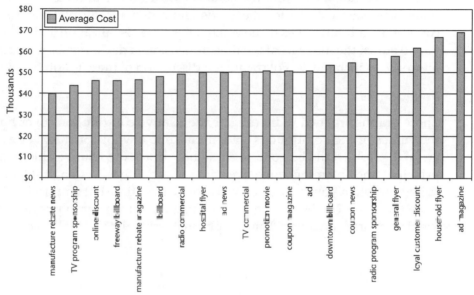

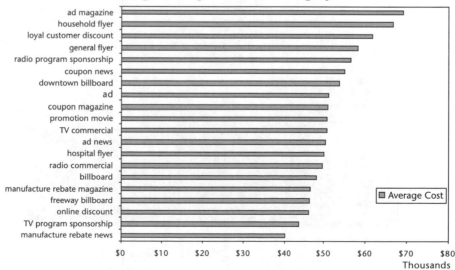

Figure 7.4 Column and bar graphs of average cost by promotion category.

Area, Line, High-Low-Close, and Radar Graphs

Like most data visualization types, area, stacked column, line, and high-low-close graphs can be used to graphically display summarized data from your prepared business data set. The most common use for area, stacked column, line, and high-low-close graphs is to compare continuous column values over a time dimension column. Normally, you do not need to aggregate your business data set to create the graphical data table. Most visualization tools will use the time dimension column for the x-axis and automatically plot the associated continuous column values to the y-axis. Often, the visualization tools will enable you to adjust the intervals of the time dimension in days, weeks, months, quarters, or year increments. Following is a discussion of these graph types.

Area Graphs

These graphs are used to investigate the relative contributions over time that the values of each continuous column make to a whole picture. For example, an area graph would be good to show how much the relative amounts of the principal and interest change over time of a mortgage. Area graphs are best suited for when you want to show a change over time but emphasize the total of all the series combined. Figure 7.5 illustrates an area graph using the Bond Yield prepared data set. This graph enables you to visually compare the

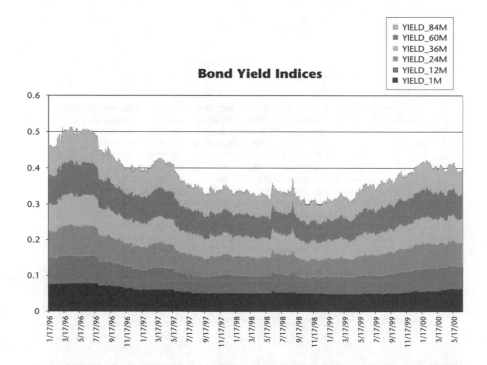

Figure 7.5 Area graph of bond yield indices from 1/17/1996 through 5/17/2000.

difference of the 1-, 3-, 6-, 12-, 18-, 24-, and 36-month bond yield indices within a single visualization.

Line Graphs

Line graphs plot the values of the continuous columns as a specific point, then "connect the dots" in order to give you some idea of the relationship of consecutive points. This type of graph may also be used to show how column values change over time. Unlike bar and column graphs, line graphs imply continuous change rather than a number of discrete observation points. For this reason, line graphs are better at implying a trend. However, just because a line graph implies trends does not necessarily mean the trend is real. You should be careful when interpreting such graphs that you do not automatically assume intermediate values by the line placement. In general, line graphs are best at showing changes in a series over categories or time. A line graph suggests that the data is continuous, so if you were to measure a point between two points in your data set, the value of the point is implied by the graphical line entity even though the implied point is not part of your data set.

Insert Figure 7 illustrates using a line graph to display the bond yield indices from 1/17/1996 through 12/31/1997. Unlike the area graph, the line graph can be used to show the continuous column values in relationship to the index value (y-axis). The line graph in Insert Figure 7b uses the default scale of the bond yield indices values from 0.0 to 0.1; however, the line graph in Insert Figure 7a reduces the scope of the indices values to the minimum and maximum indices values. Using a custom range enables you to focus more closely on the indices trends and changes.

High-Low-Close Graphs

High-low-close graphs plot the values of a set of three continuous columns as a single set, then "connect the dots" between sets in order to give you some idea of the relationship of the set. Normally, these graphs are used to investigate the relationship between the high, low, and close price of stocks over time. However, you can use this graph type to investigate the relationships between any three continuous dimensions that have the same observation base. For instance, Figure 7.6 illustrates how a high-low-close graph can be used to investigate the relationship between the 1-, 3-, and 6-month bond yield indices over time. The 1-, 3-, and 6-month continuous column values share the same observation base, that is, the value of the bond index for a given day. Therefore, you can use the high-low-close graph to plot and investigate their interaction. However, you will notice that with the addition of the triangle, square, and diamond graphical entities, you have to reduce the time dimension dramatically. In this case, the high-low-close graph can only display a 3-month period to maintain readability, whereas, a line or area graph can display the entire 3-year period for the bond yield business data set.

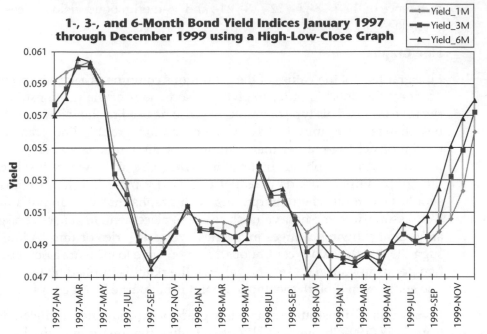

Figure 7.6 High-low-close graph of bond yield indices from January 1997 through December 1999.

Radar Graphs

These graphs plot the continuous column values as a function of distance from a central point. Each continuous data dimension, normally plotted along the x-axis using a column graph or along the y-axis using the bar graph, is displayed as a spoke radiating outward from a central point. A line connects the continuous column values for each data dimension, forming a spiral around the center. For each major interval on the y-axis, there is a dotted circle around the central point, functioning like grid lines to aid in interpreting the data.

Radar graphs enable you to see symmetry or uniformity of continuous data dimensions compared to the categorical column value. You also can compare how the continuous data dimensions compare to one another (the greater the distance between the data points on each spoke, the greater the difference between the data dimension). Further, you can see how much the data fluctuates by observing whether the spiral is smooth or has spikes of variability. Insert Figure 6 illustrates the bond yield graphical data table displayed as a radar graph. From this figure, you can quickly identify which spikes show the most variability within the 3-year period.

Histogram, Distribution, Pie, and Doughnut Graphs

Like most data visualization types, histogram, distribution, pie, and doughnut graphs are used to graphically display summarized data from your prepared business data set. The most common use for these graph types is to compare the distribution (count of distinct values) for one or more discrete columns. In the data preparation chapters, we often made use of these graphs to compare the distribution of the operational data source column to the distribution of the corresponding business data set column to verify that they were the same or similar. For comparing continuous column values, you can use box plots. Refer to Chapters 1 and 4 for a complete discussion on the use of box plots.

Histogram and Distribution Graphs

In the data preparation chapters, the column graph was referred to as a histogram graph, when it was used to investigate the frequency of the number of records grouped by distinct values for the discrete column. In these same chapters, the bar graph was referred to as a distribution graph, when it was used to investigate the frequency and distribution percent of the number of records grouped by the distinct values for the discrete column. Throughout the data preparation chapters, when we analyzed the distribution of more than one discrete column at a time, stacked column and bar graphs were used.

Pie and Doughnut Graphs

These graphs are used to show proportions of a whole. Pie and doughnut graphs are very useful for investigating how discrete column values relate to a larger sum, such as demographic data or budget information. It is easy to get a feel for the relationship between component values when they are placed in a pie graph. However, you need to be careful that you do not have too many slices in the pie, or they will become meaningless. A pie graph is typically used as a snapshot of the business data set at one moment in time. If you want to show relationships as part of a whole over time, you would use an area or line graph. If you want to look at a number of pie graphs at once, you might consider a doughnut graph. Some visualization tools also allow you to highlight slices of the pie by separating them slightly from the pie. You can use this technique to emphasize a particular category.

Insert Figure 8 shows two pie graphs of the average cost of promotion in relation to their major and minor categories for a large computer company. Insert Figure 8a shows the major promotional categories, and Insert Figure 8b shows the subcategories. Instead of displaying the average promotion cost as a dollar figure, the pie graph calculates and displays the percentage that each promotion cost contributes to the whole. Compare these pie graphs with the column and bar graphs from Figure 7.4. Although the same graphical data table was used in Insert Figure 8, the information focus is on the distribution of the promotion budget, whereas in Figure 7.4, the focus was on the actual dollar amount of the promotions. Choosing which type of graph to use will depend on the focus of your business question and the information you are trying to communicate to others.

Scatter Graphs

A scatter graph (also known as a scatter plot) is the simplest type of graph. It merely plots the data points against their values, without adding any connecting lines or bars. The scatter graph is a very neutral tool for investigating and evaluating correlations between two sets of column values. Many other graph types tend to have a psychological implication; for instance, bar graphs imply a comparison and line graphs imply continuity. The scatter graph is a useful visual data mining tool for searching for unbiased patterns in your prepared business data set.

In most cases, the scatter graph is used to show correlations between the values of two or more continuous columns. It is generally not used with time series columns (instead, line graphs are typically used). The vertical axis of a scatter graph charts the "effect" column with the highest end of the scale at the top of the graph. The horizontal axis plots the column of the "potential cause," with values increasing from left to right. Figure 7.7 illustrates how you can use

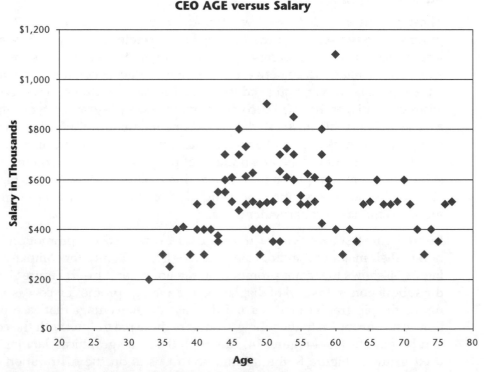

Figure 7.7 Scatter graph of CEO salary versus age.

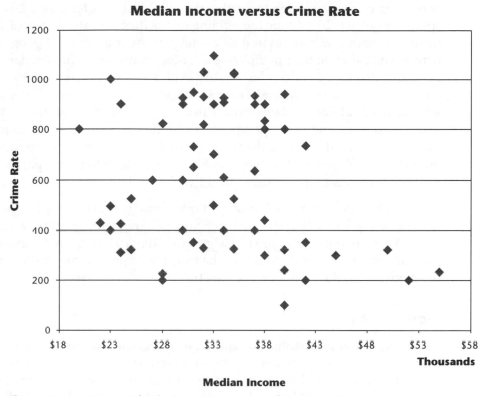

Figure 7.8 Scatter graph of crime rate versus median income.

scatter graphs to investigate the effect on SALARY using AGE as the potential cause. The graphical data table contains the ages and salaries of 60 chief executive officers from around the United States.

Figure 7.8 illustrates how you can use a scatter graph to investigate the effect on CRIME using the median household income of the U.S. state as the potential cause. The data table contains the violent crime rate per 100,000 people and the median household income in 1996 for each of the 50 states. You may notice that although the graphical data table contained information on the STATE, the scatter graph omits the STATE information and only focuses on the patterns of CRIME versus INCOME. In Chapter 8, we will discuss how to analyze and derive conclusions using scatter graphs.

Specialized Landscape and Hierarchical Visualizations

Some specialized data visualization tools allow you to investigate the hierarchical or geographical nature of your prepared business data set. For instance, Microsoft Excel includes a very simple map graph tool, whereas data visualization tools such as MapInfo have entire suites of map visualization tool sets.

You can use the map graph to display the graphical data table as a 2-D or 3-D spatial or geographic picture (depending on the data visualization tool you are using). At least one column in the data table must contain valid geographical names, such as state code or zip code. All other columns in the data table must be aggregated to the geographical entity. With some specialized map visualization tools, you can even create your own custom spatial maps. For example, gene values could be displayed on a map diagram of human chromosome pairs using a column that corresponds to the location on the chromosome map. Likewise, you could create a map of your production floor and investigate failure rates in relation to the "geographical" location where the part is being produced in your manufacturing facility.

Other data visualization tools include a tree visual tool to display the graphical data table in a 2-D or 3-D interactive picture of a tree with branches and leaves (nodes). These tools allow you to assign 1 to N hierarchies from columns in the graphical data table as the levels of the tree. The experimental unit of the data set should be at the lowest level of the tree.

Map Graphs

A map graph is best suited for spatial or geographic analysis. This type of analysis allows you to rank and sort customer data by geographic area, among other attributes, including custom trade areas, such as telecommunication coverage zones. After drilling down through customer records through visual map graphs, you may be able to target customers and areas to be compared, contrasted, and eventually used to both find new customers and determine potential up-sell opportunities among existing customers and territories. Spatial and geographical analysis often reveals patterns and trends in your prepared business data sets that would not have been uncovered in any other way. It shows customer and marketplace demographics at geographical level.

Normally, the graphical data table needs to be aggregated by the geographical attribute you are investigating. Figure 7.9 is a simple map graph of the geographical relationships among male car buyers. Although this figure is very simple, the visualization still would assist a decision maker in determining which states to target for new sports car dealerships (if you were targeting male car buyers).

Tree Graphs

A tree graph is best suited for hierarchical or structural analysis. For example, you could use a tree graph to investigate the hierarchical nature and effectiveness of your sales structure. To display a top-down tree graph of sales by year, you would assign the top of the organization to the tree root level, for example, SALES_VP, the next level of the organization to the level 2, for example,

REGIONAL_MGR, and so on until you reach the lowest level of the hierarchy. Most tree graph tools allow you to map one or more continuous columns to the tree nodes. The values for each continuous column can be assigned a graphical entity such as a box, column, bar, or disk. For example, you could map YEARLY_SALES to the height of the column and display it as the nodes in the tree graph. Most tree graph tools automatically aggregate the total YEARLY_SALES at each level of the tree. So the root level contains the total of total YEARLY SALES for the entire tree structure, level 2 of the tree divides the total by each member of level 2 (REGIONAL_MGR), and so on.

Figure 7.10 illustrates yearly profits by region, by sales branch, and by product type and demonstrates a top-down tree graph. The "root" node or start of the tree shows the aggregation of all profits for the business by product type. The second level of the tree represents three regions that make up the business and shows their contribution to the business by product type. Even without seeing the profit numbers, you can see that there are profit variations by product among the regions from the differences in the height and color of the three region boxes. The third level of the tree represents the sales branches and shows their contribution to each region and so on.

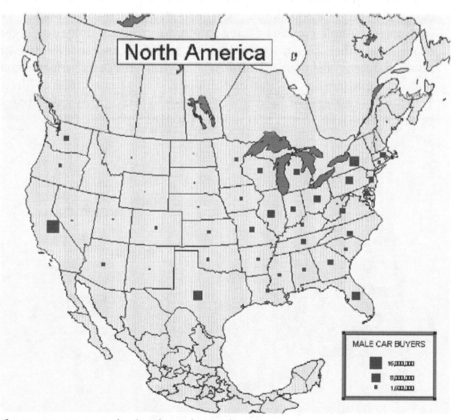

Figure 7.9 Map graph of male car buyers by state.

Figure 7.10 Tree visualization of yearly profits by region by sales branch by product type.

Some tree graph visualization products, such as Inxight Tree Studio, use a spherical graphing technique versus a top-down approach for displaying a tree graph. Figure 7.11 illustrates an interactive tree graph using Inxight that illustrates how to investigate the hierarchical nature of a prepared business data set. For instance, Inxight's Star Tree Studio enables you to create interactive tree graphs or hierarchical structure maps. These tree structures help users easily navigate large amounts of information. Users can quickly view and understand whole Web sites, information directories, catalogues, organization charts, and other large document collections. You can use these tree graphs to investigate the hierarchical structure of your prepared business data set. For more information on Star Tree Studio and this figure, refer to "Inxight Star Tree Studio Example of Bestbuy.com." Inxight Web site at www.inxight.com/products/st_studio/in_action_st.html (Inxight Software, 2002).

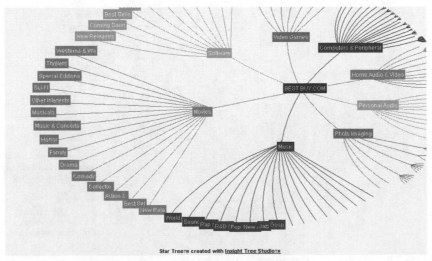

Figure 7.11 Tree graph of structure of www.bestbuy.com.

Choosing the Right Data Mining Tool

The first step to choosing the right tool is determining which tools are able to address the business question, and the second step is determining what specific tool is best suited for the particular situation. There are many data mining techniques that perform the same function using different processes, and each has its own strengths and weaknesses. Two companies may have the same business problem, but might select different tools because of differing environments.

The applicable subset of mining techniques depends on the business question under investigation and how the results will be used. However, before we explain how these issues affect your selection of tool, we need to introduce the two broad tool categories of data mining tools: *supervised* and *unsupervised* (also referred to as directed and undirected). We will introduce and discuss specific examples of supervised and unsupervised tools available in popular commercial data mining packages. From a suitable subset of tools, the best tool depends on the answers to the following questions:

- How accurate are the results of the tool?
- How interpretable are the results; can the domain experts, the data and business analysts, and the decision makers understand it?
- Does the tool produce results quickly?
- How easy is it to implement the results in a production or test environment?
- Can the tool handle the data you have available to mine?

More than likely there will be a trade-off among these issues, and empirical experiments are required for a final decision. A distinct advantage that data mining packages have over individual tools is that they provide a platform to integrate the results of multiple data mining tools. Each data mining technique has its own strengths and weaknesses. Often, combining one or more techniques can overcome some of the weaknesses of a single data mining tool.

Which Subset of the Available Tools Is Applicable?

The business questions to address and how the model will be used are two key issues for determining which subset of available tools is applicable to a situation.

Business Questions to Address

Both visual and analytic data mining tools can address business questions that at the core consist of a specific task. The output from a data mining tool is a *model* of some sort. You can think of a model as a collection of generalizations or patterns found in the business data set that address a task. Data mining tools tend to address one specific problem or task at a time, such as classification, estimation, prediction, association groupings, or clustering and segmentation. Rarely does a single data mining tool (data mining algorithm) address more than one of these specific tasks at a time. For instance, a classification data mining tool typically doesn't perform any clustering or segmentation. Often you will need to use multiple data mining tools to fully address your business question.

We first discussed classification, estimation, prediction, association groupings, and clustering and segmentation in Chapter 3. Let's review these concepts before we further explore choosing the right tool for data mining.

Classification is the process of putting an object into a predetermined distinct category. Each row in the business data set represents an object at the experimental unit level. Every day, banks categorize loan applications as acceptable or not acceptable, insurance companies decide whether to investigate a suspicious claim, and ebusinesses must determine which type of advertisement is most likely to elicit a response from a particular type of customer.

Estimation is very similar to classification. However, with estimation, each object is associated with a continuous value. For example, a telecommunication company may assign a customer a lifetime value in terms of dollars, a credit card company can estimate the dollars an individual will spend in a year, and a warranty provider estimates the number of claims a particular product is likely to generate. We may convert the estimation into categories based on intervals of the estimated value. For instance, you can map customer's lifetime value to low, medium, and high.

Most data mining techniques can be used for prediction, though it is often associated with classification and estimation. Prediction refers to attempting to determine if some event will occur in the future. In the case of classification, the difference between classification and prediction is quite subtle. You can use a classification tool to build a model to classify existing loan applications for explaining what characteristics are associated with loans that default. If you then use that same model to determine whether to give a loan to a new customer, you are using the model for predictive purposes.

Association grouping consists of identifying which entities/items are likely to coexist in some situation. The quintessential example is market basket analysis. Each time a person goes shopping, if the store has the right equipment, it can determine what items the customer has bought (coexist) in his or her visit to the store (situation). If the store were to look at all customers' buying transactions, it can determine if there are any pairs (or groups) of items that customers tend to buy at once. This information can be used for promotions, product placement, or pricing strategies.

Clustering and segmentation is the process of dividing a population of objects into subgroups of like items. We can view clustering as forming categories. For example, a retailer may segment its customers based on demographics and spending habits and then label each group based on the cluster description. The retailer may then send out product promotions that appeal to their different tastes.

How Is the Model to Be Used?

Each data mining tool produces a model of some sort. The intended use of the model plays a key role in determining if the technique is applicable. For instance, your data mining tool selection depends on whether you plan to deploy the data mining model into a production environment or whether you only plan to use the model to provide explanation and insights.

The same model may have different uses depending on the business environment. Consider a model that can predict which insurance customers are likely to cross-sell (buy another type of insurance). An Internet insurance company may deploy this model into the server software to automatically display an advertisement when a suitable type of customer logs on. An agent-based insurance company may use this model as part of its training material to explain the characteristics of customers that have a propensity to cross-sell.

Some models are easily deployable in a few lines of most procedural languages or SQL; other models require deployment using a complex program. The understandability of how the model is making its decisions is also important. Some data mining tools can provide excellent results but are black boxes, giving little insight into how they get their results.

Supervised and Unsupervised Learning

As mentioned earlier in the chapter, data mining tools consist of two categories: supervised or unsupervised. The business questions may be approached using either or both of these categories, often depending on what data is available and the expectations of the VDM project. Consider the task of differentiating between automobile insurance claims that are fraudulent or nonfraudulent. To help us, a domain expert team may have created a data set of examples that contain many columns describing the claim and added a column that labels if the claim is fraudulent or not. In this data set, the *dependent* column is another name for the label, which we try to predict from the remaining *independent* columns. After we have studied the examples, we should be able to better classify claims as being fraudulent or not, without seeing the dependent column value. Supervised learning is learning by examples where we use the examples to find patterns that differentiate between dependent column values. Classification, estimation, and prediction are typical tasks that supervised learning can address. Unsupervised learning does not have the benefit of teacher labeled examples; instead, it attempts to find patterns intrinsic to the data. Consider the previous example of identifying fraudulent claims if there were no labels in the example set. We could group the examples so that similar claims are in the same group and then try to describe each group. During this process, we may identify groups that have unusual descriptions (for example, the damage to the car may be small, but the medical cost of settling the claim is large). The description of these groups can identify potentially fraudulent claims. The aim is for the data mining techniques to find patterns that are, for example, interesting or frequent.

Each technique has its own benefits and problems. A model built using supervised learning can only learn what is implicitly contained in the examples. If there is a type of fraud that we have no examples of, then our model cannot learn this behavior, but an unsupervised learning technique may discover this type of claim. However, unsupervised learning may result in many legitimate claims being labeled as fraudulent.

Supervised Learning Tools

Functionally supervised learning tools take as input a data set consisting of independent columns and one or more dependent columns. The tool produces a *model* whose purpose is to suggest the value of the dependent column from the independent columns. A model is analogous to a machine. It contains the patterns, regularities, or generalization found in the training data set. The model can process new data and label an unseen example. The supervised learning tools available in data mining packages differ by:

- The type of dependent column they predict (binary, multi-nominal, or continuous)
- The type of patterns they can represent
- The method used to search for patterns

For example, a decision tree tool can build a model that predicts a single dependent column that is discrete. A tree structure represents the patterns as a series of decision points at each branch until we reach a leaf node. Each leaf node is associated with a particular value of the dependent column. Most decision tree tools use a quick local search technique.

Decision Trees and Rule Set Models

Decision tree tools build models that can predict a discrete dependent column. Example dependent columns may be Fraud or Not Fraud, Lifetime Value of Low, Medium, or High, and Churn or Retain. To interpret a decision tree model, you begin at the root node and follow the paths or branches extending from the root node. Each full path through the tree shows the decision rules for classifying one or more records. Depending on the column values of the record and the decision points at each node in the tree, a record's path will lead to a leaf node that is associated with a value of the dependent column.

Code Figure 7.3 demonstrates the SQL query to generate the data set we will use to illustrate the various data mining techniques. The data set is of customers' responses to a home equity loan campaign. The REPONSE column is the dependent column for supervised learning examples. In this case, the discrete column values are either 0 or 1, where 0 indicates the customer did not respond to the home equity loan campaign and 1 indicates the customer responded. In this business data set, the values of the RESPONSE column are what the data mining models will be trying to predict. Insert Figure 9 illustrates using a tree graph to show the rules discovered by the decision tree data mining tool. You can use the tree graph to visually investigate what factors (values and ranges of the other columns in the data set) were most important to why customers respond to the home equity loan campaign.

In the tree graph of the decision tree model, the root node states that if the value of the discrete column OWN_CAR is Y (yes), then follow the right path, if N (no), then follow the left path. If the record value of NUM_DEBITS_MTD was less than or equal to $442.8, then the left branch would be taken. Taking the left branch results in arriving at a leaf node whose associated value for RESPONSE is 0 (i.e., the person isn't interested in a home equity loan). You can use each path decision tree model to develop business rules that will predict which customers to include or exclude from your target marketing campaign.

```
SELECT      response,
            annual_income,
            smart_banking,
            num_debits_mtd,
            loan,
            loan_to_value_ratio,
            mortgage_age,
            occ_prof,
            age_primary,
            buying_power,
            own_car,
            use_credit_card,
            customer_financing,
            education_level,
            saving_acctn,
            teaser_rate
FROM RESPOND;
```

Code Figure 7.3 SQL query to create the training set of labeled records.

The marketing team can use the business rules you discover to selectively contact those customers most likely to respond. The power of data mining is the ability to reduce marketing costs by using models to increase your campaign's effectiveness. Chapter 8 will discuss analyzing data mining models in more detail, as well as methods for calculating your return-on-investment.

Most data mining packages use the efficient approach of incrementally building the decision tree from the root node using a number of different criteria to determine the column and decision point in a node. "Boosting" and "bagging" (see Appendix for definitions) are recent developments in the decision tree technology that use an ensemble of multiple trees to build more complex models that may be more accurate at the expense of complexity and interpretability.

Neural Network Models for Classification

Neural networks are a general class of learning techniques useful for both supervised and unsupervised learning. They are simple models of the neural connections that exist in brains. The network consists of an input layer of nodes that represent the columns to learn from, an output layer of nodes that represent the classification task, and a number of hidden layers of nodes. Figure 7.12 illustrates a simple neural network.

Each node is analogous to a biological neuron that combines its multiple inputs into a single output that it broadcasts to all connected nodes. The activation function within each node performs the combination, and there are many types of such functions. Most activation functions are of the type where the output value remains low until the combined inputs reach an activation threshold when the neuron is activated and produces a high output. Each input into a neuron has a weight that indicates its significance to the neuron.

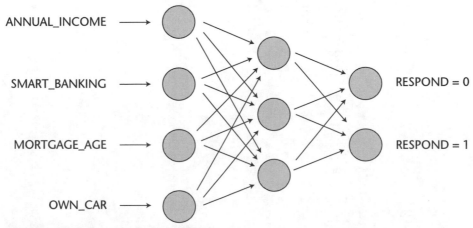

Figure 7.12 Example of a neural network.

When the neural network model is learning how to predict the dependent value, it is busily changing the weights in the network to try to obtain a good model. Most neural networks in data mining packages are examples of feed-forward networks whose weights are learned using the back-propagation algorithm.

If the activation functions take a linear combination of input values, the neural network is really just performing linear regression. The power of neural networks to find interesting patterns is evident when nonlinear activation functions such as the commonly used sigmoid or hyperbolic functions are used. The network is then effectively using a nonlinear combination of the independent columns to predict the record label, which in practice has obtained excellent results in many domains. However, the model produced by a neural network for a given activation function and network connection is a series of weights for every node that are difficult to understand and gain insight from.

Linear Regression Models

Linear regression models can estimate or predict a continuous dependent column. For instance, the data mining business question may be to predict the buying power of an individual from his or her demographic and loan-related information. The model is a simple linear equation with the dependent column being equal to the independent column values multiplied by a constant. This means that the independent columns can only be continuous value columns. Code Figure 7.4 demonstrates a linear regression model generated from the home equity loan campaign business data set.

In Code Figure 7.4, the linear regression model is attempting to calculate the value of the continuous BUYING_POWER column as a function of the other columns in the data set. If the coefficient of a column is near zero, it means it is independent of BUYING_POWER and does not appear to influence it in a way different than any another column. Columns with a positive coefficient correlate positively with the BUYING_POWER, whereas those with negative coefficients are negatively correlated.

```
Equation for BUYING_POWER
BUYING_POWER =
      0.152640 * TEASURE_RATE      +
     -0.144398 * AGE_PRIMARY       +
      0.125365 * MORTGAGE_AGE      +
     -1.111479 * LOAN_TO_VALUE_RATIO +
      0.000104 * NUM_DEBITS_MTD +
     -0.001447 * ANNUAL_INCOME + 6.299050
```

Code Figure 7.4 Example linear regression model.

Data mining tools typically build linear regression models using an approach that attempts to fit a straight line to the dependent column values with an error function that minimizes the square of the difference between the actual and calculated/predicted dependent column values.

Logistic Regression

Logistic regression models are similar to linear regression models but predict a discrete dependent column. A set of equations is used to calculate the dependent column value from the independent columns, which can be both continuous and discrete columns. From the equations, a probability can be associated with each value of the dependent column for a given record. Table 7.2 lists a logistic regression model generated from the home equity loan campaign business data set. We see that the big drivers of positive responses are the LOAN_TO_VALUE_RATIO and if an individual actively uses this bank's-credit card (two most positive coefficient scores). Customers that do not own a

Table 7.2 Example Logistic Regression Model

RESPONSE=0 (FALSE)	COEFFICIENT
Intercept	1.875
ANNUAL_INCOME	0.0
SMART_BANKING	-0.375
NUM_DEBITS_MTD	0.0
LOAN_TO_VALUE_RATIO	0.450
MORTGAGE_AGE	-0.008
OCC_PROF	0.0
AGE_PRIMARY	-0.036
BUYING_POWER	0.021
SAVING_ACCTN	-0.141
TEASER_RATE	-0.04
OWN_CAR=N	-1.008
OWN_CAR=Y	0.0
USE_CREDIT_CARD=Y	0.538
CONSUMER_FINANCING=N	0.180
EDUCATION_LEVEL=H	0.025
EDUCATION_LEVEL=M	0.0
EDUCATION_LEVEL=L	0.326

car, use smart banking, and have savings accounts (OWN_CAR, SMART_ BANKING and SAVINGS_ACCTN) are quite unlikely to respond to the campaign (two most negative coefficient scores).

You can use Table 7.2 to investigate and evaluate the coefficients of the independent columns for this logistic regression model. The dependent column value will be predicted using a logarithmic transformation of the independent columns.

Unsupervised Learning Tools

Functionally, unsupervised learning techniques take as input a collection of records and attempt to find patterns within and amongst them. The types of patterns and the search process to find them differ from tool to tool.

Association Rules

Association rules look for patterns in the form of combinations of column values that frequently occur in a record. Consider the typical market basket example database that consists of many records, each of which represents the items bought by a customer for a single trip to the supermarket. An association rule algorithm would attempt to find the most frequently occurring combination of items bought in one trip. An association rule model consists of a series of rules that state the presence of one or more items implies the presence of another item such as "IF MILK THEN COOKIES". Association rule tools are effectively trying to count every combination of items, though most tools use clever approaches to speed up the process. Different association rule algorithms typically differ in how quickly they can count the commonly occurring items and the size of the combinations allowed (pairwise or greater).

Association rule tools can find huge numbers of patterns. To focus on the patterns of interest, often the user must provide a definition of what is interesting. This definition takes the form of support and confidence. *Support* is how often the combination occurs as a portion of the entire number of records in the data set, whereas *confidence* is the number of records that contained all the items in the rule divided by the number of records that contained only the items in the "if" part of the rule.

Table 7.3 lists the association rules generated from the home equity loan campaign business data set for the RESPONSE, USE_CREDIT_CARD, and OWN_CAR columns. These rules have a minimum support of 5 percent of all records in the data set and 50 percent confidence. From this list of associations, you can see what values of the records often co-occur. For example, a positive response to the campaign is likely if the MORTGAGE_AGE is > 0.5 or the ANNUAL_INCOME > 408.5 and MORTGAGE_AGE < 30.5. In this case, the discovered association rules can be used for prediction or exploratory analysis.

Table 7.3 Example Association Rule Model

CONSEQUENT COLUMN	FIRST ANTECEDENT RULE	SECOND ANTECEDENT RULE
RESPONSE = 1.0	MORTGAGE_AGE > 0.5	
RESPONSE= 1.0	ANNUAL_INCOME> 408.5	MORTGAGE_AGE < 30.5
USE_CREDIT_CARD= Y	AGE_PRIMARY > 11.5	ANNUAL_INCOME > 278.5
USE_CREDIT_CARD=Y	ANNUAL_INCOME > 453.5	AGE_PRIMARY > 9.5
USE_CREDIT_CARD=Y	AGE_PRIMARY > 11.5	
USE_CREDIT_CARD=Y	MORTGAGE_AGE > 11.5	
OWN_CAR=N	AGE_PRIMARY > 5.5	
OWN_CAR=N	ANNUAL_INCOME < 585.0	AGE_PRIMARY > 8.5

The first column in Table 7.3 lists the consequent column value. The second column lists the first antecedent rule. The third column lists the second antecedent rule. For the home equity loan campaign, the column MORTGAGE_AGE contains the age of the mortgage is in years, ANNUAL_ INCOME contains the weekly household income, and AGE_PRIMARY contains the age of the primary mortgage holder.

K-Means and Clustering

K-means and other forms of clustering attempt to divide a collection of records into a specified number of subgroups (clusters) so that records within the subgroup are as similar to each other as possible. Functionally, clustering takes as input the collection of records, assigns each record to a cluster, and produces a model that describes the cluster in terms of the column values in the business data set. Some less frequently occurring tools assign a fraction of the record to more than one cluster. Clustering tools are iterative in nature and try different combinations of record groupings with an aim to minimize an implicit objective function. Table 7.4 illustrates a K-means model generated from the home equity loan campaign business data set. Often you develop a general descriptive profile of the customer segment based on the information discovered about each particular cluster, as well as by comparing the differences between clusters. Table 7.4 shows three clusters that contain varying number of records. Cluster 1 contains nearly 16,000 established customers. These customers have savings accounts with the bank, considerable equity in their home, and mortgages that are on average over 20 years old. Cluster 2 also contains established

Table 7.4 Example K-Means Clustering Model

CLUSTER	RECORDS IN CLUSTER	IMPORTANT COLUMNS	COLUMN VALUES
#1	15,905	LOAN_TO_VALUE_RATIO, MORTGAGE_AGE, AGE_PRIMARY, SAVING_ACCTN	3.972144, 21.128848, 13.891789, 0.806162
#2	20,095	LOAN_TO_VALUE_RATIO, MORTGAGE_AGE, AGE_PRIMARY, SAVING_ACCTN	4.61501, 22.477576, 14.649711, 0.0
#3	8,124	LOAN_TO_VALUE_RATIO, MORTGAGE_AGE, AGE_PRIMARY, SAVING_ACCTN	0.587867, 7.610288 13.568685, 0.12223

customers, but who do not have savings accounts with the bank. Cluster 3 contains predominantly new home loan customers who have little equity in their homes. Therefore, you may want to refer to cluster 1 as established customers with saving accounts, cluster 2 as established customers without savings accounts, and cluster 3 as new home loan customers.

Kohonen Self-Organizing Maps

Self-organizing maps (SOMs; also called Kohonen maps after their pioneer, Teuvo Kohonen) are a type of neural network that can be used to group records together into clusters. The pragmatic outcome of a SOM is a collection of clusters like the output of the K-means algorithm, but the two tools use quite different approaches. The SOM consists of an input layer of units and usually a two-dimensional grid of output units. One typical topological difference between neural networks for predictions and SOMs are that in SOMs each unit in the output layers is fully connected to all input layer units and there is no hidden layer. The SOM is effectively performing dimension reduction by taking the similarities between the records based on the many columns in the data set and mapping them onto a two-dimensional grid while trying to preserve and correctly represent these similarities. A two-dimensional output grid is often used because of SOM's historical use in visual pattern recognition.

We can view the output layer as being a two-dimensional topological grid that modifies itself as the SOM is trained on the records in the data set. The grid modifies or adapts itself as the SOM is fed records in the data set. Some of the units in the output layer will develop to become more pronounced and representative of the data; others will be associated with few records and add little value to the model. From the output layer we can identify those adjacent strong units that define a cluster. Unlike K-means clustering, SOMs do not require the user to specify the number of clusters to form. The SOM performs this function implicitly.

In the SOM learning process each unit in the output grid is in competition to obtain each record in the data set. When the unit wins a record, it and its neighbors adjust their weights to better match the record. The final model typically consists of a small number of units that represent many records. These units are the dominating clusters and a few units do not represent any of the observations. Though SOMs will assign each record to a cluster, like neural networks for classification they do not specify an easy-to-understand model. Instead, the user must examine the output layer to determine what collection of strong units form the clusters and then calculate the typical values for records in the same cluster. Calculating the mean for continuous columns and calculating a frequency distribution for discrete columns can achieve this.

Tools to Solve Typical Problems

Table 7.5 lists the data mining tool by the core data mining task it can address. Table 7.6 lists attributes of the resultant data mining model by the data mining tool as they are typically implemented in commercial data mining packages. You can use these two tables to help determine the applicability of the data mining tool. Often data mining packages can easily combine different tools to overcome deficiencies. For example, a decision tree can learn the behavior of a neural network, thereby adding the explanation capability to neural networks.

Which of the Applicable Tools Are Best for My Situation?

Once we identify a subset of tools, it then becomes a case of determining the best tool. You need to first determine if the tool is suited to your organization's environment and then determine its suitability to your organization's data. For example, in some organizations accuracy is very important, while in others a very accurate model is of no use unless it can be explained to regulators. Your organization may have data that contains many discrete columns, while others may contain data that is predominantly continuous columns. Often it is impossible to tell beforehand which tool is the best without conducting experiments, particularly in the area of model accuracy and performance, which we discuss in more detail in the next chapter. However, the subset of applicable tools can be narrowed down by considering, with respect to your organizational environment, the strengths and weaknesses of the type of model produced, and the type of data to mine.

Table 7.5   Data Mining Tool by the Core Data Mining Tasks They Address

DATA MINING TOOL	DIRECTED CLASSIFICATION	ESTIMATION	PREDICTION	AFFINITY GROUPING	CLUSTERING AND SEGMENTING	EXPLANATION
Decision trees	✓		✓			✓
Neural networks	✓		✓			
Linear regression		✓	✓			✓
Logistic regression	✓		✓			✓
Association rules			✓	✓		
Clustering			✓		✓	✓
SOMs			✓		✓	

Table 7.6   Attributes of Resulting Model by Data Mining Tool

RESULTING MODEL	DECISION TREES	NEURAL NETWORKS	LINEAR REGRESSION	LOGISTIC REGRESSION	ASSOCIATION RULES	CLUSTERING
Produces deployable model	✓	✓	✓	✓		✓
Produces insights into processes	✓		✓	✓	✓	✓

Table 7.7 lists the strengths and weaknesses of the implementations of typical techniques found in data mining packages. Data mining is an active research area, and new versions of existing tools and new tools may address deficiencies listed below.

Following is an explanation of the columns in Table 7.7, and a discussion of the strengths and weaknesses of data mining tools:

Effectiveness. For supervised learning, typically how accurate are the models? The accuracy and performance will vary from problem to problem, but our comments are for the overall situation. More complicated models such as boosted or bagged decision trees (see Appendix) can potentially provide better performance but at the cost of interpretability. For unsupervised learning, how good are the techniques for finding nontrivial useful patterns?

Interpretability. Interpretability relates to how easily a domain expert or non-data-mining-knowledgeable person can understand a model produced from this technique.

Ease of Implementation. How easy is it to implement the model in a production and test environment? This directly relates to the complexity of the model. A boosted decision tree or neural network model is more complicated to implement than a logistic regression model. A few lines in most programming languages can implement a logistic regression model, whereas neural networks require sophisticated constructs such as pointers to implement efficiently. We can implement a model from tools such as decision trees in nonprogramming languages like SQL, though records with missing values will cause problems.

Model Generation Time. A data mining tool searches for patterns that make up the model. How quickly this search occurs varies from tool to tool. Some tools, such as association rules, are more computationally intensive in nature, since they perform a global search, while decision trees perform a local search.

Associated Degree of Belief (Risk Assessment). Can the models associate a degree of belief or certainty for tasks such as prediction? The degree of belief can rank the predictions so that perhaps only the top-ranked, strongest predictions are used. This is particularly useful in sensitive tasks such as insurance fraud detection, where accuracy is paramount. For unsupervised learning tasks such as clustering, can a degree of belonging or distance to a cluster be calculated?

Model Can Be Visualized. Can the model be easily visualized to gain insight into how it scores new unseen examples? This is particularly important for monitoring the model after deployment. Consider a decision tree deployed

Table 7.7 Strengths and Weaknesses of Data Mining Tools

DATA MINING TOOL	EFFECTIVENESS	INTERPRETA-BILITY	EASE OF IMPLEMEN-TATION	MODEL GENERATION TIME	ASSOCIATED DEGREE OF BELIEF	MODEL CAN BE VISUALIZED	SUITABLE FOR PROOF-OF-CONCEPT WORK
Decision trees	Good	Excellent	Good	Fast	Yes	Yes	Yes
Ensemble of decision trees	Excellent	Not good	Not good	Slow	Yes	No	No
Neural networks	Excellent	Not good	Not good	Slow	Yes	No	No
Linear regression	Good	Excellent	Excellent	Fast	No	No	Yes
Logistic regression	Good	Excellent	Excellent	Fast	Yes	No	Yes
Association rules	Good	Excellent	Good	Slow	Yes	Yes	Yes
Clustering	Good	Excellent	Good	Fast	Yes	Yes	Yes
SOMs	Good	Good	Not good	Slow	No	No	No

for cross-selling purposes. We would want to visualize for presentation purposes how the model is performing with respect to different types of cases. For each path in a decision tree, we can contrast the actual behavior against expected behavior.

Suitable for Proof-of-Concept Work. Most projects start with a short phase that requires proof that data mining can add value. This requires a data mining tool to produce models that are easy to explain, can be quickly generated, and produce reasonable results. This technique may not be the final technique used, but it can demonstrate the worth of data mining to a potential problem.

More than likely there will be a trade-off between competing requirements in your VDM project, and very often empirical experiments are required to make a final tool selection decision. The Two Crows Report is an extensive review of the commercial data mining tools. For more information on this report, refer to "Data Mining '99: Technology Report" from the Two Crows Web site, at www. twocrows.com/publictn.htm. (Two Crows, 2002).

How the Different Techniques Handle Data Types

Because of their underlying computational nature and implementation in commercial data mining packages, particular techniques may or may not be well suited to the number of records, data types, number of columns, and so forth in a data set. In this section, some well-known strengths and limitations are discussed. Some data mining algorithms cannot handle a specific data type (designated by "No"), while others become very slow if this data type occurs in abundance. Table 7.8 lists how the data mining tools handle different business data sets. Your choice of data mining tool depends on the business question under investigation and also the properties of your business data set.

Following is an explanation of the columns in Table 7.8, and a discussion of strengths and weaknesses of the various data mining techniques with respect to the type of data sets they can handle:

Number of Dependent Columns. The dependent or target column is the column we are trying to predict. Some problems have multiple dependent columns; for example, is the driver likely to have an accident and will the cost of the damage inflicted be low, medium, or high. Often it makes sense to make two separate models for each dependent column, but sometimes the simplicity of one model to predict both dependent columns is desirable.

Ability to Handle Many Independent Discrete Columns. Can the tool efficiently handle many discrete independent columns per row in the business data set? A discrete column takes on a finite (usually small) number of discrete values that have no ordinal structure. Colors, gender, zip code, and state are examples of discrete columns.

Table 7.8 Properties of the Business Data Set by Data Mining Tool

BUSINESS DATA SET PROPERTY	DECISION TREES	NEURAL NETWORKS	LINEAR REGRESSION	LOGISTIC REGRESSION	ASSOCIATION RULES	CLUSTERING	SOMS
Number of Dependent Columns	1	>1	1	1	0	0	0
Ability to Handle Many Independent Discrete Columns	Excellent	Fair	No	Fair (1)	Fair	Good	Fair
Ability to handle many independent continuous columns	Excellent	Fair	Excellent	Excellent	No	Good	Fair
Ability to handle many values for discrete columns	Excellent	Fair (2)	No	Good (1)	Fair	Good	Fair (2)
Ability to handle many rows/records in data set	Excellent	Fair	Excellent	Good	Fair	Good	Fair
Ability to handle many missing values in independent columns	Excellent	Fair	Fair (3)	No	No	Good	Fair

(1) Logistic regression algorithms often try to generate interactive terms for discrete columns, which can slow down the algorithm.

(2) Some neural network packages use one in N coding to represent discrete values. This means if the discrete column has N values, it will be represented as N input neurons.

(3) Linear regression algorithms often have the option to ignore records with missing values, this option can be turned off, but the resulting models are not as effective.

Ability to Handle Many Independent Continuous Columns. Can the tool efficiently handle many continuous independent columns per row in the business data set? A continuous column is a number that may or may not be an integer. Integral examples include number of children, bank loans, and cars; real number examples include income, premium cost, and loan amount.

Ability to Handle Many Values for Discrete Columns. Can the tool efficiently handle discrete columns that have many values?

Ability to Handle Many Rows/Records in Data Set. Can the tool efficiently handle data sets with many records?

Ability to Handle Many Missing Values in Independent Columns. A record that does not have a value for a particular independent column is an example of a missing value. This can be overcome a number of ways, such as replacing the missing value, with the population mean for a continuous column or with the mode for a discrete column. However, in some circumstances this does not make sense, and we need a technique that can handle data with many missing values.

Choosing the Visualization or Mining Tool for the Case Study

According to the VDM project plan outlined in Chapter 2, Step 6 should take approximately 5 working days to complete. The tasks for Step 6 are assigned to the data and business analyst team.

The previous three chapters were devoted to ensuring that the correct columns of information were selected from the operational data sources and that data was correctly extracted, cleansed, transformed, and loaded into the exploratory data mart to create business data sets. Logical transforming were applied to the production business data set to enhance the information contained within the data set, to remove bias, and to facilitate visualizing and data mining of the customer retention business data set. The results of these efforts were two business data sets:

- The first business data set, called *customer_join,* combines information from the customer, contract, and aggregated invoice operational data source tables. This business data set contains 20 pieces of information on 464,916 Big Cellular phone customers.

- The second business data, called *customer_demographic,* adds 10 pieces of demographic information to the *customer_join* business set. Since the marketing department only purchased demographic information on a subset of the customer base, this table only contains information on 96,258 Big Cellular phone customers.

From these prepared business data sets, the first task is to select the appropriate data visualization tools to address the data visualization business questions for Big Cellular identified in the case study section in Chapter 3. The next task is to select the best data mining tools to address their data mining questions.

Choosing the Data Visualization Tools

One of the data visualization business questions that Big Cellular phone company had was how can it accurately identify their customer attrition rate and what is it costing them. From the interviews in Chapter 2, the customer service department estimated the 4-year customer attrition rate at 36 percent, the billing department estimated it at 24 percent, and the data warehousing department estimated it at 18 percent. Which figure is correct?

Figure 7.13 illustrates the use of column graphs to investigate the customer attrition rate by activation date. The column graph was chosen because we are searching for trends between discrete intervals (1996 to 1999). The domain experts define the activation date as the customer sign-up date; it ranges from 09/23/1996 to 08/12/1999. So in reality, the business data set only covers part of 1996, all of 1997 and 1998, and most of 1999. The stacked column graph in Figure 7.13a shows the record count for both the loyal and lost customers by activation year. This graph can be used to show the overall yearly growth of new customer activations, as well as the decline in lost customers. The stacked column graph in Figure 7.13b also shows both loyal and lost customer by activation year; however, only the percentages of loyal versus lost customers is used. In both column graphs, the activation year was used as the aggregation or group by column. Since the years 1996 and 1999 are not completely covered by the business data set, Figure 7.13a is inaccurate for these years. Since Figure 7.13b uses percentages to normalize the data, the years 1996 and 1999 are estimated customer attrition rates, while the years 1997 and 1998 are actual customer attrition rates. Normalization techniques are often used when a complete set of data is unavailable or when using a sample of the data set. In this case, the customer attrition rates shown in Figure 7.13b would not vary significantly even if the business data set had contained data for the entire years for 1996 and 1999.

Figure 7.14 illustrates the use of column graphs to investigate the customer attrition rate using the contract renewal date as the aggregation or group by column. The only difference between the graphs in Figure 7.14 and in Figure 7.13 is the aggregation or group by column. Which set of graphs depicts the true customer attrition rates? In the introduction to this chapter, it was stated that

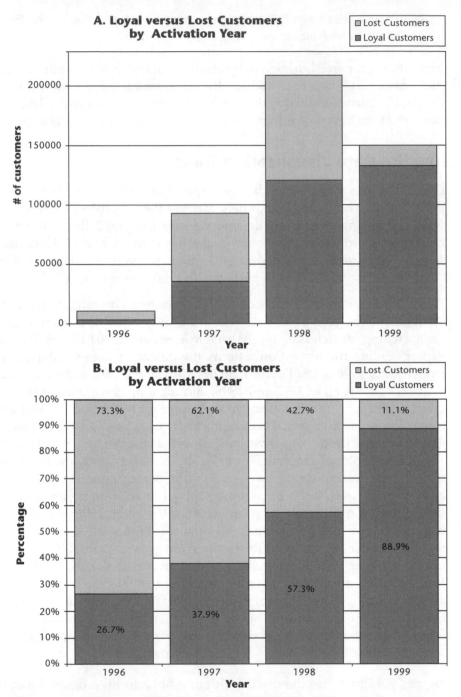

Figure 7.13 Column graphs of loyal versus lost customers by activation year.

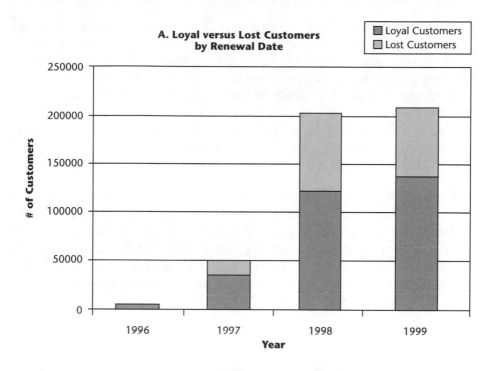

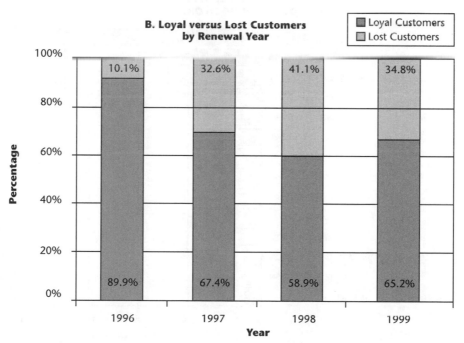

Figure 7.14 Column graphs of loyal versus lost customers by renewal year.

data visualizations send a very powerful message to people. Therefore, care must be taken to choose the right data visualization tool that effectively communicates accurate and significant information and data mining discoveries uncovered about the prepared business data set to other business analysts and the decision makers. As illustrated in Figures 7.13 and 7.14, the graphical data set selection criteria dramatically changes the information in the column graphs. In Chapter 9, we will discuss verifying the analysis. At that time, we will need to verify with the domain experts which time-based column should be used for calculating the customer attrition rates.

The magnitude of the customer attrition problem is illustrated in Figure 7.15. The bar graph was chosen because we are comparing categories of a single data dimension (churn reason). From the bar graph, you can see that approximately 35 percent of all customers from 09/23/1996 through 8/12/1999 were either canceled or dropped their service. In 12 percent of the cases, Big Cellular canceled the customer's service because the customer wasn't paying (BILLING NONPAY and REACT-BILLING NONPAY).

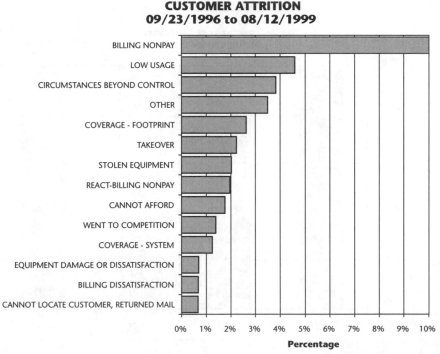

CUSTOMER ATTRITION
09/23/1996 to 08/12/1999

Figure 7.15 Distribution graph of customer attrition 09/23/1996 to 08/12/1999.

Figure 7.16 investigates the total cost of customer attrition from 09/23/1996 through 08/12/1999. The total cost of customer attrition for this time period was just over $4 million. In Figure 7.16, it is interesting to compare the dollar cost in lost revenue versus the actual number of lost (or canceled) customers from Figure 7.15. For instance, even though only 2 percent of customer attrition was REACT-BILLING NONPAY, they cost Big Cellular phone company approximately $1.3 million.

As illustrated in Figures 7.13 through 7.16, using data visualization enables you to not only investigate the business question but also to focus on different aspects of the problem. From these data visualizations, new questions have arisen that must be discussed with the business analysts, domain experts, and decision makers. For instance, what time basis should be used to determine the attrition rate (activation date or contract renewal date). More importantly, should the analysis be based on the number of customers or the total cost to Big Cellular? The answers to these questions will be addressed in Chapters 8 and 9. In Chapter 8, the visualizations are analyzed, and in Chapter 9 the analysis is verified with the domain experts and other data and business analysts before being presented to the decision makers.

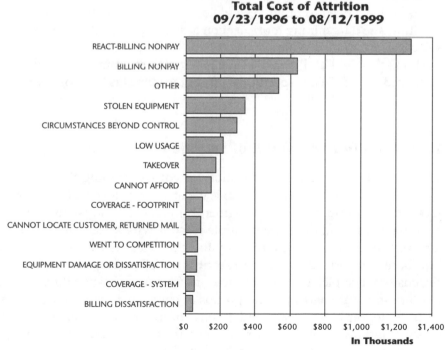

Figure 7.16   Bar graph of the total cost of customer attrition 09/23/1996 to 08/12/1999.

Choosing the Data Mining Tools

We can gain a lot of insight from visualizations of the data and raise many questions that need answers, but at times, useful patterns are too complex or too many to visually represent. This is when analytic data mining tools are useful complements to visualizations. From the discussion of the customer attrition business problem in Chapters 2 and 3, four key data mining business questions were identified:

Question 1: What are the profiles of the individuals who are leaving Big Cellular?

Question 2: Can we predict *if* an individual is going to churn?

Question 3: Can we predict *when* an individual is going to churn?

Question 4: Can we explain *why* an individual will churn?

The data mining answer to question 1 will be a descriptive model. The answers to questions 2 and 3 will be a deployable data mining model that can be implemented within the data warehouse. The answer to question 4 will be a description of the model used in question 2. Another important factor in determining the data mining tool is the type of VDM project. In this case, the customer attrition VDM project was defined and budgeted as a pilot project. Therefore, we need to build, test, validate, and deploy the models quickly. In addition, the data mining tool selection is dependent on the answers to the tool selection questions "Which subset of the available tools is applicable to my business problem and how will the resulting data mining model be used or deployed?" and "What specific tool from the subset is best for my situation?"

Tuning the Data Mining Tool Selection

The data mining solution for question 1 involves profiling the lost customers. We can profile the individuals who leave at various levels of granularity. One method is to simply have two segments, the lost and loyal customers. However, we know that there are multiple reasons why a customer left Big Cellular. We could profile the churners by these reasons, as we have in Figure 7.17, but these categories may not necessarily be the best segments, since we force the customer to pick one of these reasons for leaving Big Cellular. We can use clustering to automatically find groups of churners based on the similarity of their demographic, contract, and invoice information. We can even profile the clusters and see how the churn reason varies across them to see if there are other reasons why customers left Big Cellular.

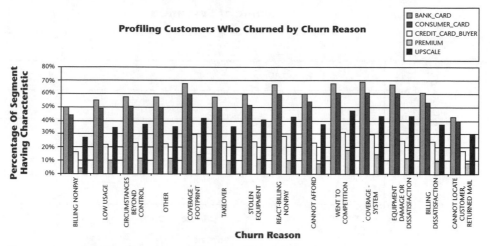

Figure 7.17   Profile of customers who churn by churn reasons.

The data mining solution for question 2 involves developing a model to classify each record in the business data set into either a Churn or Not Churn category. The data mining solution to question 4 requires explaining why the churn decision was made. The model generated to answer question 2 can be used for this purpose.

The data mining solution for question 3 is a difficult problem given that our business data set does not provide a specific date of defection from Big Cellular. We can, however, use the number of invoices to determine a customer's tenure. We can attempt to predict this information for a customer, but it will be simpler and more pragmatic to categorize customers as being recent or long-term defection chances. Figure 7.18 shows that the tenure of all customers both active and terminated in months.

In terms of data mining tasks, question 1 is a clustering task, question 2 is a prediction task, question 3 is a prediction task, and question 4 is an explanation task for the decisions made for question 2. From Tables 7.5 and 7.6, we can determine the following applicable tools:

Question 1: SOM or K-means clustering.

Questions 2 and 4: We need a tool that can perform classification and prediction, and explain the results; logistic regression and decision trees have these capabilities.

Question 3: We can use the tool found to provide best results in question 2.

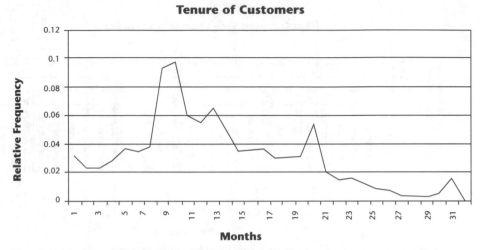

Figure 7.18 Tenure of customers in months.

These are the subsets of tools to handle the questions. We can now make use of Tables 7.7 and 7.8 to see if we can potentially narrow this down. As stated earlier, the data mining tool choice will be a trade-off between many of the features listed in the tables, and we should involve the other stakeholders in the project to prioritize them. From our knowledge of the pilot project so far, we need to quickly build and validate the results. For question 1, we can use K-means clustering, as we can quickly obtain results. For questions 2 and 4, we will need to see which technique—logistic regression or decision trees—obtain better and easily explainable results.

Summary

Step 6 focuses on choosing an appropriate data visualization or data mining tool for answering your business questions. In the first part of this chapter, we discussed which multi-dimensional graph types are appropriate for investigating comparative data visualization business questions. Then we discussed which specialized landscape and hierarchical visualizations, such as map and tree graphs, are best suited for investigation, hierarchical, or geographical business questions. In the second part of this chapter, we discussed which data mining tools are appropriate for investigating your data mining business questions and then discussed how to evaluate which data mining tools are best, based upon your specific situation.

Now that the tools have been chosen, we will focus on how to analyze and derive insights from the data visualization and data mining models. In Chapter 8, we will concentrate on how you can use data visualizations and data mining to recognize patterns and trends in your business data set, how to interpret the patterns and trends, and how to quantitatively measure the significance of the discovered trends and patterns.

Step 7: Analyzing the Visualization or Mining Tool

The second step of the data analysis phase is analyzing the data visualizations and visually evaluating the resulting data mining algorithms created in the previous chapter. Step 7 of the VDM methodology is using data visualization to acquire insight and understanding into the prepared business data set to assist you in answering your business questions. This chapter focuses on interpreting what the data visualizations are showing you about your prepared business data set and what information can be derived to answer business questions such as what are the sales trends year-to-date, what are the key business indicators as to why customers are leaving, which customer segment is most likely to buy a new product, or which customers are most likely to upgrade their service. Finally, we apply Step 7 to the ongoing customer retention business case study.

In this chapter, we provide examples of how you can use data visualization to visually mine the business data set to gain knowledge and insight about your business questions. Recall with data visualization, you act as a data mining tool. By visually inspecting and interacting with the two- or three-dimensional visualizations, you can identify interesting (nontrivial, implicit, perhaps previously unknown and potentially useful) information or patterns in the business data set.

Analyzing the Data Visualizations

The data visualization tool used depends on the nature of the business data set and its underlying structure. Furthermore, the visualization tool or technique depends on the facet of the business question you are investigating. Perhaps the best way to learn how to use data visualization to analyze and evaluate your business data set is through examples. The following is a brief list of some uses for data visualization in analyzing and evaluating your business data sets and gaining insight into your business questions. You can use:

- Frequency graphs (histogram and distribution graphs) to evaluate key business indicators such as the response rate to a marketing campaign by comparing them to other columns (data dimensions) in the business data set

- Pareto graphs (histograms and line graphs combined) to evaluate the importance of a column (data dimensions) in the business data set with respect to key business indicators such as response rate, number of failures, or fraudulent claims

- Radar graphs to search and evaluate seasonal trends or other trends in the business data set as a whole

- Line graphs to analyze and search for time-based trends and patterns

- Scatter graphs to evaluate cause-and-effect relationships

Many times when you plot the graphical data table (formatted subset of the business data set used to create the graph) using the appropriate graph type, underlying patterns are discovered. For instance, a scatter graph may show a positive, negative, neutral, threshold, or curved relationship between columns. Often you can use this relationship information and other visual discoveries and insights to help analyze and answer the business question under investigation. In addition, you can use the data visualization as a communication tool to share your discoveries and insights with other data and business analysts, domain experts, and decision makers.

Using Frequency Graphs to Discover and Evaluate Key Business Indicators

A specialized variation of the column or bar graph is referred to as a *frequency graph*. In Chapters 4 and 5, frequency graphs (histogram and distribution graphs) were used to evaluate the distribution of the values of discrete columns. In Chapter 6, frequency graphs were used to compare column values before and after the ECTL or logical transformations to verify the before and after distributions were similar. Frequency graphs can also be useful in analyzing and evaluating the distribution of key business indicators by other

```
SELECT        age,
              count(response)
FROM          response_business_set
WHERE         response=1
GROUP BY      age
```

Code Figure 8.1 SQL query to build the graphical data table for a frequency graph.

columns or data dimensions in your business data set to evaluate their strength. For instance, a key business indicator may be the response rate to your marketing campaign. You can use the distribution graphs to evaluate these business indicators by other data dimensions in the business data set, such as age range, gender, and marital status. In addition, frequency graphs are useful in searching for and evaluating problems in automated or manual processes to quickly evaluate how often problems occur and in identifying patterns that may provide a clue for identifying the causes of the problems and making process improvements.

Depending on your data visualization tool, you often need to reformat the data in your business data set in order to plot it using a frequency graph. Code Figure 8.1 shows a standard SQL statement that constructs a graphical data table that you can use for creating a frequency graph.

Figure 8.1 illustrates how a frequency graph (column graph) can be used to evaluate the distribution of customers who responded to a home equity loan campaign. In this case, the response rate distribution is being compared to the age of the customers who responded. In Figure 8.1, the response rate by mortgage age falls into a classic bell curve, a normal distribution or symmetric pattern. Whether you use a column (histogram) or bar graph (distribution), the patterns for the frequency graph will be the same—only the orientation is different (vertical versus horizontal). For instance, this frequency graph is showing you that the majority of your campaign responders are between 39 and 51 years of age.

To see if you've discovered whether customer age is a business indicator as to why a customer responded to the home equity loan, you can compare the frequency graph of responders by the age to the frequency graph of the entire customer population. Figure 8.2 shows a column graph that compares the frequency of the responders versus the population by the customer's age. To compare the two frequencies, you need to normalize the record counts per age group. For instance, the numeric range of the entire population by age results in thousands of records per age, while the numeric range of the responders results in hundreds of records per age. To solve this problem, both record counts by age are represented as a percentage of their respective total. This

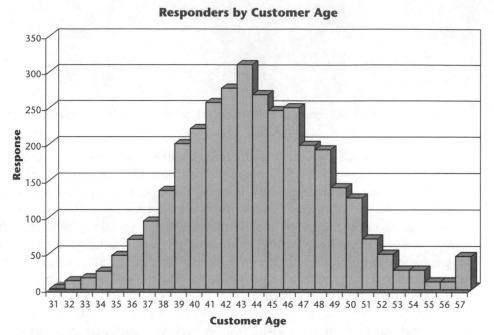

Figure 8.1 Frequency graph of responses by customer age.

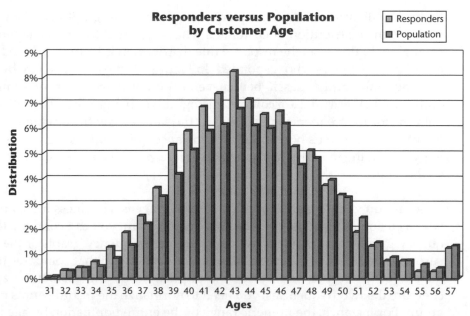

Figure 8.2 Frequency graph of the population as a whole versus the responses by customer age.

normalization technique enables you to compare the age groups using the same basic scale. As you can see from Figure 8.2, the age trends follow similar patterns. However, up to age 43, the responders tend to have higher percentages than the population. After age 49, the responders tend to have lower percentages than the population. Therefore, it appears the younger customers are more interested in the home equity loans than are older customers. The frequency graphs also provide you with descriptive information about the age ranges of your customers and those who did and did not respond to the home equity campaign.

Frequency graphs typically have one of five basic patterns: symmetric, bimodal, skewed, flat, or outlier. Figure 8.3 shows an example of bimodal, skewed, flat, and outlier frequency graph patterns using histogram graphs. In some cases, a single frequency graph may display multiple patterns. This normally indicates there are additional factors (column relationships) that must also be considered and investigated.

A *symmetric* (bell curve) frequency distribution pattern usually indicates a stable, predictable process, result, or relationship. As illustrated in the frequency graph of the home equity loan campaign responders by age in Figure 8.1, the symmetric pattern may be explained by the fact that the customer ages (primary mortgage holder) also fall into a similar bell-curved distribution.

A *bimodal* (two-humped) frequency distribution pattern may indicate an unstable process, result, or relationship, or that there are two or more sets of conditions affecting the distribution pattern as shown in Figure 8.3a. Perhaps there is another column that needs to be evaluated at the same time. For process-related business questions, you should investigate what is done differently in the steps in the process when the low points and high points occur.

A *skewed* (asymmetrical) frequency distribution pattern may indicate an unstable process, result, or relationship, but there may also be times when you can expect to see an asymmetric pattern as shown in Figure 8.3b. For example if you are examining a response time-based business question, a cluster or group of response times falling at the fastest end of the scale would be preferable to a bell curve.

Figure 8.4 was created based on the same home equity loan campaign business data set. However, the graphical data table was selected using the mortgage age instead of the customer age. This frequency graph demonstrates a combination of both bimodal and skewed patterns. You can see that customers with relatively young mortgages (under 10 years old) are very interested in obtaining a home equity loan. There is also a second wave of interested customers whose mortgages are between 15 and 17 years old. However, the overall frequency pattern is skewed to younger mortgages.

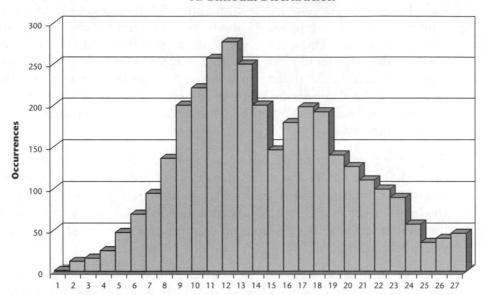

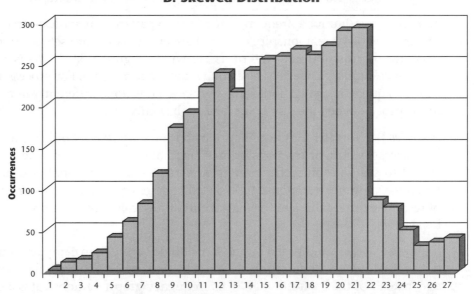

Figure 8.3 Bimodal, skewed, flat, and outlier frequency graphs.

C. Flat Distribution

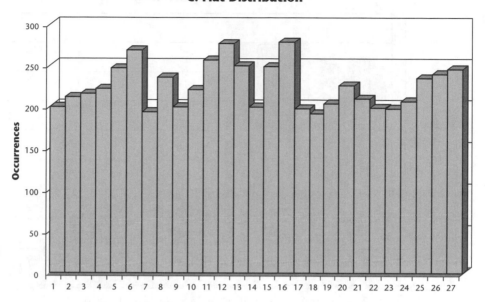

D. Normal Distribution with Outliers

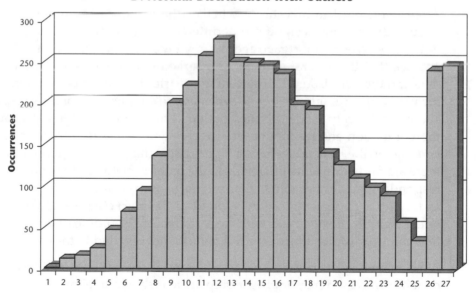

Figure 8.3 *(continued)*

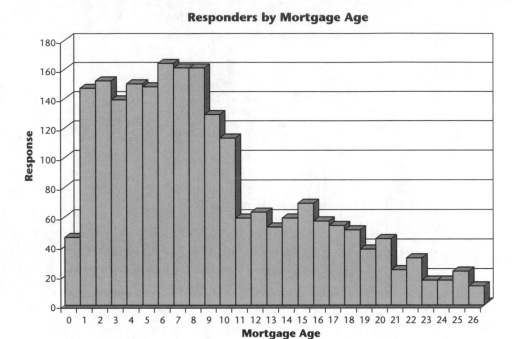

Responders by Mortgage Age

Figure 8.4 Frequency graph of responses by mortgage age.

Again, you need to investigate whether the response by mortgage age frequency distribution is significantly different from the customer population to determine whether mortgage age is a key business indicator. From Figure 8.5, you see that the general patterns are markedly different between the responders and the population. The percentage distribution of the population steadily increases up to mortgage age 8, whereas the frequency graph of responders shows a relatively flat distribution pattern. From mortgage ages 10 through 17, the population and responders are nearly equal. Then from mortgage age 18 and higher, the responders have a higher percentage than the population. Since there are fairly dramatic differences in the patterns between the population and responders, you can conclude that mortgage age is a strong business indicator as to why a customer chose to respond to the marketing campaign. The frequency graph provides you with a clearer picture or profile of your customers in general, as well as those who did and did not respond to the campaign.

A *flat* frequency distribution pattern may indicate that there isn't a stable, predictable process, result, or relationship at all as shown in Figure 8.3c. It can also indicate that you are trying to compare apples and oranges. If you get a flat frequency distribution, you will need to reexamine and redefine the process, results, or relationship being measured by stratifying the data and replotting. Figure 8.6, using the same home equity loan campaign business data set, illustrates a frequency distribution of responses by the teaser rate offered during the home equity loan campaign. After a discussion about the frequency graph with the domain experts and marketing department, it was discovered that the loan teaser rates were not evenly offered to all customers. The frequency of response by teaser rate closely resembles the frequency of the offered rates to all customers. Therefore, no insights or discoveries are gained from this frequency graph other than to confirm that the teaser rate was not a factor in why a customer did or did not respond to the home equity loan campaign.

Outliers (isolated observations) may indicate errors in your business data set as shown in Figure 8.3d. However, if the information is accurate, focusing on determining why these unique distribution patterns occurred may lead to significant process improvements or provide you with exception cases.

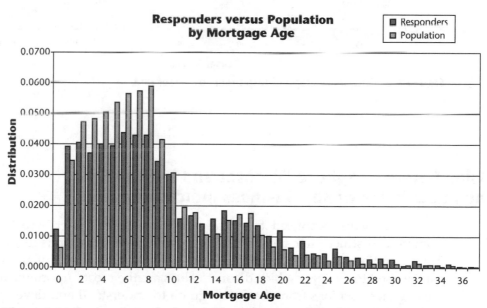

Figure 8.5 Frequency graph of responders versus population by mortgage age.

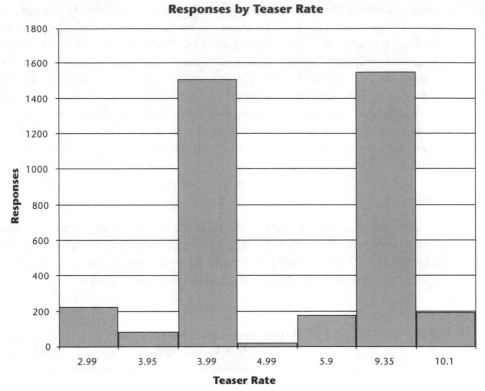

Figure 8.6   Frequency graph of responders by teaser rate.

Using Pareto Graphs to Discover and Evaluate the Importance of Key Business Indicators

As you may have noticed from the frequency graphs, there are typically numerous distinct values that define whether a person responds to a marketing promotion or characterizes the object under investigation. A Pareto graph can be used to evaluate which distinct values are the most important. You can glean generalizations from the Pareto graph to understand and develop business rules to address your business questions. The Pareto Principle states that 80 percent of the trouble comes from 20 percent of the problems. Similarly, you can develop a business rule that characterizes 80 percent of the population or problem by analyzing the business data set using Pareto graphs. This enables you to discover and focus on those values that have the greatest overall impact on improving a process or marketing campaign.

The following are examples of the type of business topics and questions that can be analyzed with a Pareto graph:

- Who is involved? A Pareto graph showing that 80 percent of the customers who responded to the market campaign were between 30 and 40 years old illustrates the answer to a "Who?" business question.

- What resources are used? A Pareto graph showing which brands of equipment resulted in fewer service calls illustrates the answer to a "What?" business question.

- Where is the physical location? A Pareto graph showing that 80 percent of all failed parts were manufactured at sites 1, 5, and 10 illustrates the answer to a "Where?" business question.

- When (date or time) did the problem occur? A Pareto graph showing that cars assembled on Mondays and Fridays account for 80 percent of the total recalls illustrates the answer to a "When?" time-based business question.

- Which areas are involved? A Pareto graph showing that lines 3, 10, and 12 are most frequently skipped on tax returns illustrates the answer to a "Which?" business question.

- How things are done? A Pareto graph showing that email is checked more frequently than voice mail illustrates the answer to a "How?" business question.

- Why or for what reasons? A Pareto graph showing that plants may die from lack of water, light, nutrients, and so on illustrates the answer to a "Why?" business question.

You first need to construct a graphical data table that you can use to create a Pareto graph. To prepare the data table, you can use a standard SQL query similar to the one illustrated in Code Figure 8.1; however, instead of the count of responders by age, you need to calculate the percent of all responders each age contributes. The query should return the percentage contribution for each value in descending percentage order. Then you need to add a column that accumulates the percentages. Table 8.1 shows an example of a graphical data table needed to create the Pareto graph based on the home equity loan campaign business data set. The cumulative percentage should equal 1 (100 percent) for the table.

Figure 8.7 illustrates a Pareto graph using the prepared graphical data table from Table 8.1. As you can see, the left-hand y-axis lists the percentage each AGE contributes to the entire data set. The column graphical entity represents those percentages based on this scale. The right-hand y-axis lists the cumulative percentages. The line graphical entity increases from left to right. It represents the cumulative percentage based on the right-hand scale. Interpreting the line graph, you can see that almost 10 percent of the customer responders are 43 years old, and if you consider both 43- and 42-year-old responders, the percentage increases to almost 20 percent. From the Pareto graph, you can see

Table 8.1 Graphical Data Table of Customer Age, Percent of Contribution, and Cumulative Percent

CUSTOMER AGE	PERCENT OF CONTRIBUTION	CUMULATIVE PERCENTAGE
43	0.093205051	0.093205051
42	0.083283223	0.176488274
44	0.08057727	0.257065544
41	0.077269994	0.334335538
46	0.075165364	0.409500902
45	0.073962718	0.48346362
40	0.066446182	0.549909802
39	0.060132291	0.610042093
47	0.059530968	0.669573061
48	0.057726999	0.72730006
49	0.042092604	0.769392664
38	0.040889958	0.810282622
50	0.037883343	0.848165965
37	0.028262177	0.876428142
51	0.021046302	0.897474444
36	0.02074564	0.918220084
52	0.014732411	0.932952495
35	0.014131088	0.947083584
57	0.013830427	0.960914011
53	0.008117859	0.96903187
54	0.008117859	0.977149729
34	0.007516536	0.984666266
33	0.004810583	0.989476849
32	0.003607937	0.993084787
55	0.003307276	0.996392063
56	0.003307276	0.999699339
31	0.000300661	1

that if you want to know how old 80 percent of the responders were, you would list all of the x-axis labels from left to right until the line graph reached 80 percent (ages 43, 42, 44, 41, 46, 45, 40, and 38). From this information, you could generalize that 80 percent of the customers that responded to the home equity loan campaign were in their early to mid 40s.

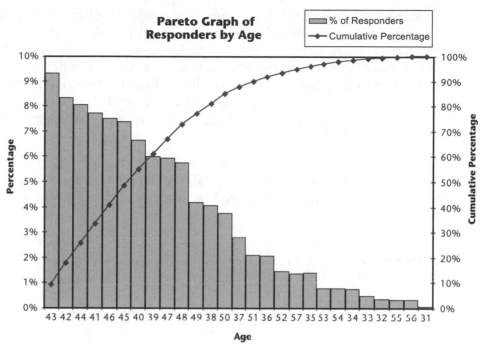

Figure 8.7   Pareto graph of responders by age.

Insert Figure 10 illustrates a Pareto graph of the home equity loan campaign responders by the age of their mortgage. In this graph, you'll notice a skewed pattern. At around 65 percent of the population, the percentage that each mortgage age value contributes drops to under 3 percent of the total. It is interesting to note that customers with mortgages under 10 years old account for 65 percent of the responders. From the graph, if you wanted to know what are the ages of the mortgages for 80 percent of the responders, you would list all of the x-axis labels from left to right until the line graph reached 80 percent (mortgage ages 6, 7, 8, 2, 4, 5, 1, 3, 9, 10, 15, 12, 11, 14, 16, and 17). From this information, you could generalize that 80 percent of the customers that responded to the home equity loan campaign had mortgages that were under 17 years old.

Using Radar Graphs to Spot Seasonal Trends and Problem Areas

A *radar graph* lets you quickly spot seasonal trends or problem areas. Just as a pie chart shows you the parts making up the whole, a radar chart lets you see individual data series as well as the accumulated whole. Suppose that the business question under investigation is "Which states should I select to launch my new cosmetic line?" From past experience, the marketing department wants to only premiere the new cosmetic line in states that will have the largest populations of working women in the next year. From a U.S. census business data set, Figure 8.8 illustrates how a radar graph can be used to show the projected versus historical working women population changes by U.S. state. From the radar graph, you can quickly spot those states where the number of working women is expected to increase dramatically next year as compared to the other states. You can visually evaluate the historical and projected trends. If you could only suggest three states for the product launch, they would be California, Texas, and Florida, since they show the highest spikes on the radar graph.

In Figure 8.8, the y-axis (population change) is marked on the first spoke. When you look at the graph, the spiral for the projected series shows a very jagged pattern or trend, indicating how the projected population of working

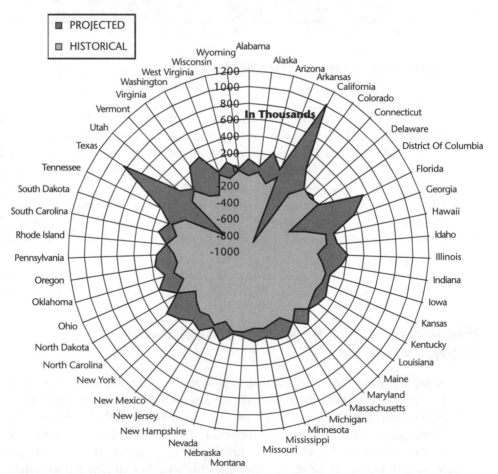

Figure 8.8 Projected versus historical working women population changes by state.

women is expected to increase for certain U.S. states. The inner spiral, the historical population, shows a smoother pattern or trend. You can see at a glance that the projected population, in most cases, is higher than the historical population. This type of radar graph works well if you are comparing continuous columns or trying to spot trends over discrete column value groups.

Suppose your business question is, "Which multivitamin compound should you add to your product to have the most benefit for your customer's hair, eyes, and skin?" Again, you can use a radar graph to compare the multivitamin compound and the effects on hair, eyes, and skin. Figure 8.9 shows a radar graph of the laboratory results testing the four compounds. You can visually see that the B multivitamin compound has the most beneficial effects on hair, eyes, and skin, since the three polygons are highest on the B spiral axis as compared to the A, C, and D spiral axes. The radar graph type enables you to quickly compare and analyze multiple dimensions to gain insight into your business data set as a whole.

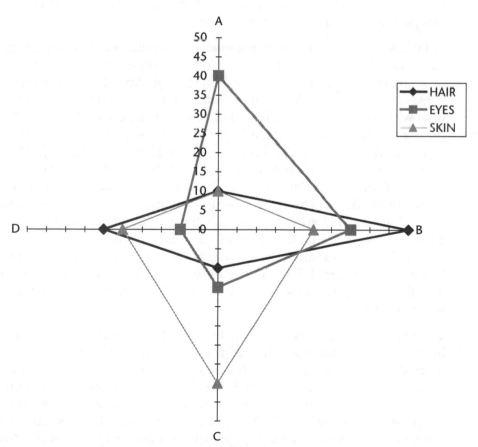

Figure 8.9 Multivitamin compound influence on hair, eyes, and skin.

Using Line Graphs to Analyze Time Relationships

Time graphs can be used to investigate and evaluate time and seasonality relationships. Time-graph types help you identify possible causes for changes by providing a visual picture that pinpoints when the changes occurred. For instance, you can use time-relationship graphs to identify causes of problems, to identify the impact of any changes made, or to determine if any new changes are even necessary. Likewise, you can use time graphs to evaluate how the object of interest or investigation changes over time.

Line graphs are normally most useful for evaluating long-term patterns; therefore, at least 24 data points are needed to construct an accurate chart. Generally, the smaller the time measurement, the more observation points needed. A useful technique for interpreting a time-relationship graph is to include a median line as part of the graph. The median or middle data point value has as many points above it as below it. If you have an odd number of data points, the median lies on the point in the center. If you have an even number of points, the median lies between the points closest to the center. Figure 8.10 illustrates a median line with the bond yield business data set for comparing the 1-, 3-, and 6-month bond yield indices.

In Figure 8.10, the inclusion of the median line helps you to evaluate the overall trend of bond yield for the entire time period you are investigating. In this case, the time period is from April 1996 through April 1999. For almost a year (1996–1997), the bond yield indices were extremely positive (above the median line) with respect to the median bond yield. During the next year (1997–1998), the bond yield indices fluctuated positively and negatively with respect to the median. Then during the last year (1998–1999), the bond yield indices remained negative (below the median line) with respect to the median. Slight changes from the median are normal and respect what is considered a common cause variation. However, rapid upward or downward *shifts* or *trends* like those that occurred after November 1996 provide you with insight into the business data set as it relates to time. These major shifts give you specific date ranges that are a subset of the entire timeline, which pinpoint when the problem or effect occurred. To identify the causes of shifts and trends, you need to examine what conditions may have changed just before or after the shift or trend occurred.

Code Figure 8.2 demonstrates how to calculate the median for the bond yield business data set using standard SQL. Refer to Chapter 5, Tables 5.4 and 5.5 for more details about the YIELD business data set. Since the bond yield line graph included the 1-, 3-, and 6-month yields, you need to calculate the median for all three continuous columns and then divide by 3 (the number of bond yield being examined). Once you have calculated the median value, you can add it as a constant to your graphical data table and plot it as an additional line.

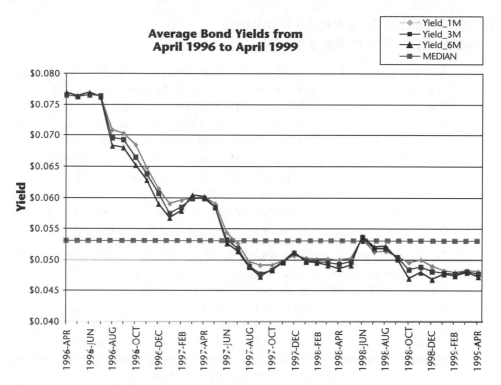

Figure 8.10   Line Graph of Average Bond Yields including a Median Line.

Clusters are also critical patterns to examine when analyzing time graphs. Clusters are created whenever a line connecting two points crosses the median. A cluster can contain a single data point or multiple data points (as long as the total number of data points doesn't constitute a shift). If a time graph has too few clusters, the data may represent a cycle, or long-term trend. Too many clusters often indicate overcompensation or problems with the business data set. The number of acceptable clusters depends upon the number of data points plotted. Circling the clusters provides a visual prompt for analyzing and evaluating the patterns. Insert Figure 11 illustrates the clusters discovered in the average bond yield line graph. Once the clusters have been identified, they can help you visually investigate whether there are any cycles and long-term trend.

```
SELECT (
percentile_cont(0.5) within group (order by yield_1m desc) +
percentile_cont(0.5) within group (order by yield_3m desc) +
percentile_cont(0.5) within group (order by yield_6m desc) )
/ 3 overall_median
FROM yield
```

Code Figure 8.2   Calculating the median constant value in SQL.

Using Scatter Graphs to Evaluate Cause-and-Effect Relationships

Scatter graphs help you analyze if you have identified likely key business indicators (important columns in answering your business question) by examining the cause-and-effect relationship between the key business indicator column values and the other column values in the business data set. In addition to indicating if there is a relationship, scatter graphs indicate the strength of the relationship. By graphing different columns from the same business data set, you can examine how different factors and conditions affect a process or business problem. It is important to note that scatter graphs only show if there is a correlation between two continuous columns. They cannot prove causation, but they can suggest probable avenues for further investigation.

To use discrete columns in a scatter graph, you first have to convert their discrete values to continuous values. For instance, you could map the discrete values *small*, *medium*, and *large* to the continuous values 1, 2, and 3. In this example, the discrete values inherently have a corresponding order from small to large. Therefore, you want to preserve that order when converting them into continuous values. Some scatter graph tools automatically convert discrete column values to numbers when computing the scatter graph, then redisplay the original discrete column value instead of its numeric placeholder.

The vertical axis of the scatter graph plots the "effect" column. The top of the graph is defined by the largest value of the effect column. The horizontal axis plots the column of the "potential cause" with value increasing from left to right. Figure 8.11 illustrates a scatter graph used to investigate the relationship between the number of service calls and the number of customers who churned (canceled their services). In Figure 8.11, the "effect" column is the number of people who canceled their service and is plotted on the y-axis of the scatter graph. The "potential cause" column is the number of customer service calls and is plotted on the x-axis of the scatter graph.

From the scatter graph in Figure 8.11, you can formulate and test your hypothesis that as the number of customer service calls increases, your customers become dissatisfied with your service and cancel. It appears that for five or more service calls, the churn rate increases; however, it also appears that with just one service call the churn rate is almost as high as with five or more service calls. Remember, scatter plots only show correlations. You will have to depend upon the domain expert's knowledge and experience, as well as other columns from the business data set, to definitely prove the hypothesis.

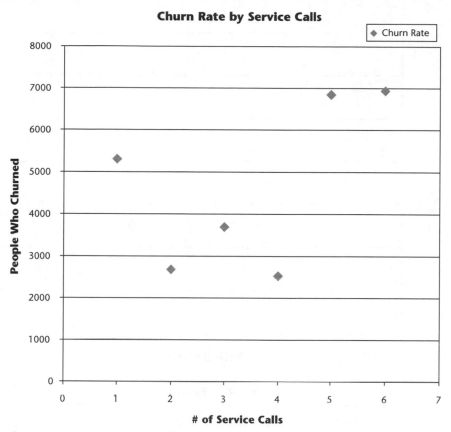

Figure 8.11   Scatter graph of lost customers by number of service calls.

The six basic patterns to look for in scatter graphs are as follows: *none, positive, negative, threshold, curved,* and *clustered.* Figure 8.12 shows examples of these six basic patterns.

As illustrated in Figure 8.12a, if there is no shape to the pattern, there is *no relationship* between the column values. For example, the height and hair color of a group of students would show no relationship or correlation. However, if a pattern was expected and *none* appeared, it may be because the plot was constructed with too narrow a range of data. A scatter graph may require at least 50 data points before a pattern is discernable. In general, the more column values plotted, the more accurate the graph and your ability to distinguish the patterns.

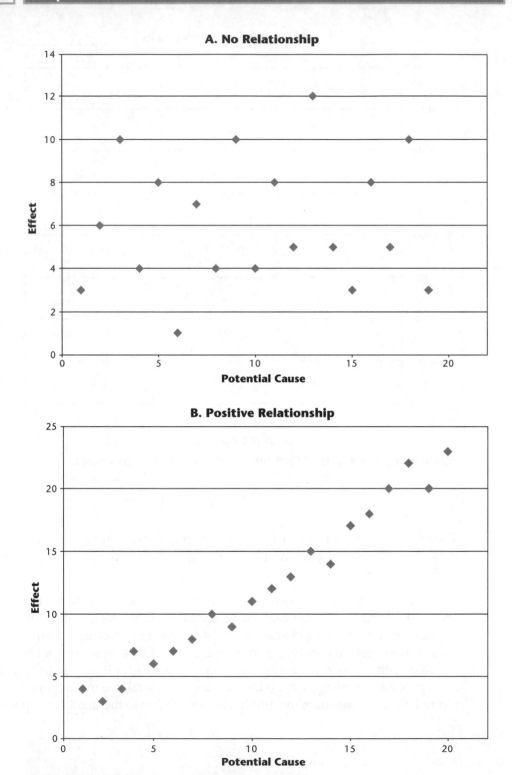

Figure 8.12   Six basic patterns in scatter graphs.

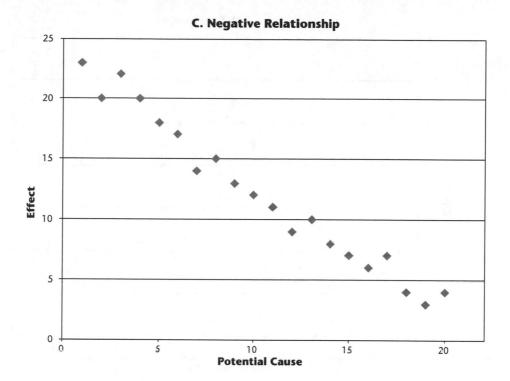

C. Negative Relationship

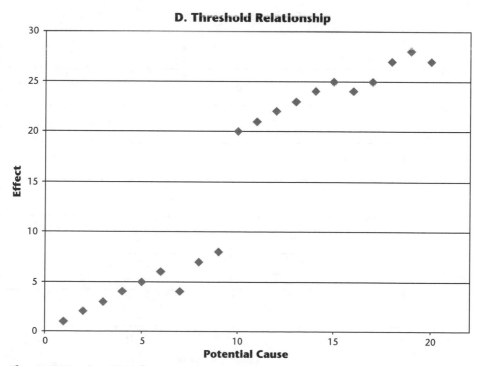

D. Threshold Relationship

Figure 8.12   *(continued)*

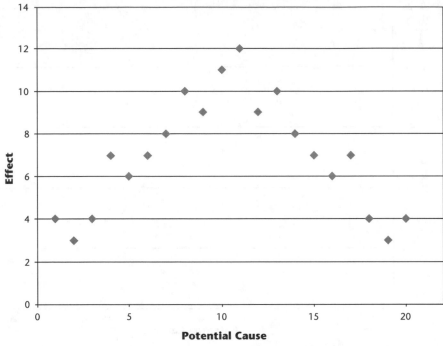

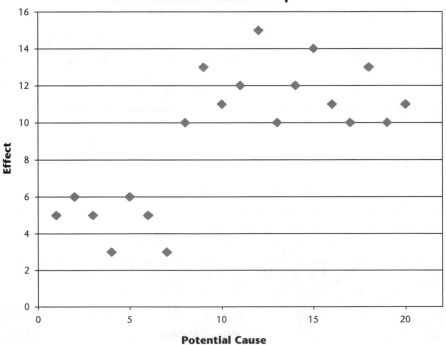

Figure 8.12 *(continued)*

In a *positive* relationship, the dots (or whatever graphical entity you are using) will form a pattern sloping from the bottom left to the upper right. As the cause (x-axis) column values increase, so will the effect (y-axis) column values. The relationship is considered stronger if the dots are closer together. For instance, if the graphical entities almost form a line from bottom left to upper right then the relationship is very strong. Figure 8.12b shows a positive cause-and-effect relationship. For example, intelligence test scores and reading skills often show a strong positive correlation. Figure 8.12c illustrates a negative cause-and-effect relationship. For example, the age of an automobile and its selling price often show a strong negative correlation. In a *negative relationship*, the dot pattern slopes from upper left to bottom right. In this case, the cause and effect are inversely related.

In a *threshold relationship*, the dot will form a pattern that takes the shape of an "L" or a "J". Figure 8.12d illustrates a "J" threshold relationship pattern. In this case, the cause and effect column values are related; it just isn't a linear relationship. The cause column doesn't have any impact until it reaches a certain level (threshold), then it begins to have an effect.

As illustrated in Figure 8.12e, in a *curved relationship*, the dots will form a curved pattern. This pattern represents a complex relationship where the cause and effect column values are positively related up to a certain point and then the effect decreases (a "frown") or the relationship can switch from negative to positive (creating a "smile").

In a *clustered relationship*, the dots will form distinct groups or clusters. Figure 8.12f illustrates a clustering or grouping relationship between the cause and effect columns. This pattern represents that groups of causes tend to have the same or similar effects. For instance, Figure 8.12f shows two distinct groups or clusters.

Once you have identified possible key business indicators or potential causes, a scatter graph can help you analyze and evaluate the relationships between causes and effects (other columns in the business data set). The domain experts, and business and data analysts can use scatter graphs to analyze and evaluate those relationships. In some cases, you may want to change the grouping of the cause column to see if the groupings have an influence on the effect column values. Juggling the column values used in a scatter graph is part science and part art, but if you make changes and begin to see improvements in a process, and you are able to detect stronger relationships, it is safe to bet that you are on the right track.

Analyzing the Data Mining Models

Visual data mining tools and techniques assist users in creating visualizations that provide insights into data mining models and their performance. This helps with decision-making and predicting new business opportunities. With visual data mining tools, the user inspects and interacts with the two- or three-dimensional visualization of the predictive or descriptive data mining model to understand (and validate) the interesting information and patterns discovered by the data mining algorithm. You can employ data visualization tools and techniques to compare and contrast the performance of different data mining models.

Data visualization techniques can be used for the five core data mining tasks. A common use of data visualization is to gain insights into the results of the model rather than the inner workings of the model itself. These types of visualizations are useful to compare and contrast multiple models from both the same and different techniques.

For some data mining tools such as linear regression, it is easy to understand the model from its textual description. However, others are quite complicated and benefit from visualization. In later sections, we will describe using visualizations to gain insights into the different type of models, specifically what patterns were discovered, as well as to evaluate the performance of the model. For instance, if you discovered a terrific model to identify customer fraud, before it could be implemented into a production environment you would probably need to explain the model to various groups of managers and decision makers, the system owners, and perhaps even regulators, to ensure that the models did not discriminate.

In addition, you can use visualizations to monitor the model deployment by comparing performance of the model during construction and after deployment. It is extremely important as soon as a model is deployed that you make sure the model performs as well in the production environment as it did in the model-building environment. It is also important to monitor the model's ongoing performance to make sure it is not becoming stale and out-of-date.

Visualizations to Understand the Performance of the Core Data Mining Tasks

In this section we discuss visualizations that provide insights into the performance of the core data mining tasks previously outlined.

Classification

The purpose of classification is to successfully categorize examples into one of a number of predefined categories. The performance of a classification technique is measured by looking at its overall ability to correctly classify cases and then investigate specific strengths and weaknesses.

The most simple performance measure is the overall accuracy of the model, which is simply measuring the proportion of all examples that the model classified into the correct category. If the model had to predict a TRUE or FALSE label for 100 examples and was correct in 80 instances, then its accuracy is 80 percent. The accuracy of a model is measured by breaking the available data into a training set and a test set. Usually, the majority of examples are placed in the training set, from which you build the model and evaluate the accuracy model on the examples in the test set. From the training set, the data mining tools make use of the independent column values to strike a balance between a generalized model and being able to correctly predict the label of every example in the training set. Data mining tools often calculate the accuracy of the model on the training set. However, normally you are more interested in how the model performs on cases it has not seen before, namely those in the test set. When trying the model on the test set the actual label is ignored and the model attempts to predict it. The classification accuracy of the training set should be approximately equal to the test set; otherwise, the model may be too specific for the training set and not general enough.

Summarizing the performance of a model by a single number has its dangers. Two models may have the exact same accuracy but one may have this accuracy for all categories, while another performs very well for most categories but performs badly for one category. Summarizing the performance of a model by accuracy is dangerous for situations where the target event is rare, such as insurance fraud. A fraud model with an accuracy of 98 percent may sound impressive, but not when we know that only 2 percent of cases are fraudulent.

Another performance measure of classification models is referred to as *lift*. The lift is measured with respect to a particular category of the dependent column, usually the category of most interest such as fraud, churn, or response to an advertising campaign. A model's lift is calculated by comparing its ability to predict the selected category relative to the proportion of this category occurring in the sample. In the sample of responses to a home equity campaign, 45 percent of customers responded favorably. If this were all you knew, the best guess model at predicting the selected category would be to label an unseen example as TRUE/1. This would result in a model whose precision at predicting a positive response would be approximately 45 percent. If the data mining model were 90 percent accurate at predicting a positive response—twice the precision of the best guess model—then the lift of the model is two-fold. Formally, lift is the proportion of the examples in a set of predictions, where the classifier correctly predicts the target event divided by the proportion of examples in the population where the target event occurs. Suppose the target event occurs in 30 percent of all examples; a classifier that could predict 60 target event occurrences per 100 examples has a lift of two. Again, summarizing model performance with one number is dangerous. A conservative model may have a large lift but only makes a few, usually right, predictions.

If the data mining technique measures a degree of belief or confidence to each prediction (most classification tools do), you can overcome this deficiency. By sorting the predictions on their confidence, you see how the model's performance varies as the progression from the strongest predictions to the weakest occurs. Rather than referring to the top n predictions, most tools divide the predictions into contiguous intervals of a fixed number of examples. Common intervals are quartiles (intervals of 25 percent of all examples), deciles (intervals of 10 percent of all examples), and percentiles (intervals of 1 percent of all examples). When we refer to the 50th percentile, we mean those observations that would be in the 50th interval if we were to divide the sorted examples into intervals of width equal to 1 percent of all examples. Often we will use the term cumulative when referring to charts where percentiles, deciles, or quartiles are used. In this situation, the graph shows the model's performance up to and including the percentile, decile, or quartile referred to. Figure 8.13 illustrates a cumulative lift chart for the performance of three models that predict the response to a home equity campaign for a single test set.

You can interpret this chart (line graph) by choosing a point on the x-axis (say 20) and finding the corresponding y-value axis (2 for decision trees) to determine the lift that occurs if you were to use the top 20 percent of predictions made by the decision tree. As expected, the lift progressively decreases as you move from the strongest to the weakest predictions. You can use the lift chart to evaluate how much of an improvement the model makes over just randomly guessing the label.

There are similar charts that you can use to investigate and compare the performance of models. For instance, a *response chart* is a line graph of the number of target events divided by the number of records in the percentile, multiplied by 100. Figure 8.14 illustrates a cumulative response chart. If you were to look at the 50th percentile, you can see that at this point the decision tree precision at predicting that an individual will respond to the campaign is 80 percent. The response at the 100th percentile will be 45 percent, which is the proportion of the sample that responded to the campaign. You can use the response chart to evaluate the precision of the model at predicting the target event.

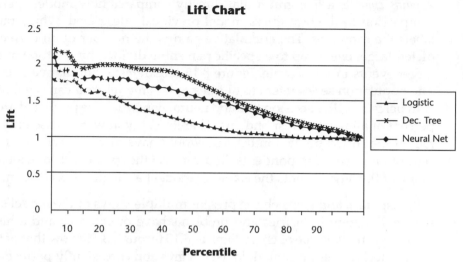

Figure 8.13   Cumulative lift chart.

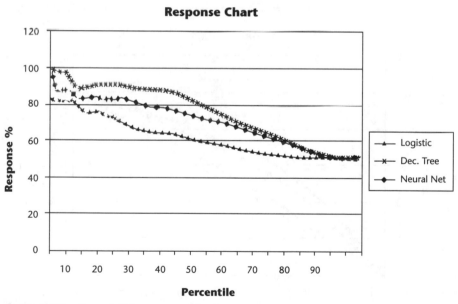

Figure 8.14   Cumulative response chart.

A *gains chart* is a line graph that directly compares how models perform in comparison to the best guess model previously described, which randomly labels the examples. The cumulative gain is the number of all correctly predicted target events up to a specific percentile divided by the total number of target events in the sample. Figure 8.15 illustrates a cumulative gains chart. The population series refers to our best guess model. You can see that by the 50th percentile, the decision tree and neural network have predicted around 80 percent of all positive respondents. Therefore, if you were to use only the top half of the sorted prediction list, you would have made a decision on 80 percent of all positive respondents. You can use the gain chart to evaluate how many of the target events the classifier model has made a decision on.

Lift, response, and gains charts present multiple views of the model's performance. Different industries and problems have preferences and a history of using a particular type of chart. Figures 8.13 through 8.15 show that of the data mining techniques evaluated, logistic regression consistently performs worse than the remaining two for the home equity loan campaign data set. Initially the decision-tree and neural-network models perform similarly, but the decision-tree model performs better until about the 60th percentile, at which the accuracy of both techniques is again quite similar.

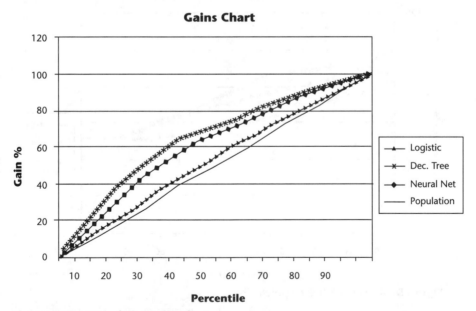

Figure 8.15 Cumulative gains chart.

Lift, response, and gains curves are useful for gaining insight into the model's performance, but a valid question is at what point is the model's performance too poor to continue using. The pragmatic answer is, when it is no longer profitable. You can determine this cut-off point by using *return on investment* (ROI) charts and *profit* charts. The ROI chart shows the profit as a ratio of the cost multiplied by 100. Suppose for the home equity example you had already built the model and now wish to use it. Every offer you sent out cost $250 to create, mail, and follow-up in person. Also suppose the revenue obtained due to a positive response is $500. Therefore, for every $250 invested, you can get $500 in return if you pick a customer who responds to your offer. For every two guesses, if you guess right once you will break even, if you do better, a profit is made. Figure 8.16 shows the return on investment chart for the various models created for the home equity loan campaign.

Another way to show the financial performance of the model is to consider a profit chart that plots the sum of revenue minus the expense. Insert Figure 12 illustrates a profit chart for the various models created for the home equity loan campaign.

From the charts in Figure 8.16 and Figure Insert 12, as expected, the ROI progressively gets smaller as the model's ability to correctly predict the target event diminishes. The rate of decrease gets quite small between the 10th and

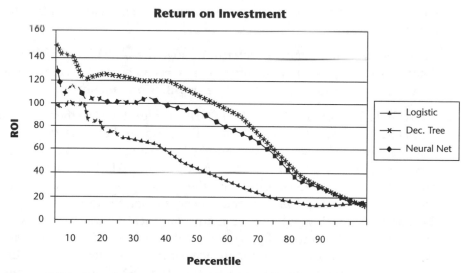

Figure 8.16 Cumulative return on investment (%) chart.

40th percentiles. Not surprisingly, if you were to use only the top 40 percent of the predications based on confidence, profits are maximized. Using predictions falling in a lower percentile will result in a diminishing overall profit. When using ROI and profit charts, you must factor in all the costs with building, using, and deploying the model. In these examples, we have ignored the cost of building and deploying the model, which will vary between the types of models.

Cumulative graphs are particularly useful for identifying the overall performance of the model. You can use non-cumulative graphs to isolate problems in the models. For example, you would expect a model to have a lift chart that progressively decreases as you progress from the strongest to weakest predictions. Non-cumulative charts are illustrated in the case study.

Thus far, the accuracy of the models described has been based upon using one training and one test set. It is important to choose these test sets randomly. You need to be careful that the results are not a statistical fluke due to unusual training and test sets. To achieve this, data mining tools use cross-validation, which consists of breaking the entire available data set into, say, 10 equally sized subsets, called folds. Then each fold is used as a test set. The classifier is built using the remaining nine folds. After performing this exercise, there will be 10 of everything: classifiers, accuracies, lifts, gains, responses, ROIs, and profit charts. You should report the average results for all 10 experiments to gain a complete understanding of performance. Comparing how the charts vary from experiment to experiment also gives an indication of the stability of the models found.

At times, you may want to determine how the classifier performs in more detail. To accomplish this, a confusion matrix can be used. Table 8.2 shows the confusion matrix for the decision-tree classifier previously built.

From Table 8.2, you see that of the 1,000 examples, the classifier's overall accuracy is 82.4 percent ((476+348) / 1000). The classifier has 348 true positives, 476 true negatives, 74 false positives, and 102 false negatives. You can see that the precision of predicting the category of TRUE or FALSE is approximately the same. A false positive occurs when the classifier says the target event will occur and it does not. A false negative occurs when the target event occurs and the classifier says it would not. In many classification tasks, the cost of a false positive is not the same as the cost for a false negative. Consider an insurance fraud situation. The cost of wrongly accusing a customer of committing fraud (a false positive) is potentially greater than the cost of not correctly predicting a fraudulent case. Now consider the same situation but for credit card fraud. Most credit card holders do not mind receiving false positive phone calls enquiring if the cardholder made a transaction; therefore it is tolerable to have more false positives.

Table 8.2 Confusion Matrix for Decision Tree Classifier

	FALSE	TRUE
FALSE	476	74
TRUE	102	348

Rows give actual classification; columns give predictions.

For the home equity campaign example, false positives can be tolerated, whereas missed opportunities will reduce potential revenue. In particular, it is beneficial to compare how column values differ between the false negatives and the true positives. Performing a simple frequency tabulation shown in Table 8.3 illustrates that the model was not useful at predicting individuals who responded and had high teaser rates.

Estimation

The performance of an estimation model is measured by comparing the difference between the actual value and the predicted value, much as we did for classification models. If the dependent column is continuous, then a confusion matrix cannot be used. Instead, you need to investigate the variance. The variance is defined as the average distance squared between the expected and actual dependent column values. Often you can use the square root of the variance (the standard deviation), as it is in the same units as the dependent column.

The linear regression model shown in Code Figure 7.4 from Chapter 7 has a standard deviation of 2.48. However, you can gain many insights by visualizing how the error fluctuates over the range of the dependent column, as in Figure 8.17. For instance, you can see that the linear regression model is most accurate when predicting the median buying power and progressively gets worse on either side. There may be a need for a first-level model to predict if the case is of someone with low, medium, or high buying power and then have three separate linear regression models, one for each category.

Table 8.3 Average Teaser Rate by Confusion Matrix Segments

	FALSE	TRUE
FALSE	6.54	6.03
TRUE	7.12	6.3

Rows give actual classification; columns give predictions.

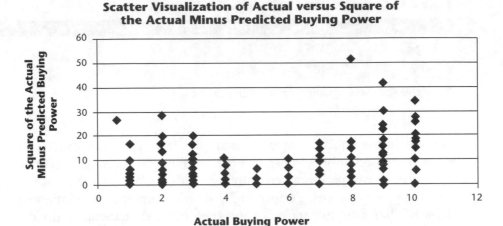

Figure 8.17 Fluctuation of the difference between actual buying power and the square of the actual minus predicted buying power.

Association Grouping

Association rule models are easy to understand but tend to produce too many trivial or non-actionable rules and are often extremely computer intensive. A Web graph tool can help to visually inspect the combination of events that co-occur and is useful for selecting the events that are worth including in the analysis by the automated association rule tool. Figure 8.18 illustrates a Web graph for a random sample of all records in the response to the home equity loan campaign. The initial data set had 15 columns, but a quick inspection shows that 5 have values that co-occur often and perhaps the analysis should be limited to only these columns. Furthermore, there seems to be a large number of records that have both missing values for USE_CREDIT_CARD and CONSUMER_FINANCING that should be investigated and potentially removed.

Clustering and Segmenting

The typical output for many of the clustering tools is a set of statistics describing the nature of the cluster. For each cluster, the output statistics contain a description and a measure of similarity or distance to other clusters. For each record, the output statistics contain the cluster that it most strongly belongs to and a measure of similarity such as distance to it. Though SOM tools do not explicitly produce this information, you can calculate it. Though some data mining clustering tools produce a single number to estimate how good a model is, like the distortion for K-Means, normally it does not provide much insight.

When evaluating a clustering model, you will primarily be interested in the following items:

- How similar are the clusters to each other?
- Do the records belong strongly or weakly to the most likely cluster?
- Are there any records that are outliers?
- What are the typical records that belong to a cluster (cluster profiling)?
- What differentiates each cluster?

You can use a variety of data visualization tools to display the output information from a clustering model. For instance, Figure 8.19 illustrates how to use a radar graph to evaluate the Euclidean distances between clusters.

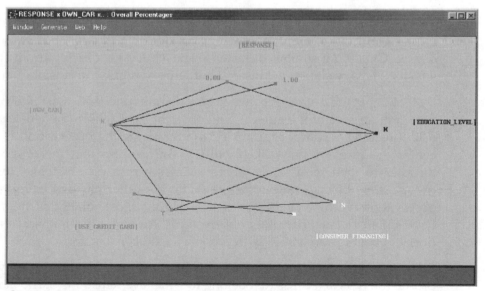

Figure 8.18 Web graph of most common co-occurring events.

Euclidean Distances between Clusters

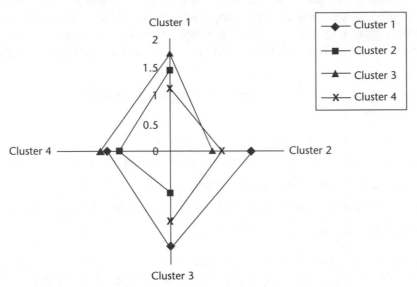

Figure 8.19 Radar graph of the distances between cluster centers.

From Figure 8.19, you can see that cluster 1 is quite different from all other clusters and is quite autonomous, as is cluster 4, though not to the same degree. Cluster 2 is similar to clusters 3 and 4 but quite different from cluster 1. Cluster 3 is very similar to cluster 2 but quite dissimilar to clusters 1 and 4.

By looking at the distances between observations and their most likely cluster, you gain an idea of the sub-populations that exist within the cluster. Figure 8.20 illustrates a scatter graph used to investigate the observation to cluster center distances by most likely cluster. You can see that the observations' distance to their most likely clusters varies across the clusters. Cluster 2's observations belong quite strongly, while the other clusters have bands of observations with varying degrees of belonging. Most notably, clusters 1 and 4 have a distinct band of outlier observations. An outlier is an observation that does not belong very strongly to even its most likely cluster.

By graphing summaries of the independent columns by the cluster, you can profile the typical records that belong to whichever cluster is particularly useful for validation. Figure 8.21 illustrates how the buying power, primary age of applicant, and mortgage age varies across the cluster. Using profiles such as these enable you to develop descriptive names for the clusters. For example, cluster 1 may be named "old-timers" because it describes long-term customers who have high buying power. Cluster 3 may be named "newcomers" because it describes newer customers who have a low buying power.

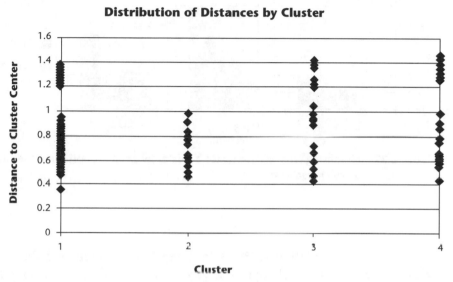

Figure 8.20 Scatter graph of the distances between observations and cluster centers.

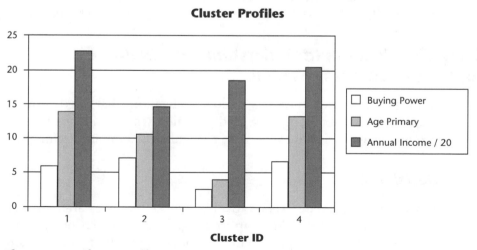

Figure 8.21 Cluster profiles.

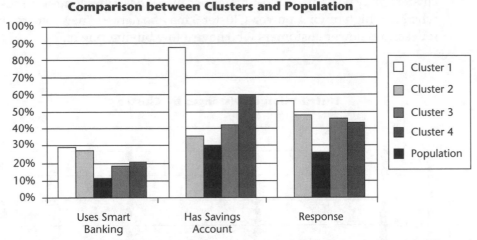

Figure 8.22 Identifying what differentiates a cluster by what proportion of the cluster has a key characteristic.

By adding the population statistics to the graph and reversing the axes, you can easily compare the change of key-column values across the clusters and the population. Figure 8.22 illustrates how the proportion of individuals who use smart banking, have saving accounts at the bank, and responded to the campaign varies across the cluster. Using these profiles, you can see what differentiates the clusters from each other and the population. For example, cluster 1 has significantly more individuals who have savings accounts with the bank, while individuals in cluster 3 did not respond well to the campaign.

Using Visualization to Understand and Evaluate Supervised Learning Models

In the previous section we described visualizations that can determine performance for a data mining task. In this section we describe visualizations that provide insights that are specific to particular data mining techniques.

Decision Trees

A decision tree can be likened to a tree whose branches are paths describing many disjoint patterns. You can investigate each branch or path in turn by assuming it is the only pattern in the model and building a confusion matrix. This would involve implementing the rule as a filter in a data mining package or a SQL query. Code Figure 8.3 shows how to take a rule and re-create the rule as a standard SQL statement.

```
-- An example rule from the decision tree previously built to predict
response to a home equity loan campaign.
IF
BUYING_POWER  <= 3 and OWNED_CAR = 'N'
THEN
RESPONSE = 1 (TRUE)
-- This rule can be translated into the following SQL:
SELECT      own_car,
            Buying_power,
            Response
FROM              response_business_set
WHERE             own_car = 'N' AND buying_power <= 3
```

Code Figure 8.3   SQL query to re-create rule.

This rule shown in Code Figure 8.3 covers 104 examples in the test set and correctly predicts 91 positive responses, giving it an accuracy of 87.5 percent. You can divide these examples into two segments, correct predictions and false positives, of size 91 and 13 respectively. It is highly unlikely that a pattern will have 100 percent accuracy, especially when modeling correlations between the dependent column and independent columns. However, you can compare the averages for independent columns for both segments to see what types of examples this rule incorrectly predicts. Figure 8.23 illustrates comparing the predictions of the rule from Code Figure 8.3. You see that the mortgage age is significantly less in the false positive segments, a common trend among all the decision-tree paths or rules. This indicates that a viable alternative could be to build two models, one for mortgage ages below a threshold and another for mortgage ages equal to and above the threshold. It is also worth seeing if the false positives contained many more missing values than the correct predictions.

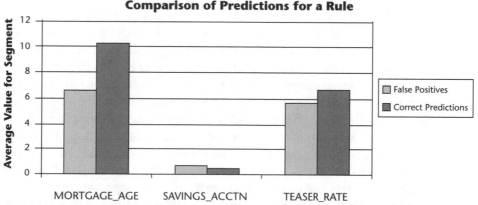

Figure 8.23   Comparing false positive and correct predictions segments.

Neural Networks

Although the inner workings of the decision process of a neural network are considered a "black box" and cannot be visualized, you can determine which independent columns are most important to the decision process by performing sensitivity analysis. For instance, assume a neural network is built that has many input-layer nodes and one output-layer node that predicts the propensity to respond to a campaign. Sensitivity analysis in its simplest form involves initially setting the value of an input-layer node to its middle value of 0.5 (most neural network packages will re-scale input columns to have a range between 0 and 1) and noting the output-layer node value. Then the input-layer node's value is changed to 0, and then 1, each time, noting the changes in the output-layer node's value. This particular node is then reset to 0.5, another input-layer node is selected, the same value changes are performed, and so on, for each input-layer node. You can then rank the independent columns by the size of the change in the output-layer node their changes of value produced. If the network has more than one output-layer node, then you can rank the independent columns for each output-layer node. Most neural network tools will perform some form of sensitivity analysis, but you may wish to perform your own type of sensitivity analysis.

You can then compare column importance with the most used columns in other models such as decision trees. You can determine the most used independent columns in a decision tree a number of ways; for example you may simply count the number of times the independent column occurs in the decision tree. Figure 8.24 illustrates normalizing these important values to sum to 1 for two models used in the response to home equity loan campaign example. You can see that the most important and most used columns in the two models differ quite significantly.

Uses of Visualizations after Model Deployment

After choosing and deploying the best model, you must still monitor it to make sure it is performing as expected. The model will not perform as expected if the data it is scoring or processing is different from the data used to build it. This may occur for a number of reasons. The independent columns may be populated differently due to changes in the information-infrastructure or data entry processes that may have occurred since the model was built, or else the model could have found patterns that are seasonal and do not apply year-round. You can monitor the performance of a deployed model by comparing the previously described visualizations both during the model-building process and after deployment to make sure they are similar. For example, the overall accuracy, accuracy of each pattern, and response curve achieved during building of a decision-tree model should be similar to those measured after deployment.

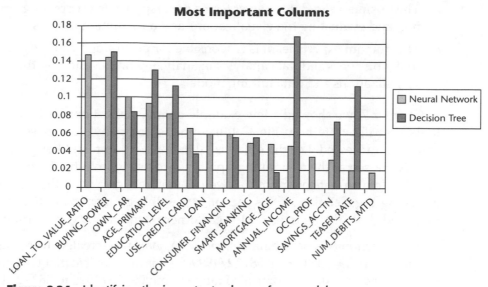

Figure 8.24   Identifying the important columns for a model.

Even if initially the model performs as expected, you should monitor the model to make sure it is not becoming out of date. A model captures patterns of some phenomenon or process and can become out of date for a number of reasons. When a model is deployed, you can directly influence the very phenomenon you attempted to model, thereby changing the patterns that occur. Consider an automobile insurance fraud model. After some time, the perpetrators of fraud will realize the frequent detection of their types of fraud (perhaps paper accidents that never actually occurred). They will more than likely change their type of fraud (to perhaps staged accidents), thereby reducing the effectiveness of the model. When this occurs, we should see a decrease in the model performance, especially the number of fraud-labeled claims.

Analyzing the Visualization or Mining Tools for the Case Study

Step 7 of the eight-step data visualization and data mining (VDM) methodology is comprised of using data visualization to acquire insight and understanding into the prepared business data set to assist you in answering your business questions. According to the VDM project plan outlined in Chapter 2, this step is estimated to take approximately 10 working days to complete. The tasks for Step 7 are assigned to the following teams:

- The business and data analyst teams are responsible for creating, analyzing, and evaluating the visualizations and data mining models.

- The domain experts team is responsible for providing business guidance to the business and data analysts in analyzing and evaluating the data visualizations and data mining models.

In Chapter 7, we showed a few example data visualizations and data mining tools that illustrate how Big Cellular phone company's business questions could be addressed. For the data visualizations, column and bar graphs were mainly chosen as the optimum graph types to use to investigate the customer attrition (churn) rate over time, as well as to investigate what the attrition rate is costing Big Cellular. In this section, we will begin analyzing the visualizations and data mining tools for the customer retention VDM pilot project.

The production business data set, *customer_join*, was created from customer invoices from 09/23/1996 to 08/12/1999. So it is only logical that the activation date or customer sign-up date also ranges from 09/23/1996 to 08/12/1999 for the data set. Therefore, the *customer_join* business data set only covers part of 1996, all of 1997 and 1998, and most of 1999. From the graphs of loyal versus lost customers by activation date (Figure 7.13) and by renewal date (Figure 7.14) in the previous chapter, the time dimension used to aggregate the business data set had a large impact on the customer churn rate. For instance, if activation date was used, the churn rate appeared to decrease over time. However, if the contract renewal date was used, the churn rate tended to linearly increase as the number of contracts increased. Therefore, we need to analyze how time affects the churn rate in more detail.

Insert Figure 13 shows a line graph that plots the number of churned versus loyal customers using the activation date as the time dimension. Four spikes appear on the line graph; three of them occur in the month of December, showing that customers tend to purchase cellular service around Christmastime. Unfortunately, the churn rate also tends to be linear with respect to the new customer activations. You'll also notice that in June of 1999 a fourth spike occurred. After this spike was discussed with the domain experts and business analysts, it was discovered that Big Cellular had run a 2-for-1 cellular promotion for that month. From Insert Figure 13, you'll notice that the trend for 1999 shows the churning customers decreasing while the number of new customer activations is increasing. Does this mean that Big Cellular is keeping more customers?

Figure 8.25 illustrates a line graph by month that plots the number of churned versus loyal customers using the contract renewal date as the time dimension. Similar to Insert Figure 13, you can see spikes in customer churn activity but only during Christmastime. Using the renewal date as the time dimension enables us to see a clearer picture of the actual loyal customer growth and churn rates. Since the majority of Big Cellular customers have yearly contracts, you see that around Christmastime there is a high rate of customer churn, since more customers have contracts up for renewal. Customers who purchased service the previous Christmas are now terminating their cellular service during the following holiday season.

Unfortunately, neither the line graph from Insert Figure 13 nor Figure 8.25 can be used to give a single customer attrition rate number. In reality, a single number doesn't exist, since it is dependent on the number of new activations and the number of active contracts over time. It will vary from month to month and tends to be very inflated during Christmastime.

In Figure 8.26, linear trend lines are added to the line graph from Figure 8.25. In addition, the date range has been reduced to November 1996 through November 1998 to minimize the seasonal spikes and account for the number of customers who will most likely churn the following Christmas season. By adding these trend lines to this 2-year line graph, you can see the overall customer attrition trend over time. The line graph shows the loyal customer trend with respect to the lost customer trend. The slope of the loyal customer trend lines is slightly steeper than the slope (increasing from left to right) of the customer attrition trend line. This slope difference indicates that fewer customers are tending to churn, or in other words, the churn rate is slightly decreasing with respect to the number of existing and new customers.

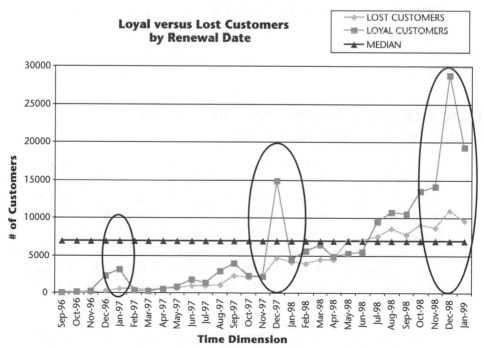

Figure 8.25   Lost versus loyal customers by renewal date.

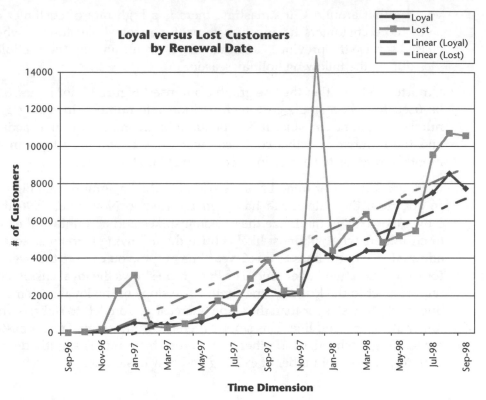

Figure 8.26 Lost versus loyal customer trends.

Using Frequency Graphs with Trend Lines to Analyze Time Relationships

Insert Figure 14 illustrates using a frequency graph to analyze the monthly churn rates for 1997, 1998, and 1999. Three linear trend lines have been added to the column graph to enable you to compare the trends for 1997, 1998, and 1999. For 1997 and 1998, the overall linear trends are decreasing. Since the business data set only contained 7 months of data for 1999, the last 5 months are estimated. However, the overall trend for 1999 is increasing. If you add up all the churn rates and divide by the number of observations, you get an average churn rate of 39.38 percent for January 1997 through July 1999. As you can see from the graphical data table, the churn rates vary dramatically from month to month. Because of the high number of new customers that sign up for service during the Christmas season, the churn rate is artificially low in December 1997 and 1998.

Using Pareto Graphs to Discover and Evaluate the Importance of Key Business Indicators

Thus far we have used data visualizations to investigate and analyze the overall churn rates for Big Cellular. However, what is the customer attrition business problem costing Big Cellular? A Pareto graph can be used to evaluate and rank the individual churn reasons. In the last chapter, a bar graph (Figure 7.16) was used to investigate the total cost of customer attrition from 09/23/1996 to 08/12/1999. Figure 8.25 shows this same graphical data set using a Pareto graph.

From Figure 8.27, you can see that the first six reasons account for 80 percent of the cost of churn. These six reasons amount to $3,305,948 in uncollected revenue from 09/23/1996 to 08/12/1999. The first two churn reasons account for almost 50 percent, as illustrated by the line graph. One of the discoveries you can discern from the Pareto graph is that perhaps Big Cellular needs to review its cancellation policy on the open invoice dollar amount. According to the domain experts and the business analysts, a REACT-BILLING NONPAY churn reason is defined as a customer who is canceled because he or she is more than 2 months delinquent on payments and has reached his or her pre-defined credit limit. A BILLING NONPAY churn reason is defined as a customer who is canceled because he or she is more than 3 months delinquent on payments. It is clear from the Pareto graph which churn reasons have the greatest effect on the total cost of churn.

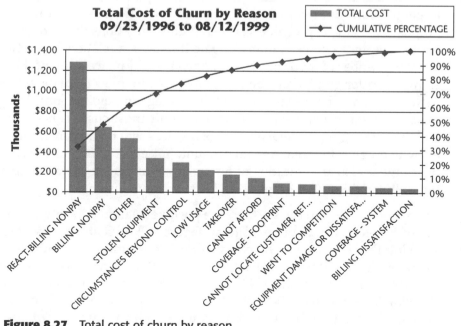

Figure 8.27   Total cost of churn by reason.

Another factor to consider is what is the total amount of revenue generated by each churn group before they were either canceled or stopped their service. This analysis may prove useful in determining whether to lower a customer's credit limit in general or cancel service before the 3-month delinquent limit is reached. Figure 8.28 is a bar graph that compares the total unpaid invoices by the paid invoices from 09/23/1996 to 08/12/1999. The churn reasons are ordered by the unpaid invoice totals. This figure also includes the graphical data table. Since the unpaid invoices are relatively a small percentage of the total paid, the graphical data table is included to assist in evaluating the cost of the customer attrition. For instance, the REACT-BILLING NONPAY group has the highest percentage of total revenue that is unpaid (6.51 percent, or $1.3 million). Although the unpaid revenue is over a half a million for the BILLING NONPAY group, their total revenue as a group is much larger, so the percentage of total revenue that is unpaid is only 1.27 percent. This type of analysis can be extremely useful in helping the decision makers decide which customer attrition groups to target or which business policies to change.

Using Scatter Graphs to Evaluate Cause-and-Effect Relationships

You can use data mining algorithms to develop business rules to profile and target the various customer attrition groups. In addition, you can use scatter graphs to evaluate potential cause-and-effect relationships. For instance, a scatter graph can be used to investigate if there is a relationship between the average number of invoices paid and the unpaid invoice amount. Figure 8.29 shows a scatter graph and a bubble graph used to investigate the relationship between the number of invoices and the average unpaid amount. The graphical data set was generated by first selecting only those customers who churned and then averaging the total number of invoices sent to them over time, as well as by averaging the total unpaid amount. Since the number of invoices sent over time is also an indication of how many months the customer spent with Big Cellular, the scatter graphs provide even more insight.

From Figure 8.29, you can see there is a positive relationship between the number of invoices and the unpaid total. Figure 8.29b illustrates a scatter graph showing that customers who churn before or around ten months leave relatively small unpaid balances (less then $20). After ten months, the unpaid balances increase dramatically ($40–$100). Figure 8.29a illustrates a bubble graph showing the same trend; however, the number of customers is also considered (size of the bubble). In this graph, you see that the majority of customers

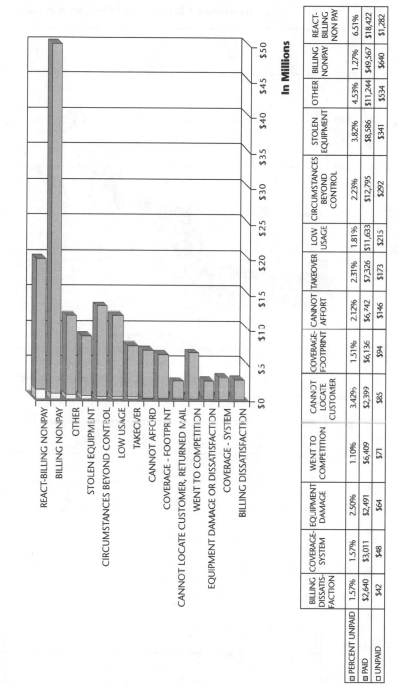

Figure 8.28 Bar graph of total unpaid versus paid invoices.

Note: *The scale of the graph is in millions of dollars per churn reason. The scale of the data table is in thousands of dollars units per churn reason.*

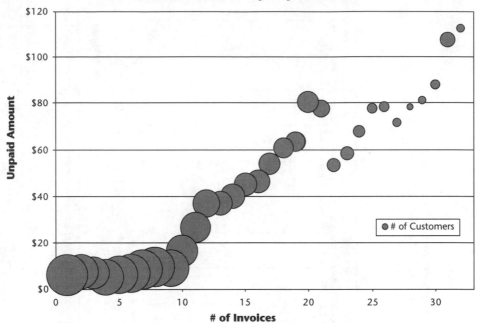

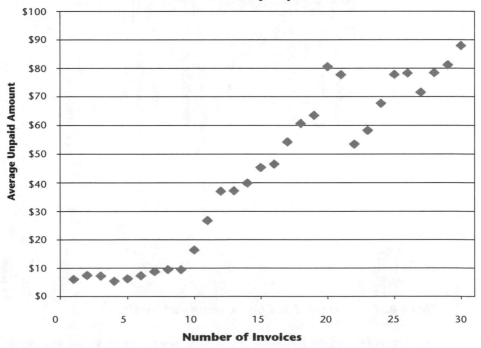

Figure 8.29 Bubble and scatter graphs of number of invoices by total unpaid.

who churn do so before or around ten months. Of the larger unpaid balances, customers who churn between ten and twenty months have balances between $40 and $80. From these graphs, you can discover insights that can help you develop new business rules for not only reducing customer attrition, but also minimizing the overall revenue impact of customer attrition.

Using Data Mining Tools to Gain an Insight into Churn

For the data mining models used to gain an insight and understanding for the customer retention VDM project, the *customer_demographic* business data set was used. Where appropriate, data visualization tools can be used for analyzing and evaluating the data mining models used to answer the key business questions. In Chapter 7 we decided to address the key business questions using the following data mining tools:

Question 1: Use K-means clustering to profile the individuals who churn.

Questions 2 and 4: Build predictive models of logistic regression and decision trees to predict if a customer will churn. Use this model to explain why customers churn.

Question 3: Build models that attempt to predict when a customer will defect.

Profiling the Ones That Got Away

To address question 1, a four-cluster model using a K-means tool was used. The CHURN_REASON column was not used in this model. The number of clusters to segment the churned population into is a key issue to address. Many data mining tools have options that will suggest the "best" number of clusters based on the intrinsic nature of the data. However, as clustering is exploratory in nature, building models using two, three, four, five, and six clusters was tried for question 1, and it was discovered that the four-cluster solution provided us with most insights and was manageable to present. Figures 8.30 through 8.33 and Tables 8.4 through 8.7 analyze and evaluate these clusters. Various columns from the *customer_demographic* business data set are used to build a descriptive profile of each cluster or customer segment. This profiling technique enables you to find and describe the different subpopulations of churners with more information than just the churn reason. We present our charts in terms of lift over the population proportion. For example, if 10 percent of all customers in the data set are from Texas and a cluster has 15 percent of customers from Texas, then the lift over to the population is 150 percent.

Figure 8.30 shows the clusters profiled by the churn reason given in the data set. The column graph displays the lift over the proportion in the population by the churn reason for each of the four clusters. Notice that the churn reasons are not uniformly distributed over the clusters.

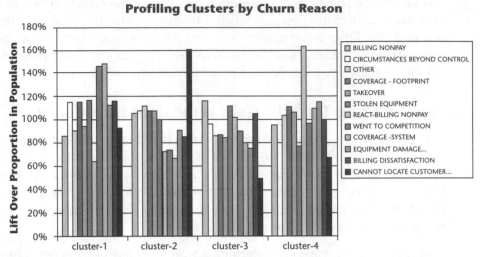

Figure 8.30 Profile of the clusters by churn reason.

Table 8.4 lists a descriptive profile of information discovered about each of the four clusters using the column graph of clusters by churn reason in Figure 8.30.

Table 8.4 Profile of Clusters by Churn Reason

CLUSTER	DESCRIPTIVE PROFILE AND OBSERVATIONS
Cluster 1	This cluster or segment of customers contains more than the average number of people who churned because they went to the competition or they did not receive the expected quality of coverage (coverage system). Conversely, the cluster contains few individuals who were forced to leave Big Cellular because they did not pay their bills (BILLING NONPAY, REACT BILLING NONPAY). These customers voluntarily left Big Cellular.
Cluster 2	This cluster or segment of customers contains a large number of people who could not be located.
Cluster 3	This cluster or segment of customer has a larger than expected number of individuals who were forced to leave Big Cellular due to nonpayment of their invoices for 3 months or had their equipment stolen and could not continue using their plan.
Cluster 4	This cluster or segment of customers contains a large number of individuals who were forcibly terminated by Big Cellular because they did not pay their invoices for 2 months but did not have their equipment stolen.

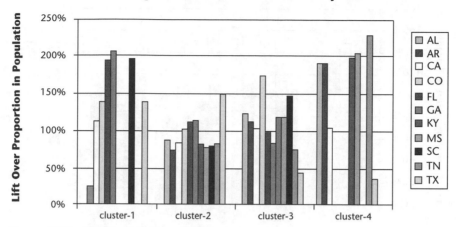

Figure 8.31   Profile of clusters by state.

Figure 8.31 is a column graph showing the clusters profiled by state. In this column graph, the lift over proportion in the population is displayed by state for each of the four clusters.

Table 8.5 continues building descriptive profile information discovered about each of the four clusters using the column graph of clusters by state in Figure 8.31.

Table 8.5   Profile of Clusters by Customer Location

CLUSTER	DESCRIPTIVE PROFILE AND OBSERVATIONS
Cluster 1	This cluster or segment consists of customers who are predominantly located in southeastern seaboard states such as Florida, Georgia, and South Carolina.
Cluster 2	This cluster or segment consists of customers who are predominately located in Texas.
Cluster 3	This cluster or segment consists of more than the expected number of customers from Colorado and South Carolina.
Cluster 4	This cluster or segment consists of customers who are predominantly located in southern states such as Tennessee, Missouri, Kentucky, Alabama, and Arkansas.

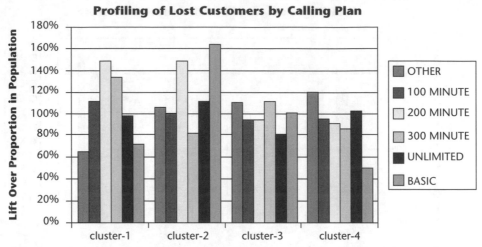

Figure 8.32 Profile of clusters by calling plan.

Figure 8.32 is a column graph showing the clusters profiled by calling plan. In this column graph, the lift over proportion in the population is displayed by calling plan for each of the four clusters.

Table 8.6 continues building descriptive profile information discovered about each of the four clusters using the column graph of clusters by calling plan in Figure 8.32.

Table 8.6 Profile of Clusters by Calling Plan

CLUSTER	DESCRIPTIVE PROFILE AND OBSERVATIONS
Cluster 1	This cluster or segment consists of customers who have more than the normal 200- or 300-minute calling plans.
Cluster 2	This cluster or segment consists of customers who predominantly have the cheaper calling plans, particularly the Basic.
Cluster 3	This cluster or segment consists of customers who have fewer than expected unlimited calling plans.
Cluster 4	This cluster or segment consists of customers who have very few basic calling plans but more than expected plans of the type "Other" (small, specialized calling plans).

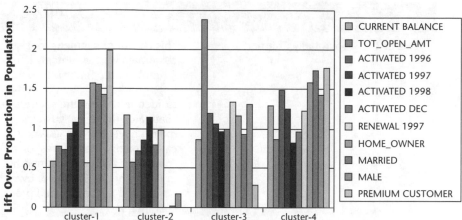

Figure 8.33 Profile of clusters by demographic and invoice information.

Figure 8.33 is a column graph showing the clusters profiled by demographic and invoice information. From this final figure, a complete descriptive profile of the segments of lost customers can be now compiled.

Table 8.7 lists the completed descriptive profile discovered concerning each cluster based upon Figures 8.30 through 8.33. In this table, a cluster "name" can be assigned based on the detailed descriptive profile of each cluster.

From the profiling exercise and information listed in Tables 8.2 through 8.5, you can now begin to understand the different types of lost customers and even why some of the customers left Big Cellular. For example, those customers in cluster 2 are renters who more than likely move frequently and do not leave forwarding mailing addresses. They churn because their invoices are returned to Big Cellular. As they tend to have cheaper plans, it may not be worthwhile chasing this type of customer. Unlike cluster 2, we wish to stop cluster 1 customers from defecting; they pay their bills in a timely fashion (even when they leave), are considered premium customers, and had relatively expensive calling plans. Cluster 4 customers are demographically similar to cluster 1 customers, as they are overwhelmingly married, own their home, and are considered premium customers. They differ from cluster 1, as they are often involuntarily terminated and reside predominantly in the southern states. Cluster 3 customers are long-time customers, who leave large unpaid balances and are not considered premium.

Table 8.7   Completed Profile of Lost Customers

CLUSTER	CLUSTER "NAME"	DETAILED DESCRIPTIVE CLUSTER PROFILE
Cluster 1	Voluntarily Churned	This cluster or segment consists of customers who voluntarily churned (went to competition). They were not happy with the system coverage and resided mainly on the southeastern seaboard. These lost customers mainly have 200- or 300-minute calling plans. They left responsibly (paid their bills). They joined mainly in December, are married, own their home, and are considered premium customers.
Cluster 2	Could Not Locate	This cluster or segment consists of customers who could not be located. These lost customers were mainly from Texas and had predominantly cheaper calling plans. They had a little higher than expected balances and are almost exclusively unmarried, young, female, and renters.
Cluster 3	Canceled for Nonpayment or Stolen Equipment	This cluster or segment consists of customers who were forced to leave (canceled by Big Cellular) because they did not pay invoices or had reported their equipment stolen. These lost customers were mainly from Colorado and South Carolina. They did not have many unlimited calling plans; however, they left with very large open account amounts. They did renew in 1997, but very few are premium customers.
Cluster 4	Canceled Premium Customers for Nonpayment or Stolen Equipment	This cluster or segment consists of customers who were forced to leave (canceled by Big Cellular). These lost customers were mainly from the southern states. They had very few basic calling plans and opened their accounts predominantly in 1996 to 1997. They are male, married, and own their home. In addition, a very large portion are premium customers.

K-means clustering analysis provides a good picture of the lost customers. It also provides insights into which customers you want to stop from defecting (cluster 1 and cluster 4). However, some issues are puzzling. Why are the customers in cluster 1 and cluster 4 who are demographically very similar apart from their location and even have similar calling plans churning for different reasons? Cluster 1 customers churn voluntarily, whereas cluster 4 customers involuntarily leave. Figure 8.34 helps to answer this question. Cluster 1 customers predominantly *proactively* join Big Cellular, whereas customers in cluster 4 *reactively* join Big Cellular due to contact by a mall vendor or a family member.

Trying to Predict the Defectors

For analyzing and evaluating the customer retention VDM project business questions 2 and 4, the data mining aim is to build a model that is independent of activation year and that attempts to predict whether a customer will defect. To achieve this goal, some columns that indirectly are surrogates of the dependent column will need to be removed from the *customer_demographic* business data set. For example, the account balance will be quite different for customers who have terminated as compared with those who are still active. Table 8.8 lists the column removed from the *customer_demographic* business data set prior to building the predictive models.

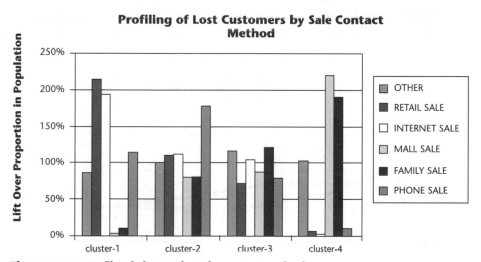

Figure 8.34   Profile of clusters by sale contact method.

Table 8.8 Columns Removed from the *customer_demographic* Data Set and Removal Reasons

COLUMNS REMOVED	REMOVAL REASON
CUSTOMERID	Unique customer token
CITY	Require general model
ZIP	Require general model
CURRENTBALANCE	Indirect surrogate for dependent column
CHURN_REASON	Direct surrogate for dependent column
TOT_OPEN_AMT	Indirect surrogate for dependent column
TOT_INVOICE_AMT	Indirect surrogate for dependent column
TOT_PAID_AMT	Indirect surrogate for dependent column
NUM_INVOICES	Indirect surrogate for dependent column
RENEWAL_YEAR	Require general model
RENEWAL_MONTH	Require general model

After the columns were removed, classification models using logistic regression and decision tree tools were built that attempt to predict which customers will churn. Tenfold cross-validation was performed for each classification tool and we present the average results.

Figure 8.35 shows a lift chart that compares the accuracy of both classification techniques. It shows that the logistic regression model initially outperforms the decision tree for about the top 20 percent of predictions but quickly performs poorly. By the 45th percentile, it is performing worse than a best-guess model. The decision tree initially has a reasonable lift that slowly diminishes.

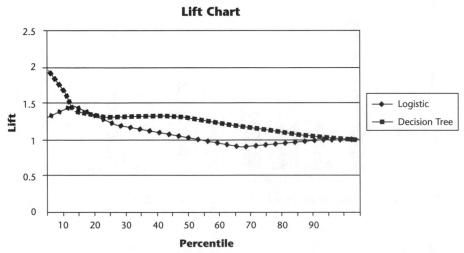

Figure 8.35 Cumulative lift chart of decision tree and logistic regression models.

Figure 8.36 shows a noncumulative lift chart that compares the accuracy of both classification techniques. It shows that the decision tree model's accuracy progressively decreases as you move from the predictions with strongest to weakest confidence. The chart illustrates that the logistic regression model potentially could be more accurate, but it does perform well with predictions of medium confidence.

As you can see from the cumulative and noncumulative lift charts, the logistic and decision tree models perform quite differently. The logistic regression performs extremely well but only for its most strongest predictions, whereas the decision tree sustains its performance over all its predictions. To determine the best model, you need to consider the financial aspect of the problem. One measurement used by Big Cellular is the percentage of lost customers. From the data visualization analysis discussed earlier in the case study, it was determined that the average percentage of lost customers was approximately 35 percent of nearly 465,000 customers (over a 3-year period), which cost the company just over $4 million. Furthermore, each lost customer cost approximately $25 in unpaid bills. If these potential lost customers can be isolated, you can save the organization money. As an initial approach, it was decided by the decision makers and marketing department that Big Cellular would develop a customer retention marketing plan to give away $50 worth of free calls. The cost to produce and mail out the offer is $2, making the total cost per customer $52. The estimated revenue for each correct prediction of a positive response will be $101, which includes the unpaid bills. If the offer is sent to a customer who was not going to defect, then no additional revenue is gained.

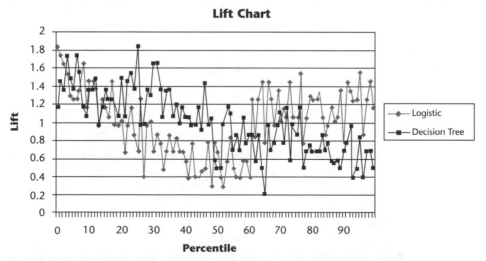

Figure 8.36 Noncumulative lift chart of decision tree and logistic regression models.

Figures 8.37 and 8.38 test and evaluate the performance of the respective models given the financial aspects of the customer retention marketing plan just discussed (even before deploying the models or sending out the first offer). You can see that ROI for the logistic regression model is initially extremely high, whereas the ROI for the decision tree is more consistent. The profit chart shows that Big Cellular can make at most about $7,500 using the logistic regression model and nearly $15,000 using the decision tree model per 2,000 customers. If the aim is to maximize the ROI, Big Cellular should use the logistic regression model's top 15 percent of predictions. If the aim is to maximize profits, Big Cellular should use the top 50 percent of the decision tree's predictions. In Chapter 9, verifying and presenting the analysis is discussed. The ROI and profit charts will be used to enable the decision makers to make informed decisions concerning which model to deploy for the customer retention VDM project.

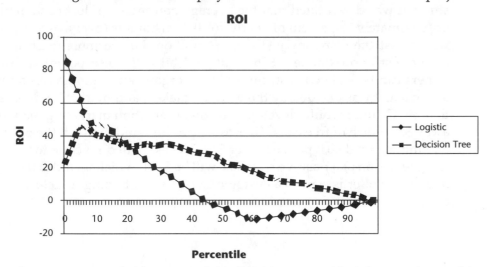

Figure 8.37 Cumulative ROI (%) chart of decision tree and logistic regression models.

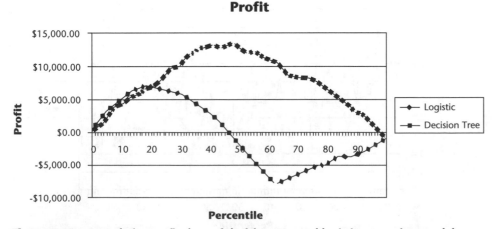

Figure 8.38 Cumulative profit chart of decision tree and logistic regression models.
Profit shown is per 2,000 customers.

Explaining Why People Leave

For analyzing and evaluating the customer retention VDM project business question 4, the rules from the decision tree model can be investigated and analyzed to gain insight into why a customer will leave Big Cellular. Since the model attempts to find correlations between individuals who churn and the independent columns, it will not explicitly tell why a customer churns. Instead, the decision tree paths or rule must be investigated with the assistance of the data and business analysts and domain experts to come up with plausible reasons why individuals are churning. Code Figure 8.4 shows a typical decision tree model containing 24 rules. A minimum number of 500 customer records support each path or rule.

```
RATE_PLAN ['100 MINUTE' '300 MINUTE' OTHER UNLIMITED]
    UPSCALE YES
    AGE_RANGE [20S 80S TEEN]
    (0.688) Churn =  TRUE {RULE #1}
    AGE_RANGE [30S 40S 50S 60S 70S 90S UNK]
        ACTIVATED_MONTH [APR AUG JUL MAY NOV OCT]
        (0.605) Churn =  FALSE {RULE #2}
        ACTIVATED_MONTH DEC
            REGION [E_N_CENTRAL MID_ATLANTIC NEW_ENGLAND
            PACIFIC S_ATLANTIC W_N_CENTRAL]
                (0.6) Churn = FALSE {RULE #3}
            REGION E S CENTRAL
                CONTRACT_FEE =< 40
                (0.514) Churn =  TRUE {RULE #4}
                CONTRACT_FEE > 40
                (0.556) Churn =  FALSE {RULE #5}
            REGION [MOUNTAIN W_S_CENTRAL]
            (0.81) Churn =  TRUE {RULE #6}
        ACTIVATED_MONTH [FEB JAN JUN MAR]
        (0.57) Churn =  TRUE {RULE #7}
        ACTIVATED_MONTH SEP
            YRS_RESIDENCE =< 5
            (0.519) Churn =  TRUE {RULE #8}
            YRS_RESIDENCE > 5
            (0.718) Churn =  FALSE {RULE #9}
    UPSCALE NO (1514)
        RATE_PLAN 100 MINUTE
        (0.782) Churn =  TRUE {RULE #10}
        RATE_PLAN ['300 MINUTE' OTHER UNLIMITED]
            MARITAL_STATUS ['DVRD FEMALE' 'DVRD MALE'
                SINGLE UNKNOWN]
            (0.655) Churn =  TRUE {RULE #11}
            MARITAL_STATUS MARRIED
                AGE_RANGE [20S 70S 80S 90S TEEN]
                (0.824) Churn =  TRUE {RULE #12}
```

Code Figure 8.4 Decision tree model to predict individuals who churn. *(continues)*

```
                              AGE_RANGE [30S 40S 50S 60S UNK]
                                  REGION E_S_CENTRAL
                                      ESTIMATED_INCOME =< 60
                                      (0.56) Churn =  TRUE {RULE #13}
                                      ESTIMATED_INCOME  > 60
                                      (0.597) Churn =  FALSE {RULE #14}
                                  REGION [MID_ATLANTIC PACIFIC W_S_CENTRAL]
                                      (1.0) Churn =  TRUE {RULE #15}
                                  REGION [E_N_CENTRAL MOUNTAIN NEW_ENGLAND
                                         S_ATLANTIC W_N_CENTRAL]
                                      (0.607) Churn =  FALSE {RULE #16}
RATE_PLAN ['200 MINUTE' BASIC]
    HOME_OWNER NULL [Mode: FALSE]
        CONTRACT_FEE =< 10
        (0.651) Churn =  FALSE {RULE #17}
         CONTRACT_FEE  > 10)
              CONSUMER_CARD YES
              (0.659) Churn =  FALSE {RULE #18}
              CONSUMER_CARD NO
                      AGE_RANGE [20S 30S 60S 70S 90S TEEN UNK]
                      (0.585) Churn =  TRUE {RULE #19}
                      AGE_RANGE [40S 50S 80S]
                      (0.586) Churn =  FALSE {RULE #20}
    HOME_OWNER OWN [Mode: FALSE] (1005)
          ESTIMATED_INCOME =< 100
          (0.683) Churn =  FALSE {RULE #21}
         ESTIMATED_INCOME  > 100
         (0.559) Churn =  TRUE {RULE #22}
    HOME_OWNER RENT
    (0.905) Churn =  FALSE {RULE #23}
```

Notes:

- The *customer_demographic* business data set columns are denoted in **bold**.
- The accuracy of path or rule is denoted in parentheses.
- The rule number is denoted in **bold italics**.
- The path or rule is built by reading to include all previous conditions. For instance, rule 1 is read as follows:

  IF

  RATE_PLAN = '100 MINUTES' or '300 MINUTES' or 'OTHER' or 'UNLIMITED'

  AND UPSCALE='YES'

  AND AGE_RANGE= '20s' or '80s or 'TEEN',

  THEN

  churn = 'TRUE'
- The accuracy of the rule #1 is 68.8%.

Code Figure 8.4   *(continued)*

Just by looking at the columns used in the decision tree, you can see that the major drivers of churn are rate plan, geographic location, activation month, contract fees, customer age, and type of customer (upscale or not). These data dimensions suggest that the reasons why individuals churn are not consistent factors (such as bad service) but vary depending on their rate plan, location, who sold the service, and their economic situation. Some interesting decision tree paths or rules that resulted in predicting that the customer was most likely to churn are listed in Table 8.9.

From Table 8.9, you can examine the rules to see if they provide insight into why customers terminated. In addition, you can combine these insights with the previously obtained clusters to gain additional insights and profile those customers by the churn rules. For instance, rule 1 describes those individuals who are predominantly in cluster 1 (Voluntarily Churned). Rule 4 illustrates that many of the individuals who activated in December and were in the

Table 8.9   Example of Decision Tree Rules for Predicting Churn

RULE NUMBER	ACCURACY OF PREDICTION	DECISION TREE PATH
1	68.8%	RATE_PLAN 100, 300-Minute, Other, or Unlimited
		UPSCALE=YES
		AGE_RANGE= 20s, 80s, or Teens
4	51.4%	RATE_PLAN 100, 300-Minute, Other, or Unlimited
		UPSCALE=YES
		AGE_RANGE <> 20s, 80s, or Teens
		ACTIVATION_MONTH=December
		REGION=E_S_Central
		CONTRACT_FEE <= $40
6	81%	RATE_PLAN 100, 300-Minute, Other, or Unlimited
		UPSCALE=YES
		ACTIVATION_MONTH=December
		REGION=Mountain or W_S_Central
10	78.2%	RATE_PLAN 100
		UPSCALE=NO

eastern south central region with low contract fees terminated. These customers belonged predominantly to cluster 4 (Canceled Premium Customers for Nonpayment). Recall that cluster 4 customers were sold their contract in malls or by family. Their low contract fee could have been because of a Christmas promotional offer. Rule 10 is quite simple and interesting. It says that nonupscale customers with the 100-minute rate plan are extremely likely to churn. These churners belong to cluster 3. This illustrates that perhaps this plan is no longer competitive in the marketplace.

Predicting When People Will Leave

For analyzing and evaluating the customer retention VDM project business question 2, predicting precisely when people will leave is difficult. It is more feasible and pragmatic to try to predict if someone is likely to terminate within 1 year or greater than 1 year from his or her activation date. The first type of model you can consider is an early warning churn model. To build the data set for this model, only those rows or records whose number of invoices is less than 12 months are selected. Since the early warning model will be month-invariant, in addition to the previously removed columns (refer to Table 8.8), the column ACTIVATED_MONTH is also removed from the *customer_demographic* business data set.

Figure 8.39 shows the lift obtained from using decision tree models versus the general model. In addition, the decision tree model to predict customers who will churn in the longer term (after 1 year of activation) is more accurate than the general model. This is because what the classifier has to predict is easier. Previously, the decision tree model was required to predict if any customers would churn, which could be for any number of reasons. In the case of prediction when customers will leave, the task is simplified by focusing only on those customers who churn within the first 12 months of their contract. This approach of simplifying the prediction task could be continued by perhaps investigating building classifiers to predict *why* the customer churned. For instance, the predicted label could be segmented into three dependent column values, such as Active, Voluntarily Left, and Involuntarily Left. The latter category would include individuals who were terminated by Big Cellular due to nonpayment of invoices.

Code Figure 8.5 shows a typical early detection decision tree model. This model attempts to predict individuals who are most likely to churn within 12 months of their contract activation.

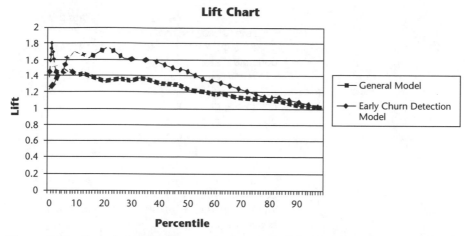

Figure 8.39 Cumulative lift chart comparing general decision tree churn model with early detection decision tree churn model.

```
RATE_PLAN ['100 MINUTE' OTHER]
(0.856) CHURN = NEARFUTURE {Rule #1}
RATE_PLAN ['200 MINUTE' '300 MINUTE' BASIC UNLIMITED]
CONTRACT_FEE =< 10
(0.666) CHURN = ACTIVE {RULE #2}
CONTRACT_FEE  > 10
     HOME_OWNER NULL (0.755)
     CHURN = NEARFUTURE {RULE #3}
     HOME_OWNER [OWN RENT]
          GENDER [FEMALE NULL UNKNOWN]
          (0.67) CHURN = NEARFUTURE {RULE #4}
          GENDER MALE
               REGION [E_N_CENTRAL MID_ATLANTIC MOUNTAIN PACIFIC
                    W_S_CENTRAL]
               (0.833) CHURN = NEARFUTURE {RULE #5}
               REGION E_S_CENTRAL
                    CREDIT_CARD_BUYER YES
                     (0.606) CHURN = ACTIVE {RULE #6}
                    CREDIT_CARD_BUYER NO
                    CONTRACT_FEE =< 25
                         ESTIMATED_INCOME =< 60
```

Code Figure 8.5 Decision tree model to predict individuals who are likely to churn within 12 months. *(continues)*

```
                              (0.625)CHURN = NEARFUTURE {RULE #7}
                              ESTIMATED_INCOME  > 60
                              (0.602) CHURN = ACTIVE {RULE #8}
                         CONTRACT_FEE  > 25
                           (0.629) CHURN=NEARFUTURE  {RULE #9}
               REGION S_ATLANTIC
                    CONSUMER_CARD YES
                    CONTRACT_FEE =< 25
                         ESTIMATED_INCOME =< 70
                         (0.556) CHURN=ACTIVE {RULE #10}
                         ESTIMATED_INCOME  > 70
                           (0.582) CHURN=NEARFUTURE  {RULE #11}
                    CONTRACT_FEE  > 25
                    (0.614) CHURN = NEARFUTURE {RULE #12}
               CONSUMER_CARD NO
               (0.636) CHURN = NEARFUTURE {RULE #13}
```

Notes:

- The *customer_demographic* business data set columns are denoted in **bold**.
- The accuracy of path or rule is denoted in parentheses.
- The rule number is denoted in **bold italics**.
- The path or rule is built by reading to include all previous conditions. For instance, rule 1 is read as follows:

    IF

    RATE_PLAN = '100 MINUTES' or '300 MINUTES' or BASIC or 'UNLIMITED'

    AND CONTRACT_FEE= < $10'

    THEN

    CHURN = 'ACTIVE'
- The accuracy of the rule is 66.6%.

Code Figure 8.5   *(continued)*

Some interesting decision tree paths or rules that resulted in predicting which customers were most likely to churn within the next 12 months of their contract activation date are listed in Table 8.10.

Table 8.10 Example of Decision Tree Rules for Predicting Churn within 12 Months of Activation

RULE NUMBER	ACCURACY OF PREDICTION	DECISION TREE PATH
1	85.6%	RATE_PLAN = 100-Minute or Other
4	67%	RATE_PLAN = 200, 300-Minute, Basic, or Unlimited
		CONTRACT_FEE > $10
		HOME_OWNER=OWN or RENT
		GENDER=FEMALE, NULL or UNKNOWN

Summary

In this chapter, we have focused on interpreting what the data visualizations are showing you about your prepared business data set and what information can be derived to answer your visualization business questions. We also focused on using data visualizations to analyze, evaluate, and gain insights into the results of data mining models. We demonstrated how these types of visualization can be useful to compare and contrast multiple data mining models that address your data mining business questions. In the next chapter, we discuss the last step of the data analysis phase of the VDM project: verifying the data visualization and data mining discoveries with other data and business analysts. Once verified, a selected number of data visualizations and data mining models will be used for the analysis presentation that is presented to the decision makers.

Step 8: Verifying and Presenting the Visualizations or Mining Models

S tep 8 of the VDM methodology is composed of three parts. First, you need to verify that the visualizations and data mining model satisfied your business goals and objectives. Next, you need to create a business presentation of the visualization and data mining discoveries to give to the decision makers. Then, based on the type of VDM project, you may need to deploy the visualizations and mining models into the production environments. Step 8 is the third and final step in the data analysis phase. In this chapter, we focus our attention on verifying that the discovered business trends and data mining models are significant in answering the business questions. The data and business analysts need to consult with the domain experts and other business analysts to verify that the analysis from the previous chapters is valid, accurate, and significant. After verifying and evaluating the analysis, we illustrate useful techniques for preparing a business presentation for the decision makers. We also discuss potential deployment options for the visualizations and data mining models. Finally, we apply Step 8 to the ongoing customer retention business case study.

Implementing the data visualization or data mining models into the production environment can be a meticulous and time-consuming process and is outside the scope of this book. However, we will discuss the overall steps of the implementation phase, as well as which steps need to be addressed based on the type of VDM project.

Verifying the Data Visualizations and Mining Models

In Chapter 6, the business data sets were verified to ensure that they represented a true, error-free, and unbiased portrayal of the operational data source information. From these business data sets, data visualizations and data mining models were created to address the business questions under investigation. Likewise, the data visualizations and data mining models you developed need to be verified to ensure they represent a true, error-free, and unbiased portrayal of real business trends to ensure the accuracy of your analysis.

Verifying Logical Transformations to the Business Data Set

While creating the graphical data table, you may have aggregated certain columns from the business data set or selected a subset of the data based upon certain criteria. You need to make certain that these aggregations and selection operations didn't introduce errors or bias into your analysis. Similarly, you may have removed columns, added calculated columns, grouped column values into ranges, or performed other transformations while building a data set to investigate. You also need to make certain these transformation operations didn't introduce errors or bias into your analysis.

In some cases, you can use the discrete and continuous column verifications techniques described in Chapter 6 to verify the graphical data table or data set used to create the data mining model. In most cases, you will need to rely on the domain experts and other business analysts to help you verify any "logical" transformations, such as profit and expense column calculations. Following are examples of verification questions that can help you to ensure the visualization or data mining model truly represents the real business trends:

- If you aggregated the business data set by a date-type column, was the date continuous over the period of investigation? For example, if you aggregated by INVOICE_DATE and your business only sends invoices on Mondays and Tuesdays, only visualizations aggregated to a weekly, monthly, or yearly granularity will not be biased. Was INVOICE_DATE the best column to use, or is there another date-type column that isn't as biased or is more appropriate in relation to the business question under investigation?

- Was the data continuous over the period of investigation? For example, if there were multiple promotions that started at different times during the period, the effects of one promotion may have crossed over to the start of another promotion. Whenever possible, it is best to isolate one cause-and-effect time period from another.

- If you grouped column values into ranges, were the groupings biased? For example, if you grouped customer incomes into High, Medium, and Low categories, you need to verify with the business and other data analysts that your definitions of High, Medium, and Low correspond to their definitions and the business definitions used throughout the organization.

■ If you used a sampling technique to reduce the size of the operation data source or business data set, did you normalize the results or transform them back into population amounts? For example, if you created a visualization of total customers or total profit by some category, the visualization totals only represent or depict the sample and not the entire population. Often, sampled data totals confuse the decision makers. Normally, they know approximately how many customers or the total profit the business makes. To transform the sample totals back into population amounts, you should divide the totals in the graphical data table by the sampling percent to calculate the population amount. For example, if you used a 10 percent sample and one of the totals in your graphical data tables is $100, you can divide $100 by 0.10 (10 percent) to get $1,000. The $1,000 is the actual total amount in the population.

■ If you are using visualization to augment traditional green bar reports, do the numbers in the visualization correspond to the totals and subtotals in the green bar reports? A simple verification technique is to cross-check the figures between the hard-copy report and the visualization amounts.

Verifying Your Business Assumptions

If ROI and profit charts were used to evaluate and choose the best data mining model, you need to verify the revenue and expense assumptions and calculations with the domain experts and the other data and business analysts. Following are example verification questions that can help you ensure the best model was selected based on realistic business factors:

■ Was the time basis the same for all ROI and profit calculations? For instance, are you measuring the expenses and revenues by month, quarter, year, or other cycle? Make sure you are using the same basis for all your calculations.

■ Did you include all the expense costs of a negative classification in the ROI and profit calculations? For instance, you need to include the cost of the VDM project, the estimated cost of deploying the model into the production environment, the estimated maintenance and monitoring costs of the model, and the mailing or solicitation costs in your expense costs.

■ Did you include all the revenue or profit from a positive classification in the ROI and profit calculations? For instance, a new customer may buy multiple services or products from your business, not just the service or product you are currently using the data mining model to target.

Verifying the data visualizations and data mining models is an important step to ensure the accuracy and integrity of the analysis. This step takes the collaboration of all the VDM teams. Whenever possible, use quantitative measurements and verification strategies instead of qualitative approaches. Make sure all teams agree on the business definitions and assumptions used for the visualizations and data mining models. It is easier to re-create a data visualization using a modified or corrected graphical data table or re-create a data mining model with a modified or corrected data set than it is to explain to the decision makers why the analysis was flawed or the total yearly sales doesn't match the yearly sales report.

Organizing and Creating the Business Presentation

Once the analysis has been verified, you can begin organizing and creating your business presentation. The key to a successful presentation is to know your target audience. Many of the data visualizations created during the analysis and evaluation process may be very interesting to you and other data and business analysts; however, they are often too detailed or complex to use for the presentation to the decision makers. For instance, a decision tree model visualization may contain hundreds of classification paths or rules, but for the business presentation, you only need to highlight the most important rules and insights. Often, providing the decision makers with a bulleted list of the most important rules has a greater impact than providing all the details.

Parts of the Business Presentation

Numerous books are available that provide advice on creating successful presentations. The presentation content will depend on your target audience and the type of VDM project: proof-of-concept, pilot, or production. It may be useful to structure your presentation into three main sections:

- Description of the VDM project goals and objectives
- Highlights of the discoveries and data mining models as they relate to the top business questions investigated
- Discussion of the next steps or call to action

Presenting the results of a visual data mining project can be particularly challenging due to the often high expectations and partial understanding that come with using new technology. As a rule of thumb, explicitly state all the assumptions, goals, and outcomes associated with each step to make sure everyone is at the same level of knowledge. This means that you may spend as much as 5 minutes per page of the presentation. A 1-hour presentation should contain no more than 45 minutes of slides, leaving 15 minutes for discussion at the end of the presentation.

It is often a good idea to prepare handouts for your presentation. If you are using a presentation product like Microsoft PowerPoint, the presentation notes feature enables you to supply more details about the slide. This is extremely useful if the slide contains a visualization or data mining model, since you can describe the visualization or data mining model in more detail as a slide note. Print the presentation in note-page format so that the top half of the handout page contains a hard copy of the presentation slide and the bottom half of the page contains detailed notes about the visualization or data mining model insights and discoveries. Your audience can use the handouts to take notes during the presentation. It also serves as a method for you to document the analysis.

Description of the VDM Project Goals

As part of the presentation to the decision makers, you should clearly restate the project goals and objects. During Step 1 of the VDM methodology, you originally defined your project goals and objectives as part of the project justification and plan. Have they changed based upon the analysis of the business data set? In some cases, perhaps you were able to build data mining models or discover trends with higher degrees of accuracy than you had originally projected. In other cases, perhaps you weren't able to attain the improvements or discoveries that you had originally projected.

For instance, your VDM project goal may have been to develop data mining models to improve overall *customer response* to a target marketing campaign by 10 percent. However, after performing the data analysis phase, you may have been able to create data mining models that could improve the *customer positive response rate* to the campaign from 7 percent to over 50 percent. Through the analysis, you may have discovered data mining techniques to improve the quality of the responders (list of responders most likely to buy the product or service), not necessarily to increase the total number of responders to the campaign. Restating the project goals and objectives as part of the presentation ensures that you and your audience are all in agreement. In this case, restate your project goal as "to improve the customer positive response rate from 7 percent to 50 percent."

Highlights of the Discoveries and Data Mining Models

This portion of the presentation consists of communicating the business insights and discoveries found through the data analysis phase. Using data visualization in your presentation helps you communicate your discoveries to the decision makers. If the data visualization is complex and can't be simplified, you may need to augment the visualization with a bulleted list of the discovered insights. Figure 9.1 illustrates this combined technique using the tree graph from the home equity loan campaign analysis example. In this example, only the left path of the tree is shown, which highlights the decision paths for those customers who were most likely to respond to the home equity loan campaign. The bulleted list next to the visualization lists the most important rules.

Chapters 7 and 8 discussed numerous visualization techniques for communicating your data visualization discoveries. For data visualizations business questions, the following graph types may be useful in highlighting your visualization insights and discoveries in your business presentation:

- Frequency graphs are useful for illustrating how key business indicators were discovered and evaluated. For example, using Figure 8.2 from Chapter 8, you can provide business insight into the home equity loan campaign responders' ages in relation to the customer base.

- Pareto graphs may be used as a visual communication tool for illustrating and ranking the most important key business indicators. For example, using Figure 8.7 from Chapter 8 and Insert Figure 10, you can provide business insights about the home equity loan campaign responders' ages and mortgage ages by showing the profile of the majority (80 percent) of the responders.

**Customers Most Likely to Respond to the
Home Equity Loan Campaign**

Business Rules for
Positive Responders

- The most important factor in customer response is whether they had clear title to their car.
- If their weekly income was greater than $488 and their monthly debits were more than $334, then they were 60% more likely to respond.
- If their weekly income was less than $488 and their mortgage age was less than 8.5 years, then they were 80% more likely to respond.

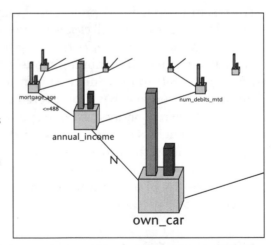

Dark columns indicate positive responses
Light columns indicate negative responses

Figure 9.1   Slide explaining the classification rules from a decision tree model.

- If the answer to the data visualization questions contained a time-based component, you can use radar graphs as a visual communication tool for illustrating the season trends or problem areas. You can also use line graphs for highlighting time-based relationship discoveries.

- In many cases, scatter graphs may be too complex to use. However, if you use a bulleted list to describe the insights and add trend lines to the graph, you may be able to use scatter graphs as part of your presentation to highlight cause-and-effect relationships between business indicators.

The majority of these graph types lend themselves to easy interpretation and may not need a bulleted list to supplement communicating your discoveries. However, if you plan to create handouts as part of the presentation, you may need to redefine the colors used for the graphical entities (columns, bars, lines, points), as well as the background color of the graph. For black-and-white handouts, avoid using light colors such as yellow for the graphical entities. In addition, only use a white background for the graph area. Even for color handouts, you should proof the readability and understandability of the printed version of the visualization. For complex visualizations, add notes to the handouts, instead of trying to fit all the information on a single presentation slide.

Chapter 8 also discussed numerous visualization techniques for communicating your data mining insights and discoveries. For data mining classification and prediction business questions, the following graph types are useful for highlighting your discoveries and their performance in your business presentation.

- Cumulative lift, response, and gain charts are useful for showing comparisons among multiple data mining models and demonstrating the strength of using each model versus guessing. In many cases, you should be prepared to explain how to interpret the graph. You may want to use a bulleted list to explain the business impacts of using one model versus another.

- Cumulative ROI and profit charts are useful for presenting the financial aspects of deploying a particular model. In the companion bulleted list, you may want to include the business assumptions used to build the charts. For example, list the cost associated with making a prediction and the benefit for a correct classification and the cost (if any) for an incorrect classification. In the presentation notes, describe how the tool is calculating the estimated revenue, as well as the estimated costs.

Figure 9.2 shows a slide with a bulleted list that explains the cumulative return on investment chart for the home equity loan campaign.

For data mining segmentation business questions, column graphs can be used as visual tools for communicating the discovered customer segments and what differentiates them from each other. Figure 9.3 shows a slide that uses a bulleted list to explain the four customer profiles discovered in the response to home equity loan campaign. You can see from this graph that the lack of a presence of using smart banking correlates well with a low response rate to the campaign. This may indicate that the campaign was communicated well to customers who used smart banking.

Call to Action

For proof-of-concept VDM projects, the call to action may be simply to gain approval to start a pilot or production VDM project. For pilot VDM projects, you may want to present potential deployment options for implementing the discoveries and data mining models in a production environment. For production VDM projects, you may want to present a high-level overview plan for deploying the discoveries and data mining models into the production environment. In all three cases, it is useful to document what you believe are the short- and long-term steps for implementing the pilot or production VDM project.

Short-term call-to-action tasks are those steps that can be accomplished in a few days or weeks and don't require colossal resource or process changes to the production environment. The following are examples of short-term call-to-action steps:

- Purchase software and hardware to support the pilot or production project.
- Request a larger sample, larger date ranges, or full exports of the operational data sources that may have only been sampled for the proof-of-concept or pilot projects.
- Request personnel resources for the pilot or production project.

Long-term call-to-action tasks are those steps that take longer to implement and frequently require process changes to the production environment. The following are examples of long-term call-to-action steps:

- Automate periodic updates to the exploratory data mart from the operational data sources or data warehouse.
- Automate the VDM data mining models into the production environment.
- Deploy automatic measurement and monitoring facilities to measure the effectiveness of the data mining models.
- Initiate a marketing project that uses the results of the pilot or production project.

Estimated Profits Using a Logistic Regression, Decision Tree, or Neural Network Model

Profit Assumptions

- Each positive response generates approximately $500 in yearly revenue.
- Each offer sent to a prospect costs approximately $250.

Suggested Method

- To maximize yearly profits, use the decision tree model to generate a customer list sorted on confidence of prediction, and use the top 45% of this list.

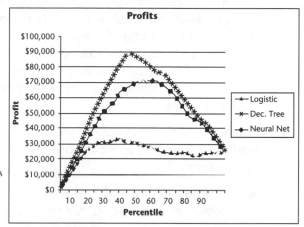

Figure 9.2 Slide explaining the estimated profits by model.

If your call to action is to gain approval to convert a proof-of-concept into a pilot or production project, you may want to list the new proposed project goals and what resources will be required for the new project. You may also want to provide an estimated project timeline. (Recall that these topics are discussed in Chapter 2.)

What Makes Each Cluster Different?

Cluster 1: Customers with savings accounts
- Have savings accounts with bank and use smart banking.
- Responded very well to campaign.

Cluster 2: Customers without savings account
- Use smart banking but do not have a savings account.
- Responded quite well to campaign.

Cluster 3: Customers who do not use smart banking
- Half as likely to use small banking compared to the other segments.
- Responded poorly to campaign.

Cluster 4: Average customers
- Largest cluster and was quite similar to overall population (although proportion who have savings accounts is a little high).

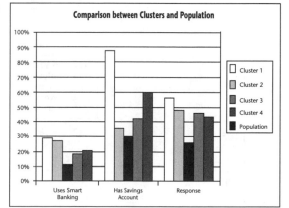

Figure 9.3 Slide highlighting home equity loan campaign customer profiles.

VDM Project Implementation Phase

Chapter 2 first introduced the closed-loop business model (as illustrated in Figure 9.4). It was used to illustrate the business stages and interactions of a production VDM project. Deploying the visualization or data mining models into the production environment can be a meticulous and time-consuming process and is outside the scope of this book. However, we will describe the steps of the implementation phase as they relate to the call to action section of the business presentation.

The number of steps of the implementation phase you need to address in your business presentation and eventually need to perform depends on your VDM project type:

■ For proof-of-concept VDM projects, the project goal is to illustrate what discoveries and insights can found in the business data set. Typically, proof-of-concept projects do not include an implementation phase.

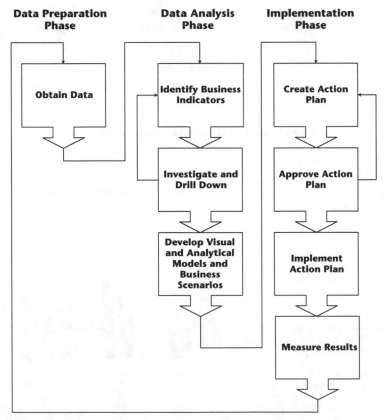

Figure 9.4 Closed-loop business model.

- For a pilot VDM project, you need to develop and investigate potential business scenarios and propose an action plan and gain approval for the action plan. Frequently, the action plan is to demonstrate how visualization and data mining model discoveries and insights address the business questions. The action plan is to gain approval to deploy those discoveries into the production environment or begin a fully funded production VDM project. In some cases, the pilot project analysis may be comprehensive enough to act on without redoing the data preparation and data analysis phases. Sometimes, you can merely use larger samples or longer date ranges, or you can resample the current operational data sources to update and verify the discoveries.

- For a production VDM project, you typically discuss and perform all the steps in the implementation phase.

Create Action Plan

The first stage in the implementation phase is creating an action plan and exploring business scenarios for implementing or deploying the "best" data visualizations or data mining models that produce the best ROI or profits based on the business goals. In this stage, the visualizations and data mining models are used to communicate the findings to the decision makers and other business analysts. During the business presentation, the discussion of the next steps or call to action is in reality an overview of the implementation action plan. The action plan needs to demonstrate how the data visualizations or data mining models will address the business questions. It should include the estimated expense, as well as the potential revenue for deploying the project into the production environment. If possible, create multiple action plans (business scenarios) to present to the decision makers that contrast the positive and negative implications of deploying each.

Approve Action Plan

The second stage in the implementation phase is gaining the approval of management to execute the action plan. The aim of the business presentation is for the decision-making team to give you approval to act upon one of the business scenarios you have just presented. As illustrated in Figure 9.3, the approval stage feeds back into the create action plan phase. Perhaps the decision makers will request more information or will ask you to analyze different aspects of the business questions and create different business scenarios to be investigated.

Implement Action Plan

Implementing the action plan once it has been approved is the next stage in the business model. In this stage, the visualizations or data mining models are prepared for production. An example of a production visualization implementation plan may be to automate the data preparation, creation of the graphical data tables, and creation of the graphs. Perhaps nightly, the refreshed graphs are posted to Web pages so that in the morning the decision makers can review the graphs containing the updated sales trends or other information. An example of a production data mining plan may be to convert the data mining model into a C program or a set of standard SQL queries or procedures that run against the data warehouse. A nightly or weekly batch procedure may be developed that creates a list of customers who have a high probability of switching to the competition or some other predicted behavior. This list of customers could then be used by the customer support center to contact each customer and proactively offer to switch them to a different rate plan (or some other proactive tactic to attempt to capitalize on or modify their predicted behavior).

The Web-ready graphs and prepared customer list deployment examples are only high-level descriptions of a deployment action plan. The actual implementation plan is often extremely complex and detailed, and it requires the collaboration of multiple departments throughout the organization, such as IT, marketing, and customer service, among others.

Measure the Results

The final implementation stage is measuring the results of the action plan. Planning how the results will be measured and performing the measurements are often overlooked in many visual data mining projects. In Chapter 3, we discussed the need for identifying measures to validate the success of the VDM project. Similarly, you need to identify quantitative indicators for measuring the results of the implementation. Did the insights from the Web-ready graphs help the decision makers and others to proactively avoid overproducing a certain part or increase margins by proactively changing discounts? Did the prepared customer list reduce the number of customers who switched to the competition? For a production project presentation, you may want to describe how the proposed deployment plan will be measured.

Before the project is implemented, the current baseline values for the measures to be used should be collected for comparison. Deploying a visual data mining project requires affecting the business process that you are trying to improve. Your measures should consider all impacts of the project, not just the direct and obvious measures. For example, if you were to deploy a credit card fraud detection project, an obvious measure would be the percentage accuracy of the predictions the model makes. However, auxiliary measures should include all other potential impacts on the business processes, such as the time spent investigating each case and the dollar amount of the fraudulent transaction.

Whenever possible, the measuring-results stage should be automated to capture effectiveness measurements. This often enables you to develop more quantitative methods for evaluating the effectiveness of the deployed visual data mining projects over time. It also provides you with a tool to proactively evaluate whether changes to the data visualizations or data mining models are required. As illustrated in Figure 9.3, the measure results stage feeds back into the data preparation phase. In some cases, the data mining model may have become less effective over time and needs to be "retrained" to discover new customer behaviors from more current data. In other cases, the business questions may have changed or new business questions may have arisen that require a new VDM project be undertaken. In either case, measuring the results is paramount to monitoring the effectiveness of the visual data mining project.

Verifying and Presenting the Analysis for the Case Study

According to the customer retention VDM pilot project plan outlined in Chapter 2, Step 8 should take approximately 5 working days to complete. The tasks for Step 8 are assigned to the following teams:

- The data and business analyst team is responsible for evaluating the analysis and creating and making the business presentation of the discoveries and analysis to the decision makers.

- The domain expert team is responsible for providing business guidance to the data and business analysts in analyzing and evaluating the data visualizations and data mining models and verifying that the visualizations and data mining models satisfy the business objectives.

In the previous two chapters, we showed a number of data visualizations and data mining tools that illustrated how Big Cellular phone company's business questions could be addressed. Before the business presentation can be created, the logical transformations to the business data sets and the business assumptions need to be verified.

Verifying Logical Transformations to the Business Data Set

During the creation and analysis of the data visualizations to answer the attrition rate and cost questions, the graphical data set was created by aggregating by the ACTIVATION_DATE date-type column. For other visualizations, the graphical data set was created by aggregating by the RENEWAL_DATE date-type column. Which column is the correct date column to use for the aggregation? The answer to this question helps to determine which graphs to use in the business presentation. Recall that seasonal trends were discovered no matter which date was used for the aggregation. After this question was discussed with the domain experts and other data and business analysts, it was agreed that the organization as a whole tends to measure customer attribution rates and costs by the RENEWAL_DATE versus the ACTIVATION_DATE date-type column.

In a sense, another transformation was how the tenure of the customer was calculated. Recall that the business data set didn't include how many months a customer had been active with Big Cellular. After this question was discussed with the domain experts and other data and business analysts, it was agreed that the total number of monthly invoices a customer received did indeed correspond to how many months the customer was active with Big Cellular.

The final transformation that needs to be verified is the removal of numerous columns from the *customer_demographic* business data set used to build the data mining models. Table 8.8 from Chapter 8 lists the columns and the reasons for their removal. However, each should be discussed with the domain experts and other data and business analysts to verify the removal reasons. After the removal reasons were discussed, it was agreed that the resulting business data set was valid and still representative of the customer population.

Verifying the Business Assumptions

From the data visualization discussed earlier in Chapter 8 of the case study, it was determined that Big Cellular lost approximately 35 percent of its 465,000 customers over a 3-year period. This cost the company just over $4 million. Furthermore, each lost customer cost approximately $25 in unpaid bills. If these potential lost customers can be isolated, we can save the organization money. The initial approach was to develop a customer retention plan to give away $50 worth of free calls. The cost to produce and mail out the offer is $2, making the total cost per customer $52. The estimated revenue for each correct prediction of a positive response will be $101, which includes the unpaid bills. If the offer is sent to a customer who was not going to defect, then no additional revenue is gained. It was decided that this was a simple but fair set of assumptions to make, and the revenue due to keeping a customer who would normally churn would depend on which cluster (see Table 8.7) the customer was part of. However, with the lack of any quantitative information on the payoff for each customer, a single average return would suffice.

The Business Presentation

The business presentation for the customer retention VDM pilot project will consist of three main sections: project goals and objectives, discovery highlights, and the call to action. The overall presentation will consist of 12 presentation slides. Visualization and data mining model details will be included in the presentation notes. In the majority of the cases, a bulleted list will accompany the visualization to highlight the insights and discoveries uncovered during the data analysis phase of the project.

Customer Retention Project Goals and Objectives

The first slide of the business presentation contains a concise description of the project goals and objectives. For the customer retention VDM pilot project, slide 1 lists the following project goals and objectives.

Project goals include:

- Finding a new, cost-effective way of retaining customers
- Reducing yearly customer attrition by 15 percent or better

Project objectives include:

- Identifying the yearly churn rate and customer attrition cost to Big Cellular
- Developing data mining models to profile churning customers
- Developing data mining models to predict likely churners and when they would churn

Slide 2 contains the list of business questions addressed in the project. For the customer retention VDM pilot project, slide 2 lists the following six business questions:

1. What are the monthly and yearly customer attrition rates and trends from September 1996 through August 1999?
2. What are the average monthly and yearly customer attrition costs and trends from September 1996 through August 1999?
3. What are the profiles of the individuals who are leaving Big Cellular?
4. Can a data mining model be developed to predict *if* an individual is going to churn?
5. Can a data mining model be developed to predict *when* an individual is going to churn?
6. Can the data mining model explain *why* an individual will churn?

Highlights of the Discoveries

This portion of the customer retention business presentation consists of creating slides and adding notes to the handouts describing the insights and discoveries uncovered during the analysis phase.

Slide 3 of the presentation (Insert Figure 14) addresses the monthly and yearly customer attrition rates and trends. You can use the corresponding slide-note page to describe the seasonal trends discovered in Figures 8.25 and 8.26 from Chapter 8. For example, you may want to list discovered insights such as a high rate or spike in the number of customers who churned was discovered around Christmastime for 1996, 1997, 1998, and 1999. This spike is caused by the tendency of Big Cellular customers to buy service around the holidays, taking advantage of the Christmas season promotions. However, after their early contract is over, they tend to churn. If you add up all the churn rates and divide by the number of observations, you get an overall churn rate of 39.38 percent from January 1997 through July 1999.

Slide 4 (Figure 9.5) addresses the monthly and yearly customer addition costs and trends. This slide illustrates business question 2. Depending on the audience, you may want to provide a detailed list of the number of customers, average cost, total cost, and so on by churn type in the handout note page for this slide. In addition to the cost by churn type, you may want to include the overall paid amounts by churn type, as illustrated in Figure 8.27 from Chapter 8.

Slide 5 (Figure 9.6) illustrates the different types of churners found using a K-means clustering technique. The four types of clusters are very different from one another and yielded some very interesting and surprising insights. As part of the corresponding handout note pages, you may want to include additional insights concerning each cluster. First, there was a segment of customers that are financially very attractive, responsible bill payers but defected because of perceived poor service. Surprisingly, a significant portion of churners left because they had moved residences and their invoices were returned to the organization. A third group of churners were relatively long-time customers who left with large unpaid balances. Finally, there was a segment of churners who were very similar demographically to the first segment but were involuntarily terminated. We note the major difference between the two segments is that the first segment proactively joined Big Cellular, whereas the fourth cluster joined Big Cellular in reaction to a mall or family solicitation.

Slide 6 (Figure 9.6) presents the financial performance of the models that predict defection. Using the cost and revenue assumptions previously described, the best model to use is the decision tree model that performs consistently and provides the highest dollar yield.

Total Cost of Churn by Reason
9/23/1996–08/12/1999

Total cost of churn
$4,029,941

- 172,772 out of 464,916 customers

- Top six churn reasons account for 80% of cost

- REACT-BILLING NONPAY average cost $114 per customer

- BILLING NONPAY average cost $13 per customer

- Overall average $23 per customer churn

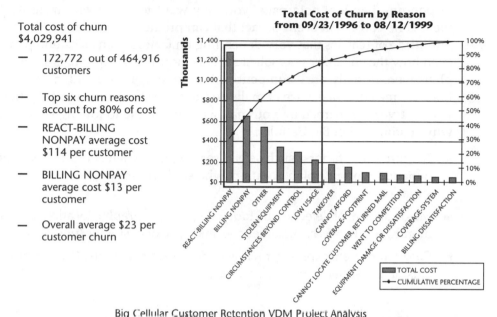

Big Cellular Customer Retention VDM Project Analysis

Figure 9.5 The different types of customers that got away.

The Clusters/Segments of the Ones That Got Away

Cluster 1: Left voluntarily

    Need to keep these customers.

    Pay on time have profitable plans.

    Are unhappy with our service.

Cluster 2: Renters

    Churned because they could not be located.

Cluster 3: Left with large account balances

Cluster 4: Demographically very similar to #1

    But were solicited proactively in malls and left involuntarily.

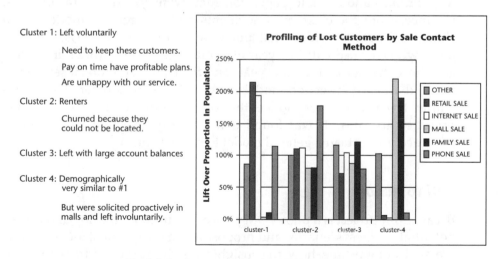

Big Cellular Customer Retention VDM Project Analysis

Figure 9.6 Financial return for models that predict defection.

Slide 7 presents in high-level detail the important factors that the decision tree model used to predict customers who were likely to churn. As part of the corresponding handout note page, you may want to list several insights. First, there is no consistent event or fact that can predict churn. Rather, there was a multitude of reasons that vary depending on factors such as calling plans and even how the customer was solicited. This indicates that perhaps some calling plans were initially price-competitive but no longer are and that the solicitation schemes that make use of malls and relatives lead to a high defection rate within 1 year. In particular, you may want to list the following insights as to why customers left Big Cellular.

- No consistent factors (such as bad service) drive defection. This varies depending on rate plan, location, who sold the service, and economic situation.

- Major drivers of defection include rate plan, geographic location, activation month, contract fees, customer age, and type of customer (upscale or not).

- Predictions help explain previously described segments. For example, cluster 4 customers who left can be predicted by the rule:

```
RATE_PLAN 100, 300-Minute, Other or Unlimited,
          UPSCALE=YESAGE_RANGE <> 20s, 80s or Teens,
          ACTIVATION_MONTH=December,
          REGION=E_S_Central
          CONTRACT_FEE <= $40
```

Slide 8 (Figure 9.7) presents an early-churn detection model. As part of the corresponding handout note page, you may want to list several insights. For instance, from the clusters of segments and the general model to predict churners, it became evident that, timewise, there were two classes of churners: those who churned within 1 year of joining Big Cellular (often involuntarily) and those that stayed for a few years and then left. Therefore, it seemed logical to build an early-detection model to predict those customers likely to churn within 1 year and other models that predict individuals who are long-term prospects to churn. It was found that the early-detection model performed more accurately than a general model to predict churn.

Call to Action

Because our project is a pilot VDM project, we need to develop and investigate potential business scenarios and propose and gain approval for an action plan. We will demonstrate how the insights we discussed address the business questions. Our aim is to gain approval to begin a fully funded production VDM project for one of the scenarios we present.

**Return on Investment for Models That
Predict if a Customer Will Leave**

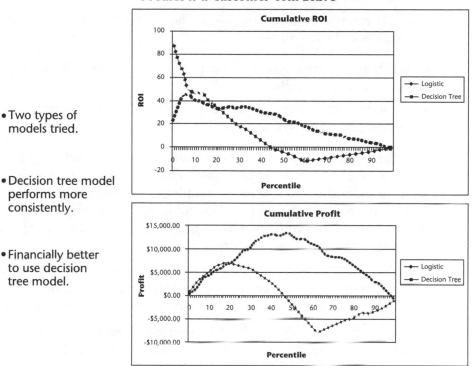

- Two types of models tried.

- Decision tree model performs more consistently.

- Financially better to use decision tree model.

Big Cellular Customer Retention VDM Project Analysis

Figure 9.7   An early-churn detection model.

Slide 9 can be used to recap the relevant data visualization discoveries and insights:

- Average annual churn rate 39.38 percent from January 1997 through July 1999

- Christmas promotions do not result in long-term customers

- Customer who leave (churn) have on average $23 in unpaid bills

- 80 percent of customers who leave are involuntarily terminated because of lack of service payment

Slide 10 can be used to recap the visual data mining discoveries and insights:

- Four segments (groups) of customers who churned were discovered:
    - Responsible paying customers who leave voluntarily
    - Customers who are terminated because they cannot be contacted

- Long-term customers who terminated after many years who left large unpaid balances
- Short-term premium customers who were solicited by promotions in malls and by relatives

- Accurate data mining models can be built that predict which customers are going to eventually churn
- Accurate data mining models can be built that predict which customers are going to churn within a year

From these VDM project summary slides, we can see that Big Cellular can reduce expenses by more aggressively collecting unpaid fees and making it easier for individuals to update their address. We assume here that individuals wish to continue their service but could not be contacted. An important task auxiliary to the production VDM project is to make it easier for individuals to register their change of address.

Big Cellular can improve revenue by reducing retention by providing better service to premium customers, providing promotions that retain customers for longer tenures, and reengineer the mall and relative solicitation practices.

The case study shows that individuals were churning for a variety of reasons. However, taking advantage of this knowledge would entail multiple courses of action to address each set of reasons. For business scenario 1, a short-term, 6-month production project can be suggested. Slide 11 can be used to illustrate a general approach that ignores this knowledge but is easy to implement, as follows:

- Use general model of churn prediction to:
  - Identify potential churners with larger unpaid balances. Actively try to collect balances.
  - Identify potential churners and provide an incentive, such as $50 worth of free calls.
- Follow up on the following general issues:
  - Consider making Christmas promotions require a two or more year commitment.
  - Improve service for premium customers.
  - Reduce involuntary termination (NOBILLPAY) threshold to below 3 months.
  - Revise the mall and relative solicitation practices.

Business scenario 1 will most likely be very profitable. However, a more complex approach should yield even better returns. For business scenario 2, a long-term, 12-month production project can be suggested. Slide 12 can be used to illustrate this long-term approach that addresses the insights that individuals are churning for a variety of reasons, including:

- Use model of early detection churn prediction to identify potential churners with larger unpaid balances. Actively try to collect balances.

- Use models of churn prediction to identify potential churners. If customer falls into:

  - Segment 1: Provide an incentive; follow up with call.

  - Segment 3: Provide a loyalty incentive.

  - Segment 4: Renegotiate a longer contract.

- Follow up these general issues:

  - Reduce involuntary termination (NOBILLPAY) threshold to below 3 months.

  - Revise the mall and relative solicitation practices.

For each production project, the short-term call-to-action tasks are purchase relevant software and hardware and request personnel resources depending on the length of the project. The long-term call-to-action tasks are schedule the extraction of more data beyond the current sample, automate the update of the exploratory data mart, and initiate investigation by the operation team to deploy automatic measurement and monitoring facilities to measure the effectiveness of the project.

Summary

Step 8 is the third and final step in the data analysis phase. In this chapter, we focused our attention on verifying that the discovered business trends and data mining models are significant in answering the business questions. We also discussed preparing the business presentation and briefly discussed the implementation phase. In the next chapter, we provide an overall summary of the VDM methodology and discuss the future of data visualization and visual data mining.

CHAPTER 10

The Future of Visual Data Mining

I n this chapter, we will summarize the previous nine chapters and discuss the future of software to support the visual data mining projects. You now have a practical methodology for creating data visualizations and for performing visual data mining. Figure 10.1 recaps the eight-step data visualization and visual data mining (VDM) methodology.

As illustrated in Figure 10.1, the book was organized into three main sections that correspond to the phases of a data visualization and visual data mining project: Project Planning, Data Preparation, and Data Analysis. We will now briefly review each phase and the steps within them and then discuss the future of data visualization and visual data mining.

The Project Planning Phase

Step 1: Justifying and Planning the Data Visualization and Data Mining Project (Chapter 2) discussed how to justify and plan a VDM project and provided guidance to estimating the project time and resource requirements. Team roles and responsibilities need to be defined at this early stage for the project. The roles of the data and business analysts, domain experts, decision makers, and operations and data warehousing teams are discussed. The *data* *and business analyst team* is involved in all phases of the project. A champion of the project, this team coordinates important tasks such as justifying and planning the project and identifying the top business questions to be investigated. The *domain expert team* acts as consultants to the data and the business analyst team provides guidance to ensure the correct data is obtained and valid business indicators are discovered. They also play the important role of determining if the proposed insights and solution makes sound business sense. The *decision maker team* evaluates the business scenarios and the candidate solutions to address the business questions. The *operations team* provides network, database administration, and system administration assistance. The *data warehousing team* helps provides extracted files from the data warehouse or other business sources and other related information such as meta data.

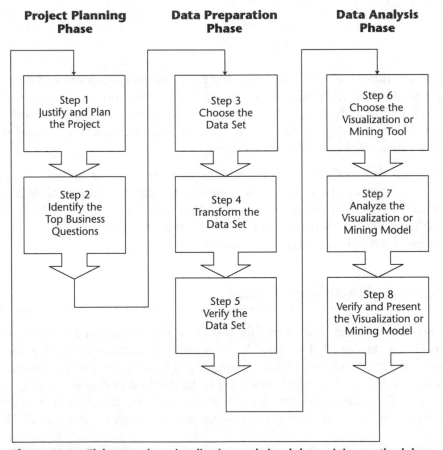

Figure 10.1 Eight-step data visualization and visual data mining methodology.

Early on, the project scope should be determined as proof-of-concept, pilot, or production. This key decision will dictate how later steps are tackled, including the complexity of the questions that can be addressed and the visualizations and models that need to be created. It is important that the project be set up as a closed-loop business model so that the resulting visualizations and data mining models feed back into the initial data set sources. This feedback allows improvement, correction, and monitoring of your production visualizations or data mining models through time. In Chapter 2, we discuss the potential challenges that may exist to creating a VDM project. When planning the project, consideration should be given to the environment and receptiveness of the organization.

Step 2: Identifying the Top Business Questions (Chapter 3) discussed three main points: how to identify the top business questions, how to map these questions to data visualization or mining tasks, and how to map your financial targets into achievable and measurable visual data mining goals. It is during this step that the various teams must work in unison. Whereas domain experts and business managers will have a sound knowledge of the core business processes, data and business analysts will understand the capabilities and limitations of data mining and the operation and warehouse teams will understand the quality of the organization's data. A successful identification of questions and mapping those questions to data mining tasks require the input and skills from all teams.

When mapping the business questions to data mining tasks, you should consider how the insights that the VDM project hopes to provide will be used. Will the insights be used as training material or as a deployable model? Chapter 3 includes a matrix that maps typical business questions to data mining tasks. Data mining tools tend to address one specific problem or task at a time, such as classification, estimation, prediction, association groupings, or clustering and segmentation. We briefly introduce these tasks in Step 2 and in more depth in Step 6. Often a business question can be better answered if it is addressed by more than one data mining task. Chapter 3 includes how to map VDM project financial targets such as ROI into achievable and measurable visual data mining goals. We conclude the chapter by discussing how to identify and measure the results of the visual data mining project. This is important not only to measure the success of the data mining project but also to convince various stakeholders that there are no secondary undesirable effects.

The Data Preparation Phase

Step 3: Choosing the Data (Chapter 4) discussed how to select the data relating to the data visualization and visual data mining questions identified in Chapter 3 from the potentially hundreds of tables of available data. This step can account for as much as 80 percent of the VDM project time. Most data in an organization was collected for the purpose of supporting the core business processes and not for data visualization or mining. Much of this information will be at different *experimental unit levels*. For example, in an organization's customer database, each row or record represents a customer; however, in the transaction database, each row or record represents a customer's transaction, of which there may be many. During the data preparation phase, it should be established what the experimental unit of the data visualization or mining study is likely to be. This is often determined by the question you plan to investigate. If the question is customer churn, then the experimental unit should be a customer, whereas fraud detection would most likely have an experimental unit at the transaction level.

We explained how creating histograms, box plots, and distribution graphs can determine if a data column should be included in the analysis and if it needs to be transformed. Once the columns are identified, they often need to be corrected, organized, and improved to make them more meaningful, accurate, and easy to use. Therefore, an important part of Step 3 is transforming the operational level data into a format that makes it amenable to data mining. We discussed how to decode columns (expand codes into English), data dimension consistency (using the same token to represent an event), and business rule consistency (always calculating a metric the same way). We also discussed unique (no value appears more than once), duplicate (can be derived from another column), and insignificant (non-value-adding) columns. Missing values for columns often occurs. You need to decide to keep, supplement, or ignore columns with missing values. If your organization has already created a data mart that can support your proposed questions, you have saved a large amount of time. In this chapter, we also addressed the issues of where to get the data, what type of data to select, and how much data to select.

Step 3 introduces the concept of using an exploratory data mart as a repository for building and maintaining business data sets that address the business questions under investigation. The extract, cleanse, transform, and load (ECTL) procedures are central to correctly populating your exploratory data mart. In a sense, the exploratory data mart is a denormalized subset of the operational data typically contained in star schemas in a data warehouse or a subject-oriented extract from OLTP systems. It is important to document the ECTL procedures so they can be replicated, referred to, and used to create a closed-loop business model. Creating an exploratory data mart may seem extreme. However, as you will probably be creating multiple business data sets from the data mart, sorting this data, and often transforming and merging it, having a data mart is more convenient than continuously scheduling and performing extracts against the operational data. The amount of data and complexity of information in the data mart will be determined by the project type (proof-of-concept, pilot, or production).

Step 4: Transforming the Data Set (Chapter 5) involved logical transformations to enhance the information contained within the data set, to remove bias, and to facilitate visualizing and data mining of the business data set. In most cases, the transformation operators are included as part of the RDBMS or embedded within the data visualization or visual data mining tool. Many data mining tools can perform complex transformations but often not as efficiently as an ECTL tool. If a transformation is required by many tools, it is worthwhile to perform the logical transformation while selecting the production business data set and making these logical transformations part of the ECTL procedures, as discussed in Chapter 4.

We discuss two general types of transformation: table level and column level. Table-level logical transformations affect the structure and number of rows within the entire production business data set. Column-level logical transformations affect the structure of the columns for a production business data set. Examples of table level transformations are:

- *Transforming weighted data sets* replace column and record weights from the data set by creating a new data set that adds new rows based on the column or record weights. Not all data visualization and visual data mining software packages can deal with weights, so this transformation is needed for these tools.

- *Transforming time series data sets* are logical transformations that restructure time series data sets with a variable number of columns into records with a fixed number of columns. Usually if a record in the original data set had m columns or values, this record will be transformed into m rows, each with a primary key, timestamp, and single column value. This table-level logical transformation creates a new data set by adding new rows based on the number of events in the time series.

- *Aggregating data sets* involves aggregating the data set to a higher experimental unit, such as when you aggregate sales information by state for presentation in a map.

- *Filtering data sets* involves using a specific subset of the data set.

Column-level logical transformations can be divided into two groups:

- Simple column transformations can change the number of columns in the data set. Examples of transformations of this type are removing columns, changing column data type, or creating new columns based on some function of the other columns. Column-level transformations enable you to reduce the number of data dimensions in preparation for a particular visualization. For example, you can combine multiple columns (data facts) into a single column that makes a visualization clearer or enhances the accuracy of the data mining model.

- Column value grouping transformations are logical transformations of continuous and discrete values into intervals or groups or subsets and do not change the number of columns. These column-level transformations enable you to improve the understandability of your visualizations and increase the chance of discovering patterns of the data mining algorithms.

These logical transformations often help in augmenting the business data set to enable you to gain more insight into the business problems under investigation.

Step 5: Verifying the Data Set (Chapter 6). In Chapter 4, we described how to identify the operational data sources and columns to use. We demonstrated source data extraction, cleansing, transformation, and loading (ECTL) into the exploratory data mart, from which we can build our business data sets. In Chapter 5, we described how to transform data from the data mart into business data sets that can be visualized and mined to discover historical patterns and trends. In Chapter 6, we discussed how to verify that the production business data set contains the expected data and that all of the ECTL steps from Chapter 4 and logical transformations from Chapter 5 have been applied correctly, are error-free, and did not introduce bias into the business data set. By *bias* we mean selecting or transforming data that is unrepresentative of all the data available. Verifying the data set is correct before you begin building visualizations and models can save you a considerable amount of rework, and it also familiarizes you with the data.

You can verify the accuracy of the data set by comparing it to the operational source. The first phase of verifying a business data set is to ensure the integrity and accuracy of the preparation. For each ECTL, column, or table transformation, you need to ensure the data operations were applied correctly. We describe how to verify discrete columns by comparing the distribution of values before and after the ECTL transformation. You can use data visualizations to help you verify the ECTL operations. We show how to use a pie graph to compare an operational data source column before the ECTL operation with its corresponding business data set column after the ECTL operation. To verify continuous column transformations, you need to compare the minimum and maximum value, numeric average, and variance between the operational data source column and the business data set column. You can use data visualizations to help you verify the ECTL operation. We show how to use a line graph to compare an operational data source column before the ECTL operation with its corresponding business data set column after the ECTL operation.

The second phase is to ensure the logic of the data preparation. For each ECTL, column, or table transformation, you need to verify that the logic of the transformation does not distort or bias the resultant data set. For example, the date warehousing team may have taken only the first 10 percent of records from the customer warehouse in a proof-of-concept project. However, these records may represent your oldest customers and are therefore not a representative sample of your customers. Verifying the logic of these operations ensures that the business data set is a true representation of the operational source data sets.

Chapter 6 also describes how commercially available data profiling tools may help you analyze source data to identify the data element and apply data integrity business rules.

Step 6: Choosing the Visualization or Data Mining Tool (Chapter 7) discussed how to choose the data visualization or data mining model tool appropriate in investigating the business questions identified in Chapter 3.

The business question, the nature of the business data set, and its underlying structure often influence the data visualization tool of choice. Data visualization tools can be divided into two main categories:

- Multidimensional visualization tools, such as scatter, line, column, bar, and pie graphs
- Specialized landscape and hierarchical visualization tools, such as map and tree graphs

Multidimensional visualizations compare and contrast the values of one column to the values of other columns in the data set. Refer to Table 7.1 for a list of some common multidimensional graph types, as well as the types of column values that can be compared and the kinds of relationships that can be investigated.

Some data visualization tools allow you to investigate the hierarchical or geographical nature of your data set. Two common visualization tools that are available in commercial products are map graphs and tree graphs. Map graphs are suited for spatial or geographic analysis. They allow you to organize your data by geographic area, such as states, and some more complex tools allow user-defined regions such as telecommunication coverage zones. Visualizing data in a spatial or geographical format often reveals patterns and trends that would not have been uncovered in any other way. It helps you understand customer and marketplace demographic at the geographical level. A tree graph is best suited for data that implicitly contains some hierarchical structure. For example, you may wish to view the performance of your sales team according to their line management structure. Most tree graph tools automatically aggregate the specified columns at each level of the tree.

Choosing the right data mining tool involves two issues:

- Which subset of the available tools is applicable to my problem?
- What specific tool from the subset is best suited for my situation?

Because of different environments, two quite similar organizations with similar problems may choose different tools.

The applicable subset of mining techniques depends on the business question under investigation and how the results will be used. We can view the business question under investigation as consisting of some core task. Data mining tools tend to address one specific problem or task at a time, such as classification, estimation, prediction, association groupings, or clustering and segmentation. *Classification* is the process of putting an object into a predetermined distinct category. *Estimation* is very similar to classification, except that each object is associated with a continuous value. The difference between data mining tasks such as classification and *prediction* is quite subtle. If you use a model to foretell some future event, you are using the model for predictive purposes. *Association grouping* consists of identifying which entities/items are likely to coexist in some situation. *Clustering and segmentation* is the process of dividing a population of objects into subgroups of similar objects.

Each data mining tool produces a model of some sort. The intended use of the model also determines if a technique is applicable. Some data mining tools produce a model that is easily deployable into a production environment but produce no explanation of how they work. Others provide explanation and insights into the decision process.

We can categorize data mining tools as being either supervised (directed) or unsupervised (undirected). Supervised tools are given positively and negatively labeled examples of some phenomenon. The tool tries to identify what combination of data values typically coexist with a specific label. For instance, a data mining tool may be given a data set of insurance fraud claims labeled as fraud or nonfraud. The tool then tries to find which combinations of events co-occur with fraudulent claims and which combination of events co-occur with nonfraudulent claims. Unsupervised learning is more exploratory in nature and tries to find patterns of interest that are intrinsic to the data and not related to some imposed label. For example, clustering and segmentation is a form of unsupervised learning that attempts to find intrinsic classes already existing in the data. This contrasts with classification, where the classes are provided before we even begin mining the data. In this chapter, we introduce decision trees, neural networks, linear regression, and logistic regression, which are all examples of supervised learning techniques. We discuss unsupervised techniques such as association rules, K-means clustering, and self-organizing maps.

From a suitable subset of tools, the best tool will depend on issues such as effectiveness and interpretability. In the chapter, we discussed issues such as: the ability to implement the model, the model generation time, the associated degree of belief, the ease of visualizing the model, and its suitability for proof-of-concept. More than likely there will be a trade-off between these issues, and empirical experiments are required to make a final decision. Each data mining technique has its own strengths and weaknesses. Often, combining techniques can overcome some weaknesses in a particular technique. Furthermore, the underlying computational nature of the techniques determines whether they are well suited to certain aspects of the data, such as number of records, types of data, and number of missing values.

The Data Analysis Phase

Step 7: Analyzing the Visualization or Data Mining Model (Chapter 8) discussed how to use visualizations to gain insight into the data sets and data mining models associated with answering the business questions identified in Chapter 3.

The data visualization tool to use depends on the nature of the business data set and its underlying structure and the business question you are investigating. We explain how you can:

- Visualize key business indicators (such as response rate to a campaign) using frequency graphs (histogram and distribution graphs) and how to compare them with other columns in the business data set

- Determine the importance of columns in the data set by using Pareto graphs (histograms and line graphs combined) in the business data set with respect to key indicators such as response rate, number of failures, or fraudulent claims

- View seasonal trends by using radar graphs

- Analyze and search for time-based trends and patterns using line graphs

- View cause-and-effect relationships using scatter graphs

Visual data mining tools and techniques create visualizations that provide insights into data mining models and their performance. The user inspects and interacts with the visualization of the predictive or descriptive data mining model to understand (and validate) the patterns discovered by the data mining algorithm. We described visualization techniques for the core data mining tasks of classification, estimation, prediction, association grouping, and clustering or segmentation. Some data mining tools such as linear regression produce easy-to-understand models. However, others produce complex models that can benefit from visualization. We described how to visualize specific aspects of a particular data mining model, such as a decision tree or neural network.

You can also employ data visualization tools and techniques to compare and contrast the performance of different data mining models. Most data mining models predictive abilities can be evaluated and compared to each other, enabling you to decide on the best model that addresses your business questions. You can visualize the model performance using lift, response, and gains charts. A lift chart shows the improvement a model makes over just randomly guessing the occurrence of the target event. A response chart evaluates the precision of the model at predicting the target event. A gains chart illustrates how many of the target events the classifier model has made a decision on.

Most models associate a confidence with each decision. Often, you need to know at what point the model's performance is too poor to continue using. Should you use the top 20 percent, 30 percent, or 40 percent of the most confident predictions? You can determine this cutoff point by using *return-on-investment* (ROI) charts and *profit* charts. The ROI chart shows profit as a ratio of the cost multiplied by 100, and a profit chart plots the sum of revenue less the expense.

You can use all of these visualizations to monitor the model deployment by comparing performance of the model during construction and after deployment. As soon as a model is deployed, you must make sure the model performs as well in the production environment as it did in the model-building environment. For example, changes to production environment may have occurred since the operational file extracts. It is also important to monitor the model's ongoing performance to make sure it is not becoming stale and out-of-date.

Step 8: Verifying and Presenting Analysis (Chapter 9) introduced you to the final step of the VDM methodology. Chapter 9 discussed the three parts to this step: verifying that the visualizations and data mining model satisfy your business goals and objectives, presenting the visualization and data mining discoveries to the decision makers, and if appropriate, deploying the visualizations and mining models in a production environment.

Verifying the visualizations and data mining models begins by considering the transformations to the data set that were performed for a specific visualization or data mining model. The techniques we describe in Chapter 6 can be employed for this purpose. Next, the business assumptions need to be verified, particularly the projected return for correctly predicting the event of interest (such as customer defection, fraud, and so on).

The format of the presentation of the results is described next. The presentation should contain three main parts: description of the VDM project goals and objectives, highlights of the discoveries found in the project in terms of addressing the top business questions, and discussion of the next steps or call to action. When creating slides, you should supplement the visualization with bullet points that explain key points. The description of the project goals was addressed in Step 1, and the visualizations of the data set and data mining models were shown in Chapter 8 (Step 7). For proof-of-concept VDM projects, the call to action is usually just gaining approval to start a pilot or production project. Pilot projects require presenting potential deployment options for implementing the discoveries and data mining models in a production environment. Production VDM projects require a complete high-level overview for deploying the discoveries and data mining models into the organization's production environment. In all three cases, it is useful to document what you believe are the short- and long-term steps for implementing the pilot or production VDM project. Short-term call-to-action tasks, such as purchasing software and hardware to support the pilot or production project, are accomplished in a few days or weeks. Long-term call-to-action tasks, such as automatic and periodic updates to the exploratory data mart from the operational data sources, often require changes to the production environment.

It takes considerable time and care to deploy a visualization or data mining model into the production environment without significant negative effects. The details of implementations of visualizations and models into a production environment are beyond the scope of this book, but we describe the implementation phases as related to the call to action. Proof-of-concept projects do not include an implementation phase. Pilot projects need to investigate and describe potential scenarios and implementation action plans. The aim of presenting the action plan for pilot projects is to gain approval to begin a production VDM project. Production VDM projects discuss and perform all the steps in the implementation phase.

The process of enacting an action plan consists of three stages: creation, approval, and implementation. In the first stage, the visualizations and data mining models are communicated to the decision makers and other business analysts. It is worthwhile to create several action plans of contrasting implications to the decision makers. The second stage involves gaining approval and support to execute the action plan. The decision-making team should approve one of the presented business scenarios. The final stage is implementing the action plan. Implementation plans are often extremely complex and are coordinated among many departments in the organization. An important part of implementation is creating a closed business loop model that measures the results of the action plan. You need to plan how the results will be measured, as well as perform the measurements. The current baseline values for the measures need to be collected for reference. Automating the measuring of results enables more quantitative and systematic methods to track and evaluate the effectiveness of the deployed visual data mining projects over time. In a closed-loop business model, the measured results feed back into the data preparation phase.

Trends in Commercial Visual Data Mining Software

As commercial visual data mining products mature, the applications of visualization to each phase will continue to become more usable and useful. This section discusses how visual data mining projects may look in the future by exploring the following common trends:

- The availability of more types of visualizations
- The changing of visualizations from being static charts to dynamic interactive representations of information
- The ability to visualize more data and more complex data
- The role of industry standards

We can view these trends as being four dimensions that visualization for data mining purposes can develop. These dimensions are not exclusive from each other. Current commercial data mining software only uses a few examples from a few of the visualization categories that have been documented and tried in the visualization community. A natural progression of visualizations for data mining purposes is from visualizations that are static views of data to presentations of information that the user can interact with a number of ways. Most current visualization techniques focus on data that can fit into a table of a fixed number of columns. However, a considerable amount of data does not exist in this format (such as text). Converting this type of data into tabular format is possible, but semantic knowledge may be lost in doing so. Finally, how the visualization is represented and stored is an important factor that is gaining attention with the introduction of data mining standards such as PMML and JSR 073.

These trends, along with the availability of enterprise charting systems (ECSs), will together have a great effect on all the steps of a visual data mining project. Enterprise charting systems sit on an organization's central servers and are accessible to many users via a client viewing system such as Web browsers. The use of emerging ECSs will enable the various teams in the visual data mining project to more easily specify and deploy chart-centric data mining applications for business intelligence. Such ECSs are tied to the data sources and are constantly kept up-to-date, instead of remaining as static reports. The use of

ECSs will enable a simpler specification of a closed-loop business model discussed in Step 1. If the various charts used in the visual data mining project are always current each time they are displayed, they are likely to become more widely used on a day-to-day basis.

More Chart Types and User-Defined Layouts

Most software supports the basic visualizations we have used in this book, such as line graphs, scatter plots, and radar plots, that have many uses and have been the mainstay of business intelligence applications. The information visualization community has spent considerable time developing new types of visualizations. Broadly speaking, there are six categories of data visualization techniques: geometric techniques (i.e., scatter plots), hierarchical techniques (trees), pixel-oriented techniques (circle segments), graph-based techniques (directed acyclic graphs), icon-based (shape coding, such as stick figures) techniques, and hybrid techniques (combinations of the previously mentioned techniques). Data mining packages typically only have a few examples from the first two categories. Pixel-oriented techniques visualize a column value as a colored pixel rather than as a polygon, such as a square or a pie segment. This enables a considerable amount of information to be displayed on the screen. Graph-based techniques visualize information represented as a graph. A graph in this context means a structure of nodes that are connected to each other in ways that are typically more complex than a tree. Icon-based approaches visualize the column values as features of a common icon and allow multidimensional data to be displayed in two dimensions. For example, in Figure 10.2 the facial features such as face, nose, mouth, and eye shape convey additional information beyond the two dimensions of face placement.

Not all categories or examples of each visualization category may be applicable to visual data mining, but there are a considerable number of techniques that could potentially benefit VDM projects. For example, tree charts or graphs are particularly useful to visualize hierarchical information but can become too large for complex structures such as Web site maps. Hyperbolic trees are like tree charts, but all branches radiate out from the root node that occupies the center of the chart, as illustrated in Insert Figure 15.

Other techniques such as parallel coordinates are a fundamentally new way of representing information. In this technique, each column is represented as a horizontal or vertical axis, and the N axes (in an N column table) are organized as uniformly spaced lines. Each N-dimensional row is mapped to a polyline that passes through all axes, crossing each at a position proportional to its

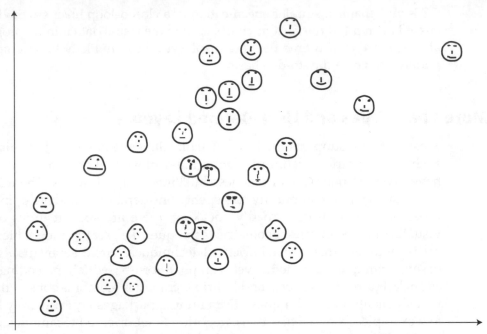

Figure 10.2 Visualization of multidimensional data set using Chernoff Faces.
Copyright © H. Chernoff. (Chernoff, 1973).

value for that column. Parallel coordinates has a multitude of applications in data preparation (outlier detection, identifying unusual/interesting columns) and model performance presentation. An example of a parallel coordinates visualization is shown in Insert Figure 16.

As visual data mining projects become more in use, their effect on key business processes will become more important and come under greater scrutiny. The effect of a data mining project on a business process is easier to determine if the process can be displayed visually. The effect of a data mining project to improve the production of a product is better understood if the production process is displayed visually with before-and-after shots presented. For example, a VDM project to predict computer network intrusion would be more easily monitored if the results of the project were visualized as an overlay onto the network structure. Map and tree graphs are forerunners of these visualizations, which consider geometric and spatial layout. However, a user-defined layout enables the presentation of results, effects, and ongoing monitoring of visual data mining projects.

Similarly, as visual data mining projects become more common and permeate organizations, the decision-making team will need better access to the performance and effects of the project. Common forms of presentation to executive business intelligence users are digital dashboards. Digital dashboards present to decision makers key performance metrics presented as indicators not unlike those on a car dashboard. From the digital dashboard the user can monitor the performance metrics.

Though the possible uses of visual data mining are wide, several industries have been particularly receptive to visual data mining projects. Areas such as customer relationship management (CRM) have already developed types of charts specific to the key questions in the field and will continue to do so. The retention case study is an example of a typical customer relationship problem. Lift curves, response curves, and gains charts are standard forms of displaying the performance of models in the target marketing industry.

Finally, the popularity of data mining tools that are currently treated as black boxes, such as neural networks, will make visualizing how they make decisions a desirable part of future data mining packages.

Dynamic Visualizations That Allow User Interaction

Most visualizations currently available in commercial software are static in nature. The data is read in once and displayed. The user cannot easily interact with the visualization. *Dynamic visualizations* allow users to get their hands on the data, by rotating, zooming in or out, and panning visualizations. In three-dimensional visualizations, simple forms of interaction such as rotation and zooming add a new aspect to the information presented and improve the ability to gain useful insights. More complex forms of interaction will enable the user to combine multiple visualizations and even use the visualization as a query tool. *Brushing* involves synchronizing two or more visualizations of the same set of data. For example, if you had a scatter plot of a data set and a radar graph of the same data set, selecting a set of data points in one of the visualizations will automatically highlight those exact data points in the other. This powerful combination of visualizations allows the user to have multiple but synchronized views of the same data set.

If a visualization allows selection of specific subsets of data points by clicking on them or even drawing a bounding box around them, then this specification can be used to subset these points—a process known as *drill-through*. Similarly, in a scatter graph a visual query can be specified by drawing a polygon of some sort around the points of interest. Because visual data mining projects are iterative in nature through the various steps we have outlined, storing and retrieving multiple viewpoints in a visualization will be beneficial. Dynamic visualizations can extend to visualizing data that is constantly changing. The data can be changing in real time, or we can view an animation of the year's sales by month in real time.

Size and Complexity of Data Structures Visualized

The definition of a large database to mine has constantly increased. Many organizations now have terabytes of data, and although a key step in the VDM methodology is data transformation, including removing insignificant columns and rows, many significant columns and many rows will still remain. Traditional visualization techniques like bar graphs are ill-equipped to display large numbers of columns and rows unless the data is aggregated. This is because the visualization unit is a polygon (such as a bar or pie) of considerable size that limits the amount of information that can be displayed. Pixel-oriented techniques, such as circle segments, allow each pixel in the visualization to convey some piece of information, therefore allowing more information to be displayed on the screen.

In VDM Steps 4 and 5, we discussed how to transform data to have a fixed number of columns. The reason for the transformation was that most data mining tools and visualization techniques expect data in this format. Visualizing unstructured data like text documents or data that contains a variable number of columns per record will enable data mining projects to extend even further into traditional fields and also into new areas. Text documents pose an interesting challenge, as their inherent complexity means that a visualization can be used to both verify insights and also navigate through the document collections themselves.

Standards That Allow Exchanges between Tools

Each data mining package has its own set of proprietary visualizations, data mining algorithms, and presentation tools. Models, visualizations, and even transformations cannot be easily intermixed among different tools. This incompatibility creates a problem, as one data mining package may have excellent analytic data mining capabilities but poor visualization capabilities. Until now, the practitioner would have to concoct a complex scheme to export a model (for instance) from one tool to be visualized in another. However, recently industry standards such as the XML-based Predictive Model Markup Language (PMML) standard and Java (JSR 073) standards are trying to remove these barriers. The benefit of these standards is that a complex model or set of transformations can be described succinctly. This enables online serving of visualizations, as well as the ability to share models among different packages.

Summary

This chapter summarized the eight-step VDM methodology. We discussed how visual data mining projects may look in the future by exploring some common trends, such as the availability of more types of visualizations, the changing of visualizations from being static charts to dynamic interactive representations of information, the ability to visualize more data and more complex data, and the role of industry standards. We hope that you are now able to apply the methodology to your real-world problems and begin receiving the benefits of data visualization and visual data mining to solve your business issues.

Glossary

aggregation.   This is the process of summarizing multiple rows of data using one or more operations over some specified set of columns. Aggregation operations are capable of producing summary statistics, transposing a table, or even producing arrays based on the original data set.

attribute (labeled discrete column).   This is a column used as input by a predictive model. When performing predictive modeling, columns in the data are divided into attributes (which provide the inputs) and the label (which represents the output of the model).

backfitting.   This process applies the full data set to a model built from a smaller sample. The resulting model retains its original structure. The purpose of backfitting is to allow a model's internal distributions to accurately reflect the full data while maintaining the model's error estimate.

backpropagation.   This is the most commonly implemented approach in data mining packages to train a neural network. Training a neural network involves finding the best set of weights for the inputs into each node or unit. Initially, the set of weights are usually randomly set. The backpropagation approach to training calculates the error that the current set of weights in the neural network would produce and then adjusts the weights to minimize the error, by propagating the error through the network. *See* feed-forward neural network.

bagging.   This method attempts to improve the accuracy of a single model by building multiple models of the same type from random samples of the data set. The ensembles of models then vote on the classification of a test set instance. Bagging is typically implemented for decision trees in data mining packages but can be implemented for most techniques. *See* boosting.

binning.   This process places partitions or groups continuous columns into discrete groups, transforming real data into categorical (discrete) column values. For example, a continuous range of ages can be binned as 0-18, 19-25, 26-35, and so on. These groups or bins are defined as regions of a continuum that do not overlap.

boosting.   Typically found in decision tree implementations of data mining packages, boosting, like bagging, attempts to improve the accuracy of a single model by building multiple models. After the first model is built, another model is built that attempts to overcome the known errors. Then the errors in the resultant tree are investigated and another model is built to overcome them, and so on. The end result is an ensemble of trees that are progressively more specialized at overcoming errors. *See* bagging.

brushing.   This feature allows the user to select the same data points in more than one visualization at a time. When you select something in a visualization that supports the sending of brushing events, it will also become selected in any other visualization that is currently open and that supports the receiving of brushing events.

classifier.   This is a predictive model that attempts to describe one column (the label) in terms of others (the column values). A classifier is constructed from a data set where the label is known, and it may be later applied to predict column values for a new data set where the label column values are unknown. Internally, a classifier is an algorithm or mathematical formula that predicts one discrete value for each input row. For example, a classifier built from a data set of iris flowers could predict the type of a presented iris given the length and width of its petals and stamen. Classifiers may also produce probability estimates for each value of the label column.

clustering.   This method determines which elements in a data set are imilar. It works to group records together according to an algorithm or mathematical formula that attempts to find centroids, or centers, around which similar records gravitate. It is the process of dividing a data set into mutually exclusive subgroups, without relying on predefined classes.

conditional probability. This is the probability of some event (A) given that some other event (B) has occurred. Written P (A | B) and read "probability of A given B".

confidence. Referring to an association rule (X —> Y), confidence quantifies how often X and Y occur together as a fraction of the number of records in which X occurs. For example, if the confidence is 50 percent, X and Y occur together in 50 percent of the records in which X occurs. Thus, knowing that X occurs in a record, the probability that Y also occurs in that record is 50 percent. Also called *predictability*.

cross-validation. A common method of estimating predictive error, cross validation splits that data set into k equal-sized pieces called folds (typically 10). k predictive models are built, each tested on a distinct fold after being trained on the remaining folds. The process can be repeated multiple times to increase the reliability of the estimate.

decision tree. This is a predictive model based on a branching series of tests. Each test examines the value of a single column in the data and uses it to determine the next test to apply. The results of all tests determine which label to predict. A decision tree is a representation of a decision procedure for determining the class of a given instance. A decision tree can consist of :

- Leaf nodes (or answer nodes) that indicate a class name
- Non-leaf nodes (or decision nodes) that indicate an attribute name branches to another decision tree for each value of that attribute

The top-down induction of decision trees is a popular approach to learning. This approach uses attribute-based descriptions and the learned concepts are represented by decision trees. It is possible to categorize conjunctive and disjunctive descriptions of concepts with if-then rules, which can be lifted from the trees. These rules often offer a more flexible representation than the decision trees themselves.

entropy. A measure from information theory, entropy refers to the degree of disorder of data. The higher the entropy of a data set, the more diverse and mixed its values. Many of the mining algorithms operate by dividing data to minimize entropy.

error rate. This is the rate of correct or incorrect predictions made by the model over the data set. Error rate is usually determined by using an independent test data set that was not used at any time during the learning process. More complex accuracy estimation techniques, such as cross-validation, are sometimes used, especially with data sets that contain a small number of instances.

evidence. This is the degree to which a probability estimate affects an eventual prediction.

expected confidence. This is the frequency of occurrences of the RHS item in the data set. So the difference between expected confidence and confidence is a measure of the change in predictive power due to the presence of the LHS item. Expected confidence gives an indication of what the confidence would be if there were no relationships between the items.

experimental unit. In data mining terminology, this is defined as the level or degree of facts about the subject.

feed-forward neural network. This is a commonly implemented neural network whose topology/structure always means that the direction of the connections between the input layer, hidden layers, and output layer always flow from the input layer to the output layer. *See* back propagation.

holdout. This is the fraction of the data set (commonly two-thirds) that is used to train a model so that the remainder may be set aside for testing.

KDD. Short for knowledge discovery in databases, KDD is the same as data mining. A formal definition of KDD is the extraction of interesting (nontrivial, implicit, previously unknown, and potentially useful) information or patterns in large databases.

inductive learning. This process is when the teacher provides examples for the learner, and the learner generalizes the given examples to induce general rules. Because human learning is mostly based on experimental observation (empirical learning), it is easier for us to produce good examples than to generate explicit and complete general rules.

In general terms, learning concepts from examples can be symbolically represented as follows. Let U be a universal set of objects (there is no limitation on the size of U); then a concept C can be categorized as a subset of objects in U. Learning concept C means learning to recognize objects in C. If X is any object in universe U, then the learner can recognize whether X is in C.

The objects in the preceding paragraph are described in terms of their attributes. These attributes have a number of possible values. For example, a person can be described in terms of the attributes "height," "hair color," and "eye color," and the "height" attribute could have values "tall" or "short." The induction task is to develop a classification rule that can be used to determine the class of any object from the value of its attributes.

All inductive learning systems address the same task of inducing classification rules from examples. These systems often generate knowledge in the form of decision trees, which are able to solve difficult problems of practical importance.

label column.   This is the single column that a predictive model is attempting to predict. The user must select the label in advance. For example, *Customer Response* is a good candidate for the label column of a consumer marketing data set.

lift.   This is the ratio of confidence to expected confidence of a rule created by association rule generators. Generally, the greater this number, the more interesting the rule. In the context of classification, lift measures the classifier's performance at predicting a particular target event relative to the target event's occurrence in the sample.

lift curve.   A method for assessing predictive accuracy of a model, the lift curve visually displays the advantage a classifier provides over random determination of the label column.

mean.   This can be thought of as the number found by adding the values of data in a sample, then dividing by the number of pieces of data. The mean is usually denoted by x-bar, and is popularly called "average." For example, the mean of $(1 + 2 + 3)/3$ is 2.

median.   This is the middle number when numbers are arranged in order of size.

model.   This is a description based on observed phenomena, often omitting certain details. A model may imply prediction. For example, if a direct-mail model is formed, it implies "This is what we think a direct mail customer looks like." The learner can change values and observe the effects of the change on the operation of the system.

predictability.   This is an alternative term for confidence. *See* confidence.

prevalence.   This is an alternative term for support. *See* support.

prior probability.   For a class label, this is the probability of seeing the label in the data for a randomly chosen record, ignoring all attribute values. Mathematically, this is the number of records with the class label divided by the total number of records.

range.   This is the difference between the largest- and smallest-possible value of a column.

record weight. This is a numerical value applied to each row in the data. If supported, the mining tool treats a row with a weight k as if there were k copies of that row.

regressor. This is a predictive model where the label takes on a continuous value. Regressors are very similar to classifiers.

return-on-investment. This is a financial term that measures the worth of a project by measuring what benefits (return) accrue from an investment. Also known as ROI.

row. This is a record in a relational table.

rules. These are prescribed patterns of behavior applied to the handling of data, such as rules of association or rules of classification. A rule is also the unique path followed in a decision tree to get from root to leaf in order to classify the records. A rules-based system performs inferences by applying a set of if-then rules to a set of facts following a given procedure.

skewness. This refers to the lack of symmetry in a frequency distribution.

standard deviation. A measure of dispersion of data, standard deviation is defined as the square root of variance.

support. This quantifies how often X and Y occur together in the file as a fraction of the total number of records given an Association Rule X —> Y (X implies Y). For example, if the support is 1 percent, X and Y occur together in 1 percent of the total number of records. Also referred to as *prevalence*.

test data set. This consists of records in the data set that have been set aside to test the error rate of a classifier after it has been induced.

training data set. This is a subset of the data set, segmented off before major data manipulation, used to build a classifier or model. It consists of records in the database for which the label has been determined, based on descriptive attributes. It is used by the inducer to learn how to construct the classifier.

References

Barquin, R. and H. Edelstein, editors. 1997. *Planning and Designing the Data Warehouse*. Upper Saddle River, NJ: Prentice Hall.

Berry, M. and G. Linoff. 1997. *Data Mining Techniques: For Marketing, Sales, and Customer Support*. New York: John Wiley & Sons.

Chernoff, H. 1973. "The Use of Faces to Represent Points in k-Dimensional Space Graphically." *Journal of the American Statistical Association*. Vol. 68: pp. 342, 361-367.

Cleveland, W. 1993. *Visualizing Data*. Summit, NJ: Hobart Press.

Freedman, D., R. Risani, and R. Purves. 1998. *Statistics*. Third Edition. New York: W. W. Norton & Company, Inc.

Harris, K. 1999. "Mapping Crime: Principles and Practice." Crime Mapping Research Center. www.ojp.usdog/gov/cmrc.

Harris, R. 1999. *Information Graphics: A Comprehensive Illustrated Reference*. Oxford: Oxford University Press.

Inxight Software, Inc. 2002. "Inxight Star Tree Studio Example of Bestbuy.com." From Inxight Web site at www.inxight.com/products/st_studio_in_action_st.html.

Jaisingh, L. 2000. *Statistics for the Utterly Confused*. New York: McGraw-Hill.

Keller, P. and M. Keller. 1993. *Visual Clues*. IEEE Transactions on Visualization and Computer Graphics Volume 4. Los Alamitos, Calif.: IEEE Computer Society Press.

Kimball, R. and M. Ross. 2002. *The Data Warehouse Tool Kit, Second Edition*. New York: John Wiley & Sons.

Oracle Corporation. 2001. "Lowestfare.com Targeting Likely Internet Purchasers." From Oracle Web site at: http://otn.oracle.com/products/datamining/pdf/lowestfare.pdf.

Pyle, D. 1999. *Data Preparation for Data Mining*. San Diego: Academic Press.

Rousseeuw, P. and A. Leroy. 1987. *Robust Regression and Outlier Detection*. Wiley Series in Probability and Mathematical Statistics. New York: John Wiley & Sons.

SAS Institute Inc. 2002. "SAS CRM a Good Call for Telco Giant." From SAS Web Site at www.sas.com/news/success/sprint.html.

SPSS Inc. 2002. "Dayton Hudson Corp." From SPSS Web site at www.spss.com/spssatwork/template_view.cfm?Story_ID=4.

SPSS Inc. 2002. "Marketing Dynamics." From SPSS Web site at www.spss.com/spssatwork/template_view.cfm?Story_ID=25.

Tufte, Edward R. 1983. *The Visual Display of Quantitative Information.* Cheshire, CT: Graphics Press.

Tufte, Edward R. 1990. *Envisioning Information.* Cheshire, CT: Graphics Press.

Tufte, Edward R. 1997. *Visual Explanations.* Cheshire, CT: Graphics Press.

Two Crows. 2002. "Data Mining '99: Technology Report." From Two Crows Web site at www.twocrows.com/publictn.htm.